THE OTHER OREGON

T0345887

The Other Oregon

People, Environment, and History
East of the Cascades

THOMAS R. COX

Oregon State University Press   Corvallis

Library of Congress Cataloging-in-Publication Data

Names: Cox, Thomas R., 1933– author.
Title: The Other Oregon : People, Environment, and History East of the
    Cascades / Thomas R. Cox.
Description: Corvallis : Oregon State University Press, 2019. | Includes
    bibliographical references and index.
Identifiers: LCCN 2019037459 | ISBN 9780870719752 (paperback)
Subjects: LCSH: Oregon, Eastern—History. | Oregon, Eastern—Social
    conditions. | Oregon, Eastern—Environmental conditions.
Classification: LCC F876 .C68 2019 | DDC 979.5/5—dc23
LC record available at https://lccn.loc.gov/2019037459

♾This paper meets the requirements of ANSI/NISO Z39.48-1992 (Permanence
of Paper).

 Oregon State University
OSU Press

Oregon State University Press
121 The Valley Library
Corvallis OR 97331-4501
541-737-3166 • fax 541-737-3170
www.osupress.oregonstate.edu

For:

All those who love this hard,
haunting, somehow beautiful land

Contents

Maps and Illustrations

Preface

Some years ago my younger daughter arrived on the Linfield College campus in McMinnville, Oregon, to begin her undergraduate career. Upon learning she was from San Diego, her dormitory roommate, a dyed-in-the-wool Oregonian, launched an attack on California and all things Californian.

"But I was born in Oregon," my daughter protested.

"Where?" the roommate demanded.

"Redmond."

"Oh, that doesn't count."

Although Redmond is actually west of the geographical center of the state, it is in the rain shadow of the Cascades—on the "dry side" of the mountain range that runs north to south, splitting the state into two dissimilar entities. The land east of the Cascades makes up some two-thirds of the state, yet somehow it is not viewed as a part of the "real" Oregon. This view is not limited to my daughter's roommate. One of the Oregon "ungreeting cards" popular in the 1960s made the point clearly; it announced: "People don't tan in Oregon, they rust." Sunshine, aridity, and sagebrush may dominate east of the Cascades, but like Redmond, somehow those do not figure in most conceptions of the state. And the purveyors of the stereotypes of popular culture are not alone. Once the period of exploration, fur traders, cattle kings, and Indian wars was over, most historians of Oregon have given the eastern realm short shrift—or have ignored it altogether. Some simply dismiss the area as unimportant. Portland State's Carl Abbott recently wrote, "Many Americans like to imagine the West as a vast land of sagebrush and deserts, mountains and forests, cougars and caribou. Sure, it has plenty of landscapes to match the western movie image, but almost nobody lives out there in the empty West."

What my daughter experienced was hardly new. Growing up in Redmond in the 1940s and 1950s, my friends and I used to bewail the inattention to our section by the state's politicians and the metropolitan press. Eastern Oregon ought to be a separate state, we argued. And when I arrived at Oregon State as an undergraduate, I was both surprised and pleased to learn that classmates from Ontario, on Oregon's eastern border, had engaged in the same discussions. Meanwhile, various and sundry fraternity brothers chided me for being from the "great desert," to which I responded that I would rather bask in the sun like a lizard than be a "mossback" from "the great swamp." The stereotypes on which these exchanges were based, like most such, were oversimplifications. Vast stretches east of the Cascades—south from Bend, between Klamath Falls and Lakeview, and in the Blue and Wallowa Mountains—are forested, and north of the Blues mile after mile of onetime bunchgrass steppe now sport highly productive wheat ranches. Nor is the Westside a vast swamp; major portions of the Willamette, Rogue, and Umpqua Valleys receive so little rain they have never been forested in modern times. Yet, all in all, west of the Cascades is a well-watered land, while relative aridity dominates east of the range.

Thus the stereotypes persist, and they are not limited to the fantasies of teenagers or rivalries of undergraduates. An old prospector, scouring the sun-drenched Pueblo Mountains in far southeastern Oregon, long ago commented on Western Oregon and its people: "Too many trees," he opined, "It gives them a narrow vision, they can't see out."

One can accept that the prospector had touched on a basic truth without falling into the maw of environmental determinism. As nineteenth-century historian Theodor Mommsen reputedly said, "Don't speak to me of environmental determinism. Where once lived the ancient Greeks now live the Ottoman Turks!" The relatively dry, challenging environment east of the Cascades presented opportunities quite different from those of the Willamette Valley; this harsh land drew people of a different sort, people who brought with them values and attitudes that shaped the economy, society, and outlook of the area and thus laid the foundation for the east-west divisions that, in spite of an ongoing influx of outsiders, have continued to the present day. The region's identity remains shaped by the land and the ways that people have survived—and even prospered—on it. And for those who have not prospered, a certain pride remains in simply having persevered in this challenging place.

More lies behind these differences than relative levels of precipitation: the contrasts are cultural as well as environmental. Some years ago Dorothy Johansen, in her presidential address to the Pacific Coast Branch of the American Historical Association, sought to explain the palpable differences between Oregon, Washington, and California—although her "Oregon," like that of my daughter's roommate, clearly lay west of the Cascades, particularly in Portland and the Willamette Valley. Echoing Louis Hartz's fragment thesis, she argued that original settlers set the tone for each of the three states and thus shaped their societies in the years that followed. In his bicentennial history of the state, Gordon Dodds took much the same position—as did I some years ago in trying to delineate the sociopolitical differences among Oregon, Washington, and Idaho through a study of the state parks movement in each. All of us reflected the earlier argument of Earl Pomeroy, that settlers of the American West brought with them cultural baggage that shaped what they did and what they built. Experience in its varied forms reinforced the mix.

Growing up in Central Oregon conditioned me to accept the ideas of Johansen and company even before I encountered them in academia. My classmates and I were well aware that Bend, Redmond, and Prineville, located only some twenty miles apart, were quite different communities, each shaped by its own past. Far more separated them than long-standing athletic rivalries. Bend was a sawmill town in which early leadership came from a core of relatively affluent and well-educated people, often with ambitious development schemes; Redmond was a quiet agricultural town servicing a hinterland of modest irrigated farms; Prineville—the oldest of the three—was a rough-and-tumble community with roots in ranching (although by the 1950s lumbering was also playing a significant role) and a history of vigilante activity and organized sheep shooting by cattlemen.

Some members of the new western school of historians have attacked the fragment thesis and its offspring as "consensus history," claiming they tend to homogenize the past by ignoring minorities and groups that do not fit dominant norms. Such was never the intention of Johansen, Hartz, Dodds, or Pomeroy. Delineating dominant values and attitudes is a far cry from denying the presence of contrasting outlooks. They did not do so, nor do I in the pages that follow. Yet even if one subscribes to the idea that early settlers established norms that long continued, delineating the character of the world east of the Cascades remains difficult.

Even more than the Central Oregon of Bend, Redmond, and Prineville, the area east of the Cascades is a complex mosaic, yet it has a shared sense of identity. As Bill Robbins once observed, regions can be viewed as "mentally bounded places" that "rest at the borders between geography and history." Anthropologists put it differently, maintaining that ethnocognitive views influence a wide variety of activities ranging from economic ties to marriage patterns. Geographers Edward Ullman and Donald Meinig have taken yet another tack, arguing that commodity flows tie the Northwest together and that rivers play a major role in shaping the patterns of trade. But their approach has limited value in analyzing Eastern Oregon, where commodities move in a multitude of directions and, when present, rivers are seldom channels of commerce. The places talked about while friends sit around a fire in the evening—or in the towns to which they go to find a bar or a girlfriend—do more to define communities than patterns of commerce or lines drawn on a map for governmental administrative purposes. Similarly, William Bowen has shown that, in the early Willamette Valley, kinship ties and geographic origins were more important than commerce in shaping communities. The same is true in Eastern Oregon. Jordan Valley is a case in point. Located in the far eastern reaches of the state, it has a history rooted in the experiences of its Basque community, which, through counterparts in southwestern Idaho and northern Nevada, is more oriented to Boise and Winnemucca than to the county seat a few miles to the north in Vale and, through its ranching heritage, is tied to southern Harney county more than to agrarian northern Malheur County, the entity of which it is a part. As anthropologist William Pilcher demonstrated in his study of Portland's longshoremen, people do not need to live closely together to share a sense of community.

Defining the mental boundaries in so diverse a land as Eastern Oregon is challenging—even for those who have spent a good share of their lives there. A high school classmate journeyed east one summer to the John Day country for an extended visit. Although she had lived on ranches in Central Oregon and on its High Desert, she was amazed by what she saw: by the huge bluffs that towered over the river, their sides marked by steep talus slopes of basalt tumbling from lava high above over fossil-bearing sedimentary layers below; by the dry rock-strewn washes that cut their way to the river until passing cloudbursts filled them with a torrent of mud and debris that flooded across roadways and swelled the river's brown flow; by the river itself, with its smattering of streamside cottonwoods, willows, and the like but no real riparian belt; by the sparse growth of dried cheatgrass that covered hillsides, providing nourishment for cattle for a few days each spring; by the trails worn by those cattle as they continued to crisscross the slopes looking for sustenance after the cheatgrass dried and became unpalatable—even the sagebrush on these slopes was stunted, and junipers, so ubiquitous in Central Oregon, were few and scattered; by the small pastures, alfalfa fields, and old orchards that occupied spots where the canyon widened to furnish a bit of irrigable bottomland; and by weather-worn towns—little more than wide spots on the highway that wound along the river—that supplied the area's scattered ranches: Dayville, Monument, Spray, and Kimberly each had fewer than two hundred people but were metropoles compared with Service Creek, which sported a service station, restaurant, and cabins—and a population of two when I last visited. Knowing I had spent summers working in the area, my friend looked me up on her return. Wide-eyed, she said, "I never knew there was such a place—it was like visiting the moon!"

Other areas east of the Cascades are equally distinct, and their differences, like those my classmate detected, are cultural as much as physiographic. Yet however much it may be evident to visitors, the sociocultural makeup of Eastern Oregon's various regions has received scant attention from scholars. Some years ago geographer Isaiah Bowman took steps in that direction in *The Pioneer Fringe*, so too did Peter K. Simpson in *The Community of Cattlemen*, but there is little else. Autobiographical studies help fill the void: William Kittredge's *Hole in the Sky*, Ellen Waterston's evocative essays in *Where the Crooked River Rises*, and Dayton Hyde's *Yamsi*. Still, such works have been few, and almost without exception limited in geographical scope. Meanwhile, novelists, seeking to tell stories rooted in this land, have done as much as historians in catching its flavor. I draw on their insights without apology—and on local newspapers and histories, which reflect grassroots concerns and attitudes better than do most more broadly or technically focused sources.

East of the Cascades, identities are layered. On the one hand, we have "Central Oregon," the "John Day country," the "Klamath Basin," and so on, but we have also a larger, harder to define "Eastern Oregon." Efforts to identify what binds Eastern Oregon's diversity into a conscious, if not entirely cohesive, whole remain unwritten. Anthropologist Luther Cressman noted that the Eastern Oregon where he unearthed prehistoric remains was "a different world from that of the moist, lush Willamette Valley. . . . Different lifeways marked the two environments." Marion Weatherford pinpointed what may be the overarching characteristic in his history of Arlington: "What rugged individuals these Eastern Oregon people are!" His characterization was seemingly reflected in recent presidential elections. Republicans John McCain, Mitt Romney, and Donald Trump carried Eastern Oregon, yet all three lost in the state as a whole. Indeed, a Democratic presidential candidate has not carried Malheur County since 1940. The pattern puts Eastern Oregon politically closer to Idaho and its libertarianism than to the rest of Oregon.

This book is an ambitious—some might say foolhardy—effort to tell the story of this vast, varied land. Oregon State College's Joseph Ward Ellison, who taught Oregon history when I was an undergraduate there, thought seeking to delineate the differences between Eastern and Western Oregon hardly proper work for an historian. I disagreed then and still do. I knew it to be a story with some familiar actors, but also many who were little known, and I thought it a story worth telling. As I have at last proceeded against Ellison's long-ago advice, I have found it not an easy story to tell, for it is a diverse land lacking a focal point or an industry around which the rest revolves. Moreover, much of Eastern Oregon is unfamiliar territory even to many lifelong Oregonians. Indeed, the larger world paid the region little heed until early 2016, when protesters occupied the headquarters of the Malheur National Wildlife Refuge. When they did, droves of reporters arrived from outside but, almost without exception, showed limited understanding of the region and the events they were covering.

My hope is that, out of the kaleidoscopic portrait that follows, a "feel" for the region will emerge, a sense of what it is that ties Eastern Oregon together and provides a sense of shared identity little understood—or even recognized—beyond its borders. The centers of political and economic power are far distant, little shaped by Eastern Oregon's residents, and play a limited role in shaping its self-identity. Similarly, with a population of recent arrivals who have come from a host of sources, kinship ties and the shared past they represent have little influenced regional self-identity. Rather, as the following pages demonstrate, identity is deeply rooted in the land and the peculiar characteristics thereof, an identity that grew out of the prolonged and ongoing dance between Eastern Oregon's people and their environment. This is, in other words, both a history of people and their actions *and* an environmental history of the land itself. Both stand in sharp contrast to the better-known story of the Oregon that lies west of the Cascades.

Finally, as one might deduce from this preface, this book is something of a personal statement and incorporates elements of reminiscence, hardly the norm in historical studies. For that I offer no apology, only the wish that these elements add understanding for those who come to these pages from other places and times.

Thomas R. Cox
McCammon, Idaho

1

This Varied Land

In 1863, as gold miners poured in to newly discovered digs around Canyon City in Oregon's John Day country, Brigadier General Benjamin Alvord, in charge of the army's District of Oregon, worried that major clashes with Paiute bands inhabiting the area would soon erupt. Scattered raids had already occurred. Seeking to rein in the Snakes, as he called them, in February 1864 Alvord ordered Captain John M. Drake to take companies of Oregon volunteers to John Day country to conduct pacification efforts.

Drake and his men were not particularly successful, for the Paiutes were scattered and elusive; indeed, conflict with them would continue to 1868 and beyond. But if their military efforts were hardly memorable, Drake's men have a lasting place in the annals of Oregon's vast, interior domain. On July 19, 1864, Drake wrote the Reverend Thomas Condon, minister of the Congregational church in The Dalles: "Last week during my absence from our camp on Beaver Creek, a tributary of Crooked River . . . some soldiers made a discovery that I take to be of interest geologically." Bored with sitting in camp while Drake led a detachment in pursuit of a reported band of warlike Paiutes, some of the rest of his men wandered over area hills and found a variety of mammal fossils and marine shells. Intrigued, the soldiers—joined soon enough by Drake himself—began combing the area with enthusiasm. As Drake put it, "I found our camp converted into a vast geological cabinet: everyone had been gathering rocks." He quickly dispatched a collection of the finds to Condon.

Drake had reasons for the shipment. Soon after Condon arrived in The Dalles in 1862—the same year Drake arrived there—he had displayed an interest in, and considerable knowledge of, the relatively new science of geology. From time to time he gave public talks on the subject and was frequently seen investigating the hills behind the crude frontier town. Condon was fascinated by Drake's shipment and promptly began maneuvering to get to the area to see for himself what was to be found there.[1]

The Indian threat was too great for Condon to venture there on his own, but the following year he accompanied an army unit traveling to Harney Basin to bring supplies to the isolated post there. Drake's cavalry provided his protective escort. On its return to The Dalles, the body passed along the South Fork of the John Day. The multicolored slopes of sedimentary rock overtopped with basalt, the weathered hills, and the erosion-sculpted shapes of soft, exposed rock fascinated Condon. To his eye the sedimentary layers clearly represented eons of time—and with his geologist's pick he was soon unearthing fossils.[2]

Over the years Condon would return to the John Day country time and again and widen his fieldwork to other areas as well. Others came too, and as Condon made ever more finds—and shared them with leading geologists of the day—a picture gradually emerged of a shallow sea that slowly gave way to a well-watered subtropical land with lush vegetative growth and a fauna of primitive beasts, many long gone, others ancestral to modern forms. Eastern Oregon had clearly not always been an arid—or even semiarid—land. As geological explorations expanded beyond the John Day Basin, the picture became more complex and confusing, but Condon developed an explanation for the apparent anomalies, an explanation he would detail in 1902 in *The Two Islands and What Came of Them*.[3]

Simply put, Condon posited that in the long-ago Cretaceous Period the waters of the Pacific lapped on the uplift that sports the various mountain ranges now known collectively as the Rockies. West of the shoreline lay a vast, shallow sea on whose bed many of the sediments Condon explored had been deposited. Older rocks, those found in today's Blue and Siskiyou Mountain complexes, rose from the primordial sea as "islands" whose rocks dated from much earlier—the Triassic and Jurassic. Subsequently a volcanic ridge—the Cascades—arose miles to the west, isolating a great inland sea whose bed gradually rose leaving the area a vast, relatively level grassy plain on which a variety of terrestrial forms flourished. As the Cascade Range rose, it gradually cut off the interior from the warm, water-laden winds of the Pacific; the area became increasingly dry. Repeatedly, huge lava flows poured from volcanoes and giant fissures, overtopping the sedimentary rocks laid down in the Tertiary Period and thus helping preserve the fossil record for Condon and others to unravel.

As subterranean pressures mounted, extensive faulting followed, creating huge escarpments like Abert Rim, Steens Mountain, Mount Emily, Winter Rim, and a variety of lesser uplifts. Related subsidence occurred on the downslope side of many of these, sometimes—as at Upper Klamath Lake and the Grande Ronde Valley—creating graben valleys with uplifts on either side of a sunken floor. These and other low-lying areas gradually filled with water, especially during the pluvial late Pleistocene, creating huge inland lakes—Modoc, Chewaucan, Fort Rock, Lahontan, and others. As the climate turned drier, these gradually receded, leaving saline lakes, playas, and alkali flats. Over the millennia, climatic and geological processes thus created the arid and semiarid domain that is the Eastern Oregon of today.

In time the emergence of plate tectonic theory and the growing complexity of evidence as geological investigations continued would result in modifications of Condon's simplistic picture, but it still suffices to explain the vast and very basic differences between the lands west and east of the Cascade Range. Condon may not have filled in the details, but with unusual prescience he had pointed the way.[4]

Casual visitors, speeding across the long, straight stretches of highway between the Blues and the Nevada border, often develop a picture of the area as a land of interminable sagebrush plains, largely bare grayish hills, and occasional dark lava outcroppings. There seems little of note and even less population. "Towns" on the map—Wagontire, Riley, Millican, Brothers, Valley Junction, Blitzen, Burns Junction—never had significant populations and now are deserted or nearly so.[5]

This is not just the case in Oregon's southeastern quadrant. The Blue Mountains fail to offer the long straight stretches of highway found in the lands to the south, but are equally sparsely settled. A number of little communities, some now ghost towns, hunker on the lower slopes or nearby, tapping the mountains' timber and grazing lands; but with few exceptions there is a dearth of settlement in the mountains themselves. Indeed, to travel westward through the Blues one must leave major highways and travel dirt and gravel roads. The population is insufficient to require anything better. Interstate 84, across and to the north of the Blues, takes one past communities of some size—Baker City, La Grande, Pendleton, Hermiston, The Dalles—but also past long, nearly empty stretches with tiny, widely spaced towns like Boardman, Rufus, Mosier, Arlington, and Biggs. Secondary highways running south from I-84 yield more of the same: Condon, a county seat, has but 655 people; Moro and Fossil, also county seats, have even fewer; Shaniko, an oft-visited ghost town, has but a handful of residents. Thus this seems to many a largely empty land with tiny nodes of settlement, a land with little of note that repels more than it attracts.

The impression is misleading. One does not have to be a "desert rat" to find this land intriguing, its stories numerous. The emptiness helps define and shape the people who live there, and at the same time leaves much of the land uncluttered by works of human artifice or lush vegetative growth obscuring much of what could otherwise be seen and learned. Historian Robert Bunting noted that, in Oregon, "it is land and not the Puritan migration, the American Revolution, or the Civil War that stands at the center of [its] . . . history, art, and literature." Speaking of the American West as a whole, John Caughey made the same point: "This is a land where the environment has to be taken into account." Nowhere is this truer than east of the Cascades, where to tell the story of the people one must recount that of the land and what has been done with it and to it.[6]

But if the miles of sagebrush steppe leave the viewer convinced this is a land of sameness, that impression is well off the mark. Even allowing for the vast differences among the Great Basin, Blue Mountains, and Columbia Plain, any appearance of uniformity within their subdivisions is misleading. Even the sagebrush lands vary. On the backcountry drive from the rim above Warner Lakes to Frenchglen, the sagebrush is seldom more than a foot high. East of there, on the slopes of Steens Mountain, it is immense. John Scharff, longtime superintendent of the Malheur National Wildlife Refuge, reportedly once bragged of Steens Mountain sagebrush: "It's real timber boys. This fall my first job is to run some lines and cruise and scale it."[7]

Highways contribute to the illusion of sameness. They follow the easiest and lowest routes, avoiding mountainous stretches, often by following river courses. Traveling the John Day Highway, one can only guess at what the hulking masses looming above hold. Similarly, one cannot grasp the story of Steens Mountain without making the ascent to its summit and peering down into Kiger Gorge, or understand the lower Deschutes— from Warm Springs to the Columbia—and the place the river has had in the area's history from any highway (and only partially from aboard the myriad of white-water boats and inflatable rafts that descend its rapids each year). There is more to this land than can be learned from its major thoroughfares.

In Eastern Oregon the past seems especially close and relevant. It is, of course. Much of its settlement dates from the twentieth century, and even the oldest communities from fewer than fifty years before that; the constructions of the earliest settlers and the fields they cleared may still be detected. Yet it is not just the built environment of white settlers that is readily apparent—so is the geological past.

A historian friend once described this land as one with the bare bones of the earth sticking out, visible for all who would see.[8] Of course skeletal structures not only shape the body that develops around them, they also set the limits of what is possible. The geological past of the region, the past that Thomas Condon did so much to uncover, has a greater—or at least more evident—relevance in Eastern Oregon than in most places. Many geological sites in this region have gained national recognition for being both spectacular and informative: Crater Lake, the various units of the John Day Fossil Beds National Monument, the lava country from Bend south to Newberry Crater, the stunning canyonland of The Cove-Palisades State Park on Crooked River, Steens Mountain, Hells Canyon. The list of lesser-known instructive places is even longer—including as it does Fort Rock, the moraines of Wallowa Lake, Lost Forest, Borax Lake, the Owyhee Canyon, and the edenic valley of the upper Metolius River.

Change has occurred in modern as well as geologic times. Weather cycles have modified the landscape in important ways. When Thomas Condon collected there in 1877, Fossil Lake, once quite large, was "a small pond." In the years since, it has dried up completely. Goose, Warner, Harney, and Silver Lakes became temporarily dry (or nearly so) in the 1930s, and not for the first time.[9] While growing up in Warner Valley, near the string of shallow lakes nestled at the foot of the massive Hart Mountain fault block, young William Kittredge explored long-inundated areas that had become so dry that fires burning in the peat and duff became a major problem, and he found scores of arrow points and other artifacts showing that the area had been dry before, well before the coming of whites. When rainfall increased in the 1950s and the lakes rose again, they not only inundated many sites of Kittredge's boyhood but also so enlarged Silver Lake that

Oregon had to relocate portions of Highway 31, the link between Bend and Lakeview.[10]

Worse, during the first decades of the century, rainfall increased—not much, but enough to encourage thousands of settlers to flock to the High Desert near Millican and Brothers, north from there around Post and Paulina, and to the vast stretches south and west of Burns.[11] Soon enough they learned the truth: the growing season was too short for successful agriculture and the normal rainfall inadequate. By 1930 geographer Isaiah Bowman found only nineteen of the seventy "homes and shanties" within sight of the highway between Bend and Burns still inhabited—and the number was continuing to decline. Today little remains save a few desiccated, windswept skeletons of buildings, some memoirs, and novels by Anne Shannon Monroe and H. L. Davis that chronicle the struggles of long-gone residents.[12]

Other changes have been less dramatic, but important nonetheless. Photographs of Deep Canyon, located between Redmond and Sisters, showed almost no junipers in the 1920s, but by the 1940s and 1950s junipers had become the dominant vegetation, having arrived in the wake of heavy grazing that reduced native bunchgrass, thereby providing openings for junipers to take root. The process has continued, there and elsewhere; junipers sucking up much of the limited water have reduced moisture available for grasses and thus the value of the land for grazing.[13]

Rangelands changed elsewhere too. Overgrazing by cattle and sheep destroyed much of the bunchgrass that had dominated the landscape when whites first arrived, opening the way for wind erosion that in places blew away the light, scanty topsoil and left a sterile, pebbly surface. In naturally occurring deserts, this "desert pavement" acts as a welcome protection for the soil—but the bunchgrass steppe was not a true a desert. Sometimes the roots of the sagebrush that remained when grass was gone held the immediately surrounding topsoil in place, leaving individual sagebrush plants growing atop mounds of dirt; the result could remind a viewer of a land sprinkled with huge flower pots out of which sagebrush grew, while the land between them had been lowered as it was scoured by the wind.

Throughout the region cheatgrass replaced native bunch grasses and became a blight to man and beast; its prickly awns probed and festered in the lips, noses, and mouths of grazing animals, in the feet of carnivores, and in the ankles of humans.[14] Its shallow root systems did little to slow wind or water erosion. The plant itself was tender enough to serve as food for herbivores for only a brief period each spring, and it covered the land so densely that catastrophic range fires repeatedly erupted. As Aldo Leopold put it in 1941, westerners felt helpless in the face of the unwanted invasion, viewing cheatgrass as "a necessary evil, to be lived with until kingdom come." Unnoticed by Leopold, well-intentioned range managers may have played a role in the takeover. Eileen McVicker does not recall any cheatgrass when she was growing up near Steens Mountain until "one year a man came with free seed and an offer to pay the ranchers to keep so many acres free of livestock for a year so the seed could get established. . . . My dad and all the other ranchers around our area signed up for the program, and my dad fenced off a part of our land. The cheatgrass got well established all right; it spread all over the country like wildfire." McVicker went on, "I always thought this man was from the Taylor Grazing Office, but we blamed them for everything bad, so I may have been wrong about that."[15]

The Blue Mountains have had wet-dry cycles too. Since the retreat of glaciers at the end of the Ice Age some twelve thousand years ago, swings in climate, primarily precipitation, have caused forests in the Blues to come and go, replaced with dry grasslands at least three times. The current forests go back only 2,500 years—perhaps as few as a thousand—and even these have advanced and retreated and their species mix changed over time. Tree ring studies show that during the last three centuries droughts have occurred in the Blues roughly every thirty-seven years.[16]

Even within the long-term cycles, changes took place in the Blues. The normal processes of ecological succession were ever at work. Ponds became marshes, marshes became meadows, and meadows were gradually invaded by first one species of tree and then another. The mountain environment was dynamic indeed.[17]

Changes occurred in the area north of the Blues too, but since photographic evidence is scanty and tree-ring analysis, a primary tool for long-term climate studies, hardly applicable in this unforested regime, the details are less clear; still, works on the interior Pacific Northwest as a whole hint at a long-term pattern not unlike that in the forest areas. Records of the National Oceanic and Atmosphere Administration's National Climatic Data Center provide a detailed picture for the years from 1895 to 2012. These show that Oregon's zone 6, the Umatilla Plateau region, experienced drought from 1912 to 1930, 1959 to 1978, and 1998 to 2004. That these resulted in significant biotic changes is doubtful; grasslands are remarkably resilient.[18]

Yet to talk of the regions' three major areas—the Columbia's grassland plains, the mountainous midsection, and the drier lands to the south—and the changes therein obscures an important aspect of Eastern Oregon: differences are found within as well as between them. William O. Douglas observed "the moods of the foothills are as variable as the seasons of the year or the hours of the day."[19] Moreover, rain shadows make areas downwind from mountains and fault blocks more arid, the vegetation there different and sparser. By the time water-bearing storms arrive east of Steens Mountain they have been wrung so dry that the Alvord Desert's annual rainfall averages a mere five inches. Different plant and animal communities emerge in response to each increase in aridity.[20]

Elevation is a key factor. As one ascends, the air cools, evaporation rates slow, and changes in plant-animal communities occur. Some people arriving from well-watered lands in the East, where lowlands tended to be well-forested and mountain heights sparsely vegetated or bare, often find the pattern odd, but the phenomenon is not restricted to Eastern Oregon. Alexander von Humboldt observed it in South America's Andes; Dietrich Brandis (mentor of both Gifford Pinchot and Henry Graves, the first chiefs of the United States Forest Service) in India; and C. Hart Merriam in the Grand Canyon–San Francisco Mountain area of northern Arizona. More recently Frederick Gehlbach has observed it along the US-Mexico border and characterized the relatively well-vegetated highlands as so many islands in a desert sea. It is a characterization that could be applied equally effectively to places like Pine Mountain and the Maury Mountains, standing apart from Eastern Oregon's main forested areas—and on a larger scale to the Blue Mountains themselves. It applies even on Steens Mountain, which rises to 9,733 feet through belts of sagebrush, juniper, and mountain mahogany into the subalpine and alpine zones (although there it sports stands of aspen rather than the usual evergreens).[21]

Temperatures are affected by exposure to the sun as well as elevation. South-facing slopes receive more sunlight than north- or east-facing and thus are hotter and—with higher evaporation rates—drier. Thus, within the Blues, as well as elsewhere, there is a patchwork of local ecosystems, a patchwork that belies travelers' impressions of a land of monotony and sameness. Hardscrabble Ridge at the southern edge of the Ochocos is a classic case; assigned to a Forest Service lookout there in the 1950s, I found its southern slope a steep, rocky, brush-covered incline, while its north slope was covered by pine forest. Distance from moderating influences also affects temperatures—influences such as prevailing winds off the Pacific and the buffering of temperatures by nearby lakes. In 1934 the little town of Seneca, which sits in a basin high above where the Blues drop off to the John Day Valley to the north and slide more gradually down to the Great Basin to the south, had the lowest winter temperature recorded for any Oregon community: −54° Fahrenheit.[22]

How a dominant sense of identity and values could emerge in such a varied land with little population and little uniformity—save for an overarching sparseness of precipitation—and whether in fact it did, are the central issues addressed in this book. The difficulties faced and the frictions that emerged out of this dance between people and their land is the subtext.

2
Probings

In 1937 forest ranger Walter J. Perry contacted Luther Cressman with news of caves he had found in the Paisley and Fort Rock areas. He thought they might be of interest to the sociologist-turned-anthropologist from the University of Oregon. Perry was an amateur paleontologist who had worked as a volunteer on Cressman's dig in Catlow Valley the preceding summer, so he had an informed idea of the sorts of things Cressman sought. Perry was correct in his judgment. Finds at the sites would revolutionize understanding of the prehistory of the northern Great Basin, bring Cressman to national attention, and greatly increase public awareness of the antiquity of early man in Eastern Oregon—thanks especially to seventy-five sandals crafted from cords made from shredded sagebrush bark, sandals that somehow caught public attention as few archeological finds do.

For many years, the dominant view in archeological circles had been that the northern Great Basin was settled from a cultural hearthland in the Southwest—an interpretation that would have made Eastern Oregon marginal and relatively inconsequential, and settlement there probably not more than a thousand years old. Based on what he found at Paisley, Fort Rock, and elsewhere, Cressman disagreed. People had been present in Eastern Oregon far earlier; settlement went back to the late Pleistocene, for he had found artifacts in association with remains of animals extinct in the New World for close to ten thousand years.[1] Moreover, rather than being a peripheral area of little consequence, "Eastern Oregon, the land of the now-dry lakes, was once a segment of the migration corridor of early Indian populations in their movements from the northern Bering land bridge into the American Southwest." Members of the "establishment" fought back, rejecting the work of this self-trained upstart, work that reduced the centrality of their own areas of expertise; some even implied that Cressman had faked his evidence.[2]

Luther Cressman at Fort Rock Cave. Credit: University of Oregon Archives.

In time Cressman's interpretation would prevail. His key finds at Fort Rock and the Paisley Caves were beneath an undisturbed layer of pumice that had come from the eruption of Mount Mazama (in whose remnant Crater Lake now rests). At the time, geologists dated the eruption at between 4,000 and 10,000 years ago. Carbon-14 dating of a later sandal find validated Cressman's view; the sandal was between 6,200 and 6,700 years old, far older than the Basketmaker culture of the Southwest, which existed around 3,000 years ago and had been considered either the source from which the northern Great Basin had been populated or the antecedent of later cultures found there.[3]

Others followed in Cressman's footsteps. Subsequent finds at Rimrock Draw Rockshelter (near Riley) show a radiocarbon age of 15,800 years, while spear points unearthed at Paisley Cave are 13,200 years old—as old as the famed Clovis points from New Mexico and elsewhere, but clearly not Clovis. Specialists now divide the area's prehistory into five major periods that resulted from adjustments to environmental and other changes; these periods extend from the Paisley (15,500 to 12,000 years ago) to the Boulder Village Period (3,000 years ago to the present). This later work stands on the foundation built by Cressman. Indeed, an important recent collection of studies on the northern Great Basin is titled *Archaeological Researches in the Northern Great Basin: Fort Rock Archaeology since Cressman.*[4]

All the breakthrough finds have not been only in the northern Great Basin. Cressman himself did work at Lower Klamath Lake, a site on the upper Deschutes River destined to be flooded by Wickiup Reservoir, and sites along the Columbia set to be inundated by The Dalles Dam. More newsworthy than these, however, was the discovery of the remains of what came to be known as Kennewick Man, found after Cressman's death and quite independent of his finds.

While watching hydroplane races on the Columbia River on July 28, 1996, two young men happened upon a human skull. Local officials recognized it was far from contemporary and called in archeological assistance. Additional bones were recovered, making a nearly complete skeleton. Initial carbon-14 dating placed the remains at 8,400 years old (other tests put them somewhat later). In a suit filed under the Native American Graves Protection and Repatriation Act, the Umatilla tribe claimed the remains (which they dubbed the Ancient One), arguing they had oral traditions that went back ten thousand years and that they had been residents of the area since "the dawn of time." Other area tribes joined in support of the Umatillas.

Scientists studying the remains at first provided no support for the Umatillas' claim. Craniometric and DNA studies suggested a greater affinity to Jomon-Ainu (proto-Japanese) and Polynesian populations than to mainstream Native Americans. These findings lent credence to the thesis that North America had been populated by more than one wave of immigrants coming across the Bering land bridge or by sea. Further, Douglas W. Owsley of the Smithsonian Institution found isotopic evidence showing Kennewick Man had not even been from the Columbia Basin; his diet had been primarily seals or other marine mammals. The Ancient One was "just passing through," he said.

That was hardly the end of it. Subsequent studies strengthened the Umatilla's position, and the tribe was able to gain possession of the remains and give them a proper Native American burial. Kennewick Man had taken debates in a new direction. But they stand on the shoulders of Luther Cressman, whose arguments—that human habitation east of the Cascades was genuinely ancient and that the region had been a major migration route as people moved south—underlie the entire discussion.[5]

In October 1805, Captain Meriwether Lewis and then-lieutenant William Clark were also "just passing through." On October 16 they arrived at the confluence of the Snake (which they called Lewis's River) and the Columbia, near where the bones of Kennewick Man would later be found. Three days later Clark reported spotting what "I take to be Mt. St. Helens," named earlier by George Vancouver during his maritime explorations of the Northwest coast. Further downstream, the party named Cataract River (later known as the Deschutes) and Beacon Rock.[6] In doing so, Lewis and Clark were following the established practice of naming places explorers found as they probed the North American interior. As elsewhere, the Pacific Northwest's interior had long since been explored; the places "discovered" by Lewis and Clark had already been named by Native Americans.

Although Lewis and Clark engaged in the cultural imperialism of the time, renaming sites as they went, they were more sensitive observers than was common among their Caucasian contemporaries. They recorded Indian place-names and terms, noted the character of the peoples they met, and with some sensitivity differentiated among the cultures with which they came in contact.

As the party neared the confluence of the Snake and Columbia, they emerged from a canyon-girt world and, for the next many miles, were able to see the land for a considerable distance on either side of the river. They were not impressed. It seemed a sagebrush- and cactus- covered expanse of little note. The Nez Perce, Clark had noted, owned "emence numbers of horses," but as the party continued downstream they descended into a river world bounded by basalt uplands that obstructed their landward view. Focusing their attention on the fishing villages along the river, they seemed unaware of the vast numbers of horses belonging to the Umatilla and Cayuse.[7] There is considerably more discussion of horses during their return journey through the area, but they still failed to grasp the equestrian nature of the society that existed a short distance back from the banks of the Columbia.

Horses had been absent from the Americas since the late Pleistocene, and their reintroduction revolutionized Native American life.[8] Comanches were instrumental in the process. They obtained horses from Spanish settlements in the Southwest, and through trade and raids horses were spread northward from one Indian group to another, especially along the western flanks of the Rockies where Shoshonean peoples—with whom the Comanches had cultural and linguistic ties—lived. By the early seventeenth century, horses were present in small numbers on the upper Snake River plain, and they spread west from there.[9] The Cayuse remembered their first sighting of horses; hunting near the Malheur River, a group spotted some "Snakes" (probably Shoshoni, but perhaps Paiutes) "riding elk or deer." Soon realizing their mistake, Cayuse began acquiring horses of their own. Territorial expansion followed. As Robert Ruby and John Brown put it, the Cayuse should pay tribute to "the animal on which they rode to power."[10]

The mobility that horses made possible changed Native societies. The high grassy plains, until then largely empty of humans, took on new importance. The Cayuse and Nez Perce, who obtained horses earlier than most, established territorial claims on the plains; gradually the Umatillas and others edged their way into such places too.[11] The advent of horses also led the Cayuse into the Blues, for the mountains supplied excellent summer grazing. Soon enough they and their neighbors learned that grazing lands could be improved by annual burning. The "light burning" involved—what early foresters referred to dismissively as "Paiute forestry"—reshaped the mountain forests, just as annual burning did the grassland plains.[12]

A host of cultural changes came with the acquisition of horses—many of them the result of trips to the buffalo grounds across the Rockies, trips that were influential in the transfer of plains cultural patterns into the Northwest. Moreover, as Donald Meinig has noted, the introduction of "this valuable animal resulted in more mobile relationships which heightened trade, trespass, thievery, and petty quarrels." These and other important changes were well under way by the time Lewis and Clark arrived in the area. The horse, Meinig summarized, had by then opened "a new way of life."[13]

Northern Paiute life changed even more dramatically than that of the Cayuse. Just how long the Paiute had been present in Oregon's Great Basin is not clear; they may have introduced the Boulder Village culture archeologists date from about 2,000 BCE. Ethnolinguistic studies support this view, suggesting Northern Paiutes migrated into the area from near Owens Valley, Mono Lake, and the southern Sierra Nevada.[14] What combination of push and pull factors led to this population movement is unknown, but one suspects it was more push than pull—the resource-scant Great Basin would hardly have attracted people who were not desperate. Folklore lends support to this view. Northern Paiute tales recount how the land had once been covered with water, and as it dried up the Creator (Numüna) made the plants and animals that would be typical of the area for years to come. Then, "some kind of man happened along after the water dried. He was called Nümüzo'ho [Cannibal]. . . . He was a big man and ate other men. He had a big kettle or rock, and in it he ground all the Indians that he killed. . . . That meant there was someone coming from the south eating all the Indians." Cannibalism is, of course, a last resort of people on the verge of starvation, rampant at the time.[15]

The Northern Paiute were not a tribe, but a thinly spread linguistic group whose members shared cultural similarities that stemmed in large part from the limitations of their lands. They lived in small, autonomous bands—often little more than family units—and, because they had to roam widely, living off whatever the land had to offer, they had few possessions to weigh them down in their quest. William Kittredge put it simply, "The country did not reward them for owning things." In sum, they were an impoverished people living on an impoverished land. Among themselves, they were identified not by language (dialects differed, but all were Numic speakers) or by place of residence so much as by their basic foodstuffs: seed-eaters, marmot-eaters, root-eaters, and so on.[16]

When Lewis and Clark passed through the area, the Paiutes near the lower Deschutes apparently still lacked horses, but when they—or rather some of them—acquired horses, their lives quickly changed.[17] With greater mobility, their history of living off the land soon morphed into living off whatever could be found there—including the possessions of others. Similar changes came to other Paiute groups. Mobility brought larger territories, greater contact (including warfare) with others, larger band sizes to meet offensive and defensive necessities, and, of course, more possessions and greater affluence for some. The successful stealer of horses received great honor.[18]

By the time whites began arriving, Northern Paiute bands were raiding north of the Blue Mountains, to steal horses and would-be slaves from the Umatilla and Cayuse, and contending with the Tenino—who, residing far from Comanche-Shoshoni sources, long had few horses—for control

of hunting and gathering lands in the Deschutes River country that both groups claimed. As Gregory Michno has put it, the Teninos and Paiutes "would not pass up any chance to fight each other." But the advantages lay with the area's Paiutes—known as the Hunipuitokas or Walpapi—and they established dominance over much of Central Oregon. The Redmond Caves, which had once provided campsites for Teninos headed south to seasonal hunting and gathering sites, were permanently abandoned as the area fell under the sway of Paiutes.[19]

But not all Paiutes (or their Shoshoni and Bannock cousins) acquired horses. For those that did not, life changed less than for those who did— except that now they were more open to aggression from mounted bands that often arrived from considerable distances. As mountain man Warren Ferris observed, "poorer classes, who do not possess horses . . . pass their lives in single families" living off what they are able to gather from the land. He judged it "the most miserable" existence imaginable.[20] Fur trader Peter Skene Ogden was equally appalled at how basic this life was. After investigating an Indian "hut" near the mouth of the Malheur River, he wrote,

> I had often heard that these wretches subsisted on ants, locusts and small fish not larger than minnies [minnows]. . . . I found that it was the case. . . . One of their dishes, not of a small size, was filled with ants. They collect them in the morning . . . before the thaw commences. The locusts they collect in Summer and store up for their Winter eating. . . . It appeared strange, and the only reason I can give . . . is the poverty of this country.[21]

As Native Americans, both afoot and on horseback, probed areas east of the Cascades searching for sustenance and fresh opportunities, whites also began moving in. Unlike Native Americans, many were looking not for riches or places to live but for routes to Western Oregon. Like Kennewick Man—and Lewis and Clark—they too were "just passing through." And for good reason. Compared with the attractive pictures of the Willamette Valley then circulating, Eastern Oregon seemed grim and unappealing, a trial to be endured en route to the Promised Land rather than a place to build one's future. Others moved into the area for what could be described as geopolitical reasons: seeking to keep Americans out, in the case of the

Hudson's Bay Company, or to discern routes to California, in the case of American champions of Manifest Destiny.

Wilson Price Hunt, leading the so-called Overland Astorians, was in the forefront of American incursions. The dynamic and ambitious John Jacob Astor had seen opportunity in the Northwest and founded the Pacific Fur Company to compete with Britain's Hudson's Bay Company for the riches from beaver pelts found there. Astor planned to erect a trading post near the mouth of the Columbia and dispatched two parties for that purpose, one by sea the other by land. Hunt was in charge of the latter.[22]

After overwintering in Missouri, Hunt's party departed for the Northwest on April 22, 1811, planning to follow the route of Lewis and Clark. The plan was soon abandoned for a more southerly route. When they reached the Snake River, frequent falls and rapids necessitated abandoning attempts to use canoes. The party then ran short of food and nearly starved trying to find a way through Hells Canyon. As Hunt put it, for twenty days they had "worn ourselves out futilely trying to find a passage," only to eventually turn back and strike off cross-country in a northwesterly direction. Two weeks later, still desperately short of food and exhausted from floundering through snow, they reached "a beautiful valley several miles wide and very long. A pretty stream meanders there and the beaver seem to be plentiful." It was the valley that would come to be known, appropriately, as the Grande Ronde.

Continuing on, the party crossed the mountains and descended to reach a thirty-four-teepee village of "Sciatogas and Tushepohs," probably Cayuse and Nez Perce: "The residents had at least two thousand horses." A week later they reached the Umatilla River and, six days later, the Columbia, which they followed downstream until, on February 16, the "fog dissipated in the afternoon . . . and soon afterward we saw Fort Astoria."[23]

As it turned out, Donald McKenzie and a group of twelve men who had separated from Hunt's party in Idaho were already there, having arrived in Astoria on January 18. John Day and Ramsey Crooks were less fortunate. Left behind near present-day Weiser, Idaho, because of Day's ill health, the starving pair followed Hunt and company across the Blue Mountains to the Umatilla, where Natives nursed them back to health. But their troubles were not over; struggling on, they faced one problem after another until, in May, a group of trappers heading downstream were hailed by the gaunt, bedraggled, nearly naked pair—the John Day River, near the mouth of which they were rescued, was named in honor of one of the unfortunate pair. For his part, McKenzie would stay on in Oregon, trapping in the Willamette Valley and then in southern Idaho and Eastern Oregon. It was he who named the Owyhee and Malheur Rivers—names that spoke volumes of his view of the area.[24]

Nor was that the end of it. The *Tonquin*, the ship sent to help establish Fort Astoria, was lost soon after its arrival, together with much of the outpost's trade goods. Lacking other means of getting word to Astor, Robert Stuart departed by land on June 29, 1812, more or less retracing Hunt's route. After crossing the Blue Mountains he encountered one of Hunt's former guides near the confluence of the Owyhee and Snake Rivers; he told Stuart there was an easier route than that Hunt had taken over the pass to Teton Valley. As Stuart wrote, "I without loss of time offered him a Pistol a Blanket of Blue Cloth a looking Glass and a little Powder and Ball, if he would guide us to the other side, which he immediately accepted." Two days later the Indian disappeared with his gifts and Stuart's mount— but his information remained in Stuart's mind and no doubt influenced his decision to veer south and led Stuart to South Pass, which he crossed on October 22. The gentle, twenty-mile-wide pass was the last-discovered link in what would become the Oregon Trail.[25]

In 1834 a company led by Nathaniel Wyeth and Jason Lee traveled the length of the Oregon Trail to the Willamette Valley, the first immigrant party to traverse its entire length. Then in 1840 a party led by mountain man Joe Meek took a wagon from Fort Hall in southern Idaho to Marcus Whitman's mission at Waiilatpu (near present-day Walla Walla), thus suggesting the practicality of taking the possessions to start a new life through to the Willamette Valley. A flood of would-be settlers soon followed; the first large group, the Great Migration of 1843, included between seven hundred and a thousand immigrants. In the years that followed thousands more would make their way west over the route (and thousands more would follow it part way before branching off to California).

British policy makers and Canadian fur traders found American inroads in the Northwest unsettling, but concern focused as much on the competition in the fur trade and potential American territorial claims as on fear of an influx of settlers—although these concerns were, of course, intimately interconnected. In 1823 Hudson's Bay Company, now united with the rival North West Company, named Peter Skene Ogden chief trapper for the Snake River division of its Columbia Department. In that capacity, Ogden led a series of five expeditions between 1824 and 1830 to probe the interior. On these trips Ogden sought to trap out the area, creating a "fur desert" that would serve as a buffer against American intrusions. His was the first in a long series of developments aimed at tapping and exporting Eastern Oregon's resources. Unlike Lewis and Clark and their successors, he was not just passing through.[26]

In 1825–1826, Ogden journeyed down the Columbia from Fort Nez Perce (located at the mouth of the Walla Walla River) to the "River of the Falls." His party crossed to the west side of the Deschutes, "bade farewell to the Columbia" and headed south. Passing the site of present-day Dufur on Fifteen-Mile Creek and continuing on through Tygh Valley, Ogden noted the area had been "formerly stocked with beaver, but the Nez Perces Indians had destroyed all." Things got worse. The country became "covered with rocks and stones" and word arrived that Finan McDonald, who had set out with others ahead of Ogden to trap along the upper Deschutes, had collected only 460 beaver "owing to the poverty of the country." Near its confluence with Crooked River, Ogden's party recrossed the Deschutes and worked its way southeast through the Crooked River country. Troubles continued to mount. Hunters found little game to feed the cavalcade; thefts of horses had been something of a problem all along, but now "we require to watch by day and night"; like Tygh Valley, this area had been trapped out by the Nez Perce; moreover, the river was too frozen for effective trapping. After crossing the Ochocos, on January 11, starving and with but few beaver to show for their efforts, the party reached the upper John Day. The route, Ogden wrote, "cannot be surpassed in badness." They struggled on until, on February 2, they reached the Snake River. Here, Ogden observed, "as far as the eye can reach, [there is] nothing but lofty mountains. A more gloomy country I never yet saw." Continuing south, Ogden's men trapped on the lower Malheur and the Owyhee. Since those rivers seemed to hold plenty of beaver, Ogden left Antoine Sylvaille there to continue trapping, planning to rejoin him on his return. Ogden then swung east across present-day southern Idaho before finally turning back, traversing Central Oregon once again, and crossing the Cascades to the Willamette Valley. The party arrived at the Hudson's Bay Company's Fort Vancouver on July 17. It had been a trying trip—especially the outward struggle across Central Oregon and the John

Day country. It certainly had not been a journey that would encourage others to follow, yet follow it Ogden himself did on a second expedition in 1826–1827.[27]

This time Ogden's party crossed the Deschutes some miles upstream from its mouth on a rickety Indian "bridge made of slender wood"—and lost five horses "thro' the bridge." From there, they more or less followed the route that in time would be that of a military wagon road and along which Thomas Condon would collect. They had difficulties with Indians while traveling through the Deschutes River country, repeatedly losing horses to them. Angling south of their route of the year before, they reached the Harney Basin on November 1. In the vicinity of Malheur and Harney Lakes, the "trappers did not see a vestige of beaver" and, except for waterfowl, other animals were scarce too. It was disappointing, for Antoine Sylvaille had reached that area as he trapped up the Malheur and had reported beaver abundant on a river flowing into the lakes, a river that today bears a corruption of his name—the Sylvies.[28]

In spite of Ogden's frustration with the thefts of horses—at one point in 1825 he had written, "the sooner we can get rid of the Indians the safer our horses will be"—he was a careful and not unsympathetic observer of Native peoples. Of the Harney Basin Paiutes, he wrote,

> It is incredible the number of Indians in this quarter. We cannot go 10 yds. Without finding them. Huts generally of grass of a size to hold 6 or 8 persons. No Indian nation so numerous as these in all North America. I include both Upper and Lower Snakes, the latter as wild as deer. . . . What a fine field for the [missionary] society; one equal to it not to be found. They lead a most wandering life. . . . Unfortunate creatures what privations you are doomed to endure. . . . Many a day they pass without food and without a murmur. Had they arms and ammunition they might resort to buffalo, but without . . . the war tribes would soon destroy them. The country is bare of beaver to enable them to procure arms. Indian traders cannot afford to supply them free.

Lacking firearms and with few horses, the Paiutes seem not to have given Ogden the degree of difficulty experienced earlier in the expedition, but still, impoverished as they were and with little to trade, they had to steal the few horses they acquired, a prospect against which Ogden's party had to be perpetually on guard.[29]

Short on food and supplies, Ogden summed up the situation: "prospects gloomy." He planned to leave the Harney Basin for the Clammitte [Klamath] country, where he hoped conditions would be more satisfactory, but his scouts had difficulty finding water and game for the journey. Finally, "with general gloom prevailing in camp, with all in starving condition," Ogden raised camp and headed west. Snow soon added to the party's difficulties, and with no game in sight Ogden feared "our horses will fall to the kettle."[30]

In spite of everything, Ogden managed to make it to the upper Deschutes and from there south into Klamath country. Finan McDonald had edged into the area the year before, supposedly the first white man to do so, but Ogden now ventured farther. He went down the Klamath River nearly to the sea, and then back north across the Siskiyous to the headwaters of the Rogue.[31] The details of these travels are obscure, but clearly they were extensive, and the information he learned about the Klamaths provided a foundation for much subsequent activity. Oddly, on May 14, when the time came to end his expedition and make his way to a Hudson's Bay Company post, he returned by way of the Harney Basin.[32] Once again experiencing difficulties there, Ogden wrote, "I have done my duty examining this barren country, but our loss has been greater than our profit." Two days later, he added, "The country must be explored as long as we can find water or the means of advancing. Unfortunately this country has been too long neglected." On June 3, he added, "If I escape this year, I will not be doomed to endure another" such expedition. But survive it he did. On July 16 his party reached the Snake downstream from its confluence with the Malheur. There, "not wishing to lose any time," Ogden left the main body to hurry on to Fort Vancouver.[33]

Conditions soon began to change. In the face of relentless trapping, beaver populations plummeted; more important, the market for beaver pelts collapsed as tastes in dress changed in Europe. Prime pelts that had sold for some $6 a pound between 1828 and 1833 had dropped to around $2.60 by 1841. Trapping continued, but the once-great profit incentives were gone. Meanwhile, Americans were growing more interested in farmland than the fur trade, and their government more active than ever in pursuing geopolitical opportunities in the continent's western reaches. These two concerns met in the person of John C. Fremont who, between 1842 and 1853, led five exploring expeditions into the West.

In 1841 Senator Thomas Hart Benton and other champions of Manifest Destiny pushed through Congress a $30,000 appropriation for a survey of the Oregon Trail. Second Lieutenant Fremont was selected for the task and, in 1842, with Kit Carson as his guide, pushed west up the North Platte to South Pass. The following year he mapped the trail through to Fort Vancouver. His "Report and Map"—in its various popular permutations—would guide thousands to Oregon. Following the discovery of gold in California, many thousands more would swing south near Fort Hall, guided by Joseph Ware's *Emigrants' Guide to California*, published in 1849, a guide that drew on Fremont's third expedition as well as his first two.

Fremont's explorations along the Oregon Trail revealed little new about Oregon east of the Cascades, but his subsequent travels certainly did. Following his arrival at Fort Vancouver in 1843, Fremont returned to The Dalles to seek a route south to California. He traveled up the Deschutes: "The country," he reported, "is abundantly watered with large streams, which pour down from the neighboring range. These streams are characterized by the narrow and chasm-like valleys in which they run, generally sunk a thousand feet below the plain. . . . The road across the country, which would otherwise be very good, is rendered impracticable for wagons by these streams."[34] He then swung southeast. On December 16, 1843, struggling through ice and snow, his party emerged from pine forest at the rim of a huge fault block escarpment: "At our feet—more than a thousand feet below—we looked onto a green prairie country, in which a beautiful lake, some twenty miles in length was spread along the foot of the mountains." Descending into sunshine and warmth, Fremont promptly labeled his find Summer Lake, the escarpment above Winter Ridge—names they bear to this day. His find was not an unmixed blessing: the lake proved to be alkaline.[35] Continuing south, Fremont's party entered ostensibly Mexican territory, seeking in vain for a good pass across the Sierra Nevada (a search that made him the first white to see Lake Tahoe).

Fremont, by then a captain, would return to the land east of the Cascades in 1845. After heading for the headwaters of the Arkansas, Fremont drove west to California—perhaps anticipating war with Mexico would soon erupt and wanting to be on the scene when it did. Fremont quickly wore out his welcome in California and was ordered to leave.[36] He took his time, but eventually did, traveling up the Sacramento to the Pit River and from its headwaters near the Oregon border made his way west. He traveled along Lost River to Tule Lake (long known as Rhett Lake) and, reaching the outlet of Upper Klamath Lake, made his way north along its western shore to some Native villages near the later site of Fort Klamath. There Archibald Gillespie caught up with him and supposedly delivered secret instructions. Fremont promptly began moving south along Upper Klamath's rugged eastern shore, headed back to California. As he later recalled, "I resolved to . . . return forthwith to the Sacramento Valley in order to bring to bear all the influences I could command [in the expected] war with Mexico. . . . This decision was a first step in the conquest of California."[37]

Trouble was brewing in the Klamath country too. Before they caught up with Fremont, Gillespie's small group had been stalked by Indians for a hundred miles or more, and on May 9, as they made their way south, Fremont's command was attacked—probably by the same Indians who had been shadowing Gillespie. Three of his men were killed, and, although those who attacked were probably Modocs, Fremont took revenge the next day by attacking and destroying the Klamath village of Dokdokwas at the mouth of the Williamson River. Within a week he was back in California, but the ill-will generated by his impetuous attack on the Klamaths remained.[38]

Taken all in all, Fremont's expeditions yielded less new information than Peter Skene Ogden's, and antipathy between whites and Indians would surely have developed regardless of what happened at Dokdokwas. Fremont was the first to recognize the endorheic nature of the Great Basin—a great enclosed area into which rivers flowed but from which there were no outlets—a condition that helped both to explain the world in which Luther Cressman was to work and to shape the environmental debates of a later generation. Yet Fremont's greatest contribution was of another sort. He did more to encourage migration over the Oregon Trail than anyone else and through that brought inexorable change to the nation. Lewis and Clark and Fremont's other predecessors had probed the route west earlier, but Americans had not yet been ready for a great overland migration. By the mid-1840s they were. Between 1846 and 1869, some four hundred thousand settlers traversed the Oregon Trail.

In spite of the vast traffic that developed over the Oregon Trail, the passage was always daunting and hope of a better route ever-present. After crossing the Snake River into Oregon south of present-day Nyssa, the trail continued northwest to the Malheur, then turned north up Willow Creek, crossed to Farewell Bend on the Snake, and then entered the canyon of Burnt River. Stephen Meek—Joe's older brother—seized on the idea of continuing west up the Malheur (rather than turning north up Willow Creek), crossing the High Desert near Malheur and Harney Lakes, and then swinging northwest toward the Deschutes River and The Dalles.[39] Such a route, the elder Meek thought, would avoid the Oregon Trail's tortuous section along Burnt River and across the Blue Mountains. Meek claimed to have been in the area previously, although he may simply have heard of it from trappers who had worked the Malheur as far as Harney Basin (perhaps some who had accompanied Ogden or Sylvaille, but probably not Ogden himself)—with a garrulous raconteur such as Meek one could never be sure of the truth.[40]

Meek was in Fort Hall in 1845, looking for employment, and signed on to lead a train of some five hundred wagons through to Oregon. As the group proceeded west, he persuaded some of the leaders to try a "shortcut" that would avoid crossing the Blue Mountains and rumored Indian troubles to the north. Some 40 percent of the train agreed to try his proposed route; two hundred wagons, some thousand people, and well over two thousand cattle were soon headed up the Malheur.[41]

The travails that followed are well documented, for at least six diarists left records of the experience. One provided what must have been the almost-universal view: "The new route was a trackless waste, covered, for the most part, by immense fields of sage-brush that grew tall, strong, and dense. Through these sage-fields we were obliged to force the oxen, the teams taking turns, day about, in breaking their way."[42] Samuel Parker, one of the captains of the train, was blunt: "Tuck what is caled meeks Cut of[f]. . . . A Bad cut of[f] fore all that tuck it." At another point, he wrote that there was "Swareing without end," much of it directed toward Meek. Ere long some were even arguing Meek should be hanged.[43]

Finally the group struggled over Stinkingwater Pass and into Harney Basin. What awaited them was unexpected. Since Ogden's visits, Malheur Lake had dwindled to a stagnant, marshy pool. Confused by this, Meek seemed unsure of what to do next, and several members of the party lost confidence in his leadership. The party found water at Silver Lake,[44] but when Meek proposed following its little tributary northwest toward Crooked River, dissidents insisted they head west, directly overland to the Deschutes. They prevailed, and things quickly became worse. As James Field, one of the more level-headed wagon captains, observed, Meek "well knew that there was a scarcity of grass and water across here and so informed them, but . . . they would have him go it, and now blame him for coming the route they obliged him to [take]."[45]

Dissension continued, and the party split. By the time the two groups rejoined in the scablands south of Shaniko, food was nearly gone, and people were dying from illness and malnutrition. Relief parties from The Dalles aided the destitute immigrants, but before they limped into the frontier outpost more than twenty-three of the party had died; another twenty-five more would do so in The Dalles. Samuel Parker summed it up neatly: "I will just say pen and tong[ue] will both fall short when they gow [*sic*] to tell the suffering the company went through."[46]

In spite of the disastrous experience of Meek's train, the desire to find a viable route through the Harney Basin did not die. Hoping to induce more settlers to come to the southern Willamette valley, a group set out in 1852 to scout out a trail across the Cascades near Diamond Peak. The plan was for immigrants to follow Meek's route to the Deschutes and then turn south to link up with a new, toll-free road over the mountains. The plan almost died aborning. In 1853 Elijah Elliott, who had heard of but not seen the trail, led a wagon train west over Meek's route.[47] The party ran into trouble and began running short of supplies before reaching the Deschutes, and Elliott hurried ahead with part of the train to seek help. Reaching the Deschutes (where the party camped at today's Pioneer Park in the city of Bend), Elliott became confused. Mistaking the South Sister for Diamond Peak, the key landmark indicating the crossing point, he led his party across the Cascades into the rugged upper McKenzie River watershed. Bogged down by heavy timber and almost impassable terrain, members of this "Lost Wagon Train" nearly starved before being saved by a rescue party from the valley. The main body, following behind, turned south at Bend and successfully located Diamond Peak and blazes cut to mark the new trail. Though this second group experienced great difficulty on the largely uncleared route, they actually managed to reach the Willamette Valley well before Elliot's group was found and rescued.[48]

A train the following year was more successful but the route, by then known as Elliott's Cutoff, never became popular. These experiences, like those of Meek's party earlier, did little to convince immigrants that the area east of the Cascades was anything more than an inhospitable place to hurry across—although in 1853 James McClure did remark on the beauties of the upper Deschutes and noted that the "desert we have just crossed is covered with the finest kind of bunch grass."[49]

Two years later William Keil's utopian community took a modified route, leaving Burnt River to make their way across the Blues on a middle route over Dixie Pass. Their experience was harrowing—sufficiently so that no later wagon trains took the route—but Keil's group made it across the Ochocos to The Dalles, proceeded on to Washington's Willapa Bay, and subsequently moved south to settle in the Willamette Valley.[50]

Meek and later immigrants who took all or part of his cutoff were not alone in seeking a better route to the Willamette Valley. In 1843 brothers Jesse and Lindsay Applegate, emigrating from Missouri, each lost a child on the Columbia River portion of the Oregon Trail. Seeking a better alternative, the two, together with nine others, set out on June 25, 1846, to scout out a southern route. From the Willamette Valley to the Rogue they traversed relatively well-known terrain, but when they turned east they entered largely unfamiliar territory—although Ogden and Fremont had provided glimpses of what to expect.[51]

After reaching Lower Klamath Lake, the party passed north of Tule Lake, made their way across the rugged Modoc Plateau[52] to Goose Lake, crossed the Warner Mountains at Fandango Pass (just south of the Oregon-California border), and from there worked their way southeast across the Black Rock Desert to the Humboldt River, where they intersected the main California Trail. Most of party remained there to allow their horses to graze and recover, while Jesse proceeded on to Fort Hall, where he persuaded some 150 immigrants to try his trail. Their trip was trying, and one of those initial immigrants, J. Quinn Thornton, later wrote a series of attacks on Applegate and his so-called trail. Improvements gradually made the route better, and although it never became a major thoroughfare to the Willamette, it did play a significant role in settlement of the Rogue River Valley. In 1853, probably its peak year, some three thousand immigrants used the trail.

The timing of the opening of the Applegate Trail was hardly propitious, coming as it did on the heels of Fremont's clashes with Natives whose lands it traversed. Attacks by Modocs became regular occurrences along the route, and in 1852 a massacre occurred at Bloody Point on Tule Lake in which eighty whites were killed. Paiutes and Pit River Indians added danger on portions of the trail farther east and south. The journal of Ananias Rogers Pond, who traversed a portion of the trail in 1849, reflects the constant fear of attack by Indians, especially during the leg from the Black Rock Desert to Fandango Pass. Near the latter he wrote, "All Travellers say they [the Indians] are troublesome in these parts & it appears they are."[53] Still, it seems difficulties of the trail, not fear of attack, kept the trail from becoming popular.

Negative opinions of the region were reinforced by the Williamson-Abbot Pacific Railroad Survey of 1855. The Army Corps of Engineers had assigned Lieutenants Robert Williamson and Henry Larcom Abbot to investigate the feasibility of a rail route from the San Francisco Bay area to Portland. To examine possibilities east of the Cascades, they proceeded up the Sacramento and Pit Rivers. From near the headwaters of the latter, the group swung west past Tule Lake and Lost River following the Applegate Trail to Upper Klamath Lake. There the party turned north past Klamath Marsh to the Deschutes River country. Near the headwaters of the Deschutes they located a promising-looking pass over the Cascades, probably the same one Elliott had traced three years earlier.[54] While Williamson investigated, Abbot pushed north to the Mpto-ly-as (i.e., Metolius), a major western tributary of the Deschutes. Following it, he soon found himself in a "very wild and beautiful" world of yawning, basalt-rimmed canyons. Building a railroad through the area would be daunting, if not impossible. As Abbot put it in his official report, "The impracticality of the [rail]road is most sufficiently manifest" north of the Metolius, for between it and The Dalles were seven major canyons to cross, as well as the Mutton Mountains (an eastern spur of the Cascades).[55]

Abbot reached The Dalles on September 11 and quickly doubled back to the Metolius-Deschutes country hoping to find a pass over the Cascades near Mount Jefferson, a pass that, if found, would make a trans-montane railroad north of the Klamath area feasible. He made his way across the range, reaching the Willamette Valley in mid-October, but failed to find

"Wild and beautiful": Pacific Railroad Survey lithograph of Seekseekqua Creek near its confluence with the Deschutes River canyons based on field sketch by Lt. Henry Abbot. Credit: Div. of Work and Industry, National Museum of American History, Smithsonian Institution.

a usable pass. Had Abbot ventured a bit farther south, he would probably have found Santiam Pass—a viable, but hardly ideal, crossing that independent trapper Joseph Gervais had been using for some years—but he did not.[56] A rail route, it seemed, would need to cross the Cascades near the head of the Deschutes or veer east and avoid the Deschutes "valley" altogether. In any case, Abbot observed, the regions he surveyed "are unsettled, and, as a general thing, [so] barren in their character . . . [that] the country is unfitted to support a civilized population."[57]

Although Abbot and Williamson failed to find feasible routes for a railroad, they did accumulate a massive amount of geological, biological, and ethnographic information on the areas they traversed, information that would provide the basis for generations of scholarly study. But in the short run their expedition provided support for the view that Central Oregon was a marginal area unreachable by railroads and hardly worth the trouble in any case.

All this probing by whites had a tremendous impact on the Native peoples of the area—and on Indian-white relations as well. Not all of it was negative. The Cayuse, Umatillas, and others found they could profit by trading fresh stock and supplies to immigrants staggering into their territory over the Oregon Trail. Even the Coeur d'Alene, who lived well north of the trail, found it profitable to drive horses and cattle south to trade with those in incoming wagon trains. Horses brought $40 to $100 apiece, so those in a position to engage in the trade were able to obtain a variety of goods previously unavailable, goods that improved their standard of living in many ways and through further transfers gradually made their way to Native people well distant from the trail itself.[58]

The acquisition of the goods of white society did not always come by peaceful means. Native groups had a long tradition of raiding. For the Shoshoni, Bannock, and Paiute, who had long lived off whatever they could find in their harsh environment, stealing from whites or other Natives who chanced into their lands was a natural outgrowth of their traditional means of support. Such action carried no moral or geopolitical implications; it was simply what one did to survive. Fur traders, explorers, or immigrants who wandered into their land were fair game.

Whites were outraged by the attacks and thefts. They saw them as the actions of an unpredictable, bloodthirsty people who could never be trusted and could be kept at bay only by force. No attempt at understanding the Indian situation, let alone sympathizing with them, seemed worth the effort. Ananias Pond reported that a member of his train "discovered an Indian among the Oxen and Shot him through the head." More humane than most, Pond wrote "I deprecate [sic] . . . taking the life Even of an Indian on Suspicion." Five days later, an ox broke its back in a fall, but the owners were unable to bring themselves to shoot it to put it out of its misery—yet they "appear rather anxious to shoot Diggers." Such attitudes were certainly not restricted to Pond's wagon train.[59]

Other factors also contributed to the likelihood of clashes. Immigrants brought smallpox and other diseases with them, and although Native peoples did not fully understand what was involved, they saw the connection between the advent of wagon trains and the deaths that followed. When missionary Marcus Whitman treated victims of smallpox and whites recovered but Indians died, Native frustration boiled over. The Whitman massacre of 1847 resulted, and the white response—the Cayuse War of 1848–1850 and the hanging of alleged leaders—followed. In 1855, after a subsequent intertribal alliance collapsed in the face of white military actions, the Cayuse would end up on the Umatilla Reservation southeast of Pendleton.[60]

Smallpox also broke out among the Modocs after immigrants began moving through their territory on the Applegate Trail (as did scarlet fever). Whether this led to the rise of Modoc militancy such as was manifested at Bloody Point in 1852 is not clear, but that may well have been the case.

The impact of livestock that immigrants took through Indian country is more difficult to assess. Diarists frequently noted grasslands along the trail were virtually denuded by the end of summer. Tribes with large herds, such as the Cayuse, must have suffered as a result. The subsequent arrival of gold miners and settlers only made matters worse. Under the circumstances, Natives had ample reason to try to bar whites from their lands—or at least even accounts a bit through raids and thefts.

After some five decades of probing by explorers, trappers, and immigrants, Eastern Oregon was little changed; it remained a hard land where life was never easy and conflict a matter of course. Still, the period had set in motion forces that would lead to new sources of friction and reshape old ones.

The legacy of Indian-white friction and distrust helped shape later events, but so did other things. Although immigrants had seen nothing to make them halt to settle before reaching the Willamette Valley, some discerned spots where the possibilities of settlement seemed real enough. The Grande Ronde Valley, the area around Bend on the upper Deschutes, and the grasslands of the Harney Basin became ever more attractive in the mind's eye of those who, upon arriving in the Willamette Valley, found the best claims already taken up and life there harder than had been anticipated. Soon a trickle back across the Cascades began. Andrew Jackson Tetherow, who had survived Meek Cutoff with his father, Sol Tetherow, was among the returnees, moving to a homestead on the Deschutes in the late 1870s.[61]

Other things drew whites east of the mountains. As panning for gold gave way to hydraulic sluicing and hard-rock mining in California, many of the forty-niners (and later arrivals as well) began seeking their fortunes more widely. Gold strikes in Idaho drew many in that direction, and in crossing through Oregon some found rich deposits in the Blue Mountains. People soon flocked to the area.

A sort of human detritus was left by the era of probing. Joseph Gervais and his annual trans-Cascade trips to trap east of the mountains—trips that continued long after the heyday of the fur trade had passed—could be said to represent this sort of continuity. But perhaps the best example was provided by Jean Baptiste Charbonneau, the son of Sacagawea born during the Lewis and Clark expedition. After growing up, Charbonneau worked as a guide for Duke Friedrich of Wurttemberg in 1823, spent time in Europe, and then returned to the West where he worked as a fur trapper and trader, military scout during the Mexican-American War, and gold prospector in California's Placer County. In 1866, seeking to return "to familiar scenes," he left California for Eastern Oregon, where he died on May 16 near the tiny community of Rome in today's Malheur County. According to the *Owyhee Avalanche*, he died of pneumonia. Charbonneau's gravesite on an isolated, windswept hill is on the National Register of Historic Places.[62] With his death, events inaugurated by Lewis and Clark had come full circle. By the time Charbonneau died, he was an anachronism, a symbol of times long past.

3

Questing for Gold

In 1856, Major General John E. Wool, in charge of the Department of the Pacific, issued an order banning white settlement east of the Cascades in Oregon and Washington. Wool directed that

> No immigrant or other whites, except Hudson's Bay Company
> persons having ceded rights from the Indians, will be permitted
> to settle or remain in Indian country. . . . These orders are not
> however to apply to miners engaged in collecting gold. The miners
> will, however, be notified that should they interfere with the
> Indians or their squaws, they will be punished and sent from the
> country.[1]

As Major Gabriel Rains, commandant at The Dalles, had put it the year before regarding the land east of the Cascades, "If any country has ever merited the title 'Indian country,' this is it." He and Wool intended it should remain so.[2]

Their view was not shared by authorities in Oregon and Washington Territories. To them the interior Northwest was an extension of the settlers' frontier, not yet settled but destined to be—and the sooner, the better. Indian troubles needed to be brought to an end by restricting tribes to reservations. If necessary, force should be used to bring this about. Preparing the way for settlement, on January 11, 1854, Oregon created Wasco County, encompassing all its territory east of the Cascades (some 130,000 square miles, for at the time Oregon Territory extended to the Rockies). As an early historian put it, Indian troubles created "a need for local government [that] preceded the creation of towns."[3] Colonel Rains scoffed at the action; there were, he claimed, only thirty-five white residents in the entire area, and most of those not bona fide settlers but people who lived by stealing horses, selling whiskey to the Indians, and trading with people in wagon trains passing through to the Willamette Valley. There was a seed of truth in his statement. Aside from The Dalles, the only node of settlement in Eastern Oregon was in the Umatilla Valley, and after Wool issued his order in 1856, the military took rather unsuccessful steps to get it removed.[4]

Indian-white clashes had marked the area ever since the Whitman Massacre of 1847 and the Cayuse War that followed. In the mid-1850s the Cayuse, still smarting, desperately sought allies for renewed combat many thought inevitable. Wool lacked sufficient forces for a quick victory, but the governors of Oregon and Washington Territories, George L. Curry and Isaac I. Stevens, impatient to rescue the area from "barbarism," issued calls for volunteer militia to force the area's tribes onto reservations. Even this heavy-handed approach was too restrained for some of the troops (as well as various settlers and newspaper editors west of the Cascades). For them extermination was the proper solution, and they repeatedly acted in ways seemingly aimed at bringing that about. On July 17, 1856, a party of Cayuse camped in the Grande Ronde suffered an unprovoked attack by a force of Washington Territorial Volunteers under Colonel Benjamin F. Shaw. Forty Indians were killed. One may question the propriety of Shaw's troops operating in Oregon (and of Oregon Volunteers who crossed into Washington Territory's Walla Walla country), but a half century later a writer in the Portland *Oregonian* still viewed Shaw's action as "a master stroke to rescue the country from barbarism."[5]

Wool was convinced that clashes resulted from actions by whites as often as by Indians. He saw the former as both triggering conflict and causing its continuation, while the "practice of the Volunteers of killing [Indian] friends as well as enemies . . . greatly increased the ranks of the hostiles." Speaking of the attack by Shaw's troops, he wrote, "The whole object was to plunder the Indians of their horses and provoke a prolongation of the war." He assured Governor Stevens that "the war with the Indians will be prosecuted with all vigor, promptness, and efficiency. . . . I think I shall be able to bring the war to a close in a few months, provided the extermination . . . is not determined on . . . private war prevented and volunteers withdrawn.[6]

The matter was not so simple. Wool was at loggerheads with the territorial governors of Oregon and Washington, who shared the hostility to Indians that Ananias Pond and others had seen on the overland trails. Stevens and Curry wanted Indian depredations punished, wagon trains protected, tribes confined to reservations, and the remaining land opened to white settlement. The governors' call for militia was aimed at forcing an uncompromising settlement on their terms.[7] Wool opposed such a course, but to no avail. Indeed, the territorial legislatures of both Oregon and Washington petitioned to have Wool removed from his command. Before that could happen, Colonel George Wright, who commanded the Fifth US Infantry Regiment and had been placed in charge of the new Military District of Oregon, repeated Wool's order of exclusion. But Stevens, Curry, and their allies won out. In 1857 Wool was reassigned to duty on the East Coast. Soon after, his successor, Brigadier General William S. Harney, rescinded Wool's non-settlement order.[8]

Even if Wool's order had stayed on the books, the course of subsequent events would probably not have been much changed. Wool specifically exempted gold seekers from his exclusion order, and it was from this quarter that Eastern Oregon's first big influx of whites came. Beginning in 1850, gold discoveries in southwestern Oregon demonstrated that not all the West's precious metal was in California. A major gold rush centered on Southern Oregon's Jacksonville area was soon under way.[9]

Attention soon turned to areas east of the Cascades, spurred by memories of earlier finds there. Members of Meek's wagon train had stumbled on gold in the upper Malheur drainage but had not recognized it for what it was until later; and four Germans had found gold in the western reaches of the Ochocos in 1849. Repeated searches failed to locate these lost "mines"—the Blue Bucket and Four Dutchmen—but memory of them helped encourage the flood of gold seekers who flooded into Eastern Oregon in the 1850s and 1860s.[10]

In 1855 gold was found near Fort Colville in Washington Territory; in 1860 richer finds occurred in the Clearwater drainage; other strikes followed. Miners departed from California, where placer mining had passed its peak—and from Portland, the Willamette Valley, and elsewhere—to seek their fortunes in these locales.[11] On October 23, 1861, as his party crossed Eastern Oregon headed for Fort Colville, Henry Griffin chanced upon a rich new treasure trove on a tributary of Powder River. Within a year the town of Auburn sprang up there; in a short time it was the largest in Oregon, with a population of five thousand, some sixty stores, and a thousand houses. An estimated $10,000,000 in gold poured from the area's mines. But Auburn was a fleeting phenomenon. When the state legislature created Baker County in 1862, Auburn was named county seat; it remained such until 1874, by which time nearby gold production had plummeted and the town had been largely abandoned. In the end, it was not the strike there, but finds near the John Day River that had the greatest consequence.[12]

On June 8, 1862, William A. Allard, a member of a party of Californians headed for the Auburn diggings, found gold in Canyon Creek, a small tributary of the upper John Day River. Allard's find was extraordinarily rich, panning out at $18 to $20 a pan. The first claim was filed in early July, and a flood of others followed. One early arrival noted that on the trail to the diggings one could always see wagon trains ahead bound for the mines and yet others behind. Within a year some five thousand people were working Canyon Creek gulch, many more working the nearby Prairie diggings on the John Day proper, and a host of others panning nearer the river's headwaters—around Granite, Dixie, Greenhorn, Whitney, and elsewhere. Hard-rock mines soon joined placer mining and dredging and took extraction to a new, more industrialized—and destructive—level. Gold mining settled the John Day country, but in the end also devastated a considerable portion of it.[13]

Not everyone flocking to the area was a miner. There was the usual assortment of camp followers, saloon keepers, and gamblers, as well as storekeepers, teamsters, homesteaders, and others. Before the end of 1862, a train of thirty-two wagons arrived from near Red Bluff, California; included in the party were women and children. Among the new arrivals was Cincinnatus Heine ("Joaquin") Miller—an ex-Pony Express rider, newspaper editor, and sometime attorney—who would become Grant County's judge before gaining fame as a poet.[14]

The influx included a sizable number of Southerners. Miller had left Eugene after his pro-Confederate newspaper was shut down by authorities, and Dixie gained its name because of the predominance of Southerners there. In nearby Granite, also founded in 1862, Lincoln supposedly received but a single vote in the election of 1864.[15] Missourians—fleeing the devastation of the Civil War or conscription, or seeking refuge as Confederate general Sterling Price's ragtag army disintegrated—turned to the gold fields for safety and fresh opportunity. When the first store owner arrived in what would become Mitchell, he was amazed at the number of sons of the South who descended from the hills to provide customers for his goods (and his moonshine). More Southerners arrived from California. Many poured in over the Yreka Trail, a route from that northern California town (itself the center of an earlier gold rush). Others came via The Dalles from parts of the Willamette and Rogue River Valleys where Southerners had congregated. Taken together, these sources created a population that worried Unionists. In 1864, fear of outbreaks on Election Day and a Confederate flag-raising in Canyon City led to troops being ordered to the area. It is easy to overestimate the Southern influence in Eastern Oregon. No study of the makeup of its population similar to those of the Willamette Valley of the 1850s has been done—nor, in light of the limited data available, does one seem possible. Clearly, the state's Copperhead phobia—fear of Southern sympathizers in the state, hiding like poisonous snakes in the grass—rested on a shaky foundation, and many claims regarding Southern influence in Oregon were overblown.[16]

Still, it is evident the early gold seekers were predominantly young, single, white males: men seeking fortune and adventure rather than family farms and having little concern for building stable, lasting communities. David Newsom, a prosperous Willamette Valley farmer, described the situation. Oregon, he wrote, is made up of two classes of people: settlers and miners. Farmers who arrived in the 1850s and 1860s came to stay and build up the country, but the miners were "*adventurers, whose aim is to make their 'piles,' and then leave!*" Newsom added that many newcomers flocked to the mines simply to escape the Civil War and took to mining because they refused to work at any "decent" job. The miners, he added, claim Oregon (apparently meaning Eastern Oregon), is "only fit for coyotes and Indians."[17]

Newsom's picture was oversimplified. To be sure, gold drew miners by the thousands, but also people to supply their needs, and a ripple effect was quickly under way that affected The Dalles, Portland, and beyond. California's gold rush jump-started Oregon's economy, and the mines of Southern Oregon and the interior Northwest continued the process. The population of The Dalles rose from 250 to 2,500, while thousands more milled around awaiting passage upriver or transport overland to Canyon City. For a time, the incoming horde overwhelmed The Dalles, which was plundered and ruled by a mob. In addition to supplying Canyon City, The Dalles became a major supplier for Boise, Lewiston, Walla Walla, and other growing inland towns. Bloch-Miller & Company, located in The Dalles, became the largest outfitter in the state—and the largest buyer of gold. Direct shipments from Portland burgeoned too; like The Dalles, Portland and San Francisco enjoyed a major business stimulus from the interior Northwest's mines.[18]

The John Day mines were difficult to supply, the route to them long and tortuous. From The Dalles to Canyon City, pack strings initially used old Indian trails that Ogden and others had followed. Improvements were initiated in 1855, opening the way for freight wagons. Freighting soon became a "very lucrative" business, and beginning in May 1864, freighters were joined by four-horse stagecoaches carrying mail and passengers. Stage stops along the route supplied fresh horses, food, and simple lodging. Paiutes, still roaming free, raided ranches and stage stops along the route as well as freighters and stagecoaches traveling it. Highwaymen added to the danger. One stage stop, burned to the ground by Paiutes in 1866, still carries the name Burnt Ranch.[19]

Miners needed foodstuff, and farmers and ranchers moved into Eastern Oregon to supply it. A settler farming near Canyon City found that potatoes grew well, and his crop sold quickly at exorbitant prices. Farther east, Benjamin Brown, one of the first white settlers in the area that came to be called La Grande (initially it was Brownsville or Brown's Town), arrived in 1861. Others followed, attracted by the manifest agricultural and pastoral potential of the Grande Ronde Valley and the possibility of supplying wagon trains on the Oregon Trail as well as miners. One early settler noted, "The whole valley was covered with a dense, luxuriant growth of rye and bunch grass, sometimes as high as a man's head, and always so thick and tall it was impossible to see more than a few feet. . . . Only one who has seen it can appreciate its luxuriance and beauty." In 1862 the handful of cabins in the valley were huddled together for safety from Indian attack, but the settlement was growing rapidly. On September 22, James S. McClung noted in his diary, "we came to Legrande Citty 5 houses 1 store and a Black smith shop . . . some of the people were living in their tents & waggon beds until they could build houses." Just two weeks later Henry Herr reported, "This place is composed of 75 log cabins and emegrants [sic] with us are taking up claims and commencing to build houses. There are three stores." La Grande acquired a post office in 1863 and, by the end of 1868, boasted two newspapers. Nearby, Union developed as a supply center for mines in the Wallowa foothills, its name providing a challenge to Copperhead neighbors.[20]

The discovery of gold and silver in the Owyhee Mountains of southwestern Idaho in 1863 spawned similar events. Supplies came to Silver City and the area's other mining centers over trails from Boise to the north; Chico, California, to the southwest; and Portland and The Dalles to the west. Stage stops sprang up, their operators raising hay, cattle, and horses to supply both those en route and people already in the mining towns. On the Oregon side of the border, Jordan Valley became an active center supplying the Silver City area—and a major irritant to the area's Bannock and Paiute tribesmen.[21]

Clashes between Native populations and whites during the gold rush era grew out of the limited success of earlier efforts to settle the Northwest's "Indian problem." In the mid-1850s, Joel Palmer and Isaac Stevens had succeeded in getting the Cayuse, Umatilla, Yakama, Nez Perce, Tenino, and others to agree to settle on reservations. In the early 1860s a second round of reservations were agreed to by the Klamaths, Winnemucca Paiutes, Shoshonis, and Gosiutes, but these groups were all peripheral to the vast region stretching from the Ochocos and Blue Mountains south into the Great Basin, where various Northern Paiute bands continued to roam free. To them, miners and the agents of their support were invaders of a homeland they had never surrendered. Raids on settlers, miners, and stage stations were as much a defense of territory as a search for booty. Yet the so-called Snake War—which extended from 1864 to 1868 and which historian Gregory Michno considers the West's deadliest—was not merely a contest between Native people and white invaders. Indians were engaged on both sides of the conflict. It was shaped by traditional intertribal rivalries as well as white incursions.

In 1855 Tenino and Wasco leaders signed a treaty giving up traditional lands along the Columbia and elsewhere in exchange for a 464,000-acre reservation between the lower Deschutes and the Cascade Mountains, plus annuities and technical help. Paiutes, from whose territory much of the reservation was carved, began raiding the reservation almost at once.[22] In 1859, seeking to avenge one such attack, the reservation physician, Dr. Thomas L. Fitch, organized a force of fifty-three reservation Indians and supplied them with rifles and ammunition from the military post in The Dalles. Fitch's force located and attacked a Paiute camp on the John Day, killing ten men and capturing a number of women and children.

It was a Pyrrhic victory. The Paiutes rebounded and began raiding the reservation once more—and with considerable success. In August, Fitch sent a frantic message to The Dalles: "For God's sake send some help as soon as possible. We are surrounded with Snakes—they have killed a good many Indians, and got all our stock—don't delay a single minute." Troops were dispatched and the situation quieted down, but tension rose again when the troops were withdrawn in September 1860. Thus things stood as white traffic to the mines became a flood in 1861 and 1862.[23]

Paiute attacks on miners, supply trains, and post stations led to calls for a military response, and war soon erupted. It would drag on for years as the army and various volunteer units pursued Paiute and Shoshoni bands and fought them in battle after battle.[24] Many a white (either serving in a volunteer unit or acting on his own) simply sought to punish or extermi-nate Indians, but the army had a broader purpose. General George Crook and other commanders sought, by continually pursuing and defeating militant bands, to bring them to accept—however reluctantly—that they must give up their free-roaming lifestyle and move onto a reservation (or reservations) as tribes north of the Blues had done.

Victory did not come easily for whites. The regular army was busy with the Civil War, so volunteer units initially carried the burden. Neither the volunteers nor their leaders seemed up to the task in spite of help from Tenino and Wasco scouts from the Warm Springs Reservation.[25] Paiutes would attack, disappear, and quickly reappear elsewhere, often miles away. Paiute leadership—especially that of Ocheho, Paulina, and Weahwewah—was skillful, utilizing knowledge of the land and amazing mobility to great advantage. They tried to fight only when conditions seemed favorable. In July 1864, Lieutenant Colonel C. S. Drew led troops north through Sur-prise Valley, California, into Oregon looking for hostiles. Reaching the great Warner Escarpment, he recognized the difficulty of fighting in the area; it was, he wrote, "the Sebastopol of the Snake Indians." Unbeknownst to Drew, his troops were being watched from above by Chief Paulina and his Paiutes. Paulina was preparing to attack, but changed his mind when he noticed Drew had a howitzer and learned that additional troops were approaching from the east. He opted to wait and fight another day.[26]

The army did not always have such options. Whites continued flooding into the mining areas around Canyon City, Silver City, the Boise Basin,
and elsewhere, and army units repeatedly had to protect (or rescue) them.
Local newspapers kept up a drumbeat of criticism of military commanders for their slow responses to Indian attacks; as impatience grew, local
volunteers sometimes took matters into their own hands. In July 1866,
Civil War veteran Isaac Jennings led a group of outraged civilians from the
Silver City area to avenge recent attacks. Near Juniper Mountain, above
the Owyhee, they stumbled into an ambush. Jennings' volunteers were
nearly out of ammunition and on the verge of annihilation when rescued
five days later by army units. Their besiegers slipped quietly away.[27]

During the Snake War there were some seventy-five battles and skir-
mishes; along the Owyhee River alone there were seventeen (including
the debacle near Juniper Mountain). Army units spent months, summer
and winter, seeking to bring belligerents to bay, but with limited success;
when they did force a confrontation, whites had an indifferent record—as
at Crooked River in May 1864, Three Forks on the Owyhee in 1866, on the
Malheur in January 1867, and at Infernal Caverns south of Goose Lake in
California later that same year. This last, the bloodiest battle in the war,
involved primarily Pit River Indians rather than Paiutes, but it was clearly
part of the larger conflict—and was the only battle in the long war in which
a participant earned the Medal of Honor.[28]

However problematic prosecution of the war may have been, there
was never much doubt as to its eventual outcome. The army erected a
series of forts surrounding the northern Great Basin—Forts Boise, Walla
Walla, The Dalles, Ruby, and Churchill—and a larger number of permanent camps interior to the basin. The forts could supply troops and supplies to the interior camps and, as need arose, to troops in the field; the
camps, scattered at key points, were centers for intelligence-gathering and
quick response. Their mere presence had a dampening effect on the military ardor of nearby bands. So too did the construction and improvement
of military wagon roads in the area—while at the same time these roads
speeded the influx of whites drawn by the gold rush. With this support
network and Major General George Crook's policy of year-round campaigning, the various bands were worn down bit by bit. Paulina was killed
in 1867, and Weahwewah surrendered the following year. Ocheho fought
on, but more as a fugitive than a real threat.

Paulina's death and Weahwewah's surrender were revealing. Pursuit summer and winter left hostile bands with little time to hunt or gather foodstuffs; they had to steal cattle or starve—and it was the ranchers from whom Paulina had just stolen cattle who followed his tracks, ambushed, and killed him as he and fellow Paiutes gorged on captured beef.[29] Even more revealing were the words of General Crook to Weahwewah when the latter came to parlay. The chief told Crook his people wanted peace. Crook reportedly replied, "I am sorry to hear this. I was in hopes that you would continue the war," for he could easily replace any losses, while the chief would have to wait for the tribe's children to grow up to get new warriors. "In this way it would not be very long before we would have you all killed off, and then the government would have no more trouble with you." Humbled, Weahwewah agreed to go back to hunting and gathering and stop raiding. As he put it, they had "thrown away their ropes," indicating their intent to stop stealing horses.[30]

To solidify the new reality—and responding to recommendations from A. B. Meacham, superintendent of Indian Affairs for Oregon, and his successor T. B. Odeneal—in 1872 President Ulysses S. Grant established by executive order a reservation extending north and east of Malheur Lake to the upper reaches of the Malheur River. With additional land added in 1875, the reservation included some 1.8 million acres. However reluctantly, Weahwewah's people moved onto the reservation, and, although a remnant continued to roam free, bit by bit others moved onto the Warm Springs, Klamath, and other reservations.[31]

Even as the Snake War ground on, whites continued to flock into the area. New strikes encouraged them, as did a turn from placer to hard-rock mining in older areas of exploitation. Chinese came too, especially after their employment building the Central Pacific Railroad dried up after 1869, when it met the Union Pacific at Promontory Point, Utah, completing the first transcontinental connection to California.

This was a period of intense anti-Chinese sentiment in the West. Oregon law severely restricted Chinese rights including that of landownership. But Chinese found they could profit from taking on the laborious task of reworking tailings from earlier mining and, by clustering together, were able to achieve an element of safety in culturally familiar surroundings.

John Day and Canyon City soon had significant Chinatowns, and smaller ones emerged elsewhere.[32]

Although they mined marginal sites and clustered together, Chinese were never truly safe in Eastern Oregon. Their presence exacerbated the endemic racism of the era that was reflected in a comment in the *Grant County News*: "To everyone it is apparent that the Chinese are a curse and a blight to this county." Indeed, they did provide outlets for gambling, drugs, and prostitution for the area's predominantly young, transient white population. Attacks on Chinese often resulted—and largely went unpunished. As late as 1902 the Chinese community in Baker County's Mormon Basin was burned to the ground by arsonists.[33]

The danger did not come exclusively from whites. Groups of Chinese, headed for mines in Oregon or just across the border in Idaho's Owyhee district, were attacked and massacred by Indians who saw them as every bit as much of a threat as white intruders. In one incident, a group of some fifty Chinese were killed near the Owyhee River as they made their way toward Silver City. It was but one of many such attacks.[34]

Time did little to ameliorate the difficult position of the Northwest's Chinese. Indian attacks diminished, but anti-Chinese sentiment among whites continued. Most of the better-known cases from the 1870s and 1880s occurred in the more populous areas on Puget Sound and along the coast, but none were more vicious than that which occurred where Deep Creek emptied into the Snake just upstream from the mouth of the Imnaha. In the spring of 1887, some young men from Wallowa County— the youngest age fifteen—learned that Chinese miners were successfully working a gravel bar in the Snake, and they hatched a plan to relieve them of their gold. They persuaded some local miscreants to join them and, on May 25, descended on the site. Taking up positions on high ground above where the Chinese were working, they commenced firing. Over two days, they killed at least thirty-one Chinese (and probably considerably more). The crime went unreported until bodies floated down the Snake to Lewiston, Idaho, some sixty-five miles away.

The massacre was investigated and, although not all the participants were apprehended, a trial of four of them followed. They were found not guilty. Local rancher George Craig later observed, "If they had killed 31 white men something would have been done about it," but they were Chinese and no one seemed to care. For years residents of the area knew something of the massacre and trial, but in an early version of "Don't ask, don't tell," they chose not to acknowledge it; too many were related to or knew participants in either the crime or the trial. Only with the recent uncovering of old court records has the case come to light once more.[35]

Although gold mining continued in Eastern Oregon, its heyday was over by the 1880s.[36] Still, the heritage of violence and an extractive boom-and-bust economy continued. So too did the endemic anti-Indian, anti-Chinese racism. All these had other sources as well, but the gold rush era contributed in major ways.

Progressive historians long depicted this period positively, seeing it as one during which the foundations for a lasting and productive society were laid. The interpretation oversimplifies. Little of the wealth produced by Eastern Oregon's gold rush remained in the area. Just how much flowed out of the region is unclear, for much of the production was lost in the figures for San Francisco, where the nearest federal mint was located. Most miners left soon enough, taking their remaining gold with them. Many of their boomtowns were as fleeting. Goods purchased to support mining centers came from Portland and beyond; gold flowed there to pay for them.[37] The gold rush changed Eastern Oregon, opening much of it to whites and breaking the back of free-roaming Indian bands, but to see this as unmitigated progress depends heavily on the vantage point from which one views events.

If the history of Eastern Oregon can be characterized as an ongoing interaction between people and the land—an interaction that shaped its society as residents responded to the environment and at the same time changed it—then it must be admitted that the early gold miners had a limited impact. They did little to adjust to the land, and except for scattered piles of tailings and damaged streams they changed it little. They came, grubbed out as much wealth as they could, and moved on. They were little different when they left than they had been when they arrived. Any lasting effects of the gold rush years resulted largely from the non-miners who established farms, opened businesses, and built roads to service them. In time, distinct social and cultural norms would develop, but they would be shaped far more by those who came later than by the miners themselves.

4

Grass and Cattle

Through the 1860s, cattle were shipped up the Columbia and then driven to the various mining communities of the interior. Others were driven overland from the valleys of southwestern Oregon; some became the foundation stock for small local herds. But not until the end of the Snake War did cattle rearing evolve into something more than a small-time adjunct of the mining frontier.[1] Then change came with a rush.

In 1868, John S. Devine visited southeastern Oregon and found thousands of acres of open rangeland south and east of Steens Mountain and in nearby Catlow Valley. Realizing cattle could be driven from there to Winnemucca, Nevada, and thence by rail to California, he decided to establish a ranch in the area. On his return to California, he joined W. B. Todhunter to form the Todhunter & Devine Cattle Company. The following summer, Devine and a dozen California vaqueros, along with a chuck wagon and Chinese cook, trailed 2,500 cattle from California to southeastern Oregon. Devine selected for his headquarters a site southeast of Steens Mountain on what would come to be known as Whitehorse Creek. He thus became the first permanent white resident in the sprawling domain that would become Harney County.

Todhunter, a butcher who had a substantial business supplying beef to Sacramento and its hinterlands, stayed in California to tend to marketing and look after holdings in the San Joaquin Valley. With more and more of California's Central Valley being converted to wheat production, and with fencing laws increasingly limiting open-range grazing, he had been looking for new sources of supply. Partnership with Devine solved the problem.

Todhunter & Devine flourished. Within three years the partners had between fifteen thousand and thirty thousand head of cattle in Oregon, and by 1885 an estimated forty thousand. Devine had become a powerful cattle baron. He built a large stone and timber barn for his horses and topped it with a cupola with a white horse weather vane; from this the ranch and the creek on which its headquarters were located took their names.[2]

Whitehorse Ranch was hardly a leap into the dark. Cattle operations had appeared along Nevada's Humboldt River even before construction of the Central Pacific Railroad, and development speeded thereafter. They demonstrated the value of the area's native grasslands and the practicality of overwintering cattle there.[3] The distance from the Humboldt to southeastern Oregon was not insurmountable, and the opening of the Idaho Stage Company's Chico to Boise line in 1865—a line that passed near Whitehorse Ranch—made it seem even less so.[4]

John Devine was the first great cattle king of southeastern Oregon, a man whose lifestyle as well as operations came in huge proportions. He was, one authority wrote, "about the only storybook cattleman Oregon ever had." The vaqueros who came with him brought the patterns of operation of Hispanic California, and Devine assumed the role of Hispanic grandee overseeing a vast rancho. He was a big, rugged individual with an imperious, aristocratic manner that bred enemies. He donned broad-brimmed black hats, had his saddles and gear bedecked with silver, and wore clothing with extravagant trimmings. He had a cellar stocked with imported wines, rode fine white stallions—as befitted the owner of the Whitehorse Ranch—and raised, in addition to vast herds of cattle, thoroughbred racehorses and racing greyhounds. Devine paid his men well and thus was able to keep quality employees, and he entertained visitors in high style at his expansive ranch house. He believed his land would eventually be worth millions and acted as if he already had them.[5]

But this was not California. There were no Spanish or Mexican land grants on which to base operations. Devine had to obtain his range by other means. Control of the limited water sources allowed landowners to dominate vast hinterlands, and Devine adopted any and every means to tie them up. When others attempted to move into the area, he resorted to threats and harassment to drive them away and fenced vast acres of rangeland to keep them "his." Newcomers, squeezed by Devine, responded by burning his haystacks and stealing his cattle and horses. As the number of settlers rose, Devine adopted more sophisticated methods of fending them off. He shamelessly manipulated the Oregon Swamp Land Act and other legislation to gain control of winter range. In one case, he bought a piece of land in another's name, had the sale notarized by an employee, and then transferred title to his partner Todhunter without the knowledge of either the original settler or of Todhunter. A multitude of lawsuits resulted from Devine's activities, and—justifiably—he acquired a reputation as a ruthless monopolist. But he was living beyond his means, and when the brutal winter of 1887 hit, his empire collapsed. As Peter Simpson notes, "Suspicions clung to him even after he had been forced into bankruptcy," and when Miller & Lux bought the bankrupt Whitehorse operation they "acquired much of the ill will associated with John Devine."[6]

For a time Devine stayed on, working for Miller & Lux as manager of their Whitehorse holdings, but he remained as arrogant and ruthless as ever. Ill-equipped to be an underling, he soon left Miller's employ (with the latter's support and, no doubt, to his relief) to run a smaller ranch of his own in the Alvord Basin. But the pattern he had established lived on. Miller & Lux, the French-Glenn Company, Thomas Overtfelt, Riley & Hardin, and the Sweitzer Brothers were cattle kings as surely as Devine had been.[7]

The resort to preemptive fencing—and fence cutting—continued, and occasional violence flared. William Kittredge grew up in the area and puts it bluntly: southeastern Oregon's cattlemen were "driven by an understanding of violence as a commonplace method of solving problems." David L. Shirk, who had a large ranch in Catlow Valley, clashed with Pete French who was seeking to expand into the area. A shooting resulted, but when Shirk was tried for murder the jury ruled it justifiable homicide. Lacking resources to continue the contest with the French-Glenn interests, and recognizing violence could work both ways, Shirk moved to isolated Guano Valley. Locals long debated the details of French's death and the subsequent trial; but it was clear that, like Devine, French had made as many enemies as friends in Harney County.[8]

Through direct action of the sort employed by Devine and French—and legal maneuvering when it served their purposes—big-time operators long dominated the Harney County cattle business, and except for temporary setbacks from hard winters, the number of cattle in the area continued to climb even as marketing shifted to eastern outlets served through Huntington and Ontario rather than Winnemucca. Miller & Lux, the largest operation, had started in California in 1858 with a thousand head; by 1895 it controlled 14,439,300 acres (over half of them in Oregon) and had an untold number of cattle. For his part, French's P Ranch came to be what William Kittredge has described as "arguably the finest natural set of livestock properties in the American West."[9]

Yet the great cattle barons of Harney County were in many ways anachronistic. There were far more cattlemen outside the county than in it, and many a small operator within it as well. George Smyth arrived in Harney Basin as early as 1872; other members of his clan followed, including Walt and Fred Riddle, who operated on Steens Mountain. George's son Darius ("Rye") was the first white baby born in Harney County.[10] Even before Burns was founded in 1884, towns had emerged elsewhere: Linkville, later named Klamath Falls (1867); Prineville (1868); Paisley (1870); and Lakeview (1876) all developed largely, if not exclusively, as cow towns. The operations of outfits near these centers were individually much smaller than those of the cattle kings, but collectively their output was immense. Even where towns of any significance had yet to emerge, ranchers were operating. Cattlemen moved into the Wallowa Valley in the 1860s; settlement came a decade later. Farther west, John Y. Todd, who left the Willamette Valley to ranch in Tygh Valley, constructed a bridge over the lower Deschutes in 1860 (subsequently sold to Joseph Sherar after whom it came to be named), moved upstream in 1877 to where Bend now stands, bought a relinquished claim for $60 and two saddle horses, and established his Farewell Bend Ranch.[11]

Farther north, Howard Maupin, the slayer of Chief Paulina, started a ranch in the Antelope area in 1863. He soon moved to Trout Creek, an eastern tributary of the Deschutes. Joseph Teal and Henry Coleman developed a much larger ranch on Trout Creek in the 1870s. It was a prime location. A decade earlier, searching for a route for a military road to the Harney Basin, Major Enoch Steen had described the region between the Deschutes and John Day Rivers as "a high plateau covered with a fine, luxuriant growth of bunchgrass." Teal and Coleman took advantage of the resource, and their ranch prospered until a collapse of cattle prices in 1878 initiated its decline. In 1880, seeking to recoup, Teal and Coleman joined John Todd to drive some three thousand to five thousand cattle to the railhead in Cheyenne. The effort compounded their troubles. Blackleg infected the herd and, together with other problems, wiped out would-be profits. Todd soon had to sell his holdings, ranch and all, at bargain basement prices. Teal and Coleman fared better, but continued to struggle.[12]

Ranchers were present in the Crooked River drainage even before Todd established Farewell Bend Ranch. And for good reason. Early resident George Barnes described the area effusively: "This was, certainly, as fine a country . . . as a stock man could hope to see. The bottoms were covered with wild rye, clover, pea vines, wild flax and meadow grass that was waist high on horseback. The hills were clothed with a mat of bunch grass that seemed inexhaustible. It appeared a veritable paradise for stock." A bit of hyperbole was involved, but the reality was sufficient to attract many a would-be rancher to the area. Their cattle moved north and west to markets in The Dalles and Portland, and a town soon emerged to service them. Located on the broad canyon bottom where Ochoco Creek met Crooked River, it took the name of Prineville, after Barney Prine, a blacksmith, merchant, and saloon keeper who was its colorful founder. Far removed from The Dalles and fraught with conflict, Prineville had a manifest need for authority that could provide a semblance of order, and in 1882 Crook County was carved from once-giant Wasco.[13]

Similar developments occurred in south-central Oregon. Small-time operators moved in from Western Oregon—especially from around Jacksonville and Ashland—rather than from California, which had supplied the cattle kings of Harney County. This Oregon connection was rather surprising, for much of the area was so isolated from the state's commercial centers that it was more tied to California than to Portland or The Dalles—revealingly, San Francisco papers long supplied Lakeview with its news. Incoming Oregonians established spreads north from Linkville to the Fort Klamath area and east up the Lost and Sprague Rivers, and on the rich grasslands around Silver Lake and Paisley, especially along the Chewaucan River; and around Lakeview on the lowlands around Goose Lake and Drews Creek, and in Warner Valley.[14]

Gradual consolidation of smallholdings took place as marginal operations fell by the wayside. Nowhere was this more evident than around Paisley. Californian J. B. Haggin, the key figure in the huge Kern County Land and Livestock Company, organized the Chewaucan Land and Livestock Company and, in 1900, bought out J. D. Coughlin, whose holdings provided the foundation for the company's huge ZX Ranch. With this action Haggin introduced into Lake County the sort of outside influence that had long been a factor in neighboring Harney. Ranching in the Chewaucan area gradually stabilized under the dominance of the ZX, which grew until it was, a later owner proclaimed, "not just a ranch," . . . [but] an empire"—163 miles long, 65 miles wide, and encompassing 1.3 million acres.[15]

Cattle rearing was not confined to the Deschutes-Klamath country and the vast territory south of the Blues. Indeed, cattlemen moved into the grasslands south and east of The Dalles well before they invaded central and southeastern Oregon. There they flourished, providing meat for the mining towns and animals to stock ranges in Idaho, Montana, and beyond. As in the mining country, life in the cattle towns had its rough edges. Nard Jones, who grew up nearby, described one that "had once been the scene of bad men's battles; men with two guns and nasty tongues. Men whose cattle had roamed the place where wheat grew now, and men who had stolen those cattle and been hanged for it."[16]

In the early 1870s, Alkali Canyon, where Arlington would eventually arise, was chosen as a central holding place for cattle destined for buyers from afar. The grandson of the man who built the corrals recalled that from there "thousands of cattle were sent to market." There were, no doubt, other such locations as well.[17]

But by the 1870s the good ranch sites from The Dalles to Umatilla had been taken up, and residents were increasingly directing their attention to wheat, not cattle rearing. Indeed, in 1871 the surveyor-general of Idaho noted the grazing lands of Oregon's Columbia River country were eaten out. Echoing the theme, a visitor observed that the grasses that had once blanketed the area "are fast disappearing and weeds and thistles are taking their place," and the number of sheep—able to prosper on degraded lands—was rising. Heavy winterkill in 1880–1881 added to the problems of area cattlemen. Viewed with hindsight, ranching appears to have been little more than an economic stopgap in the region's development.[18]

Ranching would continue and more stockmen would arrive, but they worked lands not suited for grain. Such areas were limited, and pressure mounted to open the rich grazing lands of the Umatilla Indian Reservation. White intruders were already encroaching on the reservation, and Cayuse and Umatilla tribesmen were sometimes killed by those who coveted their range. Encroachments speeded after allotment of Indian lands began in the late 1880s. Whites acquired a sizable portion of the reservation, both by lease and homestead claims; but by then the limits of grazing in the Umatilla country had largely been reached.[19]

Novelist A. B. Guthrie caught the situation in *These Thousand Hills*. In his story, an old-timer in the Umatilla country argued that none of the ranchers who came in 1845 had been sorry for it, the land had been good to them and would be to his son too. But Lat Evans, the son, saw things differently: "It was a good and lovely water once, the Umatilla was, before people began coming in to spoil it, bringing plows to rip up pastures and cattle to graze ranges already overgrazed and sheep to make matters still worse." Young Evans soon departed for Montana, where conditions still resembled what the Umatilla country had once been and where he could escape the heavy hand of a domineering father.[20]

Umatilla cattlemen were an anomaly. By the 1870s and 1880s, Eastern Oregon's cattle industry was in the throes of changes seen dimly north of the Blues, but much more clearly elsewhere. Nowhere were the new developments more in evidence than in northern Harney County.

Cattleman Bill Hanley, whose family had migrated earlier to the Rogue River Valley, moved to land near Malheur Lake in the late 1870s. "Go until you find a big country," his father had told him, "for you will never get any bigger than the country you are in." When Hanley arrived in the Harney Basin, he camped at OO Springs; enchanted, he vowed that someday he would have a ranch on the rich grasslands surrounding the springs. He would, but it took years; for a long time the seventeen-thousand-acre OO Ranch was a property of Riley & Hardin, cattle barons from Nevada. Hanley also acquired five other ranches and, after Pete French's death, served as manager of the P Ranch. Cut from a very different cloth than the area's pioneer cattle kings, Hanley became one in his own way—and a major public figure as well.[21]

Hanley's success was a result of hard work and an eye for the main chance more than wise investments in land. As he noted, "Nobody had any title to any land then; you just stopped where nobody was, and it suited your purpose, and took all the country had to give to help you get your start. . . . Grass was everywhere, of very fine quality." For his part, Hanley centered his first ranch, the Bell A, on "the island," a rich meadowland on the estuary downstream from where the Silvies River split before continuing on to Malheur Lake.[22]

Hanley may have been the most successful of the wave of newcomers who arrived in northern Harney Basin in the 1870s, but he was not the

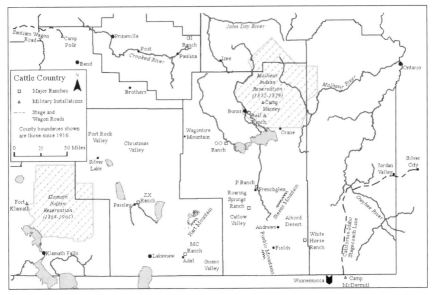

Southeastern Oregon cattle country. Credit: Kindra Blair.

first. The influx had begun with the end of the Snake War of the 1860s and grew to a flood in the decade that followed. Miller & Lux and French-Glenn joined by expanding north to take advantage of the rangeland along the Silvies River and above Malheur Lake. Friction between the cattle kings and newcomers mounted. At the same time, the increase in ranching north of Malheur Lake and the contests for the range there led to a wave of infringements on the Malheur Indian Reservation, exacerbating the problems of the already beleaguered Paiutes.[23]

War soon broke out again—although not so much as a result of territorial infringements as of the actions of reservation agent William V. Rinehart and of the Paiute's Bannock cousins from Idaho. Chief Buffalo Horn of the Bannocks was killed in early action near Silver City, and leadership devolved to Egan of the Paiutes. Told by Rinehart "nothing here is yours. It is all the government's," Egan raised the basic—unanswerable—question: "We want to know how the government came by this land . . . that he [the Great Spirit] had given to us?"[24] Mollie Jett remembered Egan, who had visited her home frequently: "He was one of the wisest and most honest Indians I ever knew," and he thought it folly to fight the whites, but in the end even Egan was driven to war. His warriors would wreak havoc as far north as Pilot Rock, but Cayuse aid failed to reach significant levels, and things soon began to unravel for the Paiutes and their allies. When Egan was wounded in a battle on Silver Creek (west of today's Riley Junction), and then killed in an act of treachery by Umapine, a Cayuse chief, the war quickly came to an end.[25]

In spite of the efforts of Sarah Winnemucca, daughter of a leading Paiute chieftain from Nevada, and of others, the Malheur Reservation was terminated and survivors scattered. Told most would be removed to the Yakama Reservation, Winnemucca was crushed: "Truly, I have not felt like this since the night Egan was killed." The order to move came just before Christmas, and as the Paiute slowly made their way across the snow-clad Blues, many died. It was the Northern Paiutes' own Trail of Tears. Yet it largely escaped the notice of whites; as William Kittredge remembered, "I never heard it talked about in southeastern Oregon; I learned it from books. . . . We knew a history filled with omissions."[26]

With the end of the war, in-migration increased—and for good reason. Bill Hanley was enthralled when he first viewed "the great Harney Valley . . . the big valley of the Oregon plains country that the Indians had fought for. I didn't wonder. It seemed a resting place for Space and all that flies or roams seemed to have found it. It was rest for all Life. I was afire with feeling for its bigness . . . grass and water and everything." Others may not have waxed so poetic, but the valley drew scores of would-be ranchers, settlers, and opportunists.[27]

As settlers streamed in, competition for rangeland took a new turn. Contempt for Indian claims to the country and their Malheur Reservation easily morphed into contempt for the claims of monopolistic cattle kings. Legal title increasingly became important, and defending it a central concern—but because of the variety of laws through which one could gain title to land, the contests were often murky and protracted.[28] Patience did not always prevail; conflicting claims were sometimes settled by direct action. Hanley remembered, "The first pioneers had all the valleys and all the hills and mountains and their wildlife to sustain themselves until they got a start. But these second [generation] pioneers were given the land only. Touch anything else at your peril." As friction between established stockmen and newcomers grew, tempers flared. Hanley recalled, "There were all kinds of secret meetings. Burns was the center. And one killing brought on another." Still, such things can be overemphasized. As Margaret Sullivan put it, unlike in Johnson County, Wyoming, "most of the conflict was nagging rather than spectacular."[29]

Historian Richard White claims that "large cattlemen were probably the most prone to violence of any economic interest group in the West. . . . [Their] predilection for violence largely resulted from the tenuousness of their own legal claims to the land."[30] But mounting violence was a result of more than competition for limited resources and questionable titles to them. Legal institutions to ameliorate conflicts were weak, ineffective, and often dominated by established interests. Principals thus frequently tried to settle disputes on their own, rather than through the machinery of government and the law. The resulting process was complicated by ego, grudges, and personal quirks, as well as by characteristics endemic to ranchland culture.

Raising cattle on the high plains of eastern Oregon rewarded quiet, self-reliant behavior. Working alone or in groups focused on shared, understood goals, cattlemen had a need for concerted effort, but limited need for interpersonal communication—Cactus Smyth professed that although he spent many an hour alone on the range, he was never lonesome. He embodied what Peter Simpson has called "interdependence alongside rugged self-reliance." Bill Hanley observed, "Most men on the plains get the silent habit—thoughts running through their minds, living in a dream . . . don't like to be disturbed, don't disturb no one." William Kittredge, who grew up farther south on his family's MC Ranch, saw the same thing: "People who had got hold of some land, people with something to lose . . . turned closemouthed and secretive." They were like his grandfather, "cherishing their own power of will, and their heedlessness, drawn to freedom they'd found by hiding out" and came to feel "they didn't have to discuss anything with anybody." Perhaps, Kittredge mused, his grandfather had not wanted his motives examined: "Certainly he thought his will should prevail." Acquisitiveness was central, "but he had standards; he wanted things done correctly. . . . He was . . . indifferent to purposes other than his own, and mainly interested in his cattle and how they were doing, beef on the hoof, for sale." A ranch family in Crook County recalled how the quest for land and the drive to succeed had gradually isolated and narrowed their own grandfather until, in the end, he had neither social skills nor broader interests. He had become one of what Kittredge called the "old bastards who congregated in the back country," men who were not above violent and underhanded methods if they led to ends they regarded as "good." As homesteader Alice Day Pratt noted, these "old Oregonians" had fixed ideas about how things should be done and what was important; they did not want these assumptions questioned: "Anything that was different was condemned without a hearing."[31]

It was not that these men were particularly antisocial. Raconteurs spun yarns around campfires and in bars—and they and their compadres sometimes wound up in jail for whooping it up too vigorously after driving cattle to railheads. Gatherings for brandings and joint drives were frequent. Informal rodeos often sprang up. Wagontire was special, "not so much a center for cattle as . . . a meeting place out in the desert. Here for a week we had feasts, lassoing the mountain sheep that were plentiful around Wagontire and killing muletail [sic] deer. . . . Then we had bucking contests and horse races. This was just the social life of range riders." Bill Brown, whose range included precious springs there, left them unfenced and open to all—yet he shot and killed Johnny Overstreet when the latter's sheep trespassed on Brown's domains in 1885. Revealing local attitudes, a jury found Brown's action justifiable. People understood and appreciated his motives, but there was no need to discuss shared values, no need to polish the verbal and analytical skills that might have been useful in a less uniform society. Even garrulous, good-humored Bill Hanley—who came to be known as "the Sage of Harney County"—was long on anecdote and short on analysis.[32]

Control of the land was not the only thing bedeviling Harney County's ranchers— newcomers and old-timers alike. Hard winters, especially that of 1889–1890, battered the open-range system. Hanley described the situation well:

> You start out in the fall with the satisfied feeling of having enough feed, with stock in good condition and everything fine. . . . Then it begins to get cold and colder. As the cold increases you gather in more stock, and still more. Feed begins to get low. You know you can't buy any for no one has a surplus. Then more snow comes, and more freezing weather, till life becomes a matter of seeing how little you can hand out, day after day, and still keep the stock alive. All your hopes are based on an early spring. But after the time for spring has come, here comes along more winter, with another big snow and another freeze-up.

When the break-up of winter finally came, most all [the ranchers] were back to where they were when they first arrived in the country.[33]

The lesson was clear: "There could be no more dependence on easy winters. There was only one way to stay in the stock business, and that was to provide plenty [of] feed. . . . When the season produced a prolific crop it must all be put away. When the season didn't it must be taken in hand and made to. Man must help Nature. . . . With land, it's the personal equation always; it's the owner that makes it valuable." Fred Otley, who settled in Harney County in 1887, was in the forefront, raising hay for his operations north of Malheur Lake.[34]

Winter feeding on this scale required draining, ditching, and irrigating of new land, as well as increasing production on meadowlands. New barns, corrals, and fences had to be built and crews and equipment acquired to put up the hay. To supplement native grasses, some planted alfalfa (Pete French did so as early as 1874; Hanley's father raised it in the Klamath country even earlier). Recognizing this new order, Hanley brought a mower and hay rake into the valley and did custom work putting up hay, thus earning funds to carry him while he built up his own herds. At the time there was only one other mower in the basin—and that was used only on its home ranch. Improvement of cattle stocks accompanied these changes—first other breeds, then Herefords replaced the earlier, less-desirable range cattle, while barbed wire provided the reliable fences required by the new order. In all this, Hanley was in the forefront, pointing the way.[35]

Marketing changed too. Completion of the Oregon Short Line from Granger, Wyoming, to Huntington in 1884 (where it met a Northern Pacific subsidiary that connected it to Portland) gave cattlemen an important new outlet, one closer than Winnemucca and with better access to Chicago and midwestern markets. Ontario, and to a lesser extent Pendleton and Huntington, became important shipping centers. But a new way to market the cattle had to be found; the old system of individual drives to Nevada would not do in the new order with more producers, many too small to warrant driving their individual herds to the railroad, or to gain favorable rail rates, or to make profitable deals when the time came to sell. Hanley found the solution. Supported by the new United States National Bank of Portland, he gathered cattle not just from the Harney Basin, but "from

Prineville, Silver Lake, Lakeview, John Day, and all the country inside [and drove them] to Huntington and Ontario." There he separated out the classes desired by customers in the Mountain States and then shipped the bulk east by rail to Nebraska, Kansas, Missouri, and Iowa, where they were fattened for urban markets. It took considerable time before returns could be realized, but the system worked and "proved one of the best ways of trading ever established in the West." In the process Ontario became "a real cattle town."[36]

The changes taking place in the Harney Basin were taking place elsewhere as well, although not always so evidently. Around Lake County's Chewaucan River, the ZX Ranch emerged as a giant operation by following the formula for success being pursued in the Harney Basin. The same was true in Crook County, especially around Post and Paulina (on the South Fork of Crooked River), where the GI Ranch, founded in the 1870s, came to control an area forty-four miles wide and sixty-nine miles long. Like the ZX, its operations were similar to those developed in Harney County. Bill Brown, the master of Wagontire Mountain (and more noted for the horses he raised than his cattle or sizeable herds of sheep), also spread his operations into land along the South Fork of Crooked River. Numerous smaller operations sprang up in Crook and Grant Counties: along Bear Creek (a year-round stream flowing into Crooked River from the south after flowing west along the southern slope of the Maury Mountains), on Big Summit Prairie (where the Lost Dutchman Mine was rumored to be located), and along the South Fork of the John Day around what came to be known as Izee (after settler Carlos Bonham's IZ cattle brand). Again, as in Harney County, rival land claims and alleged trespasses led to violence involving self-styled vigilantes.[37]

Bill Hanley put what was going on in perspective: a big cattle ranch had become "just a meat factory where they gathered up the grass, got it into commercial shape, and moved it on to the centers of population to be distributed to consumers." Although speaking of a later period, William Kittredge made the same point: "We tried to manage our ranchlands with efficiency we thought of as scientific, but our actual model was industrial." His family's MC Ranch had been "turned into a machine for feeding livestock." Examining the operations of Miller & Lux, historian David Igler detected the same trends.[38]

Bernard DeVoto, William Robbins, Gene Gressley and others have characterized such developments as the exploitation of peripheral areas by the economic core.[39] The West, they posit, was an exploited, colonial province. The analysis is suspect. People moved into the cattle country to advance their own fortunes, not as minions of outsiders. The changes they wrought were motivated by self-interest, not the desires of urban capitalists. And their goals were not necessarily economic. Richard White has observed that most were not motivated so much by a desire to get rich (although some of them certainly did), as by a search for a "competence," a sufficiency of wealth to allow them to live a comfortable life. For such folk, wealth was a means, not an end.[40] Many, of course, failed. For every Bill Hanley there were dozens who came in search of a good life and foundered, their dreams shattered. They had come in the restless quest for a better life that characterized much of America's frontier experience and would have been appalled at the idea that they were pawns of city folk— bankers, industrialists, and their ilk—from whom they felt distanced and whom they often despised.

Regardless of who ultimately benefited the most, or why, the fact remains that, from the end of the Bannock-Paiute War to the early twentieth century, Eastern Oregon's cattle industry went through basic changes. An industry that developed by mining the region's great resources of grass had moved on to an industrial mode of production wherein efficient use of raw material inputs was essential and maximizing the availability of such resources through careful management of land and water were central concerns. Ranching would continue, but it never again was what it had been during the years when John Devine and his ilk set things in motion.

Changes were attitudinal as well as economic. The outlook of Bill Hanley was vastly different from that of John Devine. Devine's frame of reference was social; the status he sought was based on the ideals of Hispanic California, not the land on which he settled. By way of contrast, Hanley developed a love of the land that shows through in page after page of his reminiscences. It was not quite environmentalism; the time for that had not yet come, but in one form or another it was shared by Cactus Smyth, Reub Long, John Scharff, and William Kittredge—and it would be a hallmark of many another Eastern Oregon resident in years to come.

5
Sheep Trails in Every Direction

In 1909, Clarence M. Bishop, together with his brothers Roy and Chauncey, purchased a woolen mill in Pendleton, Oregon. Built in 1893 as a scouring plant to clean wool before sending it to market, the facility closed when increased rail rates made it unprofitable. In 1895, the plant was enlarged and converted to a mill to weave woolen cloth for blankets for the local Indian trade. Again the venture failed; it remained idle until purchased and remodeled by the Bishop brothers with help from their family and a local bond issue. Their Pendleton Woolen Mills was soon operating and has remained active (and under family control) to this day.[1]

A woolen mill in Pendleton made sense. The town was a major stop on the Oregon Rail & Navigation Company's line, which connected to Portland as well as markets to the east and south, and community leaders were aggressively promoting economic growth. Moreover, wool production in Eastern Oregon was booming; nearby Heppner, midway between the area's summer and winter ranges, was a major sheep-shearing center; a leading sheepman recalled, "In the early days, the bunch grass was so abundant in the north end of Morrow County that it was unnecessary to arrange for winter feed." A later authority observed, "From the Columbia River Valley . . . sheep trails to the mountains pointed almost every direction," for 1905 to 1920 were the boom days of the Columbia Plateau's sheep business.[2]

Production was rising elsewhere too. Of the Hay Creek region east of the Deschutes, John Minto wrote, "this country in so far as wool production is concerned cannot be excelled in the United States," and its Hay Creek Ranch was "the greatest Merino breeding station in the world." As a leading sheepman, Minto knew whereof he spoke.[3]

The success of the Pendleton Woolen Mills sprang from more than ample nearby sources of wool, community support, and access to markets.

The Bishop brothers were scions of a family long involved in woolen milling. Their grandfather, Thomas L. Kay, born in Yorkshire in 1837, went to
work in an English textile mill as a bobbin boy at age ten. He made his way
to Brownsville, Oregon, in 1863, and by 1888 was the leading textile man
in the state. His long experience helped him gain financial support for the
successful and long-lived Thomas Kay Woolen Mill Company, which he
established in Salem.

Kay's eldest daughter, Fannie, learned the milling business from her
father. Her marriage to C. P. Bishop, a successful retail merchant (and
stockholder in the Kay mill) brought together expertise in milling and
marketing, expertise that proved immensely helpful to their sons when
they established the Pendleton Woolen Mills.[4]

Initially much of Pendleton Woolen Mills' production went into blankets for the Indian trade. This was a natural development. Colorfully deco-
rated wool blankets made using modern aniline dyes were favored dress
(and valued trade items) among western Indians. Moreover, Pendleton
bordered the Umatilla reservation, and the mill the Bishops took over had
made blankets for sale there. To tap into and expand this trade, the Pendleton Woolen Mills' predecessor had sent to England for a Jacquard loom
and hired Joseph Rawnsley, a Philadelphia Textile School graduate, to run
the challenging double-shuttle device. Rawnsley spent considerable time
on the reservation (and later in the Southwest) learning Native preferences
of colors and designs. When they took over, the Bishops kept him on. Their
mill frequently used Indians from the Umatilla reservation (including
Umapine, the Cayuse who had killed the ill-fated Paiute chief Egan during
the Bannock-Paiute War) for advertising photographs. At least five mills
in the United States were making Indian trade blankets during Pendleton's
early years; eventually it was the only mill doing so. It continues to make
them to this day, although now sales are largely to whites.[5]

The Bishops became deeply involved in the Pendleton community—
and remained so even after corporate headquarters were moved to Portland. From the first, they were major supporters of the hugely successful
Pendleton Round-Up, which in 1912 drew some fifty thousand viewers
over its three-day run. There was irony in this. The cattle industry supplied
the background for the rodeo and furnished many of its contests (and con-
testants) but no longer played a major role in Pendleton or its hinterlands.
Wheat and sheep now dominated the area.[6]

Community boosters and champions of economic growth applauded the growth of the sheep/wool industry, not only in the hinterlands of Pendleton but elsewhere as well. Yet the growth came at a price. Sheep grazed land so closely that environmental degradation proceeded apace. Grasslands were stripped, invasive species of little value proliferated, and soil erosion reduced the productivity of countless acres. As the industry evolved, its negative effects became steadily greater, but awareness of the costs were a long time coming. Not until the twentieth century would meaningful correctives be applied.

Sheep were numerous in Oregon well before the Pendleton Woolen Mills appeared on the scene. The first came on the *Tonquin* in 1811 as a part of John Jacob Astor's ill-fated attempt at building a fur-trade empire in the far West. The Hudson's Bay Company followed suit, importing sheep in the 1830s. Joseph Lease herded a band north from California in 1842, and Joshua Shaw brought a band across the plains soon after. Many of the first sheep were of poor quality, but thanks to the efforts of Joseph Watt, John Minto, and others, quality improved. It was these better animals that supplied much of the foundation stock when sheep raising moved east of the Cascades.

Initially Eastern Oregon's main areas of sheep and wool production were north and west of those of the cattle industry, areas nearer their main markets and sources of capital, The Dalles and Portland rather than Winnemucca and San Francisco.[7] Sheep husbandry began near The Dalles in 1860 and soon after near Dufur, Tygh Valley, Arlington, and in the uplands of Umatilla County. By 1867, James Small was raising sheep in the Trout Creek bottoms near Antelope. Gradually production spread south toward Prineville and the Harney Basin and east as far as the Wallowa Valley. After transcontinental connections were completed, rail rates ensured that sheep and wool would continue to be shipped westward to The Dalles (which in 1888 claimed to be the largest primary wool market in the United States) and beyond to Portland. In June 1890, dealers in The Dalles reportedly handled five million pounds of wool.[8]

Initially sheep raising was a small-time undertaking. Obtaining a few stock sheep was within the reach of nearly anyone, and husbandry was relatively simple. No extensive grazing lands were required, no troop of vaqueros to herd them; caring for sheep essentially meant guarding them, something done better afoot than on horseback. Aside from the initial cost of purchase, which was relatively small, a dog or two and some nearby grassland was about all that was needed to commence sheep raising (and sheep were not particularly demanding as to the quality of the grazing land). Owning the grazed land was hardly a prerequisite in the largely unclaimed Oregon interior. Moreover, surpluses from small local herds could be consumed on the farms and in nearby mines and towns; there was no need for major markets or distant intermediaries.[9]

Ere long, the situation began to change. A sizable herd of quality Spanish Merino sheep reached Tygh Valley in the 1870s. Local rancher John Y. Todd, who had not yet moved to the Bend area, bought the entire herd "to keep them off the [local] cattle range." He then had them driven to Idaho, where they sold at a profit.[10] Todd was prescient. Large sheep operations were in the offing, and their impact on the already-present cattle industry would be considerable. The largest and most successful of the newcomers would be the Baldwin Sheep and Land Company, established by David M. Baldwin on Hay Creek in 1873. His timing was ideal. The 1880s and 1890s were good years for sheepmen (although many were hard hit by the harsh winter of 1883–1884). Under Baldwin's successor, John G. Edwards, the operation expanded until it stretched seventy-nine miles, incorporated thirty thousand acres of pasture and hay land, and dominated vast stretches of public domain that reached into the Ochocos, providing valuable summer grazing. The ranch produced 250 tons of wool a year and 2,500 tons of irrigated alfalfa for winter feed—although it had previously been thought alfalfa would not survive in the area. Edwards purchased the best breeding stock, especially the Rambouillet strain of Merinos. In John Minto's well-informed opinion, by the turn of the century the Hay Creek operation had become "the greatest Merino breeding station in the world."[11]

Baldwin was not alone. Allan and La Follett of Prineville, E. F. Day and A. Lindsay of Heppner, and Charles Cunningham from near Pilot Rock all had sizable operations at an early date. Cunningham's career may have been the most meteoric. He reached Eastern Oregon as a poor Irish immigrant in 1869 and went to work for Major W. H. Barnhart, an established sheepman in the Pendleton area. By 1873 Cunningham had saved enough to join Jacob Frazer in a joint operation. In time he and Frazer split their holdings, and Cunningham purchased a ranch of his own. He was one of the first to see the advantages of quality animals and gradually improved his flocks until others sought him out for breeding stock. By 1894, Cunningham was running twenty thousand sheep, four thousand of them thoroughbred; by 1901 he reportedly had 155,000 head. When the Pendleton Woolen Mills came on line, it became a major buyer of Cunningham's quality wool—and has remained so.[12]

Major sheep ranches came to the High Desert later. Bill Brown and two of his brothers commenced raising sheep near Wagontire in 1882. The brothers left before long, but Brown continued to expand operations. At its height, his range extended from Wagontire to Glass Butte and to Buck Creek in southeastern Crook County; he ran some thirty thousand sheep, sheared the wool at various locations on the High Desert, and, until the Columbia Southern railroad was built to Shaniko, freighted his clip all the way to The Dalles.[13]

Richard R. Hinton followed a similar course. He homesteaded a 160-acre tract near Cross Hollows (the future site of Shaniko) in 1871 and gradually built up sizable flocks. Through careful breeding and selected outcrosses, Hinton developed his own strain, known as Columbia sheep; they were especially suited to the area and yielded ample clips and lambs with good weight. By 1900 his Imperial Stock Ranch was the largest in Wasco County and operated in several nearby counties as well. At the same time, he had large cattle herds and raised hay and grain for winter feed.[14]

Hinton was not alone in having both sheep and cattle, but the combination did not pass without comment. Herman Oliver recalls that his father raised both on their spread near John Day, and "a few cattlemen looked on us as though we were halfbreeds." Yet some major cattlemen added sheep to their range, seeing sheep as complementary to cattle operations and apt to provide a cushion when cattle prices dropped. Many believed cattle and sheep together used range better than either alone; they ate different things, and sheep fertilized the soil. What they did not realize was that together the two stripped the range clean, speeding the environmental degradation that would soon plague cattle- and sheepmen alike.[15]

In addition to the giant operations were scores of smaller ones. Their collective impact was immense. The markets for both wool and meat were strong; prices and demand were rising during the boom days of the sheep business on the Columbia Plateau.[16] The same was true for areas farther south, but getting the annual clip from there to market was not easy.

Responding, a group of investors set out in 1897 to construct a railroad from Biggs, on the Columbia, to Prineville. Progress came slowly, for the investors were short on capital. The line, the Columbia Southern Railway, gradually pushed southward, and in May 1900 reached Shaniko, sixty-nine miles south of Biggs. It never got farther. Plans for continuing on to Prineville, with a branch line to Canyon City, were abandoned. By 1905 the line was in receivership, and the Union Pacific took over, operating it through its subsidiary, Oregon Rail & Navigation Company.[17]

For all Columbia Southern's financial problems, it did what it was designed to do, hauling immense quantities of wool to the river. Shaniko grew apace and was soon advertising itself as "the Wool Capital of the World." It may well have been, for it captured a good share of the business that had once gone to The Dalles. Shaniko sat in the midst of twenty thousand square miles of wool, sheep, and cattle production—there was no other center like it anywhere east of the Cascades. Heppner continued as a sheep-shearing and shipping center, but its output, reflecting the size of its hinterland, was much smaller. Freighters were soon hauling immense loads of wool to the railhead at Shaniko. By 1901 the community boasted a bank, hotel, general store, livery stable, saloons, and a warehouse from which four million pounds of wool were sold and shipped annually, in addition to four hundred rail cars of cattle. Shipments continued in the years that followed. One million pounds of wool went out on June 2, 1903, and total shipments that year were close to five million pounds. Shipments in 1904 were similar; in June, 1,250,000 pounds of wool sold in a single day.[18]

Shaniko also served as the departure point for stage and freight service to Prineville, Bend, Canyon City, and beyond. But its boom days soon ended. In 1911 a rail line up Deschutes Canyon reached Bend. Shaniko served as a supply depot during construction, but that dried up with completion of the Deschutes line. Wool production continued in its hinterlands and was still shipped on the Columbia Southern, but Shaniko's heyday was over.

Many small operations were started by impoverished newcomers who began by working as herders for established ranchers, took their pay in sheep so as to build up flocks of their own, and then embarked on independent sheep raising—often with nothing more than a homestead claim to support the undertaking. They were, one observer declared, mere "nomadic

Wool buyers in Shaniko, 1910. Credit: Oregon Historical Society.

grass poachers." Writing in 1906, Mary Austin dismissed the sheepherder as "merely a hireling who works the flock in its year-long passage from shearing to shearing." Her assessment missed the transition from herder to herdsman-owner that contributed mightily to the hordes of sheep grazing for free on public lands. Rancher-turned-politician Walter Pierce remembered a sheepman telling him "to make this go, you have got to have lots of public dominion"—that is, "grass belonging to the government, for which he didn't have to pay anything." There was truth to the statement. Donald McLeod reported making $100,000 in 1916 fattening a band of wethers on open range on Steens Mountain in summer and the Owyhee desert in winter. He did not own land in either place.[19]

The quality of such flocks was marginal, but by selling to intermediaries who would combine several into a major band and drive them to eastern Washington, Montana, and Idaho—or, after fattening, ship them to Chicago—ranchers were able to gradually improve their situations. As more and more smallholders emerged, they moved ever farther from the Columbia Plateau. By 1880 more than 130,000 sheep were estimated inhabiting Oregon's southeastern counties; in 1897 there were 320,000 in Crook County alone; and by 1900, some 400,000 were grazing in Harney and Malheur (alongside 150,000 cattle). On Steens Mountain, a government investigator found seventy-three bands averaging some 2,500 head per band—that is, more than 450 sheep per square mile. Numbers rose almost as fast in neighboring Lake County, while on the upper reaches of the Middle Fork of the John Day, big flocks summered in the mountains—in 1897 some fifty thousand sheep (and a quarter million pounds of wool) were shipped from Grant County.[20]

Inexorably, the increasing number of sheep led to conflict with cattlemen. Friction was exacerbated in 1893 by federal action banning sheep in the Cascade Forest Reserve; according to the *Oregonian*, more than four hundred thousand sheep previously grazed there each summer. Transhumance, in which shepherds took their flocks ever higher into the mountains in search of grass as the dry summer season advanced, had been a basic element of sheep raising from time immemorial. Sheepherders from Wasco and other nearby counties, following the practice, had come to depend on Cascade grasslands; now they had to look elsewhere. A ripple effect followed; as sheepmen sought new places for summer grazing, they often found it where others—both cattlemen and sheepherders—were already ensconced.[21]

The intrusion was hardly welcome. Much of the range was already stocked beyond capacity. Deterioration of rangelands had begun, and increased numbers of sheep speeded the process. They grazed land more closely than cattle, exacerbating the shift from bunchgrass to "hard forbs" (various weedy species of limited value as feed) and to sagebrush, which was even less palatable; as early as 1883, *West Shore* magazine reported "bunch grass is nearly gone" on much of the interior range. Some cattlemen had begun to realize their rangelands were overstocked and were attempting to reduce their impact on them, but itinerant sheepmen undermined their efforts. Rancher Herman Oliver recalled, "Cattlemen were beginning to get some idea of conserving grass, so they attempted to reserve certain big ranges for later use . . . [but] invariably they would find from one to a dozen sheep outfits on the range, [and] all the grass gone." Henry Miller responded to such developments by telling the manager of Miller & Lux's Oregon holdings to "let other cattlemen use water holes in his range," but deny access to sheepmen, "as they owned no land and sheep ruined grass."[22]

In the absence of government authorities to meet the challenge, cattlemen adopted approaches to protect grazing land they considered theirs (even though they rarely held title). The Butte Creek Land and Livestock

Company, which operated near the western end of the Blue Mountains, sought to protect its grazing lands by filing claims of various sorts on a huge doughnut of timber and grassland in order to prevent sheepmen from having access to the enclosed grazing lands to which the company did not have title.[23]

More typically, cattlemen decided who had the right to which range, formed associations to work out details, and then blazed trees to mark "deadlines" beyond which sheepmen were not to go—on occasion the blazes were reinforced with warning signs bearing a skull and crossbones. Recognizing they could not halt the influx of sheep altogether, cattlemen established "driveways" along which sheepmen were to move their flocks to new areas. Armed gunmen patrolled them to keep sheep—and sheep-herders—within bounds. As time passed, harassment increased; sheep killings took place in Union County in 1887, and beginning in 1896, bands in the Izee area "were shot into or poisoned, corrals were burned, sheep camps were robbed and destroyed." The killing soon spread westward to Paulina on the South Fork of Crooked River and then northward toward Prineville and Wheeler County. A full-fledged Sheepshooters' War was under way—if "war" is the right term for something in which all the shooting was on one side.[24]

Harassment was not directed solely at itinerant sheepmen. Bill Brown, well established south of the Ochocos, had fenced large tracts of public domain to protect the winter graze of his sheep. Learning this, officials from the Department of the Interior ordered him to remove his one hundred to two hundred miles of fencing. Convinced that neighboring cattlemen had reported him, Brown informed authorities they too had illegal fences and had enclosed some thirty-five thousand acres of public domain. Brown's neighbors were outraged and took revenge—some five hundred of Brown's sheep were killed in a clandestine nighttime raid.[25]

In 1904 events reached their nadir near Silver Lake in northern Lake County. Cattlemen had declared a deadline extending from Wagontire in the northeast to Silver Lake. No sheep were to be allowed in the vast area west of the line, a deadline that would bar many sheepmen from their accustomed winter range. The audaciousness of the declaration may have made it difficult to give it credence, or perhaps local sheepmen simply had no practical choice but to ignore it. In any case, sheep were soon grazing on their usual winter range west of the deadline.

Trouble soon erupted. On February 2, five men descended on sheep corralled for the night near Reid Rock. These animals belonged to locals, not outsiders. No matter. While one man held the herder at gunpoint, the other four used knives, guns, and clubs to kill sheep. By dawn most of the three thousand animals in the band lay dead. This was followed on April 28 by an attack at nearby Benjamin Lake; an additional 2,400 sheep were killed. The attackers departed with a warning to the herder that he should "inform every sheepman he saw that the next band of sheep found in . . . [the area] would meet with the same result and they would not spare the herders hereafter."[26]

A public outcry erupted, for the killings were hardly minor dustups between disgruntled neighbors. The *Lake County Examiner* proclaimed "the lawless desperadoes . . . should be run down at any cost," and various newspapers called on Governor George E. Chamberlain to intervene. After initially insisting it was a local matter over which he had no authority, Chamberlain offered a reward for the arrest and conviction of those responsible. Soon after, the stockmen's association of Lake County added a reward of its own, as did the Oregon State Woolgrower's Association. On May 20, Lake County district attorney Lafe Conn filed warrants for the arrest of those involved in the Reid Rock and Benjamin Lake slaughters (although they were as yet unidentified). The following year Governor Chamberlain addressed the issue in his annual message to the state legislature. He denounced the "nefarious mission of slaughter" taking place in Crook and Lake Counties, called on local authorities to act, and requested that the legislature appropriate funds to apprehend guilty parties.[27]

Things did not cool down at once. Major sheep killing occurred in Klamath County in April 1905. A year later, masked men killed some 1,800 sheep east of Fort Rock by driving them over a cliff. Other killings occurred in the months that followed, but friction gradually declined. Officials introduced a system of grazing allotments in the Blue Mountain Forest Reserve soon after its creation in 1906. Forest ranger Charles Congleton, who served in the reserve's Paulina district from 1904 to 1927, considered the allotments too high for the health of the range—one authority described the Blue Mountains as "the most heavily stocked piece of National Forest in the United States"—but at least they reduced clashes over grazing rights by introducing a third-party arbiter. Congleton was succinct: "Formation of the Forest Reserve . . . ended the Range Wars." But the end did not come without concerted effort on the part of Forest Service employees. The idea of allotments faced considerable opposition, and when H. D. Langille arrived in Prineville to explain the Forest Service's intentions, he found "cattlemen would not sit in the same room with sheepmen," and he had to speak to the two groups separately. Things were little better in Klamath County, where clashes between sheepherders and homesteaders, sheep poisoning, and even murder occurred until principals worked out a compromise of sorts.[28]

The allotment system was hardly a complete solution. Allotments regulated summer range and, by reducing pressure thereon, forced grazing interests to use lowlands even more heavily than before.[29] Lowland winter range was either privately owned or was nonforested public domain, and sheep and cattle owners continued to argue over the latter as it grew ever more important to their operations. But arguments were less and less often conducted at the point of a gun or through clandestine raids. Indeed, from time to time, meetings between leading cattle and sheepmen arranged a division of the winter range. Agreement proved elusive, but finally in 1916 the parties agreed that sheep on the High Desert could be grazed south of the Bend-Burns highway, but not north of it.[30] Considering that people in the area had long taken the law into their own hands, this represented a major change. From the first, cattlemen had based their holdings more on physical possession of the range than on legal title. Now cattlemen and sheepmen were seeking ways to live side by side, if not together.

Forest Service grazing allotments and agreements dividing winter range-lands were the beginning of a new order for sheepmen, an order that was strengthened with passage of the Taylor Grazing Act in 1934. The act replaced informal agreements by extending the principle of federally assigned allotments to publicly held winter range. It affected not only established herders but newcomers as well, and in the process "sounded the death knell of the colorful but destructive itinerant sheep business."[31]

Many early sheepherders came from Scotland or Australia, but over time increasing numbers arrived from Ireland, especially County Cork. Early arrivals sponsored later ones, and they in turn others. The practice resulted in a heavy concentration of Irish in Lake County. Brothers Phillip, Mike, William, and James Barry were the first immigrants from County Cork, arriving in 1877; they brought others, mostly from Duhallow.[32]

Jeremiah Deeley and Jeremiah O'Leary came after the turn of the century. Deeley was sponsored by the Flynn brothers of Plush, who had arrived earlier; O'Leary was told not to stop in the eastern United States but "go directly to Jackie Flynn's sheep camp" in Oregon's Lake County. Later, when asked if sheepherding was a lonely life, Deeley replied, "I had lots of company, there were a lot of Irishmen herding sheep out there." There certainly were. James Deeley has compiled a list of nearly five hundred Irish immigrants in Lake County alone. Names like Lynch, Barry, O'Leary, Conn, and Flynn remain prominent in the area, and many are still engaged in sheep and cattle production. Nor were Irish shepherds limited to Lake County; they dominated on Steens Mountain, and from an early day were prominent in Morrow County, around Izee, and in Grant County. When a grazing district was set up east of Klamath Falls in the 1930s, the largest sheep operations were all owned by Irishmen.[33]

Irish immigrants came because of the manifest opportunities in Oregon. With the help of sponsors, they could get a job herding. By taking part of their pay in sheep, they could begin building up bands of their own. And by grazing their sheep on unclaimed public domain they could see their herds—and their fortunes—increase. Jerry Murphy caught these immigrants' life and hopes in "The Lonely Shepherd Boy":

> I have no home to call my own.
> To find one I won't try.
> I sleep beside the sheep at night
> A lonely shepherd boy.
>
> From the desert in the springtime
> I trailed o'er rocks and plain
> And long to see the springs and trees
> Of the mountains once again. . . .
>
> By Dog Mountain Spring and lonely glens
> Long mornings I did roam
> And by that lake where I'd like to make
> Some future day my home.[34]

But the Taylor Grazing Act closed the door on those who hoped to make their way toward the American dream by herding sheep, the sort of dream embodied in Murphy's song. The act largely eliminated opportunities for "tramp" sheepmen, landless herders who crisscrossed Eastern Oregon in search of grass for their herds and upward mobility for themselves. Without adequate free range, sheep raising was no longer profitable, and Lake County's immigration from Ireland plummeted.[35]

Basque immigrants from the Pyrenees between Spain and France followed a similar course. Superb herdsmen in their native lands, their skill and work ethic made them valued employees. Fortitude, frugality, and determination helped them succeed in a decidedly hostile social and economic environment. Concentrations of Basques sprang up in Jordan Valley (where the first permanent Basque residents arrived in 1889), McDermitt, and elsewhere in Oregon's Malheur County.[36]

Basque clannishness, cavalier attitudes toward established authority, and the barriers of a language decidedly remote from English combined with the vastness of the lands on which they worked to keep them more distant from mainstream society than the Irish in spite of many similarities in their overall situations. Basques were "a people set apart," but their isolation was relative: Mike Seminario recalled that, while herding, he traveled alone on foot with his dog and a burro laden with provisions, but he would "see a lot of people—cowboys and such. They'd come look you up. 'Course they'd come at mealtime."[37]

Tim Lequerica, who came to the United States in 1903, remembers that he and other Basques herded "wherever there was grass and water." Indeed, in many quarters the term "tramp" sheepman was almost synonymous with "Basque." H. D. Langille recalled that the forest reserves in the Lakeview area were established primarily "to escape the plague of Basque sheepmen." Because they lacked a land base, most Basques were barred from receiving Forest Service or Taylor Grazing Act allotments. As two leading authorities put it, "The Taylor Grazing Act neatly speared the itinerant Basque sheepmen on the twin horns of alien citizenship and lack of commensurate private or leased property" to qualify for allotments. In the face of this, many returned to their homeland or turned to occupations such as mining or urban employment in Boise, Winnemucca, and elsewhere. The Depression speeded the process; during the 1930s some thirty-five Basque sheepmen in the Jordan Valley area went bankrupt. As Aurora Madariaga recalled, "Everyone [was] almost broke."[38]

Yet some prospered. At the height of their operations, Tim Lequerica and his partner ran six bands of sheep totaling twelve thousand head. Other Basque herders were nearly as successful. A Basque folk song catches the independent spirit beneath it all:

> Far nobler in the mountains is he who yokes the ox,
> And equal to the monarch, the shepherd of the flocks.

Still, unlike that of the cowboy, the story of Basque and Irish sheep-herders is little chronicled. Lequerica explained, "The cowboy wrote a lot of songs telling about his occupation. He had the time. The sheepman didn't."[39]

The presence of Irish and Basque shepherds with foreign citizenship and little if any land exacerbated the hue and cry against itinerant bands of sheep scattered across Eastern Oregon, but although Basques and Irish made handy scapegoats, the actual situation was less simple than critics suggested. Vast numbers of sheep were owned by local residents, includ-ing many cattlemen who had begun running sheep to complement their beef operations. Some of these undertakings were immense. Financed by Swift and Company, A. J. Knollin drove huge bands from interior Oregon to rail markets beginning in 1887. Far from being the activity of a poor immigrant, Knollin's drives were immense undertakings tied to the indus-trializing processes reshaping American agriculture.

By 1930 the heyday of itinerant sheepmen had passed, but they held on stubbornly on Steens Mountain, where more than 145,000 sheep still grazed in 1932. Roughly 40 percent were owned in Harney County (and a good half of the owners had no land), while some 60 percent belonged to itinerant herdsmen from outside the county. The end was near, however. Economic depression combined with the modernizing forces in finance, production, and marketing favored under the Taylor Grazing Act to drive many from business. By 1937 the number of sheep on Steens Mountain had plummeted to ninety-one thousand, a fall so severe Harney County's tax collector bemoaned the resulting drop in tax revenues.[40]

Falling production hardly came as a surprise. The simple fact was that, by the 1920s, the grazing lands of Eastern Oregon had long been desperately overstocked, many once-rich grasslands had been reduced to desiccated wastelands, and others were on the fast track to that fate. On a vast tract south of the Blues, studies showed a 75 percent reduction in rangeland forage.[41] The Great Depression would bring this house of cards crashing down, but well before that the more prescient recognized that the end of the old order was in sight. In fact, by the close of the 1920s the heyday of Eastern Oregon's sheep industry had passed. The bands on Steens Mountain and in Jordan Valley's hinterland were simply the last gasps of an old order the likes of which would never be seen again.

6
From Bunchgrass to Wheat

Unlike cattle and sheep, wheat could not walk to market—and, unlike gold, was far too bulky to be carried. Oregon's wheat producers thus depended on transportation facilities—railroads, steamboats, and oceangoing vessels—to a greater degree than had been the case earlier, and no one was more instrumental in creating these essential facilities than Portland businessman John C. Ainsworth.

Ainsworth arrived in Oregon in 1851. Experienced in steamboating on the Mississippi, he joined the gold rush to California and plied his trade on the Sacramento until persuaded to move to Oregon to captain the steamboat *Lot Whitcomb*, built the year before for service on the Willamette. As trade developed, other steamers followed, and Ainsworth began to look to the Columbia and its upstream hinterland for greater opportunities than the Willamette offered. In 1860 he joined in establishing the Oregon Steam Navigation Company (OSN); two years later the firm gained control of the portages at the Cascades and The Dalles. The timing was perfect. As mining grew in the interior, OSN developed a virtual monopoly on river traffic, serving the mining centers via The Dalles, Umatilla, and other communities. The company charged all the traffic could bear, and profits poured in. The cargoes handled by the OSN's vessels included vast quantities of wheat and flour from the Willamette, Yamhill, and Tualatin Valleys, shipped upstream to meet the needs of mining centers.[1]

For twenty years the Oregon Stream Navigation Company dominated the Columbia, and for nineteen of those twenty years John C. Ainsworth was president. It was a remarkable enterprise. Built with locally generated capital, it earned huge profits year after year, profits that were invested by the company or its owners in local enterprises. In the process it helped seal Portland's position as regional leader—and Ainsworth's ascendancy as well. As he put it, sale of the OSN "made me worth more than a million. To

carefully invest this money, so that it will be of the greatest advantage to
my children is now my daily study and care." Foremost among his investments was the Ainsworth National Bank, a firm that actively supported
Portland's economic development.[2]

Conditions had undergone basic changes by the time its owners sold
the OSN in 1879. Traffic to the mines had declined sharply, and, by 1865,
wheat production in the Walla Walla area had "stopped the shipment of
flour from below." Concomitantly, downriver markets were beginning to
emerge. By 1867 flour from east of the Cascades was being sold in San
Francisco (one shipment totaled 20,000 barrels); soon thereafter the first
vessel departed Portland for Liverpool with a full cargo of wheat and flour.
Ere long, hundreds of others would follow.[3]

By then railroad magnates were engaged in cutthroat competition
building networks tying the Pacific Northwest to the Midwest and beyond.
The OSN's Columbia River transportation corridor played a vital role in
the plans of contending parties, but entering the larger world of railroad
empire builders was beyond what John Ainsworth and his partners could
manage. Sale of the OSN on the best terms possible was the logical policy—and, since there was no shortage of would-be buyers, in the end the
terms were satisfactory indeed.

Although the OSN ceased as an independent entity, it left an enduring
legacy. As railroads took more and more goods down the Columbia, they
followed the route OSN had pioneered. It long continued to dominate traffic, and wheat played an increasing role. Ainsworth and his partners had
opened the way.

Wheat was a quintessential frontier crop. Frontiersmen had planted it
since colonial times. Settlers in the Willamette Valley raised it as a matter
of course, as did Marcus Whitman at his mission at Waiilatpu and as did
later settlers in the Walla Walla Valley. But early residents in the Walla
Walla failed to realize its potential for wheat production. They sought
out the areas of low, relatively level, well-watered land that generations of
frontiersmen had previously: rich and productive alluvial sections. Even as
settlement moved beyond the Walla Walla Valley to areas along Oregon's
Umatilla River and nearby Willow Creek (as well as streams in Washington Territory), cropland remained restricted to the lowlands. At first
farmers produced for home use and for nearby consumers, not for distant

commercial outlets. But wider possibilities were recognized, and by 1880 a wheat belt had emerged, stretching from Pomeroy in Washington Territory southwest into Umatilla County. North from Pendleton, Carrie Strahorn saw mile after mile of stubble fields "spread away on every side" and wheat "firmly in place as the area's major crop." With the opening of production in the Palouse hills, the wheat belt expanded farther north. It was this area that provided much of the cargo for the growing fleet of vessels departing Portland for Liverpool and elsewhere—a fleet that numbered more than a hundred vessels a year.[4]

Getting wheat from fields to the facilities of the Oregon Rail & Navigation Company (the OSN's successor) was no easy task. Wagons carried the crop to streamside, often a distance of several miles, but in places, hulking bluffs kept wagons from continuing to the riverbanks, and grain slides were installed for the descent to loading docks. Elsewhere, residents of the Walla Walla area, located well inland from Wallula, the port that served them, joined to build the Walla Walla and Columbia River Railroad for a more cost-effective and efficient means of getting grain to the river.[5] Producers around Pendleton, at the southern end of the wheat belt, had to ship their grain by wagon to Umatilla until the Oregon Rail & Navigation Company completed a line from Umatilla to Pendleton and on across the Blue Mountains to connect with the Oregon Short Line at Huntington, giving it access to the Union Pacific's mainline. Many hailed the OR&N for providing the eastbound transcontinental connection considered essential for the Northwest's economic future, but to wheat farmers around Pendleton the line was more important for the rail connection it provided with Portland and world markets. Freight rates were consistently structured to make it cheaper to ship west to Portland, and from there to markets reached by sea, than eastward to the great milling centers in Minneapolis and elsewhere in the Midwest.[6]

Expansion of production in the Northwest's Inland Empire coincided with changes in the world market. As the Industrial Revolution accelerated in northern Europe, thousands left the countryside for factory employment; a decline in domestic grain production followed. The effect was most noticeable in Great Britain, where by 1885 the amount of land devoted to grain had fallen by one million acres, much of it converted to pasture for the sheep that supplied wool to the nation's textile mills. The shift was encouraged by repeal of Great Britain's protectionist Corn Laws in

1846—"corn" in this case meaning any grindable grain (primarily wheat), not the maize of American usage. Wheat imports rose from 2 percent of Britain's annual consumption in 1830 to 65 percent in the 1880s.[7]

Faster, cheaper transportation aided the transition. Downeasters, medium clippers, and, in time, steamships proved capable of moving vast quantities of wheat quickly and at low cost. Changes in milling technology reinforced the Inland Empire's dependence on European markets. With the development of hardened iron rollers in the 1870s, milling changed radically: it became practical to grind hard wheat into flour of uniform, high quality that was superior for making light breadstuffs. Minneapolis emerged as the nation's great milling center using hard winter and spring wheat from the Midwest.[8] The soft wheat of the Columbia Plateau, low in gluten and protein, was better suited for crackers, biscuits, pastries, and cakes; in little demand in the nation's great milling centers, it found a ready market in Europe, where soft wheat had long been raised (and depended on), and in Asia, where wheat's main use was for noodles, not bread.

Little Club and the misnamed Australian Bluestem were soft wheats well adapted to the dry summers of the Inland Empire. Moreover, their stiff stems could stand for a considerable time until machinery was available for harvest—sometimes quite a long wait. Smut, often a problem with Little Club in the Willamette Valley, was of little concern in the interior thanks to its dry summers. Both varieties were of Mediterranean origin and lacked resistance to severe cold when tried as winter wheat—which, in any case, was discouraged by the limited fall moisture.[9] The ongoing search for better varieties thus aimed largely at finding hardier (and harder) varieties that would do well in the area and help farmers penetrate Minneapolis and other Eastern markets (in 1930 the Department of Agriculture's Pendleton Field Station had 250 varieties of wheat under study). Many farmers settled on a Bluestem variety that yielded less than some alternatives but drew higher prices because its relatively hard grain was better for milling than other varieties suited to the area.[10]

The Industrial Revolution had an impact in the centers of production. Although lowlands around Walla Walla (and in more limited areas along various streams) could be farmed using techniques long familiar on the frontier, much of the land was ill-suited for such an approach. But change was coming. Walter Pierce, who eventually rose to be governor and then a congressman, arrived in Milton as a young man in 1883. He found "big wheat fields, hundreds of acres, waving in the wind. . . . The method of harvesting was new to me. Headers were used. The wheatheads [were] stacked in the field; a big threshing machine came along and threshed these stacked headings, wheat [was then] put in sacks, taken to the warehouse and loaded on trains." Pierce obtained work on a threshing machine, working "Walla Walla hours." His employer informed him what that meant: "The whistle blows at three-thirty; engineer starts steam. Four o'clock the steam starts; we commence threshing. We blow down at six-thirty for thirty minutes; eat breakfast. Then we run until twelve; blow down for one hour for dinner. Then we . . . run till six; blow down for thirty minutes. Start at six-thirty and drive until eight. Wages two dollars a day . . . two and a half if you work on the feed." Laborer Hayes Perkins summed it up neatly: "A hired man is but a domestic animal in this western country."[11]

Away from the bottoms, much of the area was made up of steep slopes that could be farmed only with heavy-duty equipment. Loess hills rose like a sea of giant dunes above the narrow, often seasonal watercourses that drained them. On their leeward sides the hills dropped off so sharply they often could not be farmed even with the most advanced machinery, but newly developed (or improved) power equipment gradually brought the less-abrupt windward slopes into production and many of the lee sides as well. As early as 1864 some recognized that the area's benchlands were suited for wheat, but initial attempts at cropping them had mixed results, slowing expansion into them. Within a few years this changed, and it came to be believed that anywhere bunchgrass grew would be good wheat country. Many now sought out hill lands in preference to the bottoms, which were more prone to frosts and often had a heavy growth of brome grass that made plowing difficult. Growing experience with dry farming and the work of agricultural experiment stations aided in bringing the hill country into production.[12]

Mechanical inventions helped the process: improved plows, springtooth and then disc harrows, seed drills for planting, headers, combines, and steam-powered and internal-combustion tractors. Huge teams of horses pulled gangs of up to a dozen plows, harrows, or drills. When Walter Pierce commenced production on his own in the 1890s, he used horse combines, utilizing "ground power, that is, the power . . . from the big wheels; there was no engine. We used from twenty-four to thirty-four horses and mules on these machines which headed and threshed."[13]

Horse-drawn wheat harvest in Wasco County. Credit: Wasco County Pioneer Association courtesy of Columbia Gorge Discovery Center and Museum.

Novelist Nard Jones, a onetime resident, remembered the transition. Describing harvest season, he wrote,

> Against the farthest hill one might see them: the long string of horses creeping slowly, looking almost like a brown worm against the yellow wheat. Or, more often now, the thresher would move rather faster, and before it there would be an awkward, lumbering tractor.

It took time to adjust to the change:

> [People] could not [en]vision a country infested with tractors, a country without stables. . . . They didn't want to fancy a place with no horses, no smell of horses, no sound of horses. Somehow they didn't like to think of their children not knowing a butt chain—just as an old seaman would hate to think of his children not knowing a halyard.[14]

Pierce was among those who adopted the new technology. He later recalled substituting a gasoline engine for ground power, a change that proved "a great success." Other changes followed. "In 1898 the crop was big and Henry Pierce and I bought the first steam combine that was ever brought to the Umatilla. It was a 'Daniel Best,'" which cut a twenty-six-foot swath. "The machine started on the Umatilla [Reservation], and cut there about three thousand acres, driving all daylight, every day." The operator was paid the "enormous salary of seven-fifty a day." Pierce concluded with a good bit of understatement: the combine "cost eight thousand dollars in California, and it was a success."[15]

Production per acre did not rise significantly with such changes, but output per man-hour did, and the shift freed up for wheat production many acres previously used as pasture or to raise oats for the horses. A system of increasingly extensive agriculture emerged based on huge, one-crop wheat ranches—one could hardly call them farms. These developments owed more to California than to earlier American agricultural frontiers.[16]

The area's rail network, which in time extended from Pendleton north to Spokane, made development possible. In turn it was made practical by wheat. Nard Jones described the scene in Weston, "Each day of the midsummer brought down more wheat; . . . yellow kernels were poured into sacks or into bulk-wagons that were pulled alongside the combine. A steady stream of these wagons went down to the scales and the warehouses below town. The tracks, deserted in Winter except for an occasional coal or wood car, were crowded with freights." Jones's novel is of life in the wheat country; earlier events intrude but little on his story. Nearby Athena was similar, although cattle raising had once been strong in the area. Alice Day Pratt, who taught there, described the town as nothing "but a wheat-shipping station" from which heavily laden wagons of grain rolled each fall. Only the "wonderful landscape of golden fields and purple fallow rolling away in every direction fully compensated for its dingy hotel, its primitive little dwellings, and its unattractive streets."[17]

West of Pendleton, wheatlands were separated by canyons that made a similar rail network impractical, and production was long inadequate to attract railroad builders. But when they eventually arrived, railroads spurred production. In the mid-1880s the Oregon Rail & Navigation Company completed a spur line up Willow Creek through the wheat-producing area around Ione and Lexington to the wool-shipping center of Heppner.[18]

Other areas struggled on without rail facilities until considerably later; those producing wheat in such places long remained dependent on expensive wagon transportation to get their crop to the Columbia. Not until 1898 did builders commence construction of the Columbia Southern Railroad, which passed through the wheat country of Wasco, Moro, and Grass Valley. In 1905, the year the line reached Shaniko, the OR&N commenced construction of a branch line to Condon in Gilliam County. The year before, construction had commenced on the Great Southern Railroad from The Dalles to and beyond Dufur; and in 1907 a spur was completed from Pendleton to Pilot Rock. Wheat production burgeoned in these areas.[19]

Although wheat prices fluctuated and producers grumbled about transportation costs, on the whole they did well. Walter Pierce recalled that he commenced farming on leased land on the Umatilla Reservation in 1897, paying from fifty cents to four dollars an acre per year for four thousand acres, half of which he fallowed every year. T. J. Tweedy, Pierce's partner, devoted full time to managing the operation, while Pierce lent money for seed, horses, machinery, labor, and rent—at 8 percent interest. In eight years, they raised five hundred thousand bushels of wheat. It cost "a trifle under" forty cents a bushel to raise and sold for an average of nearly fifty cents. Pierce concluded: "We sold out at the end of the eight year period, dividing forty thousand dollars profit."[20]

But wheat raising was a volatile business. In 1893, much of the area's crop sold for only twenty cents a bushel, well below the cost of production. Still, output continued to rise. In 1910, Umatilla County's farmers produced over five million bushels, which sold for close to eighty cents a bushel. The *East Oregonian* called it the "most successful season in many years" because of excellent weather during the harvest season, increased use of mechanized equipment, and good prices. Dozens of new combines were operating that year; one Pendleton dealer alone sold twenty-nine.[21]

Wheat farmers frequently grumbled about the price they received for grain, high freight rates, and the supposed extortion of suppliers, but corrective action was slow in coming. Farmers understood only dimly the markets on which they depended. They simply worked and then sold their wheat for what they could get. Not until 1929, and then only with federal prodding, did some seventy of the area's wheat ranchers join to create Pendleton Grain Growers, a cooperative that provided marketing and

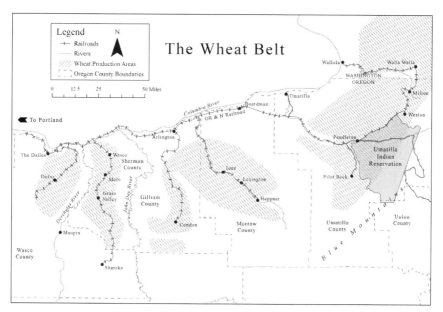

The wheat belt. Credit: Kindra Blair.

transportation services and built storage facilities at some thirty locations in Umatilla, Union, and Wallowa Counties.[22]

A distinctive society emerged in the wheat country extending north from Pendleton. Nard Jones describes it in *Oregon Detour*, set in Weston but also reflecting life in many other wheat towns—Athena, Milton, and beyond. He considered them crabbed, narrow little communities where old-timers, those descended from the early farm families, dominated and set the social norms, where people's horizons and ambitions were restricted to a limited range of concerns, and where the outside world was little understood and viewed with suspicion if not hostility. In the beginning, cattlemen and others had lent a more vibrant—and sometimes violent—tone to society, but by the end of the century wheat had dominated for so long that the early days and their influence had become dim memories.[23] In 1920, fresh from the University of Oregon, my mother was offered a job teaching English in the vicinity; although from a small town herself, she turned down the job in what she considered an overly constricted society and took up residence in Portland.

On the whole, residents of these communities were not unhappy. As Nard Jones was careful to point out, they were not the sort of people fellow New Realism novelists Sinclair Lewis and Sherwood Anderson described. Wheat ranchers "had their work to do, work they wanted. Out of that can come all the emotions needed by anyone to carry on the business of living. It was enough for them that, once again, there would be yellow wheat to harvest from the rolling hills." Donald Meinig—himself a son of the small-town world of the Palouse—notes the characteristics Jones delineated, but observes that much of this was obscured "by the massive influence of a crass materialism, strident boosterism, and frantic concern to be in the forefront of 'progress.'" In spite of Meinig's caveat, the narrowness remained, a narrowness that set the wheat ranchers and many of their towns apart from the gold seekers, cattlemen, and sheepmen who had preceded and on occasion stood alongside them.[24]

West from Pendleton, communities were different. Never exclusively wheat towns, and often founded before wheat ranchers had appeared on the scene, these communities tended to have a more varied, vibrant persona. Wheat ranchers began to enter the area in force in the 1880s—as a newspaper from The Dalles noted, "The area is fast filling up with agriculturists." George Doyle, who arrived in Sherman County in 1882, estimated that at the time "land under cultivation in the county . . . could not have exceeded 1,000 acres [and] . . . not a bushel of grain sold outside the county, for it was needed for bread and feed for the fall and winter of 1882 and 1883." Rapid expansion followed, "not a slow, steady growth, but . . . [something that] appeared almost spontaneous." In 1885, the area that four years later would become Sherman County produced some 1.65 million bushels of wheat and had become a major exporter. Development was encouraged by the completion of the Oregon Rail & Navigation Company line along the Columbia in 1882. Wheat raising on the highlands expanded and sheep range contracted, pushing pastoralism south and southeast.[25]

The shift to wheat in Sherman, Morrow, Gilliam, and Wasco Counties came late enough that much of the vibrancy that accompanied the opening of new lands remained well into the twentieth century. At the same time, cattle and sheep raising continued in parts of the Columbia River counties not suitable for wheat, thereby lending a diversity to society and the economy not seen in places like Weston and the vast wheatlands to the north of Pendleton, where grain dominated all.[26]

Until the construction of spur lines, wheat was moved to the OR&N by wagon. Arlington, Rufus, and Biggs emerged as trans-shipment points. Arlington in particular prospered, although, as local historian Marion Weatherford observed, "It may be difficult to imagine a less favorable place to start a town."[27] The town that developed there was decidedly different from Weston and its ilk. Nestled in an arid, desolate, rocky draw on the Columbia's south bank, it had little to recommend it save access to the interior, the river, and the railroad. Owen Ebi, who came to Arlington in 1882, served as the town's first night watchman and "had a pretty tumultuous and strenuous time" with rowdies who flocked to the new community. Ebi explained,

> Arlington in the early days was the supply depot for the whole interior country. Long lines of freight wagons would come here from Prineville, John Day, Mitchell, Fossil, Condon, Lone Rock and from the back of beyond. They all got their supplies here for the scattered sheep ranches and cow camps within 150 miles to the southward and they brought out . . . cattle and sheep for shipment. . . . Later when wheat began being raised in the interior all the wheat was hauled to Arlington for shipment. Naturally, with so many men constantly coming and going, this was a pretty wild town.[28]

For all this, there was a certain propriety too, a product perhaps of commercial ties the wheat counties had with Portland. Whereas the rest of Eastern Oregon voted Democratic, Gilliam, Morrow, Sherman, and Wasco Counties all voted Republican in 1896 (and in most other elections).[29]

Arlington was not alone. Being too remote to be easily served from Walla Walla, Pendleton, or The Dalles, some of the new towns—Wasco and Condon, for example—became supply centers for their hinterlands to a degree that Weston never did for its own; with this and their more varied population and history, they seemed more vibrant. In contrast, it could be said that Weston, Milton, Athena, and most other small towns to the east had hinterlands as restricted as their societies.

If the timing and patterns of settlement shaped the little wheat towns between The Dalles and the Umatilla, the same could be said of Pendleton and Walla Walla. Although these two major communities were not geographically distant, they were quite different. A half century of unrivaled development seems to have persuaded residents of Walla Walla, surrounded as they were by rich farmland, that it was their destiny to dominate the region. In 1880 one well-traveled visitor wrote, "The people seem bright, intelligent, and pleasant to meet, but [they lack] the ambitious and progressive natures of other places we had visited." They seem possessed by "self-satisfaction, possessing the thought that Walla Walla was the hub of the universe." It was, in short, a community confident in its future, a confidence bolstered at the time by the railroad building gaining pace in the interior.[30] It was a smug self-satisfaction that makes believable the oft-told tale of Walla Walla's city fathers turning down what would become Washington State University in favor of the state penitentiary, where inmates could make jute bags for use in shipping the area's wheat. And it was a self-satisfaction still depressingly palpable when I was a student there in the early 1950s, even though the city had long since been bypassed by major rail lines and highways.

Pendleton was of a different sort. Donald Meinig describes the city during the 1890s in terms that draw heavily on the rhetoric and actions of local boosters: Pendleton was, he wrote, "one of the most prosperous and progressive towns in the interior."[31] But such an interpretation overlooks as much as it illuminates. Boosters were just the tip of Pendleton's iceberg.

Nard Jones came closer to delineating the true nature of the community. As the pages of the *East Oregonian* demonstrate, from the first Pendleton was a wide-open community. Incorporated in 1880, its first city ordinance dealt with public drunkenness, fights, and the discharging of firearms in the city. By the 1920s, when Jones wrote, Pendleton was still "open, a vestige of another day," and the annual Pendleton Round-Up served to keep it so:

> Once a year, at Round-Up time, Pendleton dressed up for the effete
> East in the garb of yesterday. . . . At night there was a celebration
> in Happy Canyon that differed from the old . . . dance hall brawls
> only in point of date. Prostitutes oozed about with freedom, gay
> ladies from Seattle, Portland, Walla Walla, on their "vacations."
> The Round-Up lasted four days a year and it placed Pendleton
> on the map. But the town was never able during the remaining
> three hundred and sixty-one, to shake off the laxity of morals

which those four days bred. In fact, people weren't unproud of their viewpoint. "Pendleton people are different from Walla Walla people," they would say. "They're more broadminded. They're a different sort altogether."[32]

Jones went on: "Walla Walla was the West trying to behave itself and become cosmopolitan. . . . Pendleton was the West with its coat off and its stockinged feet on the table. It still didn't give a damn." Alice Day Pratt made a similar observation. After seeing "the dusty, dingy streets of Pendleton" a decade before Jones, she attended the Round-Up and found it "a show unsurpassed as an exhibit of native strength and physical prowess, not without brutality—a brutality that will pass away in coming years before [i.e., in the face of] the finer chivalry that evolves the gentle man." In Jones's day, Pendleton was still awaiting that transformation. C. S. Jackson, editor of the *East Oregonian*, decried community violence and the Round-Up's glorification of the past: "We must look to the present and to the future rather than to days that are gone."[33]

More went into shaping Pendleton than just the Round-Up. Its pre-wheat past of cowboys, Indian fighters, and sheepherders played a role too. And when settlers had begun to crowd into the area in the 1860s, a good portion were Missourians and others who had fled their homes in the face of destruction and desolation brought on by the Civil War. As Carrie Strahorn wrote, it was as if "the 'left wing of Sterling Price's army' had hidden itself in the sage-brush, and through narrow-mindedness and bigotry . . . tried ever to get in the way of civilization." These were hardly the sort of home-seekers from the Willamette Valley, the Northeast, and the upper Midwest who dominated in and around Walla Walla.[34]

The mix that became Pendleton was further leavened by an influx of Chinese who gave up grubbing in the tailings of worked-out gold mines to seek better opportunities in town. Ere long Pendleton had a sizable Chinese population and a warren of underground tunnels and retreats where opium, gambling, and prostitution were rampant (although whether these were actually made by the Chinese is questioned).

Railroad construction and subsequent railroad employment brought other socially marginal people to the city, as did the Industrial Workers of the World (IWW), which, during the early twentieth century, struggled to organize laborers on the wheat ranches and railroads.[35] In short, Pendleton was more than just a wheat town and would remain so for years to come.

As the major business and cultural center for a vast area, Pendleton managed to continue as the region's main population center—at least on the Oregon side of the state line.[36] Lesser wheat towns have not been so fortunate. Some, such as Lonerock, Mayville, and Hardman, have been abandoned or nearly so. Others, like Condon and Ione, hang on while trying to market themselves to tourists in search of echoes of days gone by. Nearly all struggle. New technology has led to larger and larger wheat ranches that employ ever fewer people. Meanwhile, with better roads and automobiles, many landowners have moved to larger communities so they and their families can have the schools and amenities not offered in the little wheat towns that sprang up during the 1880s. With modern communications, wheat ranchers can now manage thousands of acres of land from offices in Pendleton (or even Portland). This new breed of "sidewalk farmers" is just one more factor contributing to the ongoing decline of population in the wheat country—and to the many problems that result therefrom. Just how tied to the land—and shaped by it—these latter-day wheat ranchers are is open to question.

7
Commercializing Timber

Timber stretches across vast portions of Eastern Oregon, but it long remained beyond the reach of those who would tap it for commercial purposes. Like wheat, timber products needed transportation facilities to reach markets. For many years these were absent. There was a dearth of rivers suitable for log drives or getting lumber to market—both of which had been central in most areas where lumbering had developed earlier—and railroads did not reach the area's timbered sections until quite late. Small mills supplied local needs, but there was nothing that could be considered a lumber industry—or the seeds from which one could grow. Concerns about forest management and related environmental issues would come even later.

David Eccles introduced a new order. Born in 1849 in Scotland, Eccles emigrated with his family, who had converted to the Church of Jesus Christ of Latter Day Saints (Mormons), and made their way to Utah in 1863. Finding it difficult to make a living there, the family moved to Oregon City, where young Eccles found employment in a sawmill; with the Oregon and California Railroad, which was building south down the Willamette Valley; and with Pope & Talbot, which had a large sawmill on Puget Sound. When the Union and Central Pacific met at Promontory Point in 1869, providing transcontinental rail connections and giving Utah an economic boost, the family moved back to Ogden to be near the main body of their church. There Eccles worked as a woodcutter, house builder, teamster, and in the Union Pacific's coal mines. Throughout, the frugal young Scot saved and carefully invested his money. He founded a lumberyard in Ogden and, through sales, stayed abreast of opportunities. In 1883 he bought his first Oregon enterprise, a small sawmill in North Powder. Over the years he acquired other businesses and became Utah's first multimillionaire, but, his biographer notes, "Eccles always considered himself a lumberman."[1]

Eccles sold ties and lumber to the Oregon Short Line as it built westward from Granger, Wyoming, and in 1887 erected a small mill in Oregon to supply the Oregon Rail & Navigation Company's line from Huntington to Pendleton. Two years later he abandoned this and his North Powder mill and, with a group of partners, erected a large plant at Baker City. Known as the Oregon Lumber Company, it would run for years.[2]

The shift to Oregon was spurred by a basic reality: access to timber in Utah was problematic. According to historian Leonard Arrington, Utah's lumbermen consistently cut illegally in government timber, "protecting their efforts by paying off the inspectors one by one as they came." The manager of Eccles's mill in Schofield explained: "Every year a government agent would come to see about the cutting of the timber. We compromised, . . . each mill paying a certain amount, and the government man kept that for himself. . . . He never gave the money to the government." Eccles sought a more sustainable way of accessing Utah's timber; failing, he turned his eyes to Oregon, where conditions "both natural and governmental promised to be more amenable to the logging industry."[3]

The Oregon Lumber Company made Eastern Oregon's forests yet another source of commodity exports from the region. The firm's early success stemmed from three major factors. First, Eccles recognized that the OR&N-OSL line provided access to markets in and beyond Utah, markets that most timbered areas were poorly located to serve. Second, Baker City—"the pride of eastern Oregon" Carrie Strahorn called it—was the largest community between Portland and Utah and served a considerable hinterland, making local demand a valuable complement to more distant rail markets. Third, Eccles moved early—well before he built his sawmill there—to acquire timber in the area and, by so doing, was able to acquire stands at bargain prices. Bit by bit he added to his holdings, eventually accumulating some three billion board feet of timber.[4]

Baker City, located on the upper Powder River, was the natural entrepôt to Eccles's stands. To access them, in 1889 he incorporated the Sumpter Valley Railway and, with help from the Union Pacific, began construction of a narrow-gauge line up the Powder. Eccles slowly pushed the railroad south and west, proceeding only as fast as available capital allowed; it finally reached Sumpter in 1897. Sluicing and hard-rock mining were booming in the area, so shipments of equipment, supplies, and ore joined logs in keeping the line solvent. In Sumpter, Eccles built a second

Logs en route to Baker City on the Sumpter Valley Railroad, 1907. Credit: Baker County Library District.

large sawmill and spur lines to bring in logs from the surrounding area. In 1901, the railroad reached Whitney, across timbered heights in the watershed of the Burnt River. There Eccles built a third sawmill and more spur lines. Pushing on, the railway reached Austin in 1908. Eccles followed his by-then-familiar pattern, building a large sawmill in nearby Bates. The line was lightly ballasted and had a rough roadbed, steep grades, and numerous switchbacks, but it served Eccles and his partners well. To take further advantage of opportunities the mainline OR&N provided, Eccles also built mills in La Grande and Meacham and acquired the Grande Ronde Lumber Company, which operated north of the Wallowa Mountains.[5]

Eccles's undertaking had another side as well. As a devout Mormon, he brought many co-religionists to Oregon to run his sawmills, railroad, and ancillary enterprises. Others followed on their own, and the Sumpter Valley Railway was soon known locally as the "Polygamy Central." The LDS church would have a strong presence in the Sumpter Valley and nearby areas for years to come.[6]

Non-Mormons found reason to complain about Eccles's business practices. Indeed, his approach to acquiring timberland added to a growing, many-sided debate over the creation of federal forest reserves in Eastern Oregon. Federal inspector Harold D. Langille reported, "It is common knowledge [Eccles's] . . . employees have been supplied with funds to purchase land under the Timber and Stone Act, and it is a matter of record that their claims have been transferred to the company on the . . . day following receipt of patent." In spite of Eccles's objections, in the end federal authorities set aside the Blue Mountain Forest Reserve, which encompassed more than 3.1 million acres (including much of the territory tributary to Oregon Lumber Company's operations). Ever inventive, Eccles devised means of coping with the new realities these entities presented.[7]

Eccles's operations in the Blues were a harbinger of things to come, but for those who would follow, the wait was a long one. This may seem odd, for west of the Cascades a lumber industry had emerged much earlier. But there, the industry was oriented to markets largely reached by sea and based on Douglas-fir. Marketing was little dependent on railroads, a far cry from the situation of Eccles and his successors.

East of the Cascades, forests with commercial potential were dominated by Ponderosa pine, not Douglas-fir. The pine grew in relatively open stands, often on fairly level land, making logging less expensive than in many other areas. Pine forests stretched from north of Sisters south to Klamath Falls, from there east beyond Lakeview (and into California) and northeast almost to Silver Lake. In the Blue Mountains and its outriders, pine forests (with an admixture of other species) extended from the Idaho and Washington borders in the far northeast to near Prineville in the west.[8] But with the exception of timber accessible from the OR&N's line from Huntington to Pendleton, these stands were inaccessible. Eccles had shown what was possible when railroads came, but until then there was little lumbermen could do except look ahead and follow Eccles's lead in acquiring timberland as soon as possible. Every great lumber-producing center in Eastern Oregon, and most of the secondary ones, would come into being because of railroads, but they would be the scene of a scramble for timberland well beforehand.

Thus, for a considerable period, many of the forests of Eastern Oregon served as reserves for future use and supplied more grass for cattle and sheep than logs. The pine forests of the upper Great Lakes states and the South still filled much of the nation's demand for lumber, while the redwood and Douglas-fir forests along the Pacific shore, combined with the pineries of the Sierra Nevada, met the considerable needs of California and assorted Pacific Basin markets.[9]

Over the years Congress passed a variety of laws designed to aid in transferring western land from government to private hands: the Homestead Act (1862), the Timber Culture Act (1873), the Desert Land Act (1877), and the Timber and Stone Act (1878). These rested on a foundation of Jeffersonian thought that envisioned America as a land of agrarian smallholders who would be the backbone of democracy. Railroad land grants, designed to encourage improved transportation and thus settlement, were expected to work in the same direction. Not until the Timber and Stone Act did realization that much of the West was ill-suited for farming begin to inform policy, and even then, older ideas still held sway in most quarters.[10]

Timbermen had priorities of their own and soon found that these laws could be turned to purposes other than those for which they were intended. As opportunities elsewhere dwindled during the late nineteenth and early twentieth centuries, lumbermen turned to Eastern Oregon. The resulting scramble for timberland—and the abuses intimately tied to it—shaped and were shaped by the drive to create forest reserves in the Blues, Cascades, and elsewhere.

More was involved than competition between those who would cut forests now and those who wanted to save them for future needs. Watershed protection and control of grazing were key components.[11] Indeed, a forest reserve on Elk Creek, Oregon's first east of the Cascades, was temporarily withdrawn in 1901 (and permanently in 1904) to protect Baker City's watershed from damage by huge bands of sheep trailed through the area annually. Similarly, reserves south of Heppner, on Maury Mountain, near Dufur, and in the Warner Mountains were largely aimed at halting overgrazing. Preservationists concerned with scenery protection and outdoor recreation played a role in establishing the huge Cascade Forest Reserve (as well as Crater Lake National Park), but farther east they did little; in spite of their rugged beauty, the Wallowa Mountains (and lesser areas such as those around Aneroid Peak and Strawberry Mountain) were too far from major population centers to spur into action the Oregon Alpine Club (later known as the Mazamas) and Western Oregon's preservationist leaders such as William Gladstone Steele.[12]

Lumbermen joined those pushing for forest reserves, for they had discovered reserves could be turned to their own purposes. The "lieu" land provision of federal legislation regarding reserves was the key component. The Forest Reserve Act of 1891 had empowered the president to set aside forestland from the public domain. President Benjamin Harrison promptly reserved twenty-two million acres; other presidents followed with additions of their own. But the reserves created problems, because of the variety of state and private holdings contained within their boundaries. Responding, in 1897 Congress passed the Forest Lieu Act, which gave those with private holdings or claims within the boundaries of a reserve the right to exchange them for public domain land outside of reserves.[13]

The Lieu Act was intended to consolidate reserves by eliminating inholdings, a potential source of problems. Whether forested or not, lands within reserves that had previously been claimed using the Homestead Act or other federal legislation, acquired from Oregon's school endowment lands, or purchased from railroad and wagon road land grants could all be used as base for exchanges. Moreover, when a reserve was established, the state obtained rights to equal acreage outside it for each section of unclaimed state school land within.[14]

On the surface, such exchanges seemed reasonable, but in practice they proved anything but. One had only to file a claim for the land to become part of one's base, and, although officials in government land offices were supposed to reject claims to land not suitable for agriculture—the use envisioned in both federal and state laws—they often did not, especially when bribery or collusion were involved. Since claims were transferable, and many who took them up had no intention of farming, they quickly fell into the hands of lumbermen—indeed, Eccles and others often had people file on timberland already selected for them.[15]

The problems of collusion and fraudulent entries would have been minimized had it been possible to create a reserve in a single, quick stroke, but that was not the case. The sight of government agents investigating an area to determine its desirability as a reserve, surveying the boundaries of reserves in the offing, even informed rumors were enough to alert lumbermen, and the timber locators on whom they depended, to fresh opportunities. Hordes of would-be claimants flocked to such areas, in some cases brought en masse by lumbermen to whom they were beholden to transfer their freshly minted claims for a small payment.

When a forest reserve was being contemplated in the vast stands near Bend, the area quickly became a mecca for land-lookers and would-be claimants. Stephen Puter led 108 dummy entrymen to land he had selected there; "the concourse of vehicles," he wrote, "resembled a Sunday turnout in Golden Gate Park." Others did the same. Puter recalled that "all summer long the dusty roads between Shaniko and the Bend [*sic*] were lined with travelers, and it was soon evident that a large portion of them were under contract to convey whatever timber rights they might acquire to syndicates of Eastern lumbermen." Conspicuous in the throng were schoolteachers, dispatched during the summer from Minnesota by the Shevlin-Hixon interests, which planned to build a large sawmill in Bend when railroad connections were completed. Similar developments also took place elsewhere. Klamath Falls, looking forward to the arrival of railroads, was a center of a great scramble for timberland.[16]

But bogus claims did not go unchallenged. Oswald West, the state land agent appointed by fellow Democrat George Chamberlain to halt fraudulent practices on school endowment lands, decried individuals who "through rascality and fraud gained title to thousands of acres of valuable publicly-owned timber." He was remarkably successful, recovering one million acres of illegally claimed school land. H. D. Langille was less noted, but in 1902 he heard that "a carload of timber claim locators had arrived [in La Grande] . . . from Minnesota, had taken teams to the Wallowa country" together with land locators, and returned within a day to file claims; Langille arranged a temporary withdrawal of the area and hurried to the land office in La Grande to block the claims. All were denied.[17]

Lumbermen adopted another ploy. Recognizing that forest reserves created opportunities for claims, they began lobbying for the establishment of additional ones; sheepmen saw opportunity in them too. According to Langille, "the most controversial of all withdrawals was the . . . Blue Mountain Forest Reserve." His claim is hard to rebut; Larry Rakestraw has detailed the shenanigans involved. In due course, Stephen Puter noted, nearly "the entire [Oregon] delegation in Congress" was involved in efforts to create the reserve, which was little more than "a clever scheme to convert a quantity of school land into forest reserve scrip" for use in exchanges.

Still, as Rakestraw notes, "There was need for reserves," and gradually they proved their worth.[18]

The Oregon Central Military Wagon Road provided opportunities of a different sort. In 1864 the United States offered Oregon alternating sections of land on either side of a wagon road from Eugene across the Cascades to Fort Boise. Oregon selected a firm to construct the road, envisioned as a military supply route to the vicinity of Indian troubles and as a means of encouraging settlement. In 1872 the state's governor pronounced the road "completed," but it never assumed importance as a transportation route—and for good reason: the road's builders did only enough to secure the grant. But as a means of acquiring land from the public domain, especially timberland, the route took on considerable significance. From the first, as the *New York Times* put it, the wagon road grant and others like it in Oregon were little more than "unblushing land frauds."[19]

The route proceeded from near Eugene up the Willamette (following roughly the present-day route of Oregon Highway 58), but after crossing the Cascade summit it swung south into the Klamath Basin and then east past Goose and Warner Lakes rather than proceeding directly east toward Fort Boise. The routing took the "road" through timber and grazing land far more valuable than land along a more direct route would have been— and in the process alienated a huge acreage from the Klamath Indian Reservation. In time the California and Oregon Land Company, controlled by Eugene lumberman Robert A. Booth, came into possession of the grant. The federal government brought suit, charging the land was forfeit, for the road had never really been finished. The Supreme Court took up the case and, in 1893, ruled that 875,196 acres of unpatented lands within the grant of were indeed forfeit and should be returned to the public domain, but title to 235,568 acres of legally patented lands would stand.[20]

Booth had not perpetrated the original fraud, but certainly benefited from it. With his title secure, in 1906 he proceeded to consolidate his holdings within the Klamath reservation. The checkerboard pattern of the lands he controlled made utilization difficult, and in any case, many sections were but lightly timbered or valuable only for grazing. Booth arranged to block up his holdings by swapping less desirable acres for heavily timbered land neighboring his holdings near Yamsay Mountain north of Klamath Falls. Recognizing that the lands being exchanged were hardly of equal value, Congress appropriated $108,750 to compensate the Klamath tribes.

Timber country. Credit: Kindra Blair.

It was a gross underpayment. Observers estimated the swap profited Booth some $2 or $3 million. They were surely correct, for although Booth never logged the tract, he was able to sell it subsequently for $3.7 million.[21]

There was more to the lumber story than fraud and scandal. Over the years lumbermen in the upper Great Lakes states and Gulf South had found ways of acquiring timberland from the public domain by turning land laws to purposes other than those for which they were intended; there had been fraud aplenty, but it was far from universal. The same was true in Oregon.

Edward D. Wetmore and a group of associates from Pennsylvania provide a case in point. As timber began to run out in northwestern portions of their home state, they began to look for fresh opportunities. They were never exclusively lumbermen, but the area around Warren and Tionesta in Pennsylvania had long been an active center of lumbering, and the group had engaged in it. Early in the twentieth century, they turned to Oregon's Blue Mountains and, operating as the Kinzua Lumber Company, began acquiring timber there. Members of the group were not certain they would actually commence sawmilling in Oregon, but were convinced its timberland was a good investment, for it was still inexpensive and stands were running out in many other areas. They were certainly correct; their purchases in Oregon cost an average of only 79 cents a thousand board feet, while not long thereafter government timber in the area was selling for $3.10 per thousand.[22]

Working through timber locator Willard N. Jones, they eventually came to own some fifty thousand acres—one hundred million board feet—near the western terminus of the Blues. Jones had been an associate of Stephen Puter and had been caught up in the Oregon timber fraud scandals, but now he was working on his own as a timber locator and earning sizable commissions for his efforts. He would find promising tracts and buy up available scrip and claims, which he then used to acquire the selected tracts. In all the voluminous correspondence in the Wetmore papers, there is no indication that either Jones or Wetmore considered this illegal or even questionable. Under the law, scrip and claims were transferable, and they saw themselves as simply following the established practices of the day.[23]

The Gilchrist Timber Company and its predecessor firms followed a similar course. Running out of timber in Michigan, Frank W. Gilchrist began searching for new areas in which to operate. In 1901 he hired Frank S. Dushau and charged him with finding promising tracts, estimating the timber on them, and, if deemed worthwhile, purchasing them. In 1902 Dushau began buying in Central Oregon. By the late 1920s Gilchrist's holdings in Deschutes, Klamath, and Lake Counties totaled more than sixty thousand acres of prime Ponderosa pine forest. Not until 1937, after the Gilchrist interests had cut out their stands in Michigan and Mississippi, did the company erect a sawmill and company town on its land in Oregon. For more than thirty years, its Central Oregon holdings had been a long-term investment rather than a working forest. The record is fragmentary, but it shows few signs that Gilchrist engaged in the sorts of fraudulent practices that were hallmarks of the Eccles and Shevlin-Hixon operations.[24]

Others also acquired extensive stands in Eastern Oregon's pineries, but not all wound up building sawmills to utilize them. The Weyerhaeuser Timber Company had considerable forestland near Lakeview, and the Ochoco Timber Company (one of Robert A. Booth's enterprises), had large holdings east of Prineville. Neither built a sawmill to utilize its stands, although both toyed with the idea. Like many others, they acquired timber while it was still available, banked it while developing long-range plans, and then sold it when they decided to manufacture elsewhere.[25]

The late-nineteenth and early-twentieth-century scramble for timberland and the frauds associated therewith were a passing phenomenon. In 1905 Congress transferred authority over forest reserves to the Department of Agriculture, raised the status of its Bureau of Forestry (renaming it the Forest Service), and repealed the forest lieu provision of 1897. Gifford Pinchot, head of the Forest Service, quickly penned a directive for the management of reserves, making it clear they were for use and "the dominant industry should be considered first." Two years later Congress renamed the reserves national forests and forbade new withdrawals in the West except by act of Congress, but President Theodore Roosevelt hastened to add sixteen million acres to the system before his authority to do so lapsed, thus bringing the total to 151 million acres. With these changes, relative stability came at last to Eastern Oregon's forests.[26]

Forest Service timber sales soon made stumpage available, lessening opposition to reserves and helping mill owners manage their own stands more efficiently. At first these were small sales that primarily benefited minor operators with limited timber of their own, but they became increasingly important as private timber became less readily available and prices rose. One firm found that logs purchased from the Forest Service cost $3.75 per thousand board feet, delivered in its pond—considerably less than those it bought from David Eccles. The purchases more than doubled the company's timber base, prolonging the life of its mill sufficiently to justify the original investment in plant. The situation with the East Oregon Lumber Company sawmill, at the foot of the Wallowa Mountains in Enterprise, was similar. The company operated from 1915 to 1928, much longer than its own holdings would have allowed, because Forest Service sales made operation possible after its private stands were exhausted.[27]

Change came with Pinchot's successors, Henry S. Graves and William B. Greeley. Small, scattered sales might help marginal operators, but they did nothing to bring better management to the nation's forests. It was, Graves proclaimed, of "the utmost importance that the industrial developments supported by National Forest stumpage be permanent." Sales should be large enough, and the terms specific enough, to ensure the sustained yield management that would make permanency possible.[28]

Toward this end, Forest Service officials adopted a planning tool known as Working Circles. Taking into account public and private timber available in an area, they scheduled timber sales of a size and frequency to maintain permanent, efficient modern sawmills. This worked better in some areas than others, and computations of what was required for sustained yield were often flawed. In the Klamath forests—with their complex mixture of Forest Service, Indian, and fragmented private holdings, plus a scattered host of sawmills—planning was especially difficult. Management was also fraught with problems in the Bend area, where the two giant sawmills that dominated production engaged in the same cut-and-run policies they had pursued in the upper Great Lakes states. Although the leaders of the mills were wont to blame the Forest Service for failure to adopt policies that would lead to permanency, much of the problem rested with their own values and attitudes.[29]

Nowhere was the impact of this fresh policy more evident than in Burns. Responding to pleas from community leaders, the Forest Service surveyed the area and determined that a huge timber sale, properly regulated, could be combined with private holdings to support indefinitely a large, modern mill in Burns. Local demand for lumber was limited, so the contract crafted by the Forest Service required the successful bidder to build a railroad—a common carrier—from Crane to the mill site in Burns, a distance of some thirty miles, so that the cut could get out to waiting markets, and from there to Seneca in the midst of the stands to be tapped. Fred Herrick of Idaho won a contract for 890 million board feet to be cut over fifty years; the contract was subsequently taken over by the Edward Hines Lumber Company headquartered in Chicago (but with sawmills in Minnesota and the South). This was but the opening wedge: the Burns Working Circle encompassed roughly eleven billion board feet of timber, five-sixths of it in national ownership. The contract brought large-scale lumbering to the area for the next several decades. In time similar sales would also bring lumbering to Lakeview and Prineville and help support mills in Bend, Gilchrist, Kinzua, and elsewhere.[30]

By the onset of the Great Depression, nearly every major timbered area in Eastern Oregon hosted sawmills. A few latecomers would soon join their ranks, completing a picture that would last to the 1960s and beyond. From La Grande and Baker to Klamath Falls and Bend, timber was being turned into huge quantities of sawn material for shipment to distant markets. But although the production techniques—and the technology involved—were remarkably uniform, towns in which sawmills operated were not. There were no stereotypical lumber towns.

In areas supporting preexisting communities with established norms and institutions, lumbermen were welcomed for the employment and money they brought, but rarely came to dominate. Klamath County long had a mixed economy—ranching, farming, teamsters, and businesses that serviced the surrounding area. Far from the moderating influence of New England, which played a large part in Portland and the northern Willamette Valley, the Klamath Basin drew more of its settlers from the southern and middle border states. The Modoc War of the 1870s did nothing to smooth the rough edges of the society that resulted. In 1885 the town had only 384 residents, but four saloons. Its rough-and-tumble character was exacerbated when the first railroad (and railroad workers) arrived in 1909 and sawmills began to spring up in response. Over the years, its gritty character changed little. Inspectors labeled the city filthy; cleanup efforts seem to have done little good even when spurred by fears generated by the Spanish flu pandemic of 1918.[31] During Prohibition, stills were numerous in nearby woods, and at least one area hotel operated a speakeasy. East of Klamath Falls, Orval DuVaul remembered, "pretty much every place there was a spring there was a moonshine operation." In the 1940s brothels were still numerous, and when I resided in the area in the 1960s, Klamath County reputedly had the highest unsolved murder rate in the United States. As a local observer put it at the time, "Cowboys, Indians, and loggers make a volatile mix." The violence was hardly new; Zane Grey drew on earlier clashes in his lightly fictionalized *Forlorn River* (1927), set in the area east of Klamath Falls. Locals lionized Grey when he visited to do research for the work—and afterward eagerly tried to identify the real-life characters depicted in his novel.[32]

In Klamath Falls, local leaders long chafed over outside interests that had control of vast tracts of timber but failed to build sawmills to utilize them, thus holding back economic development.[33] In Klamath County assessors were instructed to increase their estimates of the board feet of timber in private stands, thus increasing the taxes owners would have to pay. Weyerhaeuser officials complained this was extortion, but Samuel O. Johnson, another outside timberman with interests in Klamath's forests, told a Weyerhaeuser manager his firm should go along—indeed, should buy warrants issued for local improvements—or the firm would pay down the road. Clearly, economic as well as social divisions ran deep.[34]

The situation in Burns was similar. Business leaders had lobbied the Forest Service to open area forests to production, but when development followed, control of the town remained in the hands of those who had long dominated—landowners (primarily ranchers) and the community's professional and business interests that served them. When Peter K. Simpson resided in Burns while working on *The Community of Cattlemen*, he found those in the lumber industry—even those in managerial positions—were still viewed as outsiders. The fact the Hines Lumber Company built its mill west of Burns proper and erected a company town there to house its employees served to reinforce their separateness. Moreover, many employees Hines brought in to run the mill were from the South and possessed values and attitudes distinct from those of the dominant community, thus exacerbating the divisions.[35]

Sawmills came later to Prineville, but the pattern was similar. Business leaders long lobbied for opening nearby forests, but with little success. They repeatedly castigated timberland owners for locking up the forests to serve their own interests while keeping the town economically stagnant. Area farmers were hard-pressed to keep the irrigation company on which they depended solvent—and felt oppressed by taxes and assessments as a result—contributing to the view that absentee timberland owners ought to pay higher taxes on their holdings. When major sawmills finally arrived, many of their leaders were still viewed as outsiders. John M. Hudspeth, who moved from Oklahoma to Oregon in 1936 and built his first sawmill in Prineville a decade later, was more flamboyant than most, but not altogether atypical. He was considered not only an interloper, but also a representative of a flashy nouveau-riche lifestyle at odds with that of the community at large. Through it all, as an area resident recently put it,

"Prineville remained true to its redneck roots." They were roots embedded in the community's history of vigilantes, sheep shootings, brothels, bars, and violence—roots that the lumber industry found already in place when it arrived.[36]

The coming of sawmills may not have wrought basic changes in the power structure and dominant values in established towns, but in new communities and those where sawmills were so large as to overwhelm all that had gone before, the situation was different. Bend, Kinzua, and Gilchrist were all creatures of the industry—yet, shaped by their peculiar circumstances, each was different from the others.

Bend, the most important of these, was reached by railroad in 1911. Huge Shevlin-Hixon and Brooks-Scanlon sawmills followed in 1915 and began cutting stands acquired during the area's hectic scramble for timber a few years earlier. In spite of irrigation projects that were opening land north of town, Bend was first and foremost a lumber town. It quickly became the largest community in Central Oregon—and, after Deschutes County was carved from Crook in 1916, the county seat. Management and much of the workforce of the mills came from the Great Lakes states. The workers included a considerable Scandinavian presence. They were augmented by railroad workers laid off when construction of the line to Bend was completed and homesteaders dusted out from the High Desert. Few appear to have come from the Douglas-fir region west of the Cascades, where labor unrest and the IWW were notable presences (although Great Lakes state workers brought a history of unrest and violence of their own).[37]

With its considerable scenic and recreational attributes, Bend also drew a number of well-heeled, well-educated residents who set a social tone at odds with that in many another lumber town: Harry K. Brooks, in charge of Brooks-Scanlon and the man who arranged for the building of the Pilot Butte Inn, a magnificent craftsman-style hostelry that opened in 1917; Alexander Drake, son of a US senator from Minnesota; George Palmer Putnam, scion of a leading New York publisher; Robert W. Sawyer, a Harvard-educated lawyer-turned-newspaperman; and assorted others. Putnam called them "blue-blood settlers" and noted there was "a whole nest of 'em hereabouts."[38] By the 1920s the famous and near-famous were coming to the area to enjoy its scenery and world-class trout fishing. Along Mirror Pond, a park-rimmed impoundment of the Deschutes that ran through the town, fine homes soon lined the waterway.

A harsher reality lay beneath this tranquil façade. Popular historian Stewart Holbrook lamented the passing of the wild, rambunctious days of the early lumbering frontier, but his claims were true only in a relative sense. Lumbering work remained the fiefdom of hardworking, hard-living men—even though, to Holbrook's dismay, some were now married and lived in town.[39] Revealingly, loggers and sawmill workers still referred to themselves as "timber beasts" and "sawdust savages."

Away from Mirror Pond, houses were modest at best. Bars, brothels, and occasional violence were ever-present. Still, compared with other lumber towns, Bend was respectable—in part because many of the loggers, rather than living in town, lived in Shevlin-Hixon's woods camp, which was moved from area to area by rail as cutting shifted from one locale to another; frequently the camp was miles from Bend itself. Many of Brooks-Scanlon's woods workers were nearly as transitory—and like those of Shevlin-Hixon, the places where they lived were hardly centers of propriety. Sisters was "just a little rugged town that you passed through," a place for workers to gather on a Saturday night.[40] And when Brooks-Scanlon extended its timber harvests to the Sisters area in the 1940s, the community's schools quickly became so unruly that Bill Edwards, a coach and later administrator at the tiny local high school, found other schools unwilling to schedule his teams. The spokesman for one explained, "Bill, we have to tell you the truth, we don't want your kids in our school. And furthermore, we don't want the parents." Edwards understood: "The parents got drunk at the games and had fights and the kids weren't much better." The situation was the same when the school held a dance to which parents as well as students were invited; it ended in a drunken brawl. Reveling in their reputation, students adopted the name "Outlaws" for their sports teams. Previously, the community's only significant social event had been the annual Sisters Rodeo; festivities surrounding it were also often decidedly raucous and unruly.[41]

If Bend and its logging camps presented something of a dual personality, Gilchrist and Kinzua were simpler propositions. Like Bend, they were new communities shaped by the lumber firms that brought them into being. Unlike Bend, both were company towns. But they were profoundly different, one from the other.

Kinzua came first. After hesitating for years, E. D. Wetmore and his partners decided to build a mill to saw the timber they had accumulated near the western terminus of the Blue Mountains, and a company town to house the workers. Camp Five (a logging camp now known as Wetmore) followed. Kinzua was a basic community: a company store, community hall (which, among other things, showed movies once a week and housed a bar, soda fountain, and tiny library), a gas station, a simple hotel for visitors (mostly lumber buyers), company offices, scattered houses of the most basic sort, an elementary school, and the mill—which was supplemented in due course by a "factory" that made moldings, doors, and the like. Prices in the store were outrageous, and those in Fossil, the little county seat some ten miles away, not much better; when the State of Oregon later posted a fire crew in Kinzua, the crew cook found it cheaper to send a pickup seventy-three miles to Prineville for supplies than to buy locally. When the union local went on strike in the late 1940s, the company settled quickly, but the next day prices in the company store went up accordingly.

Camp Five was smaller—and no better. The father of one of my professional colleagues had been a migrant farm worker in California. He got his first "permanent" job at Camp Five as an oiler for the log trucks and other company equipment. The son remembers his mother sweeping the floors in the company house in which they lived, a house so poorly constructed the sweepings simply fell through cracks in the floor and disappeared. Meanwhile, the father watched as neighbors cut firewood after work, and as the piles grew so did his concern; finally he asked one of them how many cords of wood it took to get through the winter. Told it generally took about twenty cords (no doubt an exaggeration) he promptly quit and returned to California.

In spite of such conditions, the workforce became relatively stable. Initially, many young, single men had been hired in Spokane and Pendleton to fill the crews; finding Kinzua's isolation unbearable, most soon quit. Their action was hardly surprising. As the *Bend Bulletin* had observed shortly before, "Lumberjacks are a notoriously restless class of men and no amounts of improvements in the camps . . . can make them entirely satisfied and they drift from one camp to another."[42] Responding, the company decided to recruit married men to replace those who had left and went to Kentucky and the Ozarks to recruit them, bringing them west in boxcars to take up their jobs. Impromptu performances of country music by the Samples family band, nearby barn dances, and hunting with coon hounds joined with soft Southern accents in setting the tone for the town. With a population of more than seven hundred, Kinzua was the largest community in Wheeler County. Education was hardly a priority. Few Kinzua residents graduated from Wheeler County High School, located in Fossil, and when one girl actually went to college, she became something of a celebrity—or, perhaps more accurately, oddity.[43]

Gilchrist, founded shortly after, stood in sharp contrast to Kinzua, although it had Southern roots of its own. Unlike Kinzua's absentee owners, the Gilchrists moved to the town they built and sought to make it a model community. Many employees had worked for the Gilchrist firm in Mississippi and brought west with them both a sense of community and a loyalty to the firm. The houses, designed by Portland architects, were well built and modern. The mill, homes, mall, and schools were planned and landscaped to be an attractive whole in which residents could take pride, and the company saw to it that occupants took care of the houses they rented and the lawns and yards that went with them. Gilchrist Timber Company's owners expected operations to be permanent and, toward that end, managed its forests on a sustained yield basis;[44] it could thus justify the expense of building the sort of community it did, a community that stood in sharp, self-conscious contrast to Bend and La Pine to the north and the little communities of Crescent and Chemult to the south. Bill Edwards recalls that Gilchrist High School was among those that refused to play his teams from Sisters.

Gilchrist's heavy-handed paternalism might have been resisted had workers brought a history of labor management hostility with them, but on the whole they did not. Still, it was never the tranquil Eden some would later choose to remember. During the waning days of the Great Depression, workers were simply glad to have a job, especially one in an attractive community that carried a promise of permanence, as had few towns in the Southern pineries.[45] But during the lumber boom that followed World War II, such considerations became less central. With increased opportunities elsewhere, the workforce became less permanent and discontent grew. In late 1945 a strike began that involved nearly all area sawmills. Gilchrist's officials were wont to blame the strike on "outsiders," but they (and John Driscoll, their champion) overlooked the fact that a majority of the company's workers voted to strike, and they stayed out long after other mills in the area had settled and reopened.[46]

In all these places, the workforce was almost exclusively white. The situation was different in Wallowa County, where the Bowman-Hicks Lumber Company hired black loggers, giving Wallowa and the nearby hamlet of Maxville a racial mixture rare elsewhere—and de facto segregation. Moreover, as one of their number recalled, "The company gave the Black workers the hardest most dangerous job[s]."[47]

A common denominator ran through all this. For all the differences from firm to firm and community to community, lumbering brought a rough reality to large sectors of Eastern Oregon. Rough work, rough men, and rough communities (Gilchrist to the contrary notwithstanding) helped shape an action-oriented, materialistic mind-set ill-prepared to cope with the urbanites and environmentalists who would later invade the area. Only the fact that most mills had closed and their workers left for employment elsewhere served to lessen the conflicts that resulted.

Yet it would be a mistake to view the industry's workers as interested only in exploiting the land and being oblivious to its noneconomic values. Fishing and hunting were favorite undertakings; Diamond Lake became a regular vacation site for Shevlin-Hixon employees. Many would have agreed with the northern Idaho logger who said, "Show me a logger who doesn't think . . . [the woods] are the most beautiful place on earth and I'll show you a man who isn't a logger." And when Bill Edwards started a conservation class in Sisters High School in the early 1950s, it enjoyed widespread support in the little logging community.[48] More than many later environmentalists realized, these were folk who provided a foundation of support for later efforts at the preservation and wise use of resources.

8

Ignoring Limits

Andrew Jackson Tetherow was twelve when his family made its way west over Meek Cutoff. One would think the experience would have seared into his brain an image of Eastern Oregon as something to be avoided. It certainly seems to have done so with his father, Sol Tetherow, who captained a major element of the train, took up a homestead in the Willamette Valley, and never returned east of the Cascades. But the son was cut from a different cloth, and in 1877, remembering the lush grasslands along Crooked River, joined the growing migration to the range country around Prineville. There his wife soon gave birth to a son, Jesse. Not just would-be settlers were moving over the Santiam Wagon Road, completed in 1868. Willamette Valley ranchers also drove their herds to the high country for summer grazing, and a heavy traffic in wool went westward to mills in Brownsville and Waterloo. Recognizing an opportunity, Tetherow moved his growing family to a homestead on the Deschutes, a short distance north and west of present-day Redmond and conveniently located near one of the two practical crossing points for the wagon road's traffic. They were the first permanent settlers in the area.[1]

In 1879, Tetherow opened a cable ferry across the river, a considerably larger stream in those days, prior to major upstream impoundments and diversions for irrigation. He operated it until 1885, when he replaced it with a heavily constructed wooden bridge (no longer used, but still present until washed away by the great Columbus Day storm of 1962).[2] Bit by bit Tetherow moved to take full advantage of the location, establishing an inn, brewery, store, and other facilities to meet travelers' needs—all while farming his homestead using water diverted from the Deschutes.[3]

By the early twentieth century, Tetherow Crossing was a major stop for immigrants from the Willamette Valley who joined the growing rush to the arid lands of Central Oregon, especially the High Desert area east of

Bend. They were part of a land boom resulting from the belief that this last frontier could yield good crops using dry-farming techniques perfected in the Umatilla and Palouse regions and elsewhere. For a time a series of wet years kept the illusion alive, and settlers' wagons continued to roll eastward—according to one report, some twenty-five wagons a day crossed Tetherow's bridge. But reality crept in, the traffic reversed, and the crossing became a stop for disheartened, financially destitute former homesteaders headed back to the Willamette Valley. As Jesse Tetherow put it, they had discovered life was no easier and the future considerably bleaker on the drylands east of the Cascades than in the Willamette Valley.[4]

The homesteading movement into Oregon's dry interior began shortly after the turn of the century. With other frontier areas filling up and the depression of the 1890s a thing of the past, the state's drylands lured as never before. As one western writer put it, land was "only the beginning. The real treasures lay no doubt in some vision of easy fields, greening up in spring, croplands flowing across the rolling plowground out back of the white-painted home place, and the gleeful crying of grandchildren at play on the lawns sloping to the mossy spring-creek—some particularly American version of promised land solace." At work too was what Bill Hanley called "the fundamental instinct to own land and be independent."[5]

The dream was less problematic in some areas than others. In better-watered locales ("better" here being a very relative term)—places like the Silver Lake Valley, Harney Basin, and the land stretching from Izee west past Post and Paulina—native grasslands made dryland farming seem feasible, but the best grasslands had been appropriated by ranchers long before the homestead rush began. Newcomers had to settle for marginal tracts and thus were little better off than those taking up claims in the heart of the High Desert. As Ivan Doig put it in connection with land in Montana his family homesteaded, it was "a land short on everything but their own capacities."[6]

After the turn of the century, immigration to Crook, Harney, and Malheur Counties became a flood spurred on by local boosters who hoped to profit from the growth; by the Hill and Harriman railroad interests, which from 1898 to 1906 used the *Pacific Monthly* to encourage settlement that would profit their lines; and by less-than-truthful blandishments from speculators and their agents. Brochures showing developed towns, fields of golden grain, and even date palms where in fact only sagebrush grew lured the unwary. Land locaters who, for a price, helped newcomers locate claims were more subtle, bringing potential settlers to the area during the few weeks of spring when grasslands had not yet been seared brown by summer heat and aridity and urging them to act quickly, before the choicest locations were all claimed.

Meanwhile, local newspapers added to the growing chorus. The *Burns Times-Herald* crowed that southeastern Oregon's desert land was "as fertile and productive when brought under the requisite conditions of moisture as any in the world." The *Bend Bulletin* went even further, publishing article after article boasting of the area's prospects. George Palmer Putnam submitted a number of similar articles to the Portland *Oregonian*. Meanwhile, the Bend Board of Trade launched a publicity campaign of its own. Coming from less arid areas, would-be homesteaders seem to have seldom asked from whence the requisite moisture would come.[7]

There were voices of caution. A contemporary history stated "agricultural possibilities of the desert are claimed to be great. . . . But little of it is good without water." The Department of Agriculture's Carl Scoville warned against exaggerated claims about the potential of dry-farming and noted that the potential in the Oregon portion of the Great Basin was "still unknown."[8] Such cautions were for naught; propaganda and maneuvering carried the day. By June of 1903, a full page of every issue of the recently established *Bend Bulletin* carried notices of desert and timber land claims. Catching the spirit of the times, the *Lakeview Examiner* described Lake County as "a small empire," which, in July of 1908, still had 2,361,608 unappropriated acres "and undeveloped resources superior to those of some entire eastern states." But the county was settling up quickly; between 1900 and 1912, northern Lake County's population rose from 229 to some 1,220. Crook County was similar; in the spring of 1911 settlers filed some three hundred land claims totaling roughly ninety-six thousand acres.[9]

Although a prolonged period of especially dry years commenced in 1911, the influx continued, peaking around 1914 when the *Bend Bulletin*, observing the quantities of goods would-be settlers brought with them, proclaimed "None are coming here broke." But the editor of the *Bulletin* had been caught up in the boosterism of the period. Representatives at annual meetings of the Dry-Farming Congress, a group dominated by agricultural specialists, viewed the immigrants more realistically. In 1911 one noted that "the average man taking up a homestead [in the drylands] has not sufficient means to develop it." He estimated not more than 10 percent were prepared to properly utilize their claims, for "as a rule, they are not practical farmers" and have "little knowledge of farming under any conditions." Another was blunt: "It is a tragedy to put an inexperienced man without means and with a family on a piece of dry ground and tell him to farm and live."[10] In spite of scattered warnings in the *Dry-Farming Bulletin* (revealingly subtitled *A Practical Book for Practical Men*) and the annual meetings of its publisher, the Dry-Farming Congress, the mere existence of these groups reinforced the notion the semiarid lands of the American West could be successfully cropped. Overlooking the caveats and nuances in such reports, would-be homesteaders seized on the idea of a promising agrarian future in the drylands.[11]

In spite of cautious evaluations by employees like Carl Scoville, the federal government lent support to visions of prosperity. "We have no useless acres," Secretary of Agriculture James Wilson declared in 1905: "We will make them all productive. We have agricultural explorers in every corner of the world finding crops so acclimated to dry conditions . . . that we will in time have plants thriving upon our so-called desert lands." Toward that end, his department established the Office of Dry Land Agriculture, which joined the developmental chorus. In 1909 Congress added its own imprimatur by passing the Enlarged Homestead Act; recognizing dryland farming required extensive acreage, lawmakers now allowed individual claims of 640 acres on non-irrigable, semiarid lands in various western states—including Oregon.[12]

Bill Hanley had spent years in Harney County and knew the fallacies involved in the dreams of incomers: in spite of what its proponents said, he declared dry-land farming "was doomed to failure. . . . The homesteaders already in the country were having it hard, with no chance to earn a living while holding down their claims, and still more were coming in, the light of hope in their eyes" and "faith in the power of the land to take care of them." Expanding on the subject, he later wrote, "The West needed settlers, but settlers out in the big plains was a mistake without . . . a means of support. A man can't take a plow and go out into the desert and make a living. It was all hardship . . . with no show to win."[13] Others agreed. Urling Coe, Bend's pioneer physician and sometime mayor, later recalled that "although the country was excellent stock range, it was entirely unfit for agriculture.

The oldest settlers had found it impossible to raise any kind of stock feed there because there was not sufficient moisture. The agriculture experts thought they knew more about it than stockmen and paid no heed to their warnings." Rancher Reub Long made a different point: "The worst thing about homesteading was that it was hard on the land. Millions of acres were plowed that should have been left . . . unshorn."[14]

Completion of the railroad to Bend in 1911 gave fresh impetus to settlement in the High Desert. The booming little town became the jumping-off place for thousands headed for the high lava plains between there and Burns and southeast to Fort Rock, Silver Lake, and beyond. Recognizing the need for water, Deschutes County drilled a well near Hampton (midway between Bend and Burns). It brought in water at 167 feet. The county was not alone. Homesteader Fred Stratton dug a 194-foot well and proceeded to sell water to neighbors for three cents a barrel. With water assured, even if in limited quantities, there was "renewed interest in getting these last untaken acres from the government."[15]

Similarly, when a rail line pushed up the Malheur to Crane in 1916, it added encouragement to homesteading in the Harney Basin and Catlow Valley. Governor James Withycombe, present at the dedication of the line, lauded it for opening a whole new realm for farming. It did, to an extent, but only briefly; the land rush was already coming to a close, and in Catlow Valley the decline would be especially precipitous. When Luther Cressman arrived there in 1932, the town of Blitzen, which served the area, was all but deserted, the government's land office, established there in 1917, had long since closed. Ere long the valley was devoid of population save for a few scattered ranchers. The same happened elsewhere. Jackman and Long list twenty-five ghost towns in the High Desert country—and their list is incomplete. The average ghost town had received a post office in 1912 and lost it by 1920.[16]

Just how many homesteaders journeyed to this last frontier is difficult to ascertain. Many who filed claims failed to take them up; others filed as a speculation rather than with any intention of establishing a farm. Some came and left so quickly they left little evidence of their passing.[17] Still, election returns provide a rough measure of the numbers involved. In the presidential election of 1904, 678 voters in Harney County cast ballots; by 1908 the figure had risen to 862 (a 24.1 percent increase since the previous presidential election); in 1912 the number had risen to 1,241 (a 44 percent increase); and by 1916 it numbered 2,329 (an 80.4 percent increase). The number of voters declined for each of the next three elections and did not again reach the level of 1916 until 1952. Isolation, indifference, and an overwhelming struggle for survival surely kept many from the polls, but the figures are indicative of the trends. Of course, some voters were those who serviced settlers from Burns and other centers, rather than actual homesteaders, but the numbers give a rough indication of the influx, for there was little other than homesteading to draw new residents during this period.

Lake County—which encompassed the Fort Rock, Silver Lake, and Christmas Valley areas, all homesteader favorites—showed similar trends. Five hundred and nine voters cast ballots in the presidential election of 1904; in 1908 the number rose to 769 (a 42.8 percent increase); by 1912 it stood at 1,065 (a 37.1 percent increase); and in 1916 it jumped to 1,897 (a 78.1 percent increase). The number voting in 1916 would not be exceeded until 1932. As in Harney County, there was little other than homesteading to draw settlers during the period. In other Eastern Oregon counties election figures are less useful, for major developments other than homesteading—irrigation schemes and railroad building, for example—were under way.[18]

In spite of the attention devoted to the High Desert country, homesteading was not limited to it. Madras, Dorothy McCall wrote, "consisted mostly of homesteaders and dust." Agency Plain to the town's north and the plateau stretching south from there past Culver and Metolius, areas northwest of Redmond, and a sizeable realm west of the confluence of the Deschutes and Crooked Rivers all drew settlers. Among them were the Ramseys, who arrived on Agency Plain from Missouri in 1900 to take up a homestead. Jim Jackson, a Wasco from the neighboring Warm Springs Reservation, crossed the Deschutes "to see what kind of people they were, these newcomers." He returned home to report "they seemed to be decent folks, but didn't know much of anything about the country and would probably need a lot of help." Over the years that followed, Jackson and his sons supplied just that, and the Ramsey family was able to hold on long after others had departed.[19]

The Ramseys were not alone in receiving help. In 1886 George Millican moved his ranching operation from near Prineville to a dry Pleistocene riverbed north of Pine Mountain, many miles east of Bend. From his ranch he watched as homesteaders poured past on their way to claim their share of the agrarian dream. Frequently asked what he thought of the area's transition from stock raising to an agricultural country, Millican replied that, owing to the scarcity of water and the high elevation, he thought it inadvisable. He had the only reliable source of water in the area, and as long as homesteaders remained in the vicinity Millican supplied them—but rains for their crops were another matter and ere long an exodus began. There were some sixty residents of the area in the early twentieth century, but by 1930 the number had dropped to one. As settlers departed, Millican was told time and again, "You are the only one here who told us the truth as to conditions. . . . We thought and were told by locaters that you and such men as the Logans and Bill Brown [just] wanted this country for your stock ranges." Millican's largesse with water may have lessened the suffering of his homesteading neighbors, but it did nothing to change the basic realities of the place, and he himself sold out in 1916 and left the area. The same happened elsewhere.[20]

Bill Hanley was another who, out of basic humanity, lent a helping hand to homesteaders. He was not alone, for the "settler had no one to turn to in his predicament but the stockman; and the stockman saved the day for him in hundreds of cases." Stockmen, Hanley noted, "helped him get feed for his horses, milk for his children, and . . . what work he has been able to get."[21] In Peter Simpson's words, Hanley and other "big cattlemen managed to graft onto their image in Harney County a certain benevolent paternalism. . . . [They] no longer operated among their smaller neighbors in the roughshod manner of earlier years." But Hanley was a speculator who seemingly saw settlement as a catalyst for increased value of his extensive landholdings. And he surely realized that, even if he lent a helping hand, the land would not support agrarian smallholders and would in time revert to ranchers.[22]

Homesteaders could hang on for a time by finding employment on neighboring ranches; collecting bounties on coyotes, mountain lions, and wolves; or, as was the case with Alice Day Pratt, who homesteaded near Post, by teaching in nearby schools. Pratt and others with dependable sources of water on their land—albeit never enough for significant irrigation—often were able to hold on longer than those without, but in the end nearly all left.[23]

Ten years after establishing her homestead, Pratt returned to New York (although she continued to hold title to her land for several more years). As she wrote, "I have known lean years and leaner years. . . . Ah, well! I . . . still cling to the dream." So did others. After 1908, a considerable if indeterminate number left the High Desert for the Bruneau River area in southwestern Idaho. New irrigation projects around Twin Falls made the area seem more attractive than Oregon's High Desert. But this too proved a will-o'-the-wisp. The reservoir behind Salmon Falls Dam leaked badly, water disappearing into the crevices in the underlying lava almost as fast as it poured in from upstream. The dam was completed in 1910, but the reservoir was not full until 1954, and by that time the area's homesteaders—including an uncle of mine—were long gone.[24]

Attempts at farming the drylands broke many a would-be settler, but they left a considerable literature in their wake—novels, poetry, scholarly studies, and a body of reminiscences and memoirs. It was a history both dramatic enough and tragic enough to excite attention, sympathy, and interpreters from well beyond the circle of people who experienced the trials of homesteading. C. E. S. Wood saw the desert as something to be defeated or, failing that, seduced; Ada Hastings Hedges viewed it as a symbol of an awesome, terrifying, indifferent cosmos and settlers as powerless to change their fates within it.[25] But perhaps the works that best caught the spirit of homesteading came from two novelists who had seen the developments firsthand: H. L. Davis and Anne Shannon Monroe. Their works were strikingly different—both in literary quality and viewpoint—but together they illustrate the range of motives, attitudes, and experiences involved in the homesteading era.

Monroe's work was a conventional, sentimental tale of limited literary merit; its characters were one-dimensional, its plot predictable. One reviewer damned *Happy Valley* with faint praise; it was, he wrote, "certain to please those readers who seek entertainment, rather than literature, in their lighter reading." Yet in spite of its shortcomings, *Happy Valley* had merits. Monroe knew the area about which she wrote (there actually is a Happy Valley district south of Burns—which she calls Twin Forks), her characters were drawn from people she knew (Bill Hanley is "Uncle John Regan" and Rye Smyth's wife is "Aunt Nell," both key figures in the story), and their experiences were informed by her own as a homesteader in the area.[26] Above all else, Monroe depicts the attitudes and values of homesteaders: dreamers drawn by an idealized image of life on the land; people seeking to escape the pressures of the city; flawed folk wanting a chance to start over and leave past problems behind; and immigrants hoping through hard work to provide a better future for their children than the Old World offered. These included people like Monroe and Alice Day Pratt—well-educated, strong-willed urbanites caught up in Jefferson's agrarian dream, people who moved to this last frontier against all logic. Such folk, even when they succeeded, never left their pasts completely behind. Monroe's protagonist, Billy Brent, brought to his new home his books, a phonograph, and his college pennants. Unlike foreign immigrants, such people were ill-prepared for the labor and deprivation of homestead life, and when Brent finally managed to get his demons behind him, he proclaimed that he "worked like a foreigner."[27]

H. L. Davis's *Honey in the Horn* was altogether different—it was awarded the Harper Prize for literature in 1935 and the Pulitzer Prize the following year, a reception completely different from that of *Happy Valley*. Yet in Davis's understanding of the frontier experience, albeit a distinctly different segment thereof, it was much the same. Davis spent his early years in the foothills of the southern Cascades among country people of little education and deep Southern roots—the sort of people Elisha Applegate described in 1866 as "butternuts . . . who rush in from the hills in long lines" to vote for the Copperheads; they were, Applegate said, waxing to his subject, "the fag end of [Confederate General Sterling] Price's long-haired, dirty faced, coarse featured, hang-dog looking tatterdemalion host."[28] Unlike Applegate, Davis had an understanding of and sympathy for these people, an understanding of what it was that led many to join the homestead rush to Oregon's interior. After Davis's family moved east of the Cascades when he was almost twelve—first to Antelope and then to The Dalles—his understanding of the harsh land and its homesteaders deepened, enabling him to craft "a story about a people whose restlessness seems endless, their defeats sure, and their successes few and fleeting." It is a story not so much about the place and what these people did there as it is about what led them to do it—in Merrill Lewis's words "what inner urges *moved* them."[29]

These were not the people who populated the pages of *Happy Valley*. Nor were they were the sort of people who left accounts of their experiences. G. P. Putnam recognized the type. A good share of the settlers, he wrote, "are discontented wherever Fortune places them. . . . In the final analysis some of our western gypsies desire nothing more ardently than a rest." It remained for Davis to give them voice, a challenging task since they themselves were but dimly aware of what drove them. Not until William Kittredge, two generations and more later, did another writer emerge who could so genuinely give voice to such people as populated *Honey in the Horn*. They were, Kittredge wrote, people who came "landless and transient and willing to live in isolation, driven by an urgency to accumulate properties—livestock before land, but always, in the long run, land. . . . It was history driven in part by a dream of some good society, even though many of the men weren't fit for society." Among these people, Kittredge counted his own father and grandfather.[30]

Those few who succeeded in hanging on could take pride in having persevered in the face of overwhelming odds, but they had little else to show for their efforts. Many, too poor to move, were simply out of options. For the most part, the legacy of the homestead era was a scattering of abandoned shacks, tracts of degraded land that had reverted to cheat grass and sagebrush, and an outpouring of onetime residents who found employment in the sawmills of Bend, Burns, and Lakeview or migrated to employment in Portland or California when World War II offered jobs there in defense industries.

In Central Oregon, the vast area that had been broken to the plow in an attempt at dryland farming had largely emptied by the 1930s—only fifty of the area's seven hundred remaining claims were occupied. The government began buying up these submarginal, drought-stricken tracts and, in 1954, began replanting them to grass. In 1960 some 112,000 acres were incorporated into the Crooked River National Grassland. Managed through the Ochoco National Forest, it stands as a monument to just how misguided efforts to homestead the area—and other areas like it—had been.[31]

But time plays strange tricks. Loie Horning recalls that after they left many were lonesome for the Fort Rock area: "I shut my eyes sometimes now and go over the scenes and things we used to do." Indeed, each September people descend on Fort Rock from all over the West. As Helen Parks explains,

> They treasure a memory of this place with its glorious sense
> of equality. No one then had possessions to speak of, and what
> little they had they shared with their neighbors. . . . Following
> generations speak of this land as their spiritual home. Nostalgia

returns them to a place where the air is clean, where the stars at night seem closer and extend to the horizon. They are drawn to a place of compelling mystique.[32]

Anne Shannon Monroe might have understood such a reaction; it is doubtful H. L. Davis ever could have.

9
Water on the Land

In May of 1909, George Palmer Putnam, grandson of the founder of New York's publishing house of G. P. Putnam's Sons, arrived in Bend. His trip had been arduous. He had taken the OR&N from Portland to Biggs, the Columbia Southern from there to Shaniko, and a horse-drawn stage to Prineville and then on to Bend. The stagecoach portion took twenty-two hours; Putnam described it as "528,000 feet of dust, mud, chuck holes, hills, rocks, ruts and bumps."[1]

Bend was small and raw, but booming—and Central Oregon was, in Putnam's words, "a region where fragrant optimism is religion." For his part, the twenty-one-year-old was looking for adventure. He had gone "a pioneering for the fun of it"—what he once called "rainbow chasing"—and selected Bend as his destination because its vast hinterland was the farthest from a railroad of any area in the United States. Putnam's love for adventure was nothing new; the first book he read for himself was Theodore Winthrop's *Canoe and Saddle*, an account of frontier wanderings from Puget Sound to The Dalles. Nor was it a passing fancy: after leaving Central Oregon, he would be involved in one adventure after another—including marriage to fellow free spirit Amelia Earhart. The town and the new arrival were made for each other.[2]

The hectic activity in Bend was the product of several factors. The scramble for timberland in the first years of the century started it, the rush of homesteaders to the High Desert spurred it on, and repeated rumors that a railroad was coming—up the Deschutes Canyon, from Shaniko, or over the Cascades—added further impetus. At least as important was the growing effort to irrigate the arid West, a movement that grew out of the work of John Wesley Powell, William E. Smythe, and others and was spurred on by the Interstate Irrigation Congress meeting in Salt Lake City in 1891. It gained force in Central Oregon because of abundant water in the

Deschutes (its low water flow exceeded that of the Westside's Willamette) and flat, fertile lands to Bend's north and east, lands largely in the public domain. Putnam soon found himself deeply involved in the community's conflicts, especially those involving irrigation, struggles he dramatized in his novel, *The Smiting of the Rock*.[3]

Irrigation in Central Oregon had begun in 1871 when Charles J. Hindman diverted water from Squaw Creek to irrigate forty-five acres. Others made small diversions soon after. In 1891 the Squaw Creek Irrigation Company incorporated and began supplying water to the Cloverdale and Lower Bridge areas.[4] But major irrigation projects did not put in an appearance until after passage of the Carey Act in 1894—and it was these projects and the controversies surrounding them that engaged Putnam after his arrival in Bend.

Competing companies jostled over water rights and key canal locations, but the main battles were between settlers on projects and the companies that contracted to furnish them with water. Company canals proved inadequate for carrying all the water promised, so they turned to selling water rights for additional land to raise money to expand capacity. But sales in these new "segregations" created larger demands. In short, the companies wanted to raise funds to meet previous commitments by taking on new ones—and there was no certainty as to how, when, or even if these new commitments could be met. Settlers protested to the companies and the state, but managers and the investors to whom they were obligated—often capitalists from outside the region—were uncompromising. Central in these struggles were Alexander Drake's Pilot Butte Development Company and its successor, the Deschutes Irrigation and Power Company (which in time morphed into the Central Oregon Irrigation Company)—or, as Putnam called it in *Smiting of the Rock*, the Bonanza Irrigation Company. Its proposal to construct a canal northward to the area of Redmond while settlers on the firm's earlier segregation were not getting the water for which they had contracted was especially contentious.[5]

There was little doubt with whom Putnam would side in the conflict. A progressive Republican, Putnam supported Theodore Roosevelt's campaigns against business abuses and attacked the Portland *Oregonian* for its support of "that species of political doctrine and activity which holds citizenship and manhood and womanhood as merely incidental to cent-per-cent gain." When Woodrow Wilson won the Democratic nomination in 1912, Putnam applauded, noting, "Wilson entirely lacks any politically damning affiliation with 'big business.'" In local affairs Putnam attacked those who would use political office to advance their own fortunes and those of their business allies.[6]

Through editorials in the *Bulletin*, meetings of the settlers' association, contacts with officials in Salem, and *The Smiting of the Rock*, Putnam weighed in on the side of the settlers. Struggles continued long after he left Bend in 1916 to become secretary to Governor James Withycombe, but the young editor had done yeoman work to ensure that eventually justice would be done. He kept the issues in front of local and state officials and gave voice to the economically oppressed. In his inaugural address in 1915—and in his subsequent appointment of Putnam as his secretary—Withycombe revealed awareness of the issues the young editor helped bring to the forefront. He called for an irrigation policy "with strict safeguards of the man on the land—until recently considered too little." He wanted "an irrigation situation reasonably satisfactory" to both the settler and the investor. In this, the governor had been preceded by his predecessor, Oswald West, who had gone so far as to have the state take over one project that had an especially egregious track record.[7]

Thus Putnam helped ensure that eventually much of Central Oregon would be home to a prosperous irrigated, agrarian economy. By 1922, the Federal Power Commission estimated some thirty-five thousand acres of Central Oregon had been irrigated—and in time water would reach far more.[8] Putnam's contribution to this is a legacy worth remembering.

The Carey Act, passed by Congress in 1894, was behind much of the difficulty plaguing irrigation development in Central Oregon. Congress had recognized that the Desert Land Act of 1877, which called on individuals to irrigate the 640-acre homesteads they claimed under the law, was a dismal failure. Yet Congress was not ready to launch a program of federal projects. Instead, through the Carey Act, it offered each of ten arid states and territories up to one million acres of public domain if they were able to settle and irrigate it within ten years. Settlers could make good on claims of 160 acres segregated from the public domain for this purpose by irrigating at least twenty of them.

Idaho and Wyoming brought major Carey Act projects on line, but success was limited in Oregon. In 1901 Oregon agreed to participate in the program on the condition private developers front the capital to build, maintain, and operate proposed diversion, storage, and distribution systems and bring enough settlers onto the land to make their projects viable. Developers could retain any profit from selling public land with irrigation rights, and settlers assumed a lien to secure payment for the cost of construction and operation. The state created the State Land Board (renamed the Desert Land Board in 1909) to oversee the program, but provided no direct control over construction or water delivery. A boom soon followed. In 1905 compilers of a regional history applauded: "Something like a stampede was made along the Des Chutes.... The rush of homeseekers had begun. About 12,000 applications for the [project] lands was made within a week by actual settlers." The figures were inflated, but reflect the mood of the moment.[9]

The state's vague rules and lax administration led to a nest of problems. The troubled history of the Tumalo project is illustrative.[10] Sixteen miles from its source near Broken Top Mountain, Tumalo Creek, a Deschutes tributary west of Bend, reached the arid Tumalo area. Though its sandy loam soil was well suited for agriculture, the area received only ten to fourteen inches of precipitation a year—and that largely outside the growing season—so the only way to make it agriculturally productive was through irrigation. Since 1883, settlers had been diverting water from the creek using short, private ditches to get water to their farms. In 1893 entrepreneurs from Prineville formed the Three Sisters Irrigation Company and announced a plan to irrigate a sizable area by drawing on Tumalo Creek. By 1902, the project's proposed size had doubled and new investors had entered the picture, including principals in the Columbia Southern Railroad who gained majority control and changed the company's name to the Columbia Southern Irrigation Company.

Between 1902 and 1905, the Harriman interests (which controlled the Columbia Southern) joined others in promoting the project as offering "profitable 80-acre homesteads." Settlers flocked to the area, and the town of Laidlaw, which served it, grew apace.[11] But this was land speculation as much as an irrigation project. The company brought in over $400,000 from land sales, but put only a fraction into its irrigation system. The firm's canals remained grossly inadequate for irrigating project lands—and so were its water sources.[12] By 1899 all of Tumalo Creek's flow had been claimed; no relief could be expected from that quarter. In 1905 settlers discovered that the first thousand acres of irrigated land had taken all the available water, yet some seventeen thousand additional acres had been sold. As they waited in vain for water, protests mounted, and efforts to convince the state to take responsibility for the project began. Two years later someone hanged in effigy William A. Laidlaw, the principal organizer of the project, and not long after that residents changed the name of their community from Laidlaw to Tumalo.

With the company foundering, Governor Oswald West pushed to have Oregon take over. Putnam was no fan of West or of government control of development. However, in the Tumalo situation, although he attempted to appear neutral—even chairing a meeting with West, company representatives, and settlers—Putnam clearly approved of state intervention.[13]

In 1913 the state legislature responded to the pressure, passing the Columbia Southern Act, which provided a mechanism for landowners who shared a water delivery system to form an irrigation district that would assess their farms for the cost of capital improvements, operation, and maintenance. Sixty-one landowners promptly formed the Tumalo Irrigation District. But the district soon repeated the errors of its predecessors. To increase water supplies, it bought storage rights at Crescent Lake, near the headwaters of the Deschutes, built an impoundment dam at the lake's outlet, and erected a diversion dam at Bend to feed the fresh complement of water into the district's canal system.[14] To raise funds for these improvements, it sold irrigation rights for additional acres. Thus, the district created anew a system with insufficient water to meet contractual obligations.

Meanwhile, the search for ways to supply water to the area continued. The high winter and spring runoffs that fed Tumalo Creek seemed to provide an answer. Irrigation engineer Olaf Laurgaard reported that "all the conditions and investigations show that [a proposed] Tumalo reservoir should make an entirely satisfactory" place to corral the runoff; responding, the Oregon legislature appropriated $450,000 to build a large dam to store high-water flows, to construct new canals and flumes, and to improve old ones. When the dam was completed on time and within budget, the Tumalo project seemed on its way at long last. Storage in the new reservoir began to climb with the winter-spring snowmelt of 1914. Settlers watched eagerly as water behind the dam rose toward its planned depth of fifty-nine feet, but when it reached twenty-five feet disaster struck. A series of breaks and sinkholes suddenly developed in the reservoir floor, one measuring some thirty by fifty feet. Children stopped on their way to school, fascinated by the sight and sound of the mad vortex of swirling water disappearing into the earth. One eight-year-old threw a board into the water and watched as it whipped around and around, stood on end, and was swallowed from sight. With it, the hopes of Tumalo irrigators disappeared too.[15]

Today Tumalo Dam stands abandoned, a stark reminder of hopes gone awry. Only a small impoundment at the south end of the planned reservoir remains, irrigating a fraction of what was originally projected. But Tumalo was not alone in facing inadequate water supplies. Carey Act projects in Harney and Lake Counties suffered the same fate. They never came to fruition, and in time land claims under them were abandoned or nullified.[16]

As one Carey project after another failed—for reasons both general and specific— Governor Walter Pierce felt compelled in the 1920s to have the state take over and complete other floundering projects, just as it had Tumalo's. On occasion it did so. Oswald West claimed that a project in Jordan Valley, completed in this way, resulted in the cheapest irrigated land in the West at a mere $34 per acre.[17]

A shortage of water was not the only problem developers faced. Canal building proved more costly than engineers expected. The area's geologic past lay behind the problem. Newberry Crater, some thirty miles south of Bend, had erupted time and again over the millennia—most recently only 1,400 years before. The eruptions, and those of associated cones, vents, and fissures, created a hidden tortuous landscape that extended from Newberry Crater north past Redmond to Crooked River; it was a landscape far more challenging than its generally level topography led engineers to expect.[18] It was not just at Tumalo Dam that this fractured landscape swallowed water. On the Pilot Butte Canal, the hard lava led engineers to reduce expenses by making the unlined canal wide and shallow. In the process, they created a waterway that lost far more through leakage than a narrower, deeper canal would have. Losses were immense, leaving the canal capable of irrigating only 13,160 of the 21,000 acres it was intended to supply.[19] To make matters worse, in the late Pleistocene rivers had cut across the land and left canyons behind—most notably Dry River, which ran from the Millican area past Alfalfa and Powell Butte to Crooked River. Irrigators had to build a 720-foot-long flume to span its gorge.[20]

Hostile climatic conditions doomed other projects. Developers of the Warner Basin project near La Pine and Crescent sought to bring agriculture

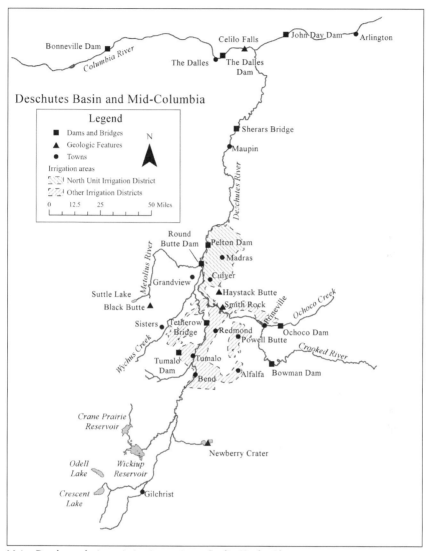

Major Deschutes drainage irrigation projects. Credit: Kindra Blair.

to one of Oregon's coldest areas, a place with *no* frost-free months. Not surprisingly, their project failed.[21]

Other projects were simply underfunded. Developers planned a seventy-five-foot-high dam on Lake Creek, near where it exited Suttle Lake. Henry J. Kaiser won the contract, but was unable to find the capital needed to commence work. Settlers waited in vain for water. Today nothing remains of their community of Grandview except the cemetery, a few stone walls (products of settlers' land-clearing efforts), and rapidly disappearing remains of old buildings.[22] A shortage of funds plagued other projects as well. Once in operation, some irrigation companies were in such desperate financial straits they increased fees charged to irrigators—sometimes to the point farmers could not earn a profit from their land.[23]

In spite of problems and failures, Carey Act projects remade much of Central Oregon. Redmond was a product of the Pilot Butte Canal, and Powell Butte and Alfalfa of the Central Oregon Canal. Together with lesser systems, these projects created a vibrant agricultural economy where previously there had been little but sagebrush and limited grazing. I recall as a young boy sitting on the porch listening to William Buckley reminisce about the pre-irrigation days, when he hauled wagonload after wagonload of market hunters' deer hides, taken in the area between Bend and the future town of Redmond, out to the railhead at Shaniko. Irrigation quickly brought an end to his enterprise.

As with other projects, settlers around Redmond had to wait for water. One of the first arrivals recalled, "When we came . . . there wasn't much here but tents." Indeed, Frank and Josephine Redmond—after whom the town would be named—lived in a tent on their homestead for some time after arriving in 1904. But in 1906 water came, a town was platted, and thereafter the community grew steadily, if not spectacularly. Jim Toney summed it up: "It was just sagebrush and nothing for a long time, and then it grew into a farming district." Jesse Tetherow described the changes differently: "We used to ride our bicycles from home [at Tetherow Crossing] to where Redmond is now and on into Powell Buttes to hunt deer." There were no canals or roads then, he added, he and his friends simply rode on wild horse trails.[24]

For a time, Redmond rivaled Bend as the leading community in western Crook County. Incorporated in 1910, it competed with Bend to become the seat of a new county locals hoped to create. But with the coming of the big Shevlin-Hixon and Brooks-Scanlon sawmills, Bend sprinted ahead—and became the county seat when Deschutes County was formed in 1916. Though considerably smaller than its rival, Redmond continued as the county's agricultural center, advertising itself as the hub of Central Oregon and, from 1906, celebrating an annual Potato Show—russet potatoes having emerged as the area's main crop. In time the Potato Show morphed into the Deschutes County Fair, a sop for losing out in the struggle to become county seat perhaps, but appropriate nonetheless.[25]

Redmond had nothing to match the residential district around Mirror Pond in Bend, but comfortable, if modest, homes emerged, especially along Buena Vista Boulevard (later renamed Canyon Drive). J. R. Roberts and M. A. Lynch arrived in 1910 to open a grocery, drug, and department store; they dominated local trade and even did a mail-order business. Roberts later recalled two days during which he hauled fifty crates a day of locally grown strawberries to Paulina, far distant on upper Crooked River (just why so many strawberries were needed in such a tiny community he did not say). About the same time, the *Redmond Spokesman* began publication, and the Bank of Commerce opened. When the Redmond Hotel burned, it was replaced in 1928 by the three-story New Redmond Hotel, a Georgian brick structure advertised as the finest hostelry east of the Cascades; it remains the largest building in town and is now on the National Register of Historic Places.

Over the years, a number of agriculturally oriented businesses sprang up: Fred Hodecker's potato-packing plant, E. O. ("Clover") Adams' seed-cleaning facility (which prospered until alfalfa replaced ladino clover in area fields), the Northwest Poultry Company's turkey processing plant, a creamery, a rendering plant, and Deschutes Grain & Feed, a large farm-supply enterprise. But perhaps the best evidence of Redmond's role as the agricultural hub of Central Oregon came in 1915, when the community joined nearby agricultural centers to create Redmond Union High School. Students from Tumalo, Cloverdale, Alfalfa, Powell Butte, Terrebonne, Lower Bridge, Opal City, and (for a time) Culver all bussed to Redmond— or resided in a boarding dormitory built in 1920. Alfalfa and Tumalo were considerably closer to Bend than to Redmond, and Cloverdale to Sisters, but joining agricultural Redmond seemed to make more sense, a conclusion reinforced in 1920 when Borden Beck joined the high school faculty as a Smith-Hughes vocational agriculture instructor, the first such east of Oregon's Cascades.[26]

In its early years Redmond had rough edges. Freighters, canal and railroad construction workers, and itinerant cowboys added a social element at odds with the area's more conservative farm families and business and professional leaders. Saloons were numerous, gambling and a small red-light district present. Local authorities turned a blind eye. But this was a passing phenomenon. Ere long Redmond became a tight-knit, conservative agrarian community under the public-spirited guidance of business and professional leaders. It developed a social tone sharply at odds with those of nearby Bend and Prineville.[27]

In Oregon, Carey Act project after Carey Act project had failed, but in the end what developed around Redmond proved the act had value. But it had limited applicability. It required vast areas of land still in the public domain to attract investors and settlers; in most irrigable locales these were no longer available, and another approach was needed. That came with the Newlands Act.

In 1902, Congressman Francis G. Newlands of Nevada introduced a bill to provide federal aid for irrigation. With backing from Frederick Newell of the Department of the Interior and the support of President Theodore Roosevelt, the bill became law. The act set aside money from the sale of arid and semi-arid public land to build and maintain irrigation projects in thirteen western states and territories. The newly irrigated land would then be sold and the proceeds deposited in a revolving fund to finance more projects. The secretary of the interior created the Reclamation Service within the Geological Survey and selected Newell to head it. Within a year, five projects had been approved, including, appropriately, one on the Truckee and Carson Rivers in Newlands' home state. The number of projects grew rapidly—by 1907, twenty-four had been approved—and to handle its growing responsibilities, the Reclamation Service was given independent status within the Department of the Interior and renamed the Bureau of Reclamation. Newlands Act projects avoided the limitations of private financing, reduced the pitfalls of speculation, and brought engineering expertise to bear to minimize chances of such ill-conceived projects as had sometimes developed under the Carey Act. The program had its critics, and their number increased as problems developed and environmentalism gained force, but for its first many years, the bureau was highly popular.[28]

Almost at once, the service-cum-bureau launched surveys of potential projects in Eastern Oregon and, under terms of the law, withdrew from homestead entry sites that were being investigated.[29] Among the potential projects were ones on the Silvies River and in the Silver Lake area. With homesteading on the High Desert in full swing, objections to the withdrawal of land for these projects erupted. Protesters were correct in claiming there was insufficient flow in the streams to make the projects feasible, and when authorities realized this, the land was reopened to homesteading—but this was hardly a solution, as has been shown: the land was also ill-suited for the needs of dryland homesteaders.[30]

Various projects were more promising. In 1916 the Ochoco project near Prineville incorporated earlier private efforts and built dams to bring water from Crooked River and Ochoco Creek to a sizeable acreage. Larger projects on the Umatilla River and in the Klamath Basin (which straddled the Oregon-California border) were also quickly approved, but a project on the Owyhee, although promising, had to wait years for implementation because accessing its potential dam site was quite difficult.

The Umatilla and Klamath projects provide a sharp contrast, one to the other. An analyst for the Bureau of Reclamation reported the former was a relatively small, straightforward irrigation project; it failed to attract national attention. The Klamath Basin undertaking, on the other hand, was huge, multifaceted, and fraught with controversy. Figures bear out the contrast. By 1919 the Umatilla project encompassed thirty-six thousand irrigable acres (not all actually irrigated) and supported 1,313 people on 507 farms; near the heart of the project, Hermiston had grown from "three or four buildings" to a population of 650. On the other hand, the Klamath project came to irrigate more than two hundred thousand acres divided among 1,480 farms; by 1918 Klamath Falls' population had grown to roughly five thousand and that of Merrill, which had incorporated only a few years earlier, had risen from two hundred to six hundred.[31]

Reports on projects reflected the view from management level; for those on the ground, things were never so simple. Locals reported investigations to determine the advisability and extent of the Umatilla project, and speculative land buying soon followed. Others homesteaded land they thought would soon be irrigated—but water was slow in coming. Among these opportunists was Samuel H. Boardman, who in 1904 filed a homestead claim near the far western end of the Umatilla project, where a town bearing his name would eventually appear. He had learned of the project and wished to be in a position to capitalize on it. Boardman later recalled, as "the years went by with no water the [other] settlers kept dropping out until there were only five of us left. . . . Thru thirteen sand-snuffing years Mrs. B and I fought that shifting desert." Finally, their savings used up, his wife left for a teaching job, while Boardman himself took work as an engineer—when he could find it.[32]

One can empathize. While teaching in Stanfield in 1911, Alice Day Pratt observed friends who had taken up claims on the Hermiston section of the project, their "weary and endless labors, the adaptations, the privations and hardships, the soaring hopes and the repressed despairs" that marked their struggles. Traveling west from Umatilla in the fall of that year, Pratt passed through the area where Boardman was homesteading and described it as dominated by "the Columbia and its sand dunes—the latter much more in evidence at that season than the river." Local boosters claimed the project "prospered beyond all expectations," but for those on the land, reality was often far harsher than such claims implied.[33]

Life was difficult on the Klamath project too. Early settlers were hard-pressed to make payments on their bills. The Klamath Water Users' Association formed in 1905; eager to have the project proceed, it entered into a contract with the Department of the Interior for water. Original estimates were that water could be supplied to KWUA farmers for twenty dollars a month, but in 1908 the Bureau of Reclamation announced the monthly charge would be thirty dollars. Members of the association denied liability and refused to pay the extra charge. There matters stood until Secretary of the Interior Richard A. Ballinger ordered construction on the Klamath project suspended. With no options left and their bluff called, the KWUA gave in. The financial struggles of others were even more intractable. Foreclosures plagued many early settlers; in 1916 a group of Russian homesteaders who had farms near the Lost River Dam, unable to make ends meet, sold out and departed. A descendant of other early settlers remembered,

> The sagebrush grew rank and high, sometimes five feet tall, causing
> hardships to both men and women, who had to grub it out by
> hand. Wind and dust blew through the hastily built cabins. Women
> worked side by side with the men in the fields, shocking grain,
> pitching hay, shoveling ditches. They made beds of meadow hay and
> furniture from used boxes. It was not uncommon for the settlers to
> work by lantern light far into the night. . . . Crops that didn't freeze or
> which weren't destroyed by winds were eaten by jackrabbits.[34]

And soon alkali buildup rendered unproductive many acres of farmland created when Lower Klamath Lake was drained. Clearly, life was difficult even on the best of projects, but in spite of this a successful mixed agriculture based on grain, potatoes, alfalfa, and cattle emerged, and Klamath County prospered.[35]

The size and complexity of the Klamath project added problems as well. There were preexisting irrigation companies in the Klamath Basin and even more claims to water rights. These had to be bought out or surrendered before the project could proceed—and the Klamath Canal Company was anything but cooperative, refusing to give up its water rights or halt diversions into its canals until richly compensated. Meanwhile, Secretary of the Interior Ethan A. Hitchcock had to gain legislative approval to ignore federal regulations pertaining to navigable waterways—which Upper and Lower Klamath Lakes clearly were—and the Oregon and California legislatures had to pass legislation of their own to allow water rights acquired under their authority to be transferred to federal hands.[36]

Bit by bit the project proceeded, with new sections still being added in the 1940s. As lands were opened to settlement, there was no shortage of applicants. In 1917 a public drawing for forty-two newly opened tracts drew 175 would-be farmers. In subsequent drawings, veterans of World War I and then World War II were given preference, and other eligibility requirements were added to assure that those acquiring land would have the wherewithal to farm it successfully. The result was a far more qualified cadre than had dominated on Carey Act projects to the north, to say nothing of those on the desert homesteads of the early twentieth century. Towns like Merrill, Malin, and Tulelake (four miles south of the state line in California) had elements of stability and respectability lacking in many other new towns. Malin, built on land previously submerged from time to time by Tule Lake, attracted a sizable body of Czech immigrants who added a special aura to the town but did nothing to undermine its respectable agrarian conservatism.[37]

Construction of two second-generation projects overlapped with that in the Klamath Basin. Work on the Vale project, utilizing water from the Malheur River and tributary creeks, began in 1927; the first units opened in 1930. Eventually the project came to serve nearly thirty-five thousand acres. The area was blessed with deep soils, a low elevation that contributed to a 159-day growing season, and adequate water supplies. Small private irrigation projects had certified the potential; in 1902 one regional history proclaimed, "All is ready for the wizard's touch" of water. Completed in 1919, the Warm Springs Dam on the upper Malheur gave a further boost to the area's

The long-delayed Owyhee Dam. Credit: Bureau of Reclamation.

potential (even as it cut off salmon runs that the Burns Paiutes utilized).[38] Under such circumstances, the Vale project enjoyed considerable success. When new sections of public land opened, the bureau graded applicants according to their estimated chances of success based on their finances and experience. Provisions in the construction contract kept land speculation (and thus prices) low, further enhancing settlers' chances. In the wake of all this, the old cattle and trading center of Vale changed and grew, but memories of its role as an important stop on the Oregon Trail remained—as did the town's oldest building, L. B. Rinehart's Stone House, which had served as a refuge for whites during the Bannock-Paiute War.[39] Like the Umatilla project, Vale attracted little attention beyond its immediate vicinity. The nearby, much larger Owyhee project was another matter altogether.

The bureau spent twenty-five years considering the Owyhee project before finally opting to go ahead. In the meantime, some small private efforts proceeded on their own.[40] As finally authorized, the Owyhee project was to irrigate 132,000 acres with water from a concrete arch dam well upstream on the Owyhee River. Although authorized in 1924, construction on the dam did not start until 1928, for access to the dam site had first to be greatly improved. When dedicated by Secretary of the Interior Ray Lyman Wilbur in 1932, the dam was the world's highest at 417 feet. Construction of the huge structure drew widespread attention, and President Herbert Hoover sent a dedicatory message. In addition to the dam, the project involved building ancillary facilities and miles of canals and laterals—the project's canal to the north ran over sixty miles to lands across the Snake from Weiser, Idaho—and, with help from the Civilian Conservation Corps (CCC), repairing and restoring the area's aging private irrigation facilities, which it had taken over.[41]

The impact on Malheur County—and parts of Idaho lying west of the Snake River around Marsing and Homedale—was immense. Between 1930 and 1950, Malheur's population doubled. By the 1940s, farm population on the project had burgeoned to 7,520 and the population in its towns to 21,250. Ontario sprinted past Vale to become the dominant community—reinforcing claims it should have been selected as county seat when Malheur was carved off from Baker County years before (an honor it had missed out on by twelve votes). Sugar beets, barley, alfalfa, onions, and potatoes all did well. The Eccles interests, now broadened well beyond lumbering, erected a sugar refinery at Nyssa. Onion- and potato-packing plants followed, helping turn a crossroads center into a significant community of more than three thousand.[42]

While the Owyhee project was inching ahead, the bureau launched a major undertaking in the Deschutes country. It was multifaceted, building on the Carey projects that had preceded it and adding ambitious new elements that private companies lacked the wherewithal to undertake. The first phase involved building huge reservoirs at Crane Prairie and Wickiup on the upper Deschutes to increase available water supplies.[43] First proposed in the early years of the twentieth century, the project garnered little support until the 1930s, when the "partnership of drought and poverty . . . finally brought engineers and irrigators together." Pushed ahead by a huge contingent of CCC workers during the 1930s, the reservoirs became mainstays of the area's irrigation systems by suppling supplemental water to forty-seven thousand acres in old Carey Act irrigation districts. Equally vital for the Deschutes project was completion of the huge, long-dreamed-of North Unit canal, which carried water sixty-five miles to fifty thousand acres of irrigable land north of Crooked River. World War II slowed work to a crawl; the canal, its giant flume over the river, and a mile-long tunnel through the hills back of Smith Rock were not completed until 1946. The flume and tunnel were the most challenging parts of the project. One observer predicted, "Every inch . . . will entail a fight." Time proved him correct.[44]

The first water reached Jefferson County's Culver area on May 18, 1946, to the accompaniment of extensive press coverage and a gala celebration centered in Madras, the county seat. My stepfather wryly noted, "Culver got the water, but Madras got the celebration," but bit by bit the project extended its reach, water eventually arriving well north of Madras. With the addition of a pumping plant at the Crooked River crossing, which allowed the tapping of supplemental water from that source, and a storage reservoir near Haystack Butte, which increased efficiency in supplying farms located many miles from the source of the water, the project was a clear success, helped along by the fact that the effects of the Newberry Crater complex—which laced Deschutes County with lava outcroppings that fragmented the landscape and left water-swallowing fissures—did not extend north of the Crooked River crossing. Lands opened by the North Unit were thus more adapted to the increased mechanization of agriculture that would subsequently develop. Some farmers in the Redmond area, including the father of a good friend, recognized greater opportunity to the north and sold their holdings to take up farms in the North Unit. Time proved them prescient. Farming has continued to prosper in the North Unit area, whereas in Deschutes County much of the land has devolved into hobby farms and sites for rural retirement.[45]

Changes in the method of bringing water to the land continued, as did changes in crops raised. Peas became important in Umatilla County (second only to wheat); pea canning and freezing plants followed; and by the 1950s the acrid smell of pea vines fermenting for silage hung heavy in the autumn air from Walla Walla to Milton-Freewater and beyond. Around Hermiston, where onions and potatoes long dominated—even as watermelons captured much of the attention—diversification (including such unexpected additions as quinoa and blueberries) added to the agrarian economy's stability. By 1972 the value of Morrow County's potato crop passed that of wheat: 140,000 acres devoted to wheat yielded a crop worth $6 million, whereas a mere 6,700 acres in potatoes generated $6.8 million.[46]

Eastern Oregon had seen its last great new irrigation project, but sprinkler irrigation grew in importance, especially because it was well adapted to fields that were not level. Moving sprinkler pipe replaced setting siphons for furrow irrigation as a standard form of summer employment for local youth until electrically powered wheel lines replaced pipes moved by hand. In time, center-pivot irrigation came to the fore—frequently drawing on groundwater rather than irrigation projects and in the process bringing water to isolated tracts in the High Desert. Agricultural economists from Oregon State University had insisted farming could never be made to pay in the area of Christmas Lake and the Fort Rock Valley, but Philip R. Pitman, E. R. Jackman, and others were more sanguine, and the Midstate Electric Cooperative, responding to their entreaties, extended service to the area in the 1950s. Rising demand for alfalfa and the co-op's inexpensive electricity disproved the specialists' dire forecasts.[47] The huge, green irrigated circles created by center-pivot operations soon became a familiar sight when flying over the area, just as in much of the rest of the arid West. The increased mechanization this shift represented was not limited to irrigation, and the result was that, while production per acre remained fairly stable, production per man-hour of labor increased sharply.[48]

Meanwhile, F. Nephi and Golden Griggs took over a bankrupt flash-freezing plant in Ontario in 1952, founded Ore-Ida foods, and developed Tater Tots, which revolutionized fast food and school cafeteria menus. They were joined by the J. R. Simplot Company, which was vaulting to leadership in potato production—supplying, among others, the McDonald's fast food chain with frozen french fries. Using the new irrigation techniques and Owyhee project water, both Ore-Ida and Simplot brought into production rolling uplands in Malheur County to complement their sources in Idaho.[49]

Viewed from the vantage point of the twenty-first century, it seems amazing all this remaking of Eastern Oregon—the transforming of natural into man-made landscapes, the capturing of wild streams and transporting their waters to distant fields—went on with but a handful of largely ignored protests. To be sure, there were complaints about the cost of projects, land speculation by irrigation companies and others, the rates charged for water, leaky flumes and canals, and the inefficiency of CCC workers, but the basic idea of changing the landscape through engineering was almost never challenged. Faith in the technological expertise of engineers ran strong during the Progressive Era and, if anything, grew stronger during the New Deal. The hubris of technocrats had not yet become an issue.[50]

Faith was also strong that irrigation would bring a new order—family farms, widespread landownership, and general prosperity—which did not always prove to be the case. Over time, as irrigated farms in Malheur County became larger and larger, they required much low-paid hired labor. By the early twenty-first century, the county was 32.8 percent Hispanic, almost four times the statewide average (in most Eastern Oregon counties, the percentage was less than 10 percent). The vast majority of Malheur County's Hispanics were poorly educated farm workers. Overall the county had an educational attainment rate well below that of both the state and nation as a whole; between 2009 and 2013, almost 28 percent of the population lived below the national poverty line. Morrow County was even worse, and Umatilla and Jefferson Counties were not far behind. All had a large base of irrigated agriculture and non-landowning farm labor. Everywhere the ideal of small family farms—which was at the heart of Progressive–New Deal irrigation efforts—and the 160-acre limit designed to ensure it were largely ignored, and the efforts of Secretary of the Interior Cecil Andrus to reinstate limits and residency requirements in the 1970s failed to reverse the shift to larger farms, often with corporate ownership employing low-paid farm labor.[51]

A primary reason for the largely unchallenged dominance of the technological reordering of the landscape was not merely exaggerated hopes for what would follow, but also the fact that the lands being altered did little to spur the imagination of nature lovers or tourists. Changing the sere, unspectacular, largely scrub-covered lands into green fields was viewed as progress. In time the sage plains of the High Desert and the spectacular canyon of the Owyhee would come to be appreciated, but that appreciation was slow in developing. Grasslands, such as those plowed under by farmers on the North Unit, were even slower in coming to be valued. The 112,000-acre Crooked River National Grassland, created in 1960 in land neighboring the North Unit, as well as the larger national grasslands movement of which it was a part, grew out of agriculture's difficulties during the 1930s rather than from any special appreciation of the lands it encompassed. Indeed, when protests finally emerged, they came not so much from defenders of grasslands per se as from those concerned with protecting wildlife. From an early date, a few, such as William Finley, fought the irrigators, but by and large protests were a product of a later day.[52]

10
Connections

On the surface, Bill Hanley and T. Egenton Hogg were little alike. Hanley was a self-made cattle king and longtime resident of the Harney Basin who was never so comfortable as when relaxing at his OO Ranch. He longed to see Harney County's isolation ended so development might proceed and cattle be more easily marketed.[1] Hogg, a onetime Confederate raider turned railroad promoter, moved to Corvallis in 1871, appropriated the title "Colonel," and began dreaming of building a railroad from Yaquina Bay across the Coast and Cascade Ranges to Prineville and then on to connect up with the Union Pacific system at Ontario. The goals of the two men were quite different, but a railroad to Central Oregon and beyond was a key element in the thinking of both.

In 1872, Hogg incorporated the Corvallis and Yaquina Bay Railroad, but his dream of a line eastward from Corvallis went nowhere until he teamed up with local banker Wallis Nash and reincorporated the railroad in 1880 as the Oregon Pacific. In addition to an extension to Ontario, they now envisioned a branch running northeast from Prineville to Umatilla and, farther along, a branch to Winnemucca. Reaching the Union Pacific system at these three points would give the Oregon Pacific both regional and transcontinental connections. A steamer line from Yaquina Bay to San Francisco would complement their railroad. The plan was audacious. It would bypass Portland and the dangerous Columbia River Bar and, Hogg prophesized, make Yaquina Bay Oregon's leading port.

The Oregon Pacific pushed east from Corvallis up the North Santiam to Idanha, fifteen miles short of the Cascade summit. Progress was slow, for Hogg and Nash had limited funds. The loss of two of Hogg's steamers on the bar of Yaquina Bay pushed him to the wall. In a desperate attempt to hold on to the railroad's right-of-way while he sought additional funding, Hogg built a short stretch of track at the summit of the Cascades (at a site known today as Hogg Rock). He used mules to pull a single boxcar back and forth over the track, thus allowing him to claim he had an operating railroad in place "over the Cascades" by the construction deadline. In a similar ploy, he built twelve miles of railroad along the Malheur River to maintain control of a critical section of right-of-way. But his efforts were in vain. Before the end of the century the company had to file for bankruptcy; further construction halted. Rail service over the portions west of the Cascades continued, but Hogg's hope for a line with transcontinental connections, dominating the trade of the coast and southern Willamette Valley at Portland's expense, died aborning.[2]

Passage through Eastern Oregon was essential for fulfillment of Hogg's plans, but development of the region was hardly central to his thinking. Not so with Hanley, who had grown disheartened as he watched railroad engineers come in "every few years making surveys . . . [and] settlers drifting in with their little herds. . . . Those that stayed always dreaming of when a railroad would come through . . . raised their children on that hope—their grandchildren." As the depression of the 1890s lifted, "surveyors were running their lines in almost every direction," but no construction followed. Tired of waiting, Hanley turned his considerable powers of persuasion and network of friendships to work to bring a railroad to southeastern Oregon whether the tycoons of the industry willed it or not.[3]

The only practical route into Harney Basin from the east was up the Malheur River, and E. H. Harriman, who controlled the Northern Pacific, Great Northern, and assorted subsidiaries, had tied up that route with surveys and claims. Hanley failed to persuade Harriman to build up the river, for his capital was tied up in upgrading lines he already had. "Harriman is only building into new territory when forced to by competition," one railroad official explained. That certainly seems to have been the case, for when a local group incorporated the California Northeastern Railroad and set about to build from Weed (south of the state line on the SP route from Portland to California) to Klamath Falls, Harriman moved swiftly to gain control. When the railroad reached Klamath in 1909—and extended northward to Kirk three years later—it was as a part of his Southern Pacific.[4]

As time passed Harriman's options along the Malheur began to run out, providing Hanley with an opening. He filed on key locations along the river and, with the help of C. E. S. Wood and other friends, pushed for state aid for construction of the line. Their plan received a great deal of publicity, and, his hand forced, Harriman finally began construction up the Malheur. He reached Vale in 1906 and pushed on bit by bit. Recognizing the Harriman interests were at last serious about completing a line to the Harney Basin, Hanley and his associates gave up their claims to right-of-way along the Malheur so Harriman could proceed unhindered. The railroad reached Crane in 1916—but by then, events had taken a dramatic turn in another direction.[5]

Harriman's lines from Huntington to Portland and down the Willamette Valley long blocked off Eastern Oregon from competitors, but early in the twentieth century James J. Hill set about to break through the "Harriman fence." Efforts in behalf of a state aid railroad may have helped stir Hill to action; in any case, he reportedly told Hanley, "You are right. You can't get the use of your country without transportation. But you don't have to get it that way [that is, through a state-aid railroad]. I will build your road for you." A bit of payback was involved. Some years before, Harriman had pushed into Seattle, which Hill considered his territory. "Now," he told Hanley, "I'm coming to Oregon with you and [will] play him a return game."[6]

In 1905 the Hill interests began construction of the Spokane, Portland and Seattle Railway. Running from Spokane to Portland along the north bank of the Columbia and connecting north to Seattle, it was designed to tie the three leading northwestern cities together and give Hill's Great Northern and Northern Pacific access to the heart of Harriman's territory. In 1908, with the SP&S completed to Portland, Hill was ready for further invasion of Harriman's domains. He purchased the Oregon Trunk, a railroad up the Deschutes that existed only on paper. Acting in secret, he acquired right-of-way up the deep, tortuous, basalt-bound gorge of the river. Sensing what was afoot, Harriman countered with surveys and right-of-way claims of his own. Soon there were two lines building upstream, Hill's Oregon Trunk on the west bank and Harriman's DesChutes Railroad on the east. Under other circumstances, Harriman might have preferred to extend his Columbia Southern from Shaniko, but by building up the Deschutes he had a chance to block Hill's intrusion. The canyon was too narrow at spots to accommodate two railroads, thus control of key sections was vital for both parties.

The contest between Hill and Harriman echoed what had transpired during the 1880s when the Oregon Short Line, a Union Pacific subsidiary, commenced building west from Granger, Wyoming, with the intention of providing its parent company with connections to Portland. At the same time, the Oregon Rail & Navigation Company was building southeast from Pendleton to make the same connection. The two clashed in the Burnt River canyon south of Baker. There was room for one line up the canyon, not two. Eventually the firms agreed that the OSL would build as far as Huntington, the OR&N from there north, and that they would share use of the trackage.[7]

No such accommodation was possible on the Deschutes, for giant egos were involved and competition between them was anything but friendly. Construction crews sabotaged one another's operations, dislodged boulders from the cliffs onto rivals working below, exchanged gunfire across the river, and engaged in donnybrooks when they met. Conflict grew when Hill's crews reached an area where there was too little room on the west bank for a railroad and crossed to the east side. Predictably, building side by side exacerbated friction.[8]

But the key battles took place in the courts, not on the banks of the river. Harriman's primary contractor, Twohy Brothers, established their headquarters and commissary at Grass Valley and constructed a ten-mile-long road from there to the river. Porter Brothers, operating on Hill's behalf, responded by purchasing a ranch across which the road ran and that controlled one of the few access routes to the river. They promptly posted "No Trespassing" signs and armed guards, preventing Harriman's contractors from getting supplies to their crews on the river below. Twohy Brothers went to court and got an injunction against Porter Brothers for blocking the road; their operatives then proceeded to the posted gate together with Sherman County sheriff Jay G. Freeman to force access to the river. Guards at the gate refused to comply with the sheriff's orders, but when he returned the next day with several deputies, they backed down. Not satisfied, Freeman proceeded to arrest several of the Porter Brothers' workers and carted them off to jail, charging them with inciting a riot by refusing Twohy's wagons permission to proceed to the river. Twenty-five miles upstream, the scenario was repeated. At a roadblock Porter Brothers had established, they stopped and unhitched Twohy Brothers' wagons and beat their drivers. Sheriff Freeman soon arrived with a court order to open the road, and when Porter Brothers' foreman refused, Freeman hauled him off to jail.[9]

Maneuvering continued. Earlier a group of Portland investors had undertaken to build a line to Bend and had acquired important right-of-way north of there. But the appeal of their Central Oregon Railroad withered as Hill and Harriman neared, and COR stock plummeted in value. Recognizing an opportunity, Hill picked up the stock and thus gained forty miles of the best right-of-way from Gateway (near Madras) to Bend.[10]

Legal battles continued, and in August 1909 Judge R. S. Bean of the US District Court in Portland ruled Harriman had no rights on sixty miles of government land north of Gateway, the only feasible site for the railroads to exit the Deschutes Canyon, but Harriman *had* acquired title to a ranch there, thus blocking Hill. Both sides were thus stymied; however grudgingly, they finally agreed that Hill's Oregon Trunk could cross Harriman's land, and in exchange Harriman received use rights on Hill's line south of there, including the vital crossing of Crooked River, which would require a state-of-the-art steel arch bridge.[11]

Bottlenecks overcome and rivalries at last under control, construction proceeded. Grading on the Madras-to-Bend section began in June 1910 and construction of the bridge across Crooked River Gorge a month later (it would take almost a year to complete). Even before it was finished through to Bend, the railroad spurred dryland wheat production around Metolius and Culver, encouraged the incorporation of Madras in 1910, and hastened a drive to peel the area off from Crook County. Meanwhile, recognizing potential advantages, residents of Culver moved their town six miles to a site on the railroad's planned route.[12]

On October 5, 1911, James J. Hill was present in Bend to drive the final spike. Bill Hanley stood next to Hill on the speaker's platform and gave a speech of his own. When the ceremony was over and the golden spike pulled, Hill slipped it into Hanley's pocket: "It belongs to you," he reportedly said, "I was building the railroad to come see you."[13]

With completion of the Oregon Trunk to Bend, railroad-building east of the Cascades slowed. Bypassed by Hill and Harriman, Prineville built an eighteen-mile spur line to connect with the Oregon Trunk—after private attempts to do so failed—but significant tapping of the Ochoco forests, which would have made the line financially sound, did not immediately follow. The City of Prineville Railroad would not turn a profit until 1939.[14] Similarly, the Nevada, California, and Oregon Railway—a lightly ballasted, underfinanced, narrow-gauge line that in 1912 reached Lakeview from Alturas, California, and points south—failed to generate significant

"Walking the plank" 348 feet above Crooked River as the railroad to Bend nears completion.
Credit: OSU Libraries Special Collections & Archives Research Center.

economic activity; the same was true for the Sumpter Valley Railroad, which reached Prairie City in 1910. Not until the 1920s, when the Southern Pacific acquired the NCO and upgraded it to standard gauge, were Forest Service officials persuaded to offer a major timber sale south of Lakeview; sawmill activity soon grew apace. For its part, the Sumpter Valley Railroad, unable to compete with trucks and autos, ceased operations to Prairie City in 1933 and concentrated on the Eccles sawmills in Bates and elsewhere that it had originally been built to serve.[15]

The heady economic climate of the 1920s generated new hopefuls. Early in the decade, the Forest Service sold cutting rights on a huge block of timber north of Burns. Fred Herrick's contract to cut the timber required him to build a common carrier railroad from Crane to Burns, a distance of thirty miles, and from there another fifty miles north to Seneca, entrepôt to the timber. Building from Crane to Burns was easy; the line went into service on September 24, 1924, and was quickly transferred from Herrick's construction company to the Union Pacific. The route to Seneca was more challenging, and before Herrick could finish the line, he ran out of funds; the Forest Service cancelled his contract, and Herrick soon filed for bankruptcy. The Edward Hines Lumber Company of Chicago picked up the pieces, completed the railroad to Seneca in 1929 and ran it as a private line until incorporating it in 1934 as the Oregon & Northwestern, a common carrier that never hauled much other than logs, supplies for Hines's operations, and a few cattle.[16]

The Condon, Kinzua and Southern was a more modest operation. In the mid-1920s, Edward D. Wetmore and his Pennsylvania associates decided to begin milling their timber near the western end of the Blue Mountains and built a twenty-four-mile-long railroad to aid in marketing. Incorporated as a common carrier, the line did little other than haul supplies to their mill town of Kinzua and lumber out to the Union Pacific's railhead at Condon. One longtime resident of the area remembers his family stretching the term "common carrier" to the limit. For Sunday outings they would ride the CK&S from Condon to Kinzua, buy ice cream cones at the company store, perhaps do a bit of fishing in Thirty Mile Creek, and then head home.[17]

More significant—and more widely noted—was the activity of Robert E. Strahorn. A onetime Indian scout, Strahorn had worked as an investment banker in Boston and then for various western railroads, helping to select, lay out, and publicize key town sites. Thanks to his advance knowledge of the routes that rail lines would be following, he made a fortune through land speculation. In the 1920s, he turned his attention to Eastern Oregon. Strahorn planned a four-hundred-mile rail system centered at Silver Lake that would tie the dead-end lines at Bend, Klamath Falls, Crane, and Lakeview together and thus provide through routes for the vast area south of the Blues. To block the Great Northern from entering the area, Strahorn combined forces with the Southern Pacific to get the Interstate Commerce Commission to withhold permission for the Oregon Trunk to connect through from Bend to Klamath Falls. Newspapers throughout the area followed developments closely.[18]

In many ways, Strahorn was a latter-day T. Egenton Hogg, long on dreams but short on capital. To overcome his shortage of funds, Strahorn worked assiduously to raise support from communities that would be served by his system. He won significant aid in Klamath Falls, where he was viewed as "a new Moses" who would lead the area's timber to market, but building his still-impoverished system faced delay after delay, and many onetime supporters turned bitterly against him. In the end, Strahorn's Oregon, California & Eastern completed only one line, a railroad from Klamath Falls up the Sprague to Bly, with a branch north up the Sycan. Completed in 1923, it opened vast stands of first-class pine forest to logging and gave a significant boost to the economy of Klamath Falls, but Strahorn's larger plans died aborning. This is hardly surprising. Much of the area he dreamed of tying together was simply too unproductive and lightly populated to support a rail system.[19]

In the end, the major rail systems—not the lines of small-time operators like Hogg, Herrick, Wetmore, Strahorn, and the City of Prineville—would have the greatest impact east of the Cascades. As in the race up the Deschutes, much of what transpired was shaped by competition between the Southern Pacific and Great Northern, the key elements in the systems that had been built by Hill and Harriman.

When the Oregon Trunk reached Bend, most assumed the line would soon be completed through to Klamath Falls, but it would be well over a decade before that happened. Although the "Harriman fence" had been pushed back to Bend,[20] the Southern Pacific continued efforts to protect its territory farther south. When the Great Northern applied to the Interstate

Commerce Commission for permission to extend to Klamath Falls, the Southern Pacific argued against the proposal, while Klamath Basin interests, and the Weyerhaeuser Timber Company, supported it.

Self-interest was at the heart of Weyerhaeuser's position. The company owned vast stands in Klamath County, but hesitated to build a sawmill there so long as the company would be dependent on a single railroad to market its cut—especially since that railroad fed into the California market, which primarily wanted box shooks instead of the more profitable sawn lumber. George Long, Weyerhaeuser's west coast manager, predicted a sawmill in Klamath Falls could be "the handsomest pearl on the string" of company holdings and argued before the ICC for approval of Great Northern's request, for it would have eliminated the problem of single-line dependency.[21]

A great scramble followed ICC approval of Great Northern's proposal. The Harriman interests pushed the Oregon Trunk not only through to Klamath Falls but eventually beyond to meet up at Bieber, California, with a Western Pacific line being built northward. The connection gave the Great Northern system access to California, as well as to Reno and other points in Nevada. To counter this, the Southern Pacific built eastward from Klamath Falls to Alturas, California, to connect with the now-upgraded NCO, thus improving its competitive position in Nevada.[22] At the same time, the Southern Pacific constructed a line from Eugene over the Willamette Pass to connect to its line at Kirk and thence to Klamath Falls. Known as the Natron Cutoff, it would soon became the main route from Portland to the San Francisco Bay area, for it was shorter, less tortuous, and had easier grades than the old mainline over the Siskiyous. In a few short years, Klamath Falls went from a relatively isolated community with a single rail outlet to a growing city with five. Responding, Weyerhaeuser built the sawmill George Long had long championed and added a rail line of its own into its timber west of Klamath Falls. The company was not alone: numerous sawmills soon sprang up in Klamath and to its north at Algoma, Chiloquin, and elsewhere.[23]

The Gilchrist Timber Company was also influenced by the new connections. It had acquired substantial holdings in Deschutes and northern Klamath Counties, but took no steps toward manufacturing until railroads began entering the area. Then, with the Natron Cutoff and Great Northern's extension south from Bend under construction, it began planning to build a sawmill on the Little Deschutes once its holdings in Laurel, Mississippi, had been cut out. With the choice of a connecting line from its proposed mill to either the SP's Natron line or to the Great Northern, the company opted for the former. However, the Great Depression slowed demand, and the company proceeded slowly. Not until 1939 did the company's sawmill and fourteen-mile-long Klamath Northern Railroad go into service.[24]

For all this activity, neither the mainlines of Hill and Harriman nor the various shortlines provided rail service to vast parts of Eastern Oregon. Railroads largely served Eastern Oregon's periphery; much of the rest remained isolated. The sort of network dreamed of by Hogg and Strahorn never came to pass. Rails opened the way for lumbering in vast stretches of the pine country, but after all this construction and all the heat of rivalries, the transportation needs of the region were still largely unmet.[25]

Highways held more promise than railroads, but that promise long remained hard to see, in part because the dynamics of roadbuilding and the debates surrounding it were decidedly different east and west of the Cascades. The Willamette and Umpqua Valleys were connected to Portland by rail by 1872 and to California a decade later; from an even earlier date steamboats plied the Willamette. These developments gave rise to a number of market and trans-shipment centers; when farmers west of the Cascades talked of farm-to-market roads, they meant roads that would allow them to get their agricultural output to these centers and that would hold up under the heavily laden farm wagons that would use them. Getting out of the mud that plagued transportation for several months each year was thus a central concern. A market road bill passed by the state in 1919 generated over $2 million annually for farm-to-market roads, but the bulk of the money was spent west of the Cascades.[26]

East of the Cascades, few areas had a pattern similar to the Willamette Valley's mixed agricultural core and the transportation routes that served it. Exceptions occurred in scattered locales such as the Grande Ronde Valley, where geographer Barbara Bailey has shown that towns sprang up along the route of the OR&N, their spacing depending on the limitations of the wagon traffic through which they reached—and were served by— their hinterlands. As roads improved, some towns declined, leaving only the more favorably located—and those were more separated.[27] A similar pattern developed elsewhere, such as in the Klamath Basin and around

Redmond, but where gold, cattle, sheep, and lumber were the main products—that is, in much of Eastern Oregon—market roads played a limited role. Indeed, in light of the area's limited capacity for mixed agriculture, roads were often more a means of bringing goods into an area than of taking them out. An early settler in the Wallowa Valley made twice-annual trips to the Milton-Freewater area to bring back produce, peddling a good portion along the way during his return to pay expenses. As with J. R. Roberts, whose store in Redmond supplied a wide variety of dry goods and produce to outlying areas (both delivered from the store and through mail order), roads were more important in supplying rural areas and improving mail and stage coach service than in getting crops out to market.[28]

With no center of focus, transportation routes ran in a variety of directions. As often as not, they were through routes following old wagon road and immigrant trails. The main road across the Blues followed the old Oregon Trail; highways developed where the Santiam and McKenzie wagon roads had once run; and when the Burns-Vale highway emerged it more or less followed Meek Cutoff. For their part, these earlier routes had tended to follow Indian trails used for generations before the arrival of whites.

Land grants for military wagon roads and trans-Cascade and Blue Mountain toll roads were the most conspicuous examples of early road-building in Eastern Oregon. Military wagon roads did not necessarily go where they would be most useful to settlers,[29] and toll roads were expensive. For example, at Smith Bridge over the Wallowa River, the charge was $1.25 per team and wagon. This was but one of many such charges. In 1868 the La Grande *Mountain Sentinel* complained that, after leaving Grande Ronde Valley, "the traveler is beset by bridge keepers, ferry owners, and owners of roads, as thick as flies in harvest." All the main highways were toll roads. Two years later the editor repeated his complaint: "A trip could not ... be made to Walla Walla or Umatilla for less than sixty dollars," a sizable sum at the time, and the route to Idaho was beset "at every turn of the road, at every crossing of every small brook, and at commencement of every pass, gulley and ravine" by toll takers. A petition asking the state to construct a wagon road from the Columbia River to Baker fell on deaf ears. Still, wagon roads had their place. The Powder River, Burnt River, and Summit Wagon Road Company, incorporated in 1881, constructed a road from Baker to the John Day area that provided a route only one-fourth as long as the one from The Dalles that had previously dominated service to the area.[30]

In 1859 the state gave counties the power to establish road districts and tax the owners of contiguous property for the cost of road construction (payment to be made in either money or labor). In lightly populated Eastern Oregon, where roads ran for many a mile through public domain, this authority was of limited use. Under the circumstances, private parties often engaged in road construction.[31] As population grew after 1870 and needs increased, county courts were besieged with petitions for new roads. Since counties were chronically short on funds, the need consistently outran construction, and private contributions continued to play an important role. The road through Wallowa Canyon to Joseph was built in 1879, "almost entirely by private contributions." Not until 1899 did the county step in to rebuild the treacherous Minam Hill portion, making it "as fine a highway as can be found anywhere in the eastern portion of the state." But counties were a weak reed for local roads to lean on, and even major through routes were often wretched. When Carrie Strahorn traveled over the Blue Mountains between Baker and Pendleton in 1880, it was a nightmare: "The road . . . was in horrible condition from the fall rains, and the regular stage had to be abandoned for an old dead axle farm wagon. . . . There were six horses all the time and part way we had eight to get through the deep and tenacious mud." Her party passed teamsters struggling to rescue their mules from a quagmire in which they were mired.

For many years there was little overall improvement. In 1902 it took stages thirty-six dismal hours to travel from Ontario to Burns, and George Palmer Putnam's critical comments about the road from Shaniko to Bend in 1910 could have been applied to many a road in Eastern Oregon. In the John Day area, pressure for an improved road down the valley grew. Thinking of incoming freight rather than market access, the *Blue Mountain Eagle* proclaimed, "Every man in the interior of the county . . . is digging up his share of the cost of hauling freight over a road that is impassable for heavily laden wagons a good part of the year." Still, progress had begun; by 1909 Klamath and other counties were taking steps to provide better local roads.[32]

The automobile revolution ushered in a new era, but what it foretold was not initially evident. As the twentieth century began, automobiles seemed more a rich man's toy than a utilitarian instrument for transporting people and goods. The much ballyhooed construction of the Columbia Gorge Highway, hardly a utilitarian undertaking, reinforced that image. So did

domination of the Oregon Good Roads Association by urbanites. The
Grange and other agrarian organizations, viewing paved highways as serving the leisure-time interests of the well-to-do, pushed for farm-to-market
roads and opposed taxes and bond issues for through routes.[33]

As the number of automobiles and trucks rose, attitudes changed.
Portland's first automobile arrived in 1899. By 1906 there were 242 in the
city, and the number grew rapidly thereafter. Increase was not restricted
to the state's urban areas. By 1910, settlers bound for the High Desert
were arriving in Bend by automobile, for railroads were still distant and
stage service from Bend to Burns hellish. The first auto apparently arrived
in thinly populated Wallowa County in 1905; by 1924 there were 1,414,
and the number was increasing rapidly. Trucks showed a similar increase,
especially after World War I demonstrated their utilitarian value. Still, the
major pressure for roadbuilding came from urban centers, where much
of the motivation was for leisure-time activity or from those interested
in tourism.[34] When the owners of the historic Barlow Toll Road, which
crossed the Cascades south of Mount Hood, sought to sell it to the state,
supporters of the idea were largely Portlanders who wanted it incorporated into the scenic Mount Hood Loop Highway that they championed;
opponents were agrarian spokesmen who saw no utilitarian value in the
loop and residents east of the mountains who wanted a trans-Cascade
route. In the end the state accepted the road as a donation.[35]

As the number of vehicles rose and their utilitarian value became clear,
opposition to through highways ebbed. With counties unable to meet the
challenge that the increasing need for such roads presented, the state
finally moved. In 1913, the legislature passed and Governor Oswald West
signed a bill to create a highway commission (made up of the governor,
secretary of state, and state treasurer), authorizing it to employ a highway
engineer and establish a highway department financed by a one-fourth mill
tax levy. The commission promptly hired Major Henry L. Bowlby, a West
Point graduate and former instructor at the University of Washington who
had worked on the Columbia Gorge Highway. The commission charged
Bowlby with producing a master plan for a state highway system.[36]

In his first report as state highway engineer, Bowlby observed that
there were more than thirty-seven thousand miles of roads in Oregon, and
that it was "not necessary today as it was four to eight years ago, [to argue]
that the motor vehicle has come to stay." On the eve of his appointment,

13,957 vehicles were registered in the state (with only twenty-five miles of paved roads); by 1916 there would be 33,917.[37]

Progress came under Bowlby, but his brusque style and autocratic financial management generated opposition. Moreover, the master plan he prepared for the state's highway system—which included 1,070 miles of primary and 1,830 miles of secondary highways—had some decidedly odd elements that displayed a limited understanding of the needs of Eastern Oregon. He proposed a Central Oregon Highway that would run from Wasco, through Prineville, to Lakeview—a route with so little utility that it would never be built—while he included no trans-Cascade route to the Portland area. He was removed as highway engineer in 1916.

In 1917 the legislature passed a revised and strengthened highway law that replaced the highway commission of elected officials with one made up of appointees. Herbert Nunn, state highway engineer under the new commission, prepared a new, more realistic master plan that included a total of 4,317 miles of highways, some two thousand of which were east of the Cascade summit. Two years later Oregon pioneered a gasoline tax to finance roadbuilding. Improvement proceeded apace. Construction of the trans-Cascade Green Springs Highway connecting Klamath Falls and Ashland was soon under way. Still, the pace of building was too slow for many, the isolation from the rest of the state too great. In 1919 state senator George Baldwin and others pushed for Klamath and Lake Counties to secede and join California (whose legislature quickly expressed a willingness to accept them). Support for the proposed highway from The Dalles through Bend to Klamath Falls—The Dalles-California Highway—soon grew, in part, the Klamath Falls *Evening Herald* suggested, to quell secessionist efforts. In 1925 the state added a ton-mile tax on trucks and buses, and the pace of building increased. By 1930, only 340 of the 4,359 miles of state highways remained unimproved.[38]

Also important was expansion of the postal service's rural free delivery system. First instituted in the 1890s, RFD service was immensely popular and grew rapidly. Legislation providing for federal aid in the construction of "post roads" followed in 1916, and Oregon took advantage. Rural mail routes proliferated, especially in Klamath County, where the scattered but growing rural population provided a pattern well suited to RFD service.[39] The federal post roads program largely financed construction of the highway from Bend to Burns, replacing the rough, unimproved old dirt road. The improvement

Springtime on the Klamath Falls–
Lakeview Highway, 1938. Credit: Lake
County Historical Society.

was desperately needed; as traveler Dallas Lore Sharp had commented in
1913, "I doubt if you could experience death in any part of the world more
times for twenty dollars than by auto-stage from Bend to Burns."[40]

Neither Bowlby's nor Nunn's plans called for a trans-Cascade route
from Central Oregon to Portland. That came in the 1920s with the Wapinitia Cutoff, which connected The Dalles-California Highway with the
Mount Hood Loop and thus eliminated the need to travel to Portland by
way of The Dalles, reducing travel time significantly. The last section was
graveled in 1929. But the cutoff was hardly ideal; it was closed in winter
and prone to breakup during spring thaws. Indeed, as late as 1936, the
state highway department stationed a truck along the highway to pull out
passenger cars stuck in the mud—nor was it alone: the Klamath-Lakeview
highway was another that could be a quagmire.[41]

The Bend Chamber of Commerce pushed for a better, faster highway
to Portland. The most promising route ran across the Warm Springs Indian
Reservation, roughly following an ancient Indian trading route and a more
recent, unpaved secondary road used primarily by locals. As early as 1932

the Oregon Highway Department began taking steps toward an improved route, but the tribes hesitated to approve, insisting among other things that the highway would need to be fenced to protect their livestock. By 1939, work had begun, but when World War II erupted it was halted for the duration. Finally completed in 1949, the Warm Springs Cutoff provided a straighter, faster route than the Wapinitia Cutoff, reducing travel time to Portland by more than thirty minutes and presenting fewer seasonal challenges. It had the additional advantage of avoiding the winding Cow Canyon section of The Dalles-California Highway and the steep grades near Maupin where the Wapinitia Cutoff crossed the Deschutes. So manifest were the advantages of the new route that traffic on the older highway slowed to a trickle. Few in the next generation of Central Oregon's young people ever travelled the Wapinitia highway; many had never even heard of it. For those of us who remember traveling the road, the reasons for this historical amnesia are clear enough.[42]

In its own way, the work of R. H. Baldock, the Highway Department's district engineer in La Grande, was every bit as important as the plans of Bowlby and Nunn. Baldock recognized that funds were insufficient to provide badly needed hard-surface roads in lightly traveled Eastern Oregon, but believed he could come up with an inexpensive substitute for paving by modifying the system developed by Scotland's John L. MacAdam, who had built all-weather roads by binding together crushed rock using water and packing it together under heavy pressure. Herbert Nunn considered Baldock's ideas impractical and tried to block the use of scarce funds on them. However, Governor Walter Pierce recognized the desirability of a cheap system of getting Eastern Oregon out of the dust and mud and, with the support of Highway Commission chairman William Duby of Baker, allowed Baldock to proceed with his experimentation. Baldock was spectacularly successful. As Pierce later recalled, Baldock "found that the rock could be held together by oil if applied in the right proportion, at the right time and under the right conditions, at a cost of less than $4000 a mile compared with a cost of more than $30,000 a mile" for earlier types of improved surfaces. Pierce, a foe of what he called the paving monopoly and always a careful watchdog of the public purse, was delighted. So were others. Within a short time oiled "blacktop" roads had spread throughout the West.[43]

Eastern Oregon's evolving highway system did more than carry automobile and truck traffic and lower the cost of goods in previously isolated communities. For communities bypassed by the main highways, the effect was decidedly negative. John Day, unserved by railroads and bypassed by major highways, remained isolated and self-focused; settlers in its outlying areas were even more so. Numerous places in northeastern Oregon, as well as Millican, Izee, Drewsey, Meacham, Shaniko, and Crane, went into sharp decline—although in the case of tiny Millican a temporary respite was provided by simply moving the little community northward to a site on the new Bend-Burns highway. Similarly, when hard-surface highways put in a belated appearance in southern Harney County, they spurred declines in places like Fields and Andrews, for good roads and modern vehicles made it easy to reach Burns and Winnemucca, where goods were cheaper and available in more variety.[44]

Elsewhere, highways reinforced—or even created—a sense of interconnectedness. The Wapinitia and Warm Springs Cutoffs strengthened Central Oregon's ties to the Portland metropolitan area while weakening those to the mid- and southern Willamette Valley that had dominated since the first settlement of the area. Moreover, they created a series of self-identified regional communities that were reflected in various ways, but especially in interscholastic athletic leagues. Bend, Redmond, Prineville, Madras, Burns, and Lakeview belonged to the Central Oregon League. The intercommunity ties strengthened by the resulting competitions resulted in a shared identity that did not extend to the communities of the Klamath Basin (even though Klamath Falls was closer to the Central Oregon communities than was Lakeview). Among smaller schools, highways long tied Cascade Locks, Dufur, Mosier, Moro, Maupin, Arlington, Culver, and Sisters together in a league—no mean feat, since Arlington was 212 miles from Sisters, and any number of schools of similar size were closer to each.

Highways and railroads were not alone in connecting residents of Eastern Oregon to one another and to the outside world. Newspapers sprang up even in tiny communities—in part to report the news (often lifted from larger papers), in part to boost community development, and in part to provide a place for the legal notices required of land filings and other actions. Some stood out for the quality of their editorship. G. P. Putnam was succeeded at the *Bend Bulletin* by Robert W. Sawyer, a Harvard graduate and trained attorney; Mary Brown, a University of Oregon Phi

Beta Kappa, long edited the *Redmond Spokesman*; C. S. "Sam" Jackson, who would in time be inducted into the Oregon Newspaper Hall of Fame, ran the Pendleton *East Oregonian* before moving to Portland to resuscitate what became the *Oregon Journal*; and Elmo Smith, a graduate of the College of Idaho who would rise to become Oregon's governor, edited the Ontario *Argus Observer* and John Day's *Blue Mountain Eagle*. Yet not all news was furnished locally; from an early date communities were supplied by stagecoach and other means with newspapers from metropolitan centers. Along with their local papers, many Eastern Oregon residents subscribed to one of the Portland dailies too. In spite of a thinly spread population, Eastern Oregon had an informed population.

Railroads may have hogged the headlines and involved more important personages, but taken all-in-all, highways did more to tie Eastern Oregon together and shape its local identities. Aided by newspapers, they helped create a people accustomed to looking beyond their immediate surroundings, to traveling long distances for work or pleasure, and to having a shared identity that set them apart from people west of the Cascades (and sometimes from other Eastern Oregonians as well). And, perhaps most important of all, they strengthened the established economy based on commodity exports.

11

The Quest for Workable Governments

In the beginning, government east of the Cascades was simple in the extreme. Aside from an army presence to protect miners and settlers from Indians and a rudimentary government in The Dalles that attempted, not particularly successfully, to provide a semblance of law and order, there was nothing. There were Wasco County deputies in the gold mining regions—and, after their separation from Wasco County, local sheriffs—but there and elsewhere people tended to settle problems themselves. After perfunctory trials, residents frequently took punishment into their own hands.

In November 1862, newly formed Baker County had a justice of the peace in Auburn. Locals argued "they might as well use him" in the case against "Tom the Spaniard," who was accused of murder. Once he was found guilty, a mob took over, beat him, and dragged him by a rope around his neck to a hanging tree a half mile away. Hubert Howe Bancroft laconically observed, "The man was dead long before the body was hanged." A similar incident occurred in the Umatilla River country in 1866.[1]

Direct action was not limited to cases of murder, nor did it always involve legal authorities, however feeble. In the absence of effective rules, miners gathered in Canyon City in June 1862, shortly after the first gold strikes, to promulgate "laws and regulations" for the John Day mining district. The extralegal framework they crafted provided the basis for settling disputes and formalizing procedures.[2] Similarly, in the absence of effective law enforcement in what would become Sherman County, local residents formed a vigilance committee and called on Wasco County to appoint a justice of the peace for the area, "as there is not one within twenty-five miles." Elsewhere, Abner Robbins, the founder of Drewsey, initially called his settlement Gouge Eye in reference to the local method of conflict resolution.[3]

The simplicity of early government and the legacy of popular tribunals is hardly surprising. So long as a modicum of order was maintained
to protect property and allow commodities to be exported and supplies
imported, little was expected of it. In the 1860s, the day of active government supporting business and social services lay far in the future—as did
the idea that government should play a role in protecting and managing
natural resources.

Wasco County provided the first civilian government in Eastern Oregon.
Created in 1854, the county embraced everything in Oregon Territory east
of the Cascades. Thus, it included large parts of what would become Idaho,
Washington, Montana, and Wyoming. Even after these areas had been
peeled away, it was still the largest county in the United States. Establishing
workable government in this vast terrain was never simple. The county's
population was tiny, and The Dalles, being its only significant community,
became county seat by default. What resulted, as the *Times-Mountaineer*
noted, was a situation in which the only court between the Willamette
Valley and the Rocky Mountains was in The Dalles, and the jurisdiction of
its justice of the peace extended from the Cascades to Fort Hall (located in
what is now southeastern Idaho).[4]

The county's government was simple in the extreme, consisting of
three commissioners, a sheriff, a judge of probate, and a clerk. That was
more than sufficient. When the commissioners met, they had little business to conduct. During the commission's first year, it granted licenses to
ferries on the Columbia, Snake, and Green; and a grocery store in The
Dalles; and passed a seventeen mill property tax designated for roads (a
mill is one-tenth of a cent). The following year it added a levy of 1 percent
on all taxable property (eight mills for the county, one for the territorial
government, and one for schools—the last in addition to the territorial
tax for schools). The taxes yielded a pittance, for military facilities were
exempt, leaving a minimum of taxable property in the county.[5]

Not until 1858 did the county have sufficient funds to construct a
modest jail and courtroom. In the interim it did the best it could. One
criminal, unable to pay his fine, was sent to Fort Vancouver for confine-
ment. Authorities there refused to accept him, so Wasco County agreed
to accept a promissory note for his fine—a note which, as it turns out,
was never paid. Subsequently, another prisoner unable to pay his fine was

simply released, "in accordance with the law." When the sheriff presented a bill for maintenance of one such individual, it was rejected because the "prisoner" had been observed wandering free in town.[6]

Difficulties continued. In 1863, one Berry Way (aka Jim Berriway and Barry Wey) robbed and murdered his partner near Canyon City. Gold had been discovered in the area the previous year, and, as the *Times-Mountaineer* later put it, "Hundreds of desperate characters had flocked thither." The county had appointed a deputy sheriff for the area; he arrested Way and, lacking a jail, tied him to a log. Way escaped, but was tracked to Boise, rearrested, and returned to Canyon City. The deputy's pay was two dollars a day and local wages were five, so rather than hire someone to guard the prisoner, the deputy—already having gone to considerable trouble—took the role of judge, called on a number of friends to serve as jurors, and conducted a brief trial. Berry Way soon "expiated his crime on the gallows."[7]

A similar situation developed in Prineville while it was still in Wasco County. In June of 1878, "two desperadoes, Van Allen and Jeff Drips, came to Prineville and attempted to 'run' it according to their own peculiar ideas." James T. Chamberlain, Wasco County deputy sheriff for the area, sought to arrest them, but they resisted. During the ensuing confrontation, Allen was killed and Drips captured. Drips was taken to The Dalles for trial and there acquitted of the charges against him. Transporting defendants some two hundred miles to the county seat was costly and time-consuming, but also ensured that witnesses were often not available for a trial. The incident convinced many in Prineville that the way to get more effective law enforcement was to form a new county.[8]

In other cases, too, distance to centers of government hindered criminal investigation and the application of the laws. So ineffectively was the murder of Silver Lake's J. Creed Conn handled by authorities in Lakeview, some ninety miles away, that Governor George Chamberlain felt impelled to intervene—to no useful effect. In the end, no one was found guilty of the crime, although a recent review of evidence has shown the strong possibility it was perpetrated by serial killer Ray Van Buren Jackson.[9]

Local residents and deputies were not alone in being frustrated by the problems of law enforcement. In Wasco County, sheriff after sheriff served only two years before being replaced by voters or opting for a simpler job such as justice of the peace. In its first ten years, the county had seven different sheriffs. The record was not much better elsewhere.[10]

City government was equally problematic. Although a municipal government began to take form in September of 1855, The Dalles did not receive a charter from the state until almost two years later. As the authors of *An Illustrated History of Central Oregon* put it, the town's "troubles would fill a good-sized volume." For nearly a decade it was dominated by "gamblers and other representatives of the 'tough' element." The influx of fortune seekers during the gold rush years exacerbated conditions; there were several murders and "numerous cutting and shooting 'scrapes.'" The authors summed up conditions with classic understatement: "Verily The Dalles was lively."[11]

Nor was the situation unique to The Dalles. In their early years, John Day, Bend, Redmond, Klamath Falls, and Ontario all experienced a degree of wide-open activity that resulted in large part from the presence of sizable transient populations of single young men engaged in mining, cattle drives, or the construction of railroads or irrigation canals.[12]

Nowhere was violence more endemic, nor local reaction more extreme, than in Prineville. Problems began while the area was still part of Wasco County, but grew once it was carved away to form Crook County in October 1882. A secret vigilance committee formed in the winter of 1881 for protection against outlaws, especially horse thieves; the group soon morphed into a body that saw itself as the area's arbiters of right and wrong and used its power to destroy those who defied its rule.

In March of 1882, Aaron H. Crooks and Stephen J. Jory were building a line fence along the edge of property Crooks claimed near Grizzly Mountain. A neighboring rancher, Lucius Langdon, considered the property his and proceeded to shoot the two from ambush. Within minutes of the news reaching Prineville a posse formed; two nights later a member caught up with Langdon, who surrendered peacefully and was turned over to Deputy Sheriff John L. Luckey. Lacking a jail, Luckey took him to a local hotel. W. H. Harrison, who worked for Langdon, was arrested too, although witnesses insisted he had been in Prineville at the time of the murders. That night a body of armed men broke into the room where Langdon and Harrison were held, shot the former, and dragged the latter through the town behind a horse and hanged him from a bridge over Crooked River.[13]

Emboldened by their success, the stockmen's association—the organizational front behind which the vigilantes operated—launched a campaign of violence that it justified as bringing law and order to the community. It sent warnings emblazoned with a skull and crossbones to any who dared challenge (or even question) its authority. One historian has put it succinctly: "Control of county and city government by these men made justice impossible." Even Deputy Luckey was intimidated. But the vigilantes' claim that they were guardians of the community was more than slightly suspect. One victim was a jockey who had refused to throw a race. Another was shot apparently because he simply dared to defy them. Then the Mogan brothers, Mike and Frank, were shot—the latter by William Thompson, a key leader of the vigilantes who made no bones about his action, but whose actions smacked more of a personal vendetta than something aimed at establishing law and order.[14]

The community had had enough. Jim Blakely and a number of others stepped forward to defy the vigilantes. After secretly touring the county to line up supporters, they set to work, challenging Thompson and Gus Winkler, another infamous vigilante, to a gunfight if they did not leave the county immediately. Emboldened by this, nearly eighty men joined Blakely's group—officially called the Citizens Protective Union but more widely known as the Moonshiners (not because of any illicit whiskey making, but because they did much of their work at night watching for vigilante actions).

Events soon came to a head. Led by Blakely and Henry Vaughan, some seventy-five armed Moonshiners marched on a saloon where the vigilantes were meeting and challenged them to come out and fight. When they did not, the Moonshiners stormed the facility. In the face of overwhelming force, the vigilantes gave up without firing a shot. When the county's first general election was held the following week, candidates put forward by the Moonshiners carried the day. Blakely was elected county sheriff. Although many of them continued to live in the community, the vigilantes' two-year reign of terror was over.[15]

In Redmond, Bend, Pendleton, and La Grande, the issue was not so much whether law and order should be established as what sort of order was wanted. In that regard, these towns were more typical than Prineville. In 1912, Governor Oswald West, a confirmed "dry" and moralist par excellence, visited Redmond and—standing Mary Ellen Lease of Populist fame on her rhetorical head—told a group of supporters that Central Oregonians ought to raise "less hell and more hogs." West had heard reports of illicit activities in Redmond from Methodist minister J. M. Crenshaw and others cut from the same puritanical cloth. West's message apparently went unheeded, for some time later Crenshaw informed West that gambling was still being carried on in the rear of the Redmond Hotel, owned by Mayor H. F. Jones. West dispatched a special deputy who sat in on a game and promptly arrested Jones and Marshall Z. T. McClay. West called for and quickly got the resignations of both.[16]

Jones defended his actions in the *Oregonian*. As a supporter put it, "The trouble is we have three or a half dozen well-meaning but misguided old women of both sexes . . . who would like to see the town conducted on puritanical lines. When Jones was mayor he gave what he called a fair, liberal administration. That is what the people want in Redmond." But Crenshaw was still not satisfied, and when he attacked Mrs. A. B. Sparks, the manager of the town's movie theater the following April, charging that movies and the manager were equally sinful, the community had had enough. The Redmond Commercial Club urged Crenshaw to change his ways or leave; the *Spokesman* weighed in, labeling Crenshaw a "man who, in the guise of a preacher, is always looking for trouble and trying to create trouble." Crenshaw responded by filing charges of defamation against fifteen prominent Redmondites. Found guilty, they were fined a mere $4.13. The Sparks Theater held a well-attended benefit to pay the defendants' fines and legal fees: admission was not less than thirteen cents and not more than thirteen dollars.[17]

The situation in Bend was more extreme. With the arrival of the railroad, the community entered a period of rapid growth—and with growth came a number of problems. Above all, there was the same question that had bedeviled Redmond: How wide-open should the town be?

Bend's government had been bumping along without accomplishing much, so at the first opportunity, seeking to provide a government adequate for the town's growth, the Bend Commercial Club and various businessmen put forward a slate of candidates for city council that they considered up to the task of providing more efficient government. At its head was mayoral candidate Urling C. Coe, the local physician. After the slate's election, Coe's first act was to order the town marshal to stop all gambling in the city. He and the council then turned their attention to the question of saloons; a score or more applications for saloon licenses were before the council, but no ordinance dealing with the matter. The council soon deadlocked between prohibitionists who wanted license fees set so high as to limit severely the number of saloons (or totally eliminate them) and those who wanted license fees low enough to allow saloon keepers to make a decent profit without having to break the law. Finally, Coe forced a decision—but, unhappy with the rather liberal outcome allowing for eight saloons, he warned that henceforth "the town would be plenty open and wild." He proved prescient, but with the liquor question out of the way—for the moment at least—the council was able to turn to other business: an engineer was hired to survey a sewer system adequate for the community's expected growth; another was employed to establish grades for the streets and sidewalks; and, in cooperation with the city attorney, Coe formulated a health code that the council adopted.[18]

But Coe soon tired of the bickering on the council; he resigned in March 1912. Without a mayor and with the council deadlocked three to three, the town was soon more wide open than ever. A murder in a "rooming house" brought conditions to widespread notice, and local ministers took up the cry for change. One presented a petition with 180 signatures, calling on the council to "eliminate from the city all dissolute women and undesirable characters who follow in their wake."[19] Still, the deadlock in the council continued.

Conditions angered not only many community residents, but also Governor West, who threatened to close down the town if a mayor was not put in place soon to take charge of matters. His statement in Redmond that Central Oregonians ought to raise less hell left no doubt as to what sort of mayor West wanted. George Palmer Putnam chafed under West's pressure, criticizing his "theatrical methods" and "inordinate attention to the affairs of local communities." But West's threats had to be taken seriously, for he had a well-deserved reputation as one who took direct and decisive action.[20]

The logjam was broken when Putnam agreed to stand for mayor as a compromise candidate. The exact sequence of events is unclear. Putnam's account in his autobiography, written thirty years after the fact, and the files of the *Bend Bulletin* tell slightly different stories; regardless, the way had at last been cleared for a government that could tackle the growing community's problems. As Putnam later wrote, "Mostly the dubious ladies left. What gambling remained became orderly and unobtrusive.

Saloon operators found wisdom in keeping strict hours and discouraging drunkenness. Rough stuff was frowned upon." His administration, Putnam summed up, "tried to set a reasonable course midway between civic virtue and something approaching the freedom a raw little frontier town wanted."[21]

The council was free at last to address the community's basic needs. It turned its attention to getting a $60,000 bond issue passed to build the sewer system planned during Coe's tenure, to improving the town's volunteer fire department, to carefully managing city finances, and to revising the city's charter and ordinances to ensure more efficient government.[22] In that day and age, not much was asked of local government, but within the narrow parameters of public expectation, Putnam's administration, like the replacement government in Redmond, did what most seem to have desired.

Oswald West took aim at Klamath Falls and Pendleton too. In Klamath, two council members were indicted for taking bribes. Infighting among council members and the chief of police followed, spurring West to send a representative to investigate. Meanwhile, in Pendleton, where saloons and rowdiness had a long history, vigilante activity broke out in 1915.[23]

La Grande presented a simpler scenario. In comparison with Pendleton, just over the Blues, La Grande was an island of moral tranquility—or, at least, it sought to be. According to local historian Jim Reavis, in the town's early years there were many arrests for "keeping a store open on Sunday" and "keeping a tippling-house open on Sunday." In 1866, Herman Weyneman was indicted for gambling—betting on a billiard game—and fined fifty dollars. Two years later Biddy Oats was indicted for keeping a house of ill-fame—to clarify, the indictment was subsequently revised to read keeping a house "for the purposes of prostitution." Oats was fined $100. Such action was hardly surprising. Churches had enjoyed a strong presence in the community from its earliest decades, and, a regional history notes, were a "force in attracting to Lagrande the better classes of citizens and in keeping elevated the moral tone of the city." Working in the same direction, La Grande also displayed an interest in education "far in advance of most pioneer settlements."[24]

The relative morality such sources attribute to early La Grande was probably largely a result of demographics. The community lacked a population of transient young men such as flocked to Prineville, Bend, Redmond,

and Pendleton; it was a trading center for a productive agricultural hinterland; it grew relatively steadily over the years, but had no great land
rush or huge influx of railroad and woods workers. As the authors of the
Illustrated History of Wallowa and Union Counties put it, "All things seem
to have worked together for the furtherance of its best interests"—that is
for stability and order.[25]

All of which is not to say that La Grande was always orderly. Following
completion of the Oregon Rail & Navigation Company's mainline through
the area, and as gold mining in the area declined, many Chinese moved
to La Grande. In 1893, spurred by the endemic racism of the era as well
as economic depression, locals attacked the Chinese community, burning
numerous buildings and forcing Chinese out of town. The cry "the Chinese must go" showed plainly that the ideal of a moral community did not
include an alien presence in its midst.[26]

City government focused on a few basic functions was a passing phenomenon. Over time citizens desired more and more. In addition to police and
fire protection, courts, water supplies, decent streets, and sewage facilities,
they came to expect libraries, parks and other recreation facilities, long-
range planning, and a variety of social and regulatory services. The increasingly complex organizational structures needed to handle these functions
increased monetary demands. To meet the evolving situation, not only
money but also more and more time and expertise were required. City
councils, filled as they were with part time, often unpaid, public servants
and meeting only once or twice a month, were hard put to meet growing
demands. They could and did hire engineers and other experts for specific
projects, but they required oversight that most council members were ill-
equipped to supply—and, in any case, councils failed to provide continuity,
for their membership changed frequently and experts came and went. The
result was that town after town stumbled along and in time many found
themselves facing financial crises.

Bend was one of the first to tackle the problem. Finding itself in financial straits, in 1929 it hired C. G. "Jude" Reiter as city manager. Reiter, a
Pennsylvania State University engineering graduate who had worked as
an army officer in the building of the Alaska Railroad and then as city
engineer of Hillsboro, was ideal for the job. Conservative, personable, and
impeccably honest, he guided Bend through the financial crisis it faced

when he came onboard and over the next twenty years directed the community on a progressive path that added parks, an improved sewer system, and waterworks that tapped pristine Tumalo Creek. His successes were noted well beyond the immediate community, and in the 1930s the League of Oregon Cities elected Reiter its president.

In time, however, things unraveled when the police chief fired three popular deputies for alleged laxities. Calls for the chief's dismissal grew, but Reiter refused, arguing he was a good man and an effective departmental leader who kept crime under control. A majority of the council supported him. But there was a seed of truth to the charges of laxity in the department: area youth were well aware of the location of Bend's bordello, and one recalls—while still underage—riding around in the back seat of "Red" Hoagland's police car, drinking beer with Hoagland's son while the father patrolled the community, apparently believing it was better to have the young men drinking in the patrol car than out in the community where they might get in trouble. In spite of Reiter's defense of the chief, critics persisted, and a recall election for a majority of the city council was understood to be a vote on Reiter and the police chief. When the three councilmen supporting them were narrowly recalled, Reiter and the chief both resigned.[27]

When Reiter had come to Bend, the city council-manager form of government was relatively new and untried. Growing out of the Progressive movement's concern for efficiency, and viewed as a substitute for the ward politics and favoritism that often prevailed in city governments, it had first been instituted in Staunton, Virginia, in 1908. Under the system, city councils established basic policies, and city managers implemented them and provided day-to-day direction of affairs. With the power to hire and fire, managers were in de facto charge of community government. Progressive members of Bend's council seized on the system as a way out of the problems facing them, and over time Bend's success encouraged many another community in Eastern Oregon to adopt it. Pendleton, La Grande, Ontario, Prineville, Baker City, Lakeview, John Day, Burns, and eventually even Sisters adopted the council-manager system. So ubiquitous were city managers that one wag commented only the old gold-mining town of Greenhorn—still technically a "city" although no one lived there anymore—seemed to lack one.

The evolution of county government followed a different path. Great distance from the established county seat and the inconveniences attendant thereon led first one area and then another to demand separation from their original county. Counties often objected because they would be losing tax base, but the state legislature repeatedly lent a sympathetic ear. Wasco, of course, was the hardest hit by defections and came to be known as the "mother of counties," since every county east of the Cascades had originally been a part of it. Baker and Umatilla Counties (both much larger than they would eventually become) were carved away in 1862. Others followed—taken from Wasco and its successors—until in 1916 Deschutes County was peeled away from Crook, making it the seventeenth county east of the Cascades; it continues to be the state's youngest.[28]

Accompanying the creation of new counties were struggles over the location of county seats. Indeed, such struggles sometimes complicated the creation—as when rivalry between Bend and Redmond delayed formation of Deschutes. Although it had a smaller population and more limited prospects and, like many other counties, had competition for its county seat, Jefferson County came into existence in 1914, two years before its southern neighbor. It came in with Culver as temporary county seat, but—on a close vote—soon settled on Madras. Hard on the heels of this close vote, Madras residents hurried to Culver and "stole" the county records for their city.[29] Other counties followed a similar course (although without the alleged thievery of records), while in Union County the seat of government passed back and forth between Union and La Grande before finally settling in the latter.

Such contests were the product of community ambition as well as community pride. Becoming county seat could bring business and help ensure a community's future. The competition was especially intense in Gilliam County. In its enabling act, the state legislature decreed that Alkali (soon to be renamed Arlington) would be the temporary county seat until voters selected a permanent site. A pioneer history described the multi-sided contest that followed as "one of the most remarkable, . . . one of the most bitter and exciting contests in the history of Eastern Oregon." It was indeed. Five communities vied for the honor, and when the election was held, Fossil—at that time located in Gilliam County—received the most votes, while Condon and Arlington tied for second. The legislature had decreed that if no community received a majority, a runoff should be held between the top two. The tie between Arlington and Condon complicated matters, but a revote was clearly needed. Local newspapers entered the lists during the run-up to the second round of voting. They were hardly genteel in their arguments. Arlington in particular, located on the northern edge of the county, came in for attack: critics charged it would be an inconvenient location for most county residents, and its harsh, unwelcoming site was ill-suited for a seat of government. Not until 1890, five years after creation of the county, did voters finally settle the matter in favor of Condon.[30] Similar circumstances occurred in Sherman County.[31]

When established by the legislature in 1874, Lake County, then encompassing both today's Lake and Klamath Counties, presented a different problem. The legislature made Linkville (later known as Klamath Falls) the temporary county seat; it could hardly have done otherwise, for Linkville was the only town in the county. But most of the new county's population resided in its eastern portions, well distant from Linkville and across intervening mountains. When the time to vote on a permanent county seat arrived, voters in the eastern precincts cast ballots for a location near Goose Lake, but they called the location by a variety of names: Bullard Creek, Bullard's Ranch, Goose Lake, and Goose Lake Valley. The clear majority was for an eastern location—and almost surely for Bullard's Ranch, to which all four names could be applied—but there was no legal winner, so Linkville continued as county seat. However, by the time the revote rolled around, in 1876, Lakeview had sprung up on twenty acres that rancher M. W. Bullard had donated for the purpose, and the "town" won overwhelming support in the eastern precincts, easily becoming the permanent county seat.[32]

Fragmentation continued. Residents of the area around Mitchell, a little community across the Ochocos from Prineville, began agitating for separation from Crook County. They were joined by individuals from Fossil and intervening centers who wanted to leave Gilliam. In 1899, the state legislature responded favorably, and Wheeler County came into being, with Fossil as its temporary county seat. In the voting for a permanent seat, Fossil triumphed over Twickenham and Spray and has continued in that capacity ever since.[33]

Fossil's triumph is instructive. Communities vied to become county seats because their champions knew they would draw business, legal and otherwise. Being county seat has done that for Fossil, whereas

Twickenham—now little more than a putting-in place for boaters on the John Day—has disappeared as a community, and Spray's population hovers below two hundred. The fate of Condon also suggests the value of becoming a county seat: When it became Gilliam County's in 1890, it had a mere sixty residents. During the next decade it grew to 230, and then, a decade later, to 1,009. To be sure, much of its growth can be attributed to the booming wheat production during those years, but no other towns in the county grew at such a spectacular rate during the period.

The creation of new counties ground to a halt after 1916, as the isolation that had fueled separatist movements eroded. In 1919, when Herbert Nunn presented his master plan for Oregon's highways, he was careful to route a highway past each county seat—something his predecessor had not done. Nunn's plan became the basic framework for the highway system that developed, reducing the isolation of many rural areas.

In time highway improvement would encourage the idea of consolidating existing counties, rather than creating new ones. In 1912, Oregon's voters considered—and rejected—a proposal to curb the creation of new counties by requiring a basic population, assessed valuation, and size while still leaving the parent county with a sufficiency of those things itself.[34] Later, Alfred Lomax, a professor of business administration at the University of Oregon, suggested consolidating some counties—a suggestion that made sense from the viewpoint of management, for county seats as small as Moro, Fossil, and Condon, and with county populations to match, were hard to justify. In 1952, Richard Neuberger went even further, proposing reducing the state's counties to seven; east of the Cascades there would be but three. Without a constituency supporting the idea, in the face of inertia, and with solid opposition in Eastern Oregon, the idea went nowhere. Adding to the hostility to Neuberger's proposal was the fact that it was the product of a Portlander, who seemed to overlook the realities of a region where terrain and winter weather promised to make travel to the seats of enlarged counties arduous in the extreme.[35]

But there *was* a problem, as Wheeler County's circumstances demonstrate. Hardly a rotten borough in the classic sense of the term, Wheeler County still came close. South of the wheat belt, and made up of rocky scabland and marginal, overgrazed range, it had not only a small population but also few prospects. In 1927, when the Kinzua Lumber Company built its sawmill, the county received a significant economic boost; ere long, with a population of some seven hundred, Kinzua was the county's largest community. But the mill closed in 1978 and the company town was dismantled, plunging Wheeler County into economic crisis. Skirting the thin edge of bankruptcy, the county had to cut back again and again on services. Today it has a lone sheriff, no jail, and only a handful of employees. Many essential services are farmed out.[36]

The governments of Eastern Oregon's better-endowed counties have played a role in shaping the evolution of government in the state, but they have hardly been leaders. Oregon's early county governments were limited in scope: their primary responsibilities were local roads, law enforcement, courts, and tax collection. Occasionally they took an activist stance, as when Klamath County sought to use increased assessed valuations of timber stands to encourage owners to utilize them rather than holding them as long-term investments. Influential citizens in Crook County urged their county to follow the same course.[37]

With time the general quiescence changed. In response to the demands of growing populations and a more complex society less exclusively devoted to commodity exports, counties gradually came to provide a wide range of public services: public health, juvenile services, hospitals, nursing homes, airports, parks, libraries, land-use planning, urban renewal, public housing, senior services, and more. But this was more evident west of the Cascades than east, for that was where social change and population growth were most in evidence.

Counties originally served almost exclusively as agents of the state, their activities either authorized or mandated by state law. However, in 1958, an amendment to Oregon's constitution allowed counties to adopt "home rule" charters, and a 1973 state law granted all counties the power to exercise broad "home rule" authority. As a result, the national Advisory Commission on Intergovernmental Relations has identified Oregon's counties as having the highest degree of discretionary authority of those of any state in the nation. But this was not an area in which Eastern Oregon was a leader. Of all the counties east of the Cascades, only Umatilla adopted a home rule charter during the twentieth century—and that not until 1993. Of the seventeen Eastern Oregon counties, only eight are today governed by the state's now-dominant system of a board of commissioners made up of three to five elected members (usually with the aid of a hired administrator not unlike a city manager). The rest—Harney, Malheur, Grant, Crook, Wheeler, Baker, Morrow, Sherman, and Gilliam—still use their original system, a "county court" consisting of a county judge (the chief administrative officer) and two part-time commissioners.[38]

The changes in Eastern Oregon's governments over the years were shaped by the great distances and thinly spread population of the area, plus forces at work outside the region, rather than by the close relationship of people and land that shaped so much else in its society or by the economy based on commodity exports on which it long depended. The people-land nexus was at best a marginal factor in the area's quest for workable governments.

12
Healing Begins

On June 28, 1934, Congress passed the Taylor Grazing Act. Designed to bring "orderly use" to the nation's rangelands, the law required land in the public domain be classified and its disposal denied except when suitable for the purpose sought. As a result, 142 million acres spread across eleven western states were closed to homesteading. Much of the remaining land was marginal grazing land in poor shape. To provide a tool for managing this public range, the act provided for the establishment of districts with licensed livestock grazing and a positive program for managing the land in them. Less than a year later, Secretary of the Interior Harold L. Ickes signed an order creating the nation's first grazing district under the act, Oregon Grazing District 1 in Klamath County.[1]

The speed with which the district emerged under the Taylor Grazing Act was no accident. Henry Gerber and other ranchers in the area had formed the Southern Oregon Grazing Association in June 1933 and began working to have the so-called Gerber Block declared a grazing district even though it would have required special legislation from Congress—a requirement that had kept the number of grazing districts in the United States to a mere handful. As secretary of the grazing association, Gerber wrote to the Department of the Interior asking for establishment of a grazing district, to members of Congress arguing the need, and to assorted people he thought might be useful allies—including J. H. Favorite of the Interior's Division of Investigations, who encouraged Gerber, provided information on existing districts, and came to Klamath County to get a firsthand look at the land. Gerber even had Klamath Falls attorney Harold Merryman draft a bill that he hoped to have presented to Congress to make the Gerber Block grazing district a reality; Merryman did it for five dollars.[2]

Gerber's efforts were aimed not only at bringing improved management to area rangeland and providing a way to get rid of itinerant sheepmen whose flocks did considerable damage, but also at halting expansion of the Fremont National Forest into neighboring public rangeland, something proposed by Walter Pierce, by this time congressman for the Eastern Oregon district. Gerber and his associates were deeply suspicious of the Forest Service's capacity to manage the land. Members of their grazing association had been using the land for more than fifty years and knew it better than Forest Service officials new to the area or, worse, operating from a distance. Conditions varied from year to year, Gerber pointed out, and management should be sufficiently flexible to adjust to these variations. Cooperative management between federal officials and local landowners could bring this about; the authoritarian, one-size-fits-all approach of the Forest Service would not.[3]

With passage of the Taylor Grazing Act, things quickly changed. Gerber had not been looking for a district under the act—indeed, he seems to have been rather oblivious to Taylor's bill until after its passage—but when he read its text, he realized it offered a better way forward than continuing to seek a grazing district through special legislation. Still, his earlier efforts had led to the accumulation of information—and allies—and cleared the way for prompt action. Two days after passage of the act, the Geological Survey[4] informed Secretary Ickes that the Gerber Block was useful only for grazing and forage crops and should be made a grazing district. Ickes responded positively and in April 1935 signed orders creating Grazing Districts 1, 3, and 4 in Oregon. Appropriately, the Gerber Block was Grazing District Number 1, making it the first grazing district established under the Taylor Grazing Act.

Friction between the Forest Service and the Department of the Interior did not come to an end with passage of the act. Ferdinand A. Silcox, chief of the Forest Service, believed the act represented an abdication of federal authority and would siphon federal funds to locals. Officially, Forest Service employees had to obey the new law, but unofficially, opposition from Silcox on down led to what Harold K. Steen has called "open Forest Service retaliation." Authors of *The Western Range*, a six-hundred-page Forest Service report published in 1936, insisted the Forest Service was "the only well-equipped department for the administration of federally owned range." Ickes responded that the report was "a thinly veiled attack on a sister department." The Forest Service's attitude no doubt stemmed, in part, from a conviction that cattlemen—like the cut-and-run lumbermen

whose activities had done so much to bring about federal forest conservation activities—were interested only in self-aggrandizement and had
little concern for long-term public good and, in part, from a technocratic
hubris that assumed that only the specially trained were qualified to make
resource-use decisions in the public interest.[5]

For its part, what Stephen Dow Beckham has called the "deep-seated
antipathy of the local ranchers toward the U.S. Forest Service" helped shape
the course of subsequent events. Nothing illustrates their attitude better
than a letter in which the advisory committee for the district, made up
largely of area ranchers, urged "the Grazing Service [to] inform the Forest
Service that that they did not want them sticking their damn nose in Grazing District 1." Not long after, the Civilian Conservation Corps built a drift
fence along the boundary with the Fremont National Forest. The fence, the
CCC's Clyde S. Stahl reported, "will discontinue all drift [of cattle] from
the Fremont National Forest. Feed for the District consumed by drift stock
is a considerable loss to [grazing district] permittees." Aside from protecting their range, district members surely took pleasure in forcing Forest
Service permit holders to keep their cattle where they belonged.[6]

That Henry Gerber had been the leading figure in the fight for a grazing district was hardly surprising. In the 1880s his father and uncle had
acquired land in the area under the Swamp Land Act; in 1895 the father,
Louis, added a homestead claim and, in 1915, purchased twenty abandoned
or failed homesteads that he incorporated into his holdings. The Gerber
Ranch had become one of the largest, most profitable in Klamath County
and continued to be even after Louis Gerber sold the original homestead
and swampland properties to the government to make way for expansion
of the Klamath irrigation project (Gerber Reservoir built in 1924–1925 by
the Bureau of Reclamation now covers most of the land Gerber sold).[7]

Henry's roots in the area ran deep. Having a long-term commitment
to the land he inherited, he sought to manage rather than exploit it,
building fences so cattle could be rotated from one tract to another and
developing scattered water holes so they would not concentrate on small
tracts of the land near water while leaving other areas largely untouched.
Acquisition of a large ranch near Red Bluff, California, further reduced
pressure on the land by allowing cattle to be wintered in the south and
then brought to the Klamath ranges in mid-May. Gerber's concern for the
health of the range was behind both his opposition to itinerant sheepmen

and his cooperation with the CCC, whose crews from Camp Bonanza did extensive work on range improvement and other projects on the Gerber Block during the 1930s.[8]

Management of the Gerber Block slowly changed. Initially, its advisory committee, made up of ranchers, determined the allotments (Animal Unit Months, or AUMs) for landholders—which assured landless itinerant sheepherders would not get them. Assigned quantities were then overseen by the Department of the Interior's Grazing Division. Essentially, in this system of participatory control of public range, local ranchers surrendered self-interested freedom of action and empowered their representatives to work with federal officials in setting and enforcing allotments. Gradually the Grazing Division took on additional chores. It engaged in land classification studies, range surveys, and evaluation of the qualifications of livestock operators. In time the addition of wildlife representatives to advisory boards broadened concerns, and through the CCC it embarked on a number of projects for public recreation as well as range management. With these changes, the range came under increasingly programmed federal management, and the Gerber Block served as an important pioneer in this participatory range management. All in all, it was a classic example of the early-twentieth-century conservation movement that sought to bring wise use to the nation's natural resources or, as Gifford Pinchot put it, "the greatest good for the greatest number in the long run."[9]

At the beginning of the twenty-first century, the three granddaughters of Louis Gerber—all daughters of Henry—still retained and lived on ranchlands in the Gerber Block area. They continued to be key players in land management working with both the BLM and Forest Service. The Gerbers also implemented projects of their own, including fencing, thinning of timber stands, and wildlife habitat improvement projects—and cooperated with Oregon wildlife biologists in reintroducing and monitoring elk in the area. In 2000, historian Stephen Dow Beckham, who has studied the area more thoroughly than anyone, summed up the legacy of the Gerbers and the district they helped bring about: "It is clear that the Gerber Block is a healthier ecosystem today than it was seventy years ago."[10]

Not just larger operators like the Gerbers benefited from grazing districts and the Forest Service's allotment system. Elsworth Hopper had a small spread on the upper reaches of the Silvies, and on February 1, 1912, obtained an allotment there on which he ran twelve head of horses. A few years before, Hopper had decamped for Montana in search of grazing land, but soon returned. The quality of Montana's grasslands was greatly exaggerated, he reported; nowhere had he found grass "as good as Silvies Valley bunch grass for growing beef." By 1930 Hopper had expanded to fifty cattle and twelve horses, and in time was able to pass his little ranch—and the allotment that supported it—to his son. It seems doubtful that without the stability provided by the allotment his operation could have survived.[11]

The Taylor Grazing Act and the agencies administering it were less welcome elsewhere. In most places there was no threat of Forest Service control. Ranchers there, accustomed to running their own affairs and ill-prepared to share decision making with others, considered federal representatives a nuisance at best and an enemy at worst.

Mike Hanley, whose family ranched in the Jordan Valley area, remembers that before the Taylor Grazing Act much of southeastern Oregon had been "over-grazed to such an extent that the open range was almost a desert." Much of the damage had been done by flocks of wandering sheepherders, although cattlemen and huge herds of wild horses contributed. To cope with the problem, ranchers in the Jordan Valley area formed a grazing association. Ralph Stanford and other area ranchers campaigned to get the Taylor Grazing Act passed, and when it came they welcomed it, for it gave the association power to halt unbridled use of the range. Under the act, operators had to have a land base to qualify for a grazing allotment, and long-term ranchers were given priority over latecomers. At last the ranchers had a tool with which to get rid of itinerant sheepmen.

The honeymoon was short-lived. Cattlemen soon found the new order of allotments and other restrictions difficult to accept. The problem was exacerbated, according to Mike Hanley, by the shortage of professionally trained rangeland managers, so many of the government's hires were "former ranchers from the area who had failed to make it on their own. The active and successful ranchers resented being told how to run their business by men who had failed and . . . didn't know as much about the operations as those still in business." Bitter lawsuits and sometimes direct confrontations between ranchers and the BLM followed.[12]

Bigtime cattle ranchers were not the only ones disenchanted with the new order. Johnie "Cactus" Smyth, a lifelong resident of Harney County and descendant of some of its first white settlers, was a small-time operator like his father before him. As he later wrote, the Taylor Grazing Act meant "the end of free range. It was a terrible thing to happen to the small rancher in the West. It was even worse happening when it did, during hard times," for this was a decade of both drought and economic depression. "I was a small boy then, but listening to the old timers and acquiring a hatred for barbed wire fences, I also hated the Taylor Grazing Act and the Bureau of Land Management . . . and will hate it [sic] the rest of my life."[13] Smyth loved the old life on the open range and wanted it preserved. Rather than pursuing his ends through the courts, he resorted to direct action. Riding his horse home from Burns in 1948, he came across "a damned drift fence with no gate" that the BLM had installed to control cattle movement. "I dismounted and found a couple of large rocks and pounded the barbed wire between the rocks until it broke. Then I threw the wires back out of the way and rode through the gap."[14]

Smyth's love of the old life was unbounded. He recalled how he and some friends ate breakfast about daylight and saddled up to ride to Acty Mountain:

> We all lined up our horses and the cook took our picture just as the sun was coming up. . . . Taking off in a gallop from camp, up Sagehen Canyon with the sun in our faces, a bunch of antelope went running across in front of us, and a little further I could see ten head of mustangs lining out over a ridge. Green grass and wildflowers everywhere, talk about your Charlie Russell paintings. This would have been a good one. And if there is such a thing as heaven, that sight to me that morning was the kind of heaven I would want.[15]

He also fondly recalled riding the Steens high country: "Up on that high rocky tableland with my horse and the night sounds all around me I wasn't lonesome." The land he loved was company enough.[16]

Lacking a base that would allow him to receive a grazing allotment, Smyth either rented pasture for his cattle and horses or turned them loose on the range to run "on trespass." On one occasion Smyth rented pasture for thirty mares because "the darn BLM was always giving me and several others hell, and trespassing us as we ran horses on the range with no permits." He also had six head of cattle and "slipped them in on the [Malheur Wildlife] refuge side of the fence." Refuge manager "John Scharff never said anything, but I paid my bill for the 30 mares."

Smyth also recalled when the BLM rounded up "a bunch of horses at Andrews that they claimed were running on trespass. But hell, the horses were on their home range where they had been running most of their lives. . . . Anyway they had [my horse] Cortez in the corrals and after we had some hot arguments I paid the trespass fee and had Cortez hauled up to my uncle Rube Blair's field at the mouth of Wildhorse Canyon," where he died of old age "a year or two later." Later, Dimples, one of Smyth's favorites, "finally turned too old to ride and I did not want him to die in my sight, so I pensioned him—turning him out on the open range where he had been born." Years later his bones were found between Ekart Grade and the Catlow Valley Rim, "where the old horses used to hang out." Time and again Smyth resorted to trespass—sometimes paying fines when caught and sometimes not—it was his way of championing the old, pre-BLM world. To Smyth the horse was king, and he hoped it always would be. Late in life he wrote that he would like to find a place "where there is lots of open range, where I could run a couple hundred head of cattle and thirty or forty horses; where I'd be in the saddle on a good bridle horse, with a long rawhide reata until the day I die." People like Smyth left few records, but he was certainly not alone in his views.[17]

Available sources fail to make clear just how widespread—or how severe— environmental degradation was, but anecdotal evidence combined with localized scientific studies are more than adequate to show that damage extended over vast areas and, in places, was virtually irreversible. Perhaps cheatgrass is the best indicator of what was happening.

In 1941 pioneer environmentalist Aldo Leopold summed up the situation in his essay "Cheat Takes Over." Cheatgrass, an annual brome, was not present in 1901 when botanist P. B. Kennedy did fieldwork in northeastern Nevada, but by the 1940s it seemed everywhere in the vast terrain south from the Blues into Nevada, Idaho, and Utah. Leopold was succinct: "The spread was . . . so rapid as to escape recording; one simply woke up one fine spring to find the range dominated by a new weed." Of value for grazing only a few days each spring, dangerous later to grazing animals that risked having its sharp awns lodge in their lips and nostrils, poor at preventing erosion because of its shallow root systems, degrading to the value of wool in which its seeds became enmeshed, and an irritant to those walking through infested ranges without high-top footwear, cheatgrass was more than just a nuisance. To make matters worse, it was highly flammable and fueled many a devastating range fire; interspersed as it often was among sagebrush, it provided flash fuel to carry a wildfire from one sagebrush plant to another. It thus was responsible for the destruction of remnants of native grasses harbored from grazing under sagebrush and thereby reduced chances of range recovery. By the time Leopold wrote, this European invader seemed a fixture, though hardly a welcome one. As he put it, "The West has accepted cheat as a necessary evil, to be lived with until kingdom come."[18]

The rapid spread of cheatgrass came in large part because of omnipresent sheep husbandry. Cheatgrass awns readily stuck in the wool of sheep, which then spread the seeds wherever they went. Cattle could be carriers too. But the Bureau of Land Management (or one of its predecessor agencies) seems to have played a role as well. Eileen McVicker, born in 1927, grew up at the southern end of Steens Mountain. She later wrote,

> I don't remember any cheatgrass when I was a little girl. What
> I remember is that one year a man came with free seed and an
> offer to pay the ranchers to keep so many acres free of livestock
> for a year so the grass could get established. I always thought the
> man was from the Taylor Grazing Office, but we blamed them for
> everything, so I may have been wrong about that. . . . My dad and
> all the other ranchers around our area signed up for the program.
> . . . The cheatgrass got well established all right; it spread all over
> the country like wildfire.

McVicker summed up the situation neatly: "The whole experiment was a real disaster." She was not alone in her judgment. After a year, the agent who had induced her father to participate came back to inspect the plot and, returning with his ankles bleeding from the cheat's sharp awns, he decided planting cheatgrass "was a very bad idea." His awareness, McVicker noted, came a year too late, the offending grass was already established.[19]

Ubiquitous though it was, cheatgrass was not alone: there were other invaders too. With a bit of hyperbole, the Biological Survey's Vernon Bailey described the situation: "Where sheep have eaten everything but the lava rocks and killed out all the native plants, even sagebrush and cactus, various exotics have volunteered to clothe the nakedness of the soil and in many areas have bravely succeeded. . . . These plants are now the principal food for thousands of sheep." Of the invaders, cheatgrass was the most noticeable and in many ways most troublesome, while the sagebrush with which it was so often intermingled had more value than many realized. If they had been good forage plants, "they would have disappeared years ago," but sagebrush "shade the ground and hold the snow, build up humus, bind the soil, conceal sage grouse and young antelope, and provide choice fuel for the campfire." None of this could be said of cheatgrass.[20]

Cheatgrass provided the most obvious indicator of widespread environmental degradation, but a composite view of more localized developments yields corroborating evidence of the ongoing environmental disaster. In 1902 the United States Geological Survey's Israel C. Russell found northern Malheur County's Willow Creek, along which the Oregon Trail once ran, dry, and the gullying that had come in the wake of overgrazing (by "sheep especially") had resulted in sub-draining that left the bordering land where meadows had once flourished supporting only sagebrush. Continuing his investigations the following year, Russell found similar circumstances along Camp Creek, a tributary of the South Fork of Crooked River, and east of there in what he called Gilchrist Valley. On Camp Creek, not only the main stem of the creek but also tributaries had "the characteristics of a young stream-cut canyon." The vertical-walled main arroyo was sixty to one hundred feet wide and twenty-five feet deep; beyond the steam bank, the valley floor was either barren or sagebrush covered. The channels had not only sub-drained surrounding land, opening the way for deep-rooted plants like sagebrush to replace native grasses, but had also carried away water from surface meadows that once supplied a summer stream flow; now the year's water supply drained away in a few short days in spring.[21] Not all the Camp Creek drainage was channelized. Some upper portions still feature healthy meadows and meandering surface streams. They serve as reminders of what the downstream portions were like before overgrazing opened the door for catastrophic change.

Similar conditions developed along Bear Creek, a tributary of the South Fork to the west of Camp Creek. In a series of interviews conducted in 1972, former homesteaders recalled the changes along the creek. Frank Scott especially remembered increased channelization. In 1920, a swale some five feet deep and twenty-seven feet wide had run past his house; it could be easily driven across. By the 1970s the swale had become a gully forty-five feet wide and twenty-five feet deep, and a bridge was needed to cross it. George Pierce reported a similar development on Little Bear Creek, and Sumner Houston remembered when water ran "on top of the ground where the creeks are cut deep now." In Houston's eyes "Irish sheep herds ruined the country. They never owned a foot of land but ran their sheep everywhere." Others agreed the root cause was overgrazing, but they included cattle and horses (especially the huge herds of Bill Brown) among the culprits.

In addition to discussions on channelization, others focused on the invasion of sagebrush into meadows and grassland. Observers along Bear Creek also noted the expansion of sagebrush, but took even more notice of the increase in junipers. One reported that when her family came to the area in 1882, they had not needed to put up much hay for winter as the hills were covered with grass; there were scattered junipers on the hills, but stands were not thick. With overgrazing they proliferated; one had once been able enjoy scenic vistas from the hills, but in time trees grew so thick it was difficult to see out. More than distant views were lost. As Sumner Houston noted, junipers "take the moisture away, making it hard for the grass to grow." He professed not to know why they had taken over, but they certainly had; between 1976 and 2000, the acreage dominated by junipers increased some 500 percent.[22]

Indirect evidence sometimes speaks louder than direct. Flash floods struck Heppner, Ione, Arlington, Mitchell, Weston, Baker, and elsewhere in Eastern Oregon during the late nineteenth and early twentieth centuries. Topographic and metrological circumstances contributed, but with lands denuded and streams channelized, the floods were also a product of a badly deteriorated landscape. The Heppner flood of 1903 was the worst. One-sixth of the town's population was killed and 140 structures (all but three of Heppner's businesses) destroyed; the torrent then surged on downstream to wreak havoc in Ione and Lexington.[23] Pendleton was struck by a flash flood in 1882, Mitchell in 1884 and 1904 (and again in 1929 and 1956). Arlington was hit a day after the Heppner flood and again in 1907. The timing of these floods, coming as they did when range conditions were near their nadir, is suggestive. Marion Weatherford made the connection explicit: "These spouts have always caused damage to property. . . . In general they became progressively worse as the land was made more barren by grazing."[24]

Damage occurred even where not easily discernible. Traveling from Redmond to Sisters one crosses Deep Canyon, an unremarkable place where the keen-eyed may spot evidence of a range fire in the late 1940s but which otherwise appears quite timeless. Yet Kenneth Gordon, late professor of zoology at (then) Oregon State College, collected photos of the canyon over a period of thirty or more years. The changes were palpable. Although no erosion or channelizing was evident, junipers and sagebrush had proliferated, bunchgrasses declined, and weedy forbs increased. Like so much else, these changes could be traced to overgrazing (largely by sheep).

Sagebrush-bunchgrass steppe was not the only place degradation occurred. Early in the twentieth century, pioneer botanist William Cusick was planning a trip to "the highest Wallowas," but he was not sanguine. "The sheep are crowding in there now," he told a colleague, and "they say there is hardly a green thing left."[25] Improvement came slowly. Supreme Court Justice William O. Douglas loved the Wallowa Mountains. By midcentury he had a summer home in the Minam River valley and hiked and camped in the high country frequently. Douglas was a champion of conservation and aware of the impact of overgrazing in the Wallowas. The "high ridges once had grass, knee-high. Reckless sheepmen and easy going rangers of the Forest Service allowed them to be denuded by overgrazing. Now they are mostly coarse sand"—although, he admitted, some pioneering plants were beginning to take hold.

Douglas was a better observer than historian; he showed almost no awareness of the restoration efforts that had been under way in the Wallowas since Cusick's day or that the lush grasslands of the lower elevations had been badly degraded too. From 1907 to 1911, Arthur Sampson, often called the father of range management, conducted studies in the Wallowas. Overgrazing was intense; some ten thousand sheep roamed the high country up to four months every summer. Their impact was severe. In Tenderfoot Basin, one of the key areas Sampson studied, grazing had reduced nonforest biomass, leaving little litter on the ground to protect surface soil. Only 5 percent of the area was covered by green fescue, the natural climax plant in most nonforest subalpine areas of the range. A follow-up study in 1942 found 73 percent of the basin eroded and 20 percent of the surface covered with "gravelly erosion pavement."[26]

Although hardly scientific, the experience of Raymond Nelson illustrates what had happened in the Wallowa country. In 1985, searching for his grandfather's gravesite on Smith Mountain, he found the spot, but no gravestone. Thinking the original must have been stolen by vandals, Nelson had a substitute made. While installing the new marker, family members found the original buried some six inches down, covered by soil from erosion on the slope above. Largely unnoticed, environmental changes had been taking place.[27]

Not just cattlemen—and old gravesites—were affected by deteriorating conditions. Elk, pronghorn antelope, and bighorn sheep suffered too. Especially hard hit were bighorns; once found all across Eastern Oregon, by the 1920s they had all but vanished. Bighorns had little resistance to scabies, which domestic sheep brought with them. This mite-caused skin disease led to loss of coat (and thus ability to cope with adverse weather conditions), caused irritation that interfered with grazing and breeding, and reduced resistance to diseases. It was almost impossible to avoid. As domestic sheep grazed, mites would rub off onto sagebrush to await passing bighorns. In the winter of 1884–1885, W. F. Schnabel found dozens of bighorns dead in a place where grass was plentiful; they had clearly succumbed to disease—probably pneumonia (also introduced by domestic sheep), to which they had little resistance, especially when weakened by scabies. Burns Paiutes reported a handful of bighorns near Wagontire Mountain in 1898, and others spotted scattered remnants elsewhere, but ere long the once-widespread California subspecies was extinct in Oregon, and their Rocky Mountain counterparts were reduced to a handful holding on in the high Wallowas and along the Imnaha River; by 1945 they too were gone. Oregon banned the hunting of bighorns in 1911 and established Steens Mountain Game Refuge in 1915, but there and elsewhere it was too little too late. Even earlier, the leading Klamath Falls newspaper conceded bighorns and antelope were probably gone from Klamath County forever, but called for the protection of remaining game of all kinds, especially deer.[28]

Charles G. Hansen did a major ecological survey of Steens Mountain in the early 1950s and became a major advocate of reintroducing bighorns to the area—even though it was still being overgrazed by sheep and cattle. He helped bring in twenty of the California subspecies from British Columbia; they prospered in a large fenced enclosure on the north wall of Steens

Mountain. In time they were released and supplied stock for reintroductions to Hart Mountain and elsewhere; eventually, however, inbreeding led to a decline in fertility. Hansen, who had continued his work with bighorns, died in 1973 in a plane crash while scouting Canyonlands National Park for potential bighorn range, but his legacy remains on Steens Mountain and elsewhere.[29]

Elk and pronghorns, less susceptible to scabies than bighorns, suffered more from deteriorating range conditions than disease. But the results were similar: numbers fell and both disappeared from much of their earlier range. By the first decade of the twentieth century, George H. Cecil, supervisor of forest reserves in Oregon, was reporting that elk, formerly abundant in the Malheur National Forest, had dwindled to twenty there, and to thirteen on the Umatilla. In 1919 a small herd of elk still remained in the Fort Klamath area; their survival, a local newspaper suggested, would be dependent on sportsmen. They were soon gone—but not permanently; in 1951 the Klamath Falls *Herald and News* noted elk had made "a big comeback."[30]

Estimates of pronghorn numbers vary and are not particularly reliable, but the general trends are clear. In 1924 the Biological Survey's Stanley Jewett estimated only two thousand pronghorns remained—and on Hart Mountain only two hundred. Just how great the drop in pronghorn numbers had been is unclear. One authority claimed their numbers had never been great and demonstrated that sagebrush, never in short supply, was their primary food and thus they competed little with cattle and sheep for forage.[31]

Both the Biological Survey and Oregon Department of Wildlife began dreaming of a refuge to save the remnant. Attempts to create one in Guano Valley failed, according to some because local sheepmen destroyed antelope to save forage and water for their flocks. Recovery did not commence until 1931, when the Boone and Crockett Club of New York and the National Audubon Society provided funds that made it possible for federal authorities to establish the Charles Sheldon Wildlife Refuge (and then the adjacent Charles Sheldon Antelope Range, a total of a half million acres) in northern Nevada—one of the last large, reasonably intact examples of a sagebrush-steppe ecosystem in the Great Basin. The Hart Mountain National Antelope Refuge followed in 1936—and both areas were subsequently kept free of domestic livestock. Utilizing the two refuges for summer and winter range, the wide-ranging herds of pronghorns gradually increased and in time spilled over into neighboring areas. The presence of undisturbed stands of sagebrush helped, for as pioneering ecologist Olaus J. Murie demonstrated, sagebrush and other browse plants were vital to pronghorn survival. The drought years of the late 1950s hit the herds hard, reducing those on Hart Mountain from an estimated two thousand to a mere seven hundred, but the setback was temporary.[32]

The refuges were the result not only of the actions of federal and state wildlife managers; they also enjoyed considerable local support, especially from the Order of the Antelope. Founded in Lakeview in 1932, the organization had members well outside Lake County, including Supreme Court Justice William O. Douglas and noted ornithologist Stanley Jewett. A male fraternal-social organization noted for its annual gatherings at the "Blue Sky Hotel" on Hart Mountain, the order championed pronghorn restoration, lent support to the tiny refuge staff, and eventually even funded research projects.[33]

The situation with elk was different. Their increased number was a result not just of reduced grazing by sheep, but also of direct action. Led by state game warden William Finley—more noted for work with birds than big game animals—Oregon brought fresh stock to the Wallowas from Jackson Hole, Wyoming, and Yellowstone National Park—over the protests of the Wool Growers Association. Forty elk arrived in Joseph by train from Rigby, Idaho, to whence they had been trucked; with the aid of locals, the elk were then hauled forty miles by wagons to Billy Meadows, where they were kept in a large enclosed area until they acclimated and numbers began to rise. For the town of Joseph, the arrival of the elk was an occasion for celebration; school was let out and people flocked to the depot to welcome them. So successful were the transplants that in 1933 an open hunting season on elk was introduced, and by 1936 Vernon Bailey could write, "Their only danger now seems to lie in overstocking the range and starvation after the food supply is exhausted."[34]

Human intervention played another role in the recovery of elk in the Wallowas. First the Forest Service, then the Grazing Division and its successors began limiting grazing on lands there. In 1906 nearly 19,000 cattle and horses and 290,000 sheep grazed the Wallowa National Forest. Bit by bit, numbers were reduced until, in 2000, domestic sheep grazing was terminated altogether. Recovery of high country ranges accompanied the reductions—although in the 1980s, in the face of drought and a burgeoning elk population, there was a temporary reversal. Elsewhere, logging

William O. Douglas, Francis Lambert, and Stanley Jewett at the Blue Sky Hotel. Credit: Oregon Historical Society.

contributed to the rising numbers. In many parts of the Blue Mountains, the removal of old-growth Ponderosa pine led to increased growth of ground-level understory on which elk browsed. Better fed than they were in old-growth forests, elk prospered. Birth and survival rates rose, encouraging a spectacular increase in the number of elk.[35]

In the wheat country north of the Blues, it was a different story. As late as 1896, Israel Russell found little evidence of erosion in southeastern Washington's wheatlands. He reported, "The hilly portion of the plateau, . . . even the steepest slopes, in many instances having an inclination of from 20° to 30°, are without rill marks. . . . [Indeed] the surfaces of plowed hillsides are smooth and unscarred by gullies." The same must have been true on the Oregon side of the border, but based on what they had learned elsewhere, experts were soon warning the area's farmers about the dangers of erosion.[36]

Farmers showed little concern. Local loess deposits were remarkably deep, so even when sheet erosion occurred, good soil remained. By the same token, when water-worn rills began to appear, farmers could simply plow across them. The growth of larger gullies also failed to incite worry; unlike in the rangelands south of the Blues, channelization did not drain away subsurface water and thus increase soil aridity. The loess soil had remarkable water-holding capacity, so only when seasonal rainfall was low did crops decline; one could hardly blame small crops on declining soil fertility when the rains provided such a convenient alternate explanation. Local boosters pointed to Sicily, whose soils, they claimed, were similar to those of northeastern Oregon and the Palouse and had been cropped successfully for two thousand years without becoming unproductive. Under such circumstances, it was easy for agriculturists to lean on their "practical" knowledge and ignore scientists with their theoretical concerns.[37]

Change came in the 1930s. Production remained high, but economic depression and falling prices combined with the specter of the Dust Bowl to finally persuade wheat farmers they should change at least some of their ways. Farmers accepted a federal program of wheat purchases as a means of price support (even as they sometimes grumbled about its implementation). In Heppner, working with the federal Soil Conservation Service, in 1941 they created one of the nation's first soil conservation districts to bring improved farming practices to the area. The passing of the self-reliant pioneer generation and the success of scientists in developing and introducing better varieties of wheat surely helped too.[38]

The activities of the Soil Conservation Service, created in 1935; of New Deal financial incentives; and of soil and water conservation districts at the local level were central to the changes that followed.[39] Contour plowing, gully stabilization, new methods of tilling (especially on fallow lands), and other means of reducing erosion, together with a degree of crop rotation—all encouraged by the SCS and local conservation districts—combined to make agriculture in the wheat country more sustainable. But except for the Conservation Reserve Program, begun in the 1950s as part of the Soil Bank and formalized in 1985, none of this was designed to restore natural ecosystems.[40] Lands that had once been cloaked with the bunch grasses that supported the vast herds of horses of the Cayuse and their neighbors now supported—and would continue to support—other grasses, the grain crops of Euro-Americans.

Except on the wheatlands, which continued to be cropped year after year, the natural processes of succession were at work in the vegetative communities of Eastern Oregon. In timberlands they proceeded in ways most foresters had not foreseen, and realization of what was happening was slow in coming. But changes slowly became apparent, there and elsewhere. With grazing reduced in the Wallowas, a series of successional changes took place that slowly led to restoration of a green fescue climax cover over wide areas. Limited reseeding speeded the process in the Blues.[41]

The situation was more problematic on lowland ranges. Aldo Leopold, who should have known better, expected cheatgrass to dominate "until kingdom come," but where conditions allowed, areas dominated by cheatgrass were invaded by rabbitbrush, then sagebrush, and eventually junipers; elsewhere sagebrush was the climax community. Although cheat remains, it is not the near-universal presence it once was. But none of this made restoration of the range easier. Even in the absence of channelization, deep-rooting sagebrush and junipers utilized so much of the available moisture that more shallow-rooted forbs and grasses were relegated to scattered locations.[42]

Established in 1934, the Squaw Butte Range Experiment Station (now the Eastern Oregon Agricultural Research Center) in northern Harney County had a mission "to increase production and economic return of livestock and related industries."[43] Faced with this charge, researchers at the station struggled to find ways to reestablish healthy rangelands. Fenced areas free from cattle and sheep showed little if any greater recovery than areas carefully grazed. It appeared a stagnated climax community dominated by sagebrush had emerged, preventing the return of the old sagebrush-bunchgrass combination.

Clearly, something more than control of grazing was needed, but just what was difficult to determine. Researchers were hampered by a number of factors. They had no solid benchmarks to determine what the pre-grazing climax community had been. Anecdotal records could be decidedly misleading, shaped as they were by the observers' limitations of time, place, and outlook. Photographic evidence was sparse and artistic renderings, which usually showed scattered sagebrush rather than dense stands, may have reflected the artistic limitations of those rendering them more than reality on the ground. In addition, early accounts generalized about sagebrush, failing to distinguish the various subspecies, and thus making analysis more difficult. Moreover, in the face of the ongoing drought of the 1930s, many grasses failed to go to seed—and blooms and seeds were the

basic means of differentiating species. Not until 1937, when C. Leo Hitchcock developed his first key to northwestern grasses based on vegetative
parts, could researchers always be sure of what they were dealing with. As
a result of all this, personnel at the experiment station disagreed among
themselves on the nature of the original ecosystem. Clearly, overgrazing
had caused degradation of the range, but "we are not all in accord as to
what . . . [its original] condition was." Under such circumstances, it was
difficult to know how to proceed.[44]

Convinced by their research that the natural processes of succession
"will not bring more than slight improvement [to the range] in our lives,
nor in the lives of our sons and daughters," Squaw Butte personnel dedicated themselves to finding means of speeding improvement. As befitted
their institutional charge, they were not seeking to restore the original
ecosystem so much as to create a new one—however artificial—that would
protect the land while furnishing good grazing.[45]

They developed methods of removing sagebrush by plowing, "chain-
ing," and then spraying with herbicides. Planting with bunchgrass followed. Various species were tried, but crested wheatgrass, a native of the
Eurasian steppe, proved most satisfactory in most situations. It was easy to
plant, grew quickly, was well adapted to the climatic and soil conditions of
the Great Basin, and was long-lived, relatively fire resistant, and withstood
regulated grazing well. In view of these qualities, it was widely adopted by
ranchers, the Bureau of Land Management, and others. In its Vale project
alone, the BLM seeded 428,000 acres with this exotic.[46]

Yet crested wheatgrass had serious limitations—although, as late as
1941, a Department of Agriculture publication showed no awareness of
them.[47] Its seeds were so tiny they provided little food for seed-eating birds
and mammals, and it flourished so well that native grasses had difficulty
competing, let alone regaining dominance. A plantation-like monocul-
tural grassland emerged that was as artificial as the stagnant, sagebrush-
dominated community it had replaced. It helped heal badly wounded
land, but—unlike in the Gerber Block and the green fescue meadows of
the Wallowas—that land had hardly been restored. Indeed, perspectives
would change with time, and many land managers would come to consider
crested wheatgrass something less than a savior and something more of a
new problem to be tackled.

13
Conflicting Uses

Chief Tommy Thompson's life spanned the last century of the Columbia River's Celilo Falls. His uncle, Stocketly, had signed the 1855 treaty in which his band—together with other Tenino and Wasco bands—had given up most of their traditional territory, some ten million acres, and agreed, reluctantly, to remove to the 461,000-acre Warm Springs Reservation. But Teninos were decidedly independent, and not everyone opted to move. Some, including Thompson's family, had stayed near the falls, and it was there, where his ancestors "had always lived and fished," that the future chief was born.[1]

Chief Thompson and others from Wy'am (Celilo Village) frequently visited the scattered fishing camps along the river, developing friendships and participating in ceremonial dances and games of skill and chance. In turn, members of other bands visited Wy'am to trade roots, berries, and venison for dried salmon. Thompson recalled,

> If the visiting Indians did not have anything to trade for fish, the local people would either give them some of their own supply or . . . lend them the necessary equipment and permit them to catch all the fish they needed from one of the established fishing stations belonging to local people. In other words, all the Indians were friends and shared their food and the means for obtaining the same with those who were less fortunate.[2]

Thompson may have overglamorized conditions, but clearly the situation led to his gradual emergence as a respected spokesman for all mid-Columbia bands and a recognized champion of Indian fishing rights in the Northwest.

Upon Stocketly's death (about 1906), Tommy Thompson became chief of the little band by Celilo Falls; he remained so until his death in 1959 at the age of 104. The village may have been small, but its chief had important duties, assigning fishing sites to those who lacked ancestral rights to particular spots and determining the days and times fishing would be allowed. It was not an easy job. When Thompson was a boy, only about twenty-five Indians went out on the rocks to fish, but by 1942, some two hundred were fishing during the height of the summer run. Diminished runs and the loss of traditional sites at Kettle Falls and elsewhere were behind the increased presence. "In the old days," Thompson recalled, "there were [few] . . . controversies concerning who should use a particular fishing rock as there were plenty of such places for the number . . . who then fished." As chief, Thompson determined who should use unclaimed or unused spots and how the use of shared spots should be allocated—and "the decision by the chief was final and respected by all other Indians."[3]

In this role, Chief Thompson stepped forward as an opponent of The Dalles Dam. In 1946 he wrote Jasper Elliott, superintendent of the Warm Springs Reservation,

> So much trouble at hand, but I got to fight for freedom of
> what belongs to me and all Indians in the nation. . . . We were
> robbed out of everything. But, I am going to cling to my fishing
> industry—I am not quitting on [the state's] closed season, for I
> know I live here year round. All I got is salmon to live on. I don't
> want this dam project. . . . There are lots of other rivers, streams
> for dams.

William A. Brophy, commissioner of Indian Affairs, joined in opposing the dam, noting Celilo Falls was one of the few remaining Native fisheries on the Columbia.[4]

But opposition was in vain. Economic development, and faith in technology as a means of achieving it, trumped Native rights and concern for the natural environment. Construction of the dam proceeded, and Celilo Falls was soon buried beneath its impounded waters.

On April 20, 1956, Chief Thompson presided at the last annual festival to welcome the salmon home. Unable to get enough salmon at the falls because unseasonable weather delayed the run, the host Wy'am had to buy

Native fisheries at Celilo Falls, 1945. Credit: OSU Libraries Special Collections & Archives Research Center.

four hundred pounds in Portland. At the gathering Thompson gave an emotional speech. "Before it was over," one attendee recalled, "the vigorous old man was weeping." Thompson died in a rest home in Hood River three years later, two years after completion of the dam. On his final visit to Wy'am Thompson was "taken in darkness past the gleaming, whirring massiveness of The Dalles Dam . . . which in life he declined to look at." At his burial, historian Katrine Barber records, more than a thousand people came to pay their respects "to a leader known for his humor and the ferocity with which he defended Native fishing rights and opposed The Dalles Dam."[5]

Eventually the Wy'am and others would be given compensation for their lost fishing sites, but the episode was sad nonetheless. As Courtland Smith asked, "How can a group of people be compensated for [loss of] a renewable resource which is an intimate part of their culture?" To that question there are no easy answers.[6]

Dam building led to other controversies in the decades following World War II. In addition to Native fishing rights, public versus private power and the competing demands of sportfishermen and power companies were hotly contested. Under these circumstances, the Snake and Deschutes Rivers shared center stage with the Columbia in the 1950s.

New Deal faith in federal action and technocratic solutions undergirded the arguments of champions of The Dalles Dam. The success of Bonneville Dam—the first such on the river—and of the Rural Electrification Administration in bringing electricity to thousands of farmers emboldened supporters in their claims. The unpopularity of Portland's power companies helped in the battle for public support. Governor Julius L. Meier put the issue plainly: "Which shall it be, private development for the further enrichment of the coffers of the power trust, or public development for the benefit of the State of Oregon and its people?" Though never so succinct, Congressman Walter Pierce shared Meier's sentiments and used his considerable influence to further New Deal public power programs.[7]

By the 1950s the tide of public sentiment was turning. President Dwight Eisenhower favored decreasing federal financial responsibilities taken on under the New Deal. He argued that prosperity was better served by local enterprise than by federal expansion. Partnership in water-resource development was one facet of his prescription. He proposed that local power companies share costs and profits, thus reducing federal investment to developments beyond the means of local enterprise. He had considerable support. The heavy-handedness and inflexibility of the Bureau of Reclamation and the Army Corps of Engineers—the two dam-building agencies—added to the growing sentiment against federal power and irrigation projects.[8]

The idea became a concrete proposal when Secretary of the Interior Douglas McKay advanced a plan for joint federal-private cooperation in building a huge dam near where the John Day entered the Columbia. Champions of federal power were appalled, especially Oregon's newly elected Senator Richard L. Neuberger.[9] An unapologetic liberal who strongly supported New Deal power policies, Neuberger challenged Republican Congressman Sam Coon—who had introduced legislation to make the John Day Dam a public-private undertaking—to debates on the issue. Hardly equipped to take on the articulate and knowledgeable Neuberger, Coon nevertheless accepted the challenge. Debates followed in each of the ten largest towns in Coon's Second Congressional District:

Baker, Bend, Burns, Hood River, Klamath Falls, La Grande, Lakeview, The Dalles, Ontario, and Pendleton.[10]

Who won is open to question. Neuberger made some of the strongest points—such as when he pointed out that, under McKay's plan, private utilities would put up only $273 million dollars, yet would gain the right to power they could sell for $5 billion over fifty years—but Coon gained both press coverage and respect. When the next round of congressional elections rolled around in 1956, Coon did better than other Republican candidates in the state—but still lost. Coon's replacement, Democrat Al Ullman, was a strong supporter of public power. When construction of John Day Dam went ahead, it was as a federal-only project.[11]

Looming in the background during the Coon-Neuberger debates was a proposal for a federal dam in Snake River's Hells Canyon. In the 1940s, the Army Corps of Engineers had proposed construction of a 720-foot-high dam in the canyon as a step in expansion of the Bonneville Power Authority. The Idaho Power Company, fearing cheap federal power invading the area it dominated, raised concern in increasingly conservative Idaho about big government, outside interference, and the aloofness of government technocrats.[12]

Although Oregon would be less affected than Idaho, in the 1950s the Snake River high dam became a major issue in Eastern Oregon's politics. Ullman had run against Coon in 1954 as a supporter of the high dam, while Coon campaigned vigorously against it. Coon won handily, but when the two faced each other again in 1956, Ullman won, carrying all five Hells Canyon counties. How much of a role the Coon-Neuberger debates played in this turnaround is a matter of conjecture, but it seems to have been considerable. Although the popular Eisenhower was running for reelection in 1956, the normally Republican Second Congressional District elected Ullman (and would reelect him time and again). Ullman carried only four of the district's eighteen counties in 1954, but in 1956 carried nine. For his part, Eisenhower carried every county in the district except Union and Wallowa, two of those that would be most affected by the damming of Hells Canyon (and both of which he had carried in 1952). Be that as it may, Congress repeatedly turned down attempts to authorize a federal high dam. In the end, Idaho Power constructed three low dams. Neuberger and his allies may have won a victory when they defeated efforts to make the John Day Dam a federal-private undertaking, but they lost when they sought a federal dam in Hells Canyon. Their defeat on the Snake, rather than their victory at the John Day site, would shape politics and policies regarding electric power in the Northwest for years to come.[13]

Fish played only a secondary role in debates over the John Day and Hells Canyon dams. Although in time fish ladders would prove to be a less-than-satisfactory solution, their inclusion at the John Day facility eliminated anadromous fishes from most of the debate. The situation was different in Hells Canyon. Fish ladders were impractical on the high dam, but the federal proposal included hatcheries to maintain upstream runs; the Idaho Power Company's plan did not. The company gave lip service to maintaining salmon runs, but without any requirement to take active steps, the company long failed to deliver. The once-sizable runs on the Snake and its tributaries upstream from Idaho Power's dams to Salmon Falls came to an end. Still, all was not lost. Conservationists were able to muster sufficient support to block Nez Perce Dam, a proposed federal dam downstream from the Hells Canyon Complex that would have blocked salmon and steelhead from the Salmon and Grande Ronde Rivers, two of the last remaining tributaries of the Snake with significant runs.[14]

The situation regarding damming the Deschutes was different: fish were a central issue from the first. In the face of a projected shortfall in the Northwest's electric power supplies, in 1949 a regional consortium proposed building hydroelectric facilities in the narrow gorge of the Deschutes River west of Madras.[15] Within a year, Portland General Electric took over the project. Protests against the proposal erupted almost immediately. Wild and scenic, the Deschutes was an iconic sportfishing stream, especially noted for its world-class steelhead runs, while the lower Metolius, which would also be flooded by the project, boasted tumbling waters that challenged even the most experienced fly-fishermen. Moreover, opponents argued that damming the Deschutes would undermine efforts to maintain viable steelhead and salmon runs on the Columbia.

Sportsmen's organizations and the Oregon Department of Fish and Wildlife protested the plan. As one opponent put it, "Oregon Trout and everyone here in Central Oregon fought that dam tooth and nail. . . . The governor disapproved it, everyone disapproved it." But when Oregon denied a permit for the dams, PGE turned to federal authorities and received authorization.[16] The issue of federal versus state authority quickly emerged, and twelve western states added support as Oregon turned to the courts for redress, claiming the federal action violated Oregon's rights as a state. It was an odd coalition: arch-conservative states like Idaho and progressive Oregon, liberals like Wayne Morse and Richard Neuberger and conservatives like Robert Sawyer of the *Bend Bulletin* and Herb Lundy of the Portland *Oregonian*. But all was for naught. The case finally reached the United States Supreme Court, which ruled eight to one against the state. Only Justice William O. Douglas dissented.

PGE hastened construction before other roadblocks could be erected. Neuberger and others continued to seek ways to halt the project, but in the end they failed. In 1958 Pelton Dam was completed and the free-flowing Deschutes, like Tommy Thompson's Celilo fisheries, came to an end.[17]

In spite of the attention dams and rivers have received in environmental histories, they were not the object of the nation's first major nonforest conservation programs. Birds played that role.[18] Amateur naturalists, including young Theodore Roosevelt, long collected bird eggs and specimens, but gradually the practice came to be frowned upon. Portland-area resident William Finley, among others, turned to nature photography as a substitute. Finley, a founder of the Oregon Audubon Society and from 1906 its president, joined those campaigning against the plume trade, for which thousands of birds were killed during the late nineteenth century to supply feathers to adorn fashionable hats for women. Finley supported the Lacey Act of 1900, designed to halt market hunting and the millinery industry's feather trade—reputedly even snatching a plumed hat off a Portland prostitute and throwing it into the gutter. In 1904 William Dutcher, national president of the Audubon Society, hired Finley as a field naturalist and asked him to investigate plume hunting on Lower Klamath, Tule, and Malheur Lakes.[19]

Finley welcomed the assignment, for he realized that, like people, "Water-birds could not live without homes," and embarked on what would be his most lasting legacy, a campaign for waterfowl refuges.[20] In 1905, he and his boyhood friend and fellow photographer Herman T. Bohlman visited Klamath Basin. Their fieldwork, done largely on Lower Klamath and Tule Lakes, reflected conditions throughout the basin. Migratory waterfowl were numerous, but threats to their habitat manifest. Three years later the young naturalists visited Malheur Lake and found similar conditions there. When pioneer ornithologist Captain Charles Bendire had been stationed at Fort Harney in the 1870s, he had observed vast numbers of egrets (or as he called them, white herons), but by the time Finley and Bohlman arrived, egrets had largely vanished, victims of the plume trade; they spent days searching for the magnificent birds and found only two. Finley concluded there probably was not a single nesting pair in the entire area. Years later the slaughter still troubled local resident E. R. Jackman, who wrote, "I am not overly sentimental about wildlife, but this episode is sickening, revolting."[21]

Corrective steps were already under way when Finley and Bohlman visited Lower Klamath and Malheur Lakes. In 1905 Congress established the Bureau of Biological Survey and charged it with responsibility for the wildlife refuges President Roosevelt had been setting aside. When Finley and Bohlman reported their findings to the Oregon Audubon Society, progress in the state gained momentum. The society appealed to Roosevelt to set aside Malheur and Lower Klamath as refuges; Finley's publications in *Bird Lore* added force to the appeal; and the president, always something of a naturalist at heart, set aside by executive order both lakes as national wildlife refuges (the Malheur refuge also included nearby Mud and Harney Lakes). They were the largest refuges established to that time.[22]

Progress was hard to see. The draining of Lower Klamath's wetlands proceeded as the Bureau of Reclamation worked to create irrigated farmland. Fires, many deliberately set, burned through its peat and dense marshland vegetation. Meanwhile, water supplies for the Malheur refuge were proving inadequate to maintain its marshes. Ranchers had preexisting rights to water from the Silvies and Donner und Blitzen Rivers and diverted most of the inflow from these major sources of water for Malheur Lake; meanwhile irrigators hatched new schemes for diking and draining the lake to create yet more farmland. Many agreed with Bill Hanley, who loved waterfowl but, oblivious to the inherent inconsistency, considered both the marshlands and water running into Malheur Lake a waste; as manager of the old P Ranch, he set about draining and ditching along the Blitzen. In the face of such developments, the refuge seemed doomed to become a dry, windswept flat.[23]

Finley was appalled and, with the support of the American Nature Association, Stanley Jewett, and others, launched a campaign to save the refuges. He went on speaking tours, wrote articles for newspapers and magazines, and—most important—produced films to dramatize the situation. His widely circulated film, *Passing of the Marshlands*, showed Lower Klamath and Malheur in 1915 with the great flocks of birds and healthy marshlands that led to their being set aside, and juxtaposed these with scenes from 1930. A caption prefacing the section showing Lower Klamath declared, "The Reclamation Service turns Lower Klamath over to land promoters," and the caption showing the Malheur as the diversions grew read, "A dry lake, no birds, and a world of dust."[24] Ira Gabrielson joined in lamenting developments: "Those who knew the wonder of the Malheur," he wrote, "saw it steadily deteriorate. An . . . aquatic paradise became, successively, a shrinking withering lake, a stinking mud hole, and finally a barren waste." Moreover, "Destruction of Malheur and Lower Klamath, both sacrificed to the greed of man, seemed especially perfidious because they had supposedly been permanently reserved for the benefit of marsh-loving wildlife."[25]

Slowly things began to change. Tule Lake and Upper Klamath were set aside as refuges in 1928. Congress passed the Migratory Waterfowl Stamp Act in 1934, and followed in 1937 with the Pittman-Robertson Act, which levied an excise tax on arms and ammunition, both acts designed to generate funds for refuges and waterfowl management. For the Malheur, the signal events were the purchase, in 1935, of the sixty-five-thousand-acre P Ranch and, in 1940, the OO Ranch. These additions brought the water of the Blitzen and the marshlands west of Harney Lake under federal management. CCC camps were soon at work on the refuge and began the long process of turning Finley's old dream into reality. Ira Gabrielson noted that Finley and Jewett "had long worked to make this an effective wildlife refuge and watched in dismay as the diversion of water had destroyed and dried it up. No one was happier . . . when the purchase of the P Ranch by the Biological Survey made possible . . . restoration of the marsh."[26]

Stanley Jewett served as interim superintendent of Malheur until John Scharff took over in 1935, commencing four decades of leadership during which local support for the refuge slowly grew. A longtime rancher, Scharff could speak in terms that registered with Harney County residents, but his commitment to the refuge and the conservation of natural resources was unwavering. As he put it, "We need open spaces, running brooks, birds in the sky and shy forest creatures to maintain the spirit" of the American people. By the time he stepped down in 1971, Malheur refuge was secure as never before. Today the John Scharff Migratory Bird Festival is an annual event in the Harney Basin. Lower Klamath too has enjoyed a comeback, in part because the soils drained for farmland were not as fruitful as expected and soon suffered from alkali buildup. Re-flooding of various tracts followed.[27]

Conflict swirled around forests as well as rivers and wetlands. On the one hand, the 1950s and 1960s ushered in the Wilderness Act, setting aside vast areas in their pristine state. On the other hand, this was a time when foresters and politicians joined in a great push to "get out the cut," felling timber with a vengeance to meet the demands of explosive postwar economic growth and employment in timber towns.

During the Great Depression, the resulting conflict would have been hard to imagine. Lumber production had plummeted across Eastern Oregon. By 1929 it had dropped to 64 percent of capacity, and President Herbert Hoover directed that no Forest Service sales be made to support the new sawmills that places like Prineville had long sought. Yet, faced with financial exigencies, a few firms continued to cut as before. The Brooks-Scanlon and Shevlin-Hixon mills in Bend ran double shifts to generate funds to pay their carrying costs, and the Hines mill in Burns—near bankruptcy and lacking funds to pay the Forest Service for cutting rights—resorted to swapping title to their private timber to pay for timber cut on federal land.[28]

World War II brought an abrupt change. Demand for lumber skyrocketed. The boom in production that followed carried on into the 1950s. With private stands increasingly cut over, Forest Service sales played an increasing role, and logging was soon being pushed into mountainous, previously inaccessible terrain.

Timber on Indian lands also became a target, nowhere more dramatically than on the Klamath Reservation. In 1953 Congress passed House Concurrent Resolution 108, which established a policy of phasing out Indian reservations and ending the dependency sponsors of the bill thought they encouraged. The Klamaths were among those considered ready for termination.[29] But if the Klamath Reservation were eliminated and the tribe ceased to exist as a legal entity, what would happen to its rich forestlands, long a source of timber for area sawmills? Many expected termination to result in sale of reservation stands to private interests, thus generating funds for distribution among tribal members. For years the Indian Service had managed stands on the Klamath Reservation on a sustained-yield basis;[30] sale to private parties would allow lumbermen to cut at a much faster rate so as to take advantage of market conditions. Tribal leader Boyd J. Jackson saw it simply as a land and water grab by non-Indians that was pushed through Congress by heavy-handed pressure from Utah's Senator Arthur Watkins.[31]

Political as well as economic considerations joined the push for increased cuts. Under President Richard Nixon, Forest Service officials were pressured to increase timber sales as a way of supporting mill towns and the regional economies of which they were a part. Area leaders such as Oregon senators Wayne Morse and Mark Hatfield—both of whom otherwise had reasonable records on conservation matters—joined in the push. "Get out the cut," became the cry. To justify increased harvests, the Forest Service had to revise its estimates of sustainable levels. Critics decried the new figures as based on "politicized science," and in time studies at the University of Montana demonstrated that they were in fact grossly inflated. Clearly, the management of national forests was on a collision course with the environmental and wilderness movements that were growing across the land.[32]

More than politics was involved. Trained in silviculture, and convinced of the value of their craft, many foresters resented challenges to their expertise from people without technical training. In Eastern Oregon various roadside timber stands had been set aside in the 1920s to maintain the illusion of the primeval conditions tourists enjoyed. By the 1950s, some foresters had come to view these strips as examples of poorly managed, stagnant forests. Officials of the Deschutes National Forest decided to "improve" the spectacular Ponderosa pine strip northwest of Sisters by selectively logging to remove, dead, diseased, and stagnant trees and to thin the stand. But when they commenced marking trees for removal with telltale spray paint, protests erupted; this was timber country, and locals well knew what those blue markings meant; they could see that the cutting would be so heavy the forest corridor would be significantly changed. Concerned by the protests, but unbowed, forest officials continued with their work but moved the rest of their markings to the side of the trees away from the highway so they were not so readily evident. Cutting soon proceeded.[33]

Forest Service actions near Sisters rested on professional self-assurance. While working in the Modoc National Forest, south of Klamath Falls, I commented to a forester that it was nice that stands around two little lakes near where I was stationed had been set aside. He replied, not too patiently, that my view would be questioned by many in forestry circles. There were those who thought it better to cut such timber carefully, bringing active management to where the public could see—and thus learn to appreciate—"proper" forestry practices.

Meeting the demand for increased cut necessitated new roads. They were not always well placed. Dayton Hyde, a conservationist who ranched northeast of Klamath Falls, complained of new, badly located roads that sliced through ecosystems, interfering with wildlife migration routes and doing ecological damage. Part of the problem, he argued, was that the foresters who laid out the roads, for all their vaunted professional expertise, were too new to the area to appreciate the subtleties of the land with which they were dealing; "They are transferred in . . . then are transferred out, often before they have achieved an understanding of the land. Long after . . . I must live with those permanent changes they have wrought, suffer for their errors, I must live out my days as neighbor to this land, and what diminishes it diminishes me."[34]

Commodity forestry and the growing environmental movement were on a collision course, but not all the threats to the environmental movement came from old-guard foresters. There were also those who saw little value in preservationist efforts. In the summer of 1950 a major fire broke out on sparsely forested high ridges above Black Canyon Creek, a tributary of the South Fork of the John Day. Lacking sufficient manpower to fight the blaze, state officials ordered a nearby sawmill closed and drafted its workers as firefighters. While the fire crew on which I was working struggled day and night to halt the blaze's spread, the mill workers huddled on top of the ridge, where pack strings brought in food and supplies and airplanes dropped water. They refused to man the fire lines. "Let it burn," one of them said, "the timber is not worth saving." Such attitudes were not uncommon in Eastern Oregon's mill towns. Yet even though the Black Canyon's stands had little commercial worth, the area had other values that in time would result in it being set aside as the Black Canyon Wilderness Area.[35]

Wallowa County's Minam River provided a more widely heralded conflict between preservationists and the champions of commercial production. In an effort to increase timber harvests, the Forest Service proposed building a road up the Minam so stands along it could be logged. A storm of protest erupted. To Supreme Court Justice William O. Douglas, the area was almost sacrosanct; he waxed lyrical in describing it.[36] Locals were as appalled as Douglas at plans to log this de facto wilderness. Hearings on the Forest Service's plan, held in La Grande, brought forth a steady stream of people who testified against it. The Black Canyon area had been too remote, its timber too scraggly to be much loved, but the Minam was another matter. Even in La Grande, with its significant sawmill industry, the pristine watershed was much loved, its unsullied banks treasured by the fishermen who trod its shore. In the end, commodity forestry had to take a back seat. Oregon made it a part of its own wild and scenic rivers system and, at the urging of Senator Mark Hatfield, Congress in due course followed suit. Today the Minam is a Wild and Scenic River running through a dedicated wilderness area.[37]

The Wilderness Act, passed by Congress in 1964, was the result of forces at work well beyond the boundaries of Eastern Oregon. Nonetheless, it would have an immense effect within the region. The same could be said of the Multiple-Use Sustained Yield Timber Act of 1960, the Wild and Scenic Rivers Act of 1968, the Endangered Species Act of 1966 (revised 1973), the Land and Water Conservation Act of 1975, and the National Forest Management and Federal Land Policy and Management Acts of 1976. Each in its own way reflected the growing environmental movement and a weakening of the overweening influence of commodity production in the management of natural resources. Little of the voluminous literature on these acts and the movement leading up to them gives more than passing mention to Eastern Oregon.[38] Still, their impact on Eastern Oregon was tremendous; not only its forests, but other types of natural environment came to be treated as never before. Numerous wilderness areas and untamed rivers came to enjoy federal protection.

Joining in the movement, Oregon declared various waterways Blue Ribbon Trout Streams, a designation that led to special management efforts—but sometimes seemed a bit incongruous. Much of the Malheur was designated such a stream, but in all my many travels along it I am yet to see a fisherman; when asked, a waitress in Juntura once told me she fished the stream, but she did not seem to consider it anything special, it was simply the river in her backyard. Similarly, although much of the John

Hydraulic sluicing at the Ellis placer near Sumpter, 1901. Credit: Baker County Library District.

Day was designated a wild and scenic river, only a few river rafters used it (the Deschutes was far more popular). Jane Kirkpatrick, who with her husband built a home on the John Day's banks—at a place appropriately known as Starvation Point—showed little love for the river itself; the land and its challenges, not the river, were the focus of their shared consciousness.[39] Conflicts over resource use, and forests and waters in particular, would continue, but the parameters of the debates were changing and would continue to do so.

Gold mining also involved conflicting patterns of land use, but unlike forests, streams, and wetlands, it long engendered little debate. Initially, miners panned and used simple sluices and rockers, but environmentally destructive hydraulic mining gradually moved to the fore. These techniques were soon joined by dredge boats, the first of which apparently operated near Ontario in the late 1890s. Soon after, C. H. Timms built his first dredge, and forty years later was still operating in Grant County. One local recalls that, while operating near Bates, Timms's dredge ran twenty-four hours a day, seven days a week. It was profitable, for wages were only forty or forty-five cents per hour, and the only times the dredge stopped were to collect the gold and when it broke down. Timms was not alone. Porter and Company's dredge, at work near Granite, and the Sumpter Valley Dredge were both larger than that of Timms; each dredged—and devastated—more than a million feet of bottomland a year. And there were others working in the Sumpter and John Day areas as well.[40]

It has been claimed that gold dredging commenced in the Sumpter Valley about 1912, bringing both bucket-line dredges and "doodlebug" washing plants, but the local newspaper repeatedly reported activity before then. Still, the *City of Sumpter* appears to have been the first large dredge in the area and a mainstay of the community's economy—until much of the town burned in 1917. Many landowners and community leaders believed selling land for dredging, or at least selling dredging rights, brought greater economic benefits than farming. The Sumpter Valley Dredge Company continued operating along the Powder River for years, ceasing, by government order, only during World War II (gold mining being considered unessential to the war effort); it recommenced after the war, continuing until 1954, by which time commercial dredging was no longer profitable. During its operation, the *City of Sumpter* recovered more than $4.5 million in gold, and the valley as a whole reportedly yielded over ten million dollars.[41]

Hydraulic sluicing had been decidedly destructive, but dredges elevated damage to even higher levels. Dredges sat on boats floating on ponds of water, which they extended as they worked, filling in behind with tailings as they went. A dredge operating near the John Day basically created a new course for the river; as a contemporary put it, the river went where the dredge went. There and elsewhere dredges worked their way along like hungry beasts, eating up farmland and leaving gravel tailings in their wake. With dredge buckets capable of digging down more than twenty feet, miles of gravel tailings resulted, while good soil washed away. Once-productive agricultural land became virtually useless; a local rancher put it bluntly: "The land was ruined forever." Yet the *Grant County Journal* was forthright in its support of efforts to attract a dredge to the Prairie City area: "Installation of a dredge on these properties would mean much to the town." Only a few—most notably Walter Pierce—spoke out against dredging. In 1937 he wrote, "Oh, such a foolish plan, to dig up good alfalfa land for little yellow rocks, then bury them down in [Fort Knox] Kentucky!! What infernal foolishness!!"[42]

Pierce was the exception. When a Baker County farmer brought suit for damage done to his land by an upstream mining operation, the jury found the company not guilty.[43] Like the Baker County jury, and my own family, most seem to have accepted damage as an unfortunate side effect of an acceptable economic activity—or simply have been unaware of the harm being done. Eddie Styskel, a family friend, was part owner and general manager of the Western Dredging Company that operated near John Day from 1937 to 1942. It was the second largest gold dredge in the state. With seventy-two dredge buckets, it dug up some six thousand yards a day.[44] En route to California from John Day, Styskel would stop at our house in Redmond, the trunk of his Cadillac laden with gold he planned to sell at the federal mint in San Francisco. So heavy was his cargo, he reported, that the rear of his car was weighted down, thus directing its headlight beams into the eyes of drivers of oncoming cars; irritated by what they conceived to be his failure to dim his lights, drivers would flash their lights at him repeatedly. A gold nugget he gave me still sits attached to a pen set on my desk. Today I see it for what it is, a symbol of a destructive heritage of land use, but for years it was merely an interesting curiosity given to a young boy who had little concept of either its value or its symbolism.[45]

While debates surrounding land use swirled in white communities both east and west of the Cascades, residents of the Warm Springs Reservation engaged in debates of their own. In the 1880s, residents of the reservation were described by Sarah Winnemucca as "a self-supporting tribe, and very rich," but when the then-current superintendent commenced work there, he described them as "the poorest of Indians." Indeed, Winnemucca's "rich" was a relative term; residents of the hardscrabble reservation were hardly affluent by white standards—and, A. B. Meacham maintained, they were badly served by the government.[46]

Moreover, Wasco Chief Nelson Wallulatum noted, in the 1920s and 1930s the tribes "had very little communication with the outside world." Unlike on the Klamath Reservation, only one sale of tribal timber took place during the period, and even that fell through before harvest. Not until the late 1940s would sales of reservation timber be consummated and tribal timber begin to bring a modicum of wealth to the confederated tribes.[47]

Divisions between modernizers and those "loath to abandon their old habits" long troubled the reservation,[48] but in 1937 the Confederated

Tribes established themselves as a self-governing body under the Indian Reorganization (Wheeler-Howard) Act and soon began to pursue programs aimed at establishing self-sufficiency. How to proceed was open to question and often set tribal members against one another. Then, in 1942, the tribe established the Warm Springs Lumber Company to utilize reservation timber while providing employment to members; it was little debated. Other projects proved more divisive.[49]

The need for education was a central issue. Vernon Jackson, scion of a leading Wasco family, had been appointed secretary-treasurer and general manager of the tribal government in 1944. In that role he pushed for a $25,000 annual scholarship fund for college education for tribal members. Others feared off-reservation schooling would draw young people away from the reservation and tribal traditions. Jackson responded, "Of course we have to retain what is good of the old Indian traditions. . . . We can't let that die out. There has to be some identification for the Indian. We don't want our young people to grow up feeling the old Indian customs aren't worth a darn." Finally one of the older members of the council spoke up: "If this thing you call education is so good, why don't you get some of it yourself?" Jackson went home that night and asked his wife, "What would you think if I was to go to college?" She replied, "When, tomorrow?" At age thirty-nine, Jackson took a leave of absence from his tribal positions and enrolled at the University of Oregon, where he majored in business administration. He graduated in 1958, the first from his reservation to get a college degree, and returned to the reservation to put his new knowledge to work. He resumed his place as secretary-treasurer of the tribal council, a position he would hold until his untimely death in 1969. Kenneth Smith, a young Wasco from another leading reservation family, followed in Jackson's footsteps, getting his degree from Oregon in 1959 and returning to become accountant for the tribal council, a member of the council from 1965 to 1968, and, after Jackson's death, its secretary-treasurer and general manager, positions he continued to hold until 1981 when he resigned to become President Ronald Reagan's assistant secretary of the interior for Indian Affairs.[50]

Jackson and Smith led the tribe in economic revitalization and growth in cultural pride. Problems remained—and were exacerbated by periodic economic downturns in the national economy—but progress was substantial. They were not alone. Younger tribal members were moving into positions of authority and influence, especially on the tribal council. In addition to eight elected members, the council consisted of the hereditary chiefs of the reservation's constituent tribes, and there, as in so many things on the reservation, younger leadership was coming to the fore. Paiute Chief James Johnson died in 1945, Warm Springs (Tenino) Chief Johnnie Simtustus in 1954, and Wasco Chief Joe McCorkle in 1958. A new vibrancy was soon apparent that stood in sharp contrast to what was transpiring on the Klamath Reservation; it gained attention as far away as New York.[51]

Jackson and Smith worked hard to further the economic development of the reservation without giving up tribal sovereignty. Outside capital, they realized, could bring with it outside control—which smacked of the governmental paternalism that had long undermined Native American communities. Tribally owned enterprises could avoid that pitfall, but finding investment capital to bring them into being was challenging. Moreover, when money materialized—such as the $4 million settlement in 1957 for loss of tribal fishing rights at Celilo Falls—there was strong pressure to distribute it on a per capita basis to tribal members.

More than a distaste for paternalism lay behind the drive for self-sufficiency. At the University of Oregon, Jackson did a comparative study of the prices received by the Warm Springs and Klamath tribes for timber sold to outside mills with the prices paid for non-reservation timber in the same markets. The tribes, he found, had been grossly underpaid. To Jackson it seemed clear the tribes could do better milling their own timber.[52]

In the midst of all this, the Pelton Dam Complex opened the way for a more cooperative approach, in which both tribal and off-reservation interests could be served. The western ends of the Pelton and Round Butte Dams would rest on reservation land. Clearly, the Warm Springs tribes had both an interest and the right to a say in the projects.[53]

Once the Supreme Court ruled the federal government, not Oregon, had the power to grant permits for Pelton Dam, PGE moved swiftly ahead. Tribal Chairman Charles Jackson signed a fifty-year agreement with PGE guaranteeing an annual payment of at least $90,000 to the tribe. An overwhelming majority of tribal voters approved the agreement, and on May 1, 1956, the reservation's three tribal chiefs joined in breaking ground for the project.[54] Two years later Pelton Dam was dedicated. Further negotiations followed as the company moved toward building Round Butte Dam. Compensation to the Indians was increased to $220,000 a year, the tribe received the right to install a hydroelectric generator at the downstream reregulating dam, and tribal control over the impounded waters was guaranteed. This last item was a source of more controversy than might have been expected. The Treaty of 1855 had given the Indians the exclusive right to fish in waters bordering the reservation; however, for years the Oregon Department of Fish and Wildlife regulated fishing on the non-reservation side of the Deschutes and Metolius and allowed non-Indians to fish there. It sought to continue to do so, but before acceding to the dams' construction, the tribe insisted that fishing in the reservoirs behind them should be under its control. Many of us who had fished for years across from the reservation were surprised to learn we now had to acquire an angling license from the tribe to fish in the impoundments. Like many others, I had assumed the boundary line would run down the middle of the lakes behind the dams. In the end, not only had world-class fly-fishing waters been inundated, but the right of non-Indians to fish on stretches of the Deschutes and Metolius had become conditional. Opponents of the dams had lost on all fronts.

There was irony in all this. Although the Warm Springs tribes supported Chief Tommy Thompson in his struggle to prevent construction of The Dalles Dam in order to save Columbia River salmon runs and traditional fishing sites, they at the same time pushed for construction of the dams on the Deschutes. Objections from the Chinook Nation and others failed to dissuade them. Salmon runs on the Deschutes and Metolius, Warm Springs spokesmen argued, were too small to have much significance; what the tribe would gain—limited recognition of its treaty rights, increased respect for its sovereignty, and funds with which to advance tribal self-sufficiency—seemed more important than the loss of anadromous fish runs above the dams.[55]

Funds for development came not just from the dams. Beginning in 1948, timber sales to sawmills in Madras and Redmond brought in additional money—Redmond's Tite Knot sawmill, where I worked in 1951, depended heavily on Warm Springs timber—and settlement of the McQuinn Strip controversy added considerable timberland to the reservation, enabling the tribe to significantly increase sales.[56] In 1964 the tribe opened Kah-Nee-Ta Village, a hot springs resort, two years later it established Warm Springs Forest Products, which purchased a sawmill and the Jefferson Plywood Company (located at Warm Springs but owned off-reservation),[57] and in 1982 it exercised its right to install a generator at the reregulating dam downstream from the Pelton Complex and commenced the sale of hydropower. These developments increased income and on-reservation employment, allowing the tribe to support an increasing number of social and cultural services even as the on-reservation population grew. Problems remained and were exacerbated by the eventual closure of Warm Springs Forest Products' operations (and eventually even Kah-Nee-Tah Resort), but bit by bit the new path charted by Vernon Jackson and Ken Smith was transforming the reservation.[58]

14
In Nature's Realm

Throughout the nineteenth century, whites sought to harvest and extract commodities from Eastern Oregon. Bit by bit, this approach was joined by another, one that cherished noncommercial aspects of the region. Though not the first exemplar of this outlook, no one illustrated its emergence better than Samuel H. Boardman. Initially Boardman, Oregon's first state parks superintendent, set out to change, not preserve, Eastern Oregon. He had little appreciation, let alone love for it. But with time his views changed.

Boardman's work as an engineer brought him to Oregon in 1903; learning of the federal Umatilla irrigation project, he quit engineering to take up a homestead claim east of Arlington, where the town bearing his name now stands. The project was slow in reaching the area, but Boardman hung on and began planting trees—"the green coverage of the creator's awning"—as a "sheer defense against the burning sands" and recruited others to the cause. Water eventually came, but too late for Boardman. With their savings used up, his wife had left for a teaching job while he took work as an engineer when he could find it. In 1910 he joined the great throng of claim-seekers headed to Bend, no doubt hoping to find fresh opportunity there, but nothing seems to have come of the trek. Then, in 1919, he went to work for the State Highway Department and, in that position, began planting trees along highway rights-of-way in the arid stretches of northeastern Oregon.[1] Boardman's tree planting came to a halt when the Grange voiced opposition to such nonutilitarian use of public funds, however limited, but it had brought him to the attention of Robert W. Sawyer and others pushing for a state parks system. In 1929, when the Highway Commission finally was ready to appoint a "parks engineer," it turned to Boardman.[2]

Boardman later recalled, "I remember the first park I blocked off. Its boundaries on the east, the Cascade Range; on the north, the Columbia

River; on the south the California line . . . the west, our incomparable coastline. I knew it was impractical, but justifiable." Remembering his years fighting aridity and dust, he included nothing in Eastern Oregon. Such views were not Boardman's alone. Scenic tastes—shaped by eastern United States and European experience and a leisure class with sufficient time and money to commune with nature—had long run to green landscapes and rugged, snow-girt mountains. There had always been "desert rats" like C. E. S. Wood who cherished the wide-open aridity of Eastern Oregon, but they were a distinct minority, and also, though they left fewer records, working-class folk—especially those in nonurban settings—who were not unappreciative of the nonutilitarian values the outdoors had to offer. A new generation less influenced by upper-class values would gradually open Boardman's eyes to things worth saving east of the Cascades.[3]

John C. Merriam was central in this shift. Merriam was the first vertebrate paleontologist on the West Coast. Although much of his fame resulted from work at La Brea Tar Pits in Los Angeles, he did fieldwork at the John Day Fossil Beds in 1899 and at Oregon's Fossil Lake two years later.[4] To Merriam, paleontology and geology were more than sciences; they were windows on the evolving world and humankind's place in it. During the 1920s he became increasingly interested in scenery preservation. Nature appreciation, he wrote, "represents to me more than that interest, that solace, that joy, that stimulus which we receive from contact with nature"; he posited that it has an educational role that leads to better citizens. States, he argued, should join municipal and national bodies in furthering its protection.[5]

The view rang true to Boardman. He often compared parks to sermons and, after a trip to California, complained to the head of California's parks that his holdings were too developed:

> There seemed a strong tendency to intrude with man-made
> things among the God-given things that you originally obtained
> to conserve. . . . In park after park I observed the lines of the
> technician's blueprint intertwining and overpowering the living
> designs of the great Architect. Maybe the times call for this but it
> seems sacrilegious to me. To me a park is a pulpit. The more you
> keep it the way He made it, the closer you are to Him.[6]

Romantic, and hardly the stuff of hardheaded science, these views nonetheless undergirded his preservation efforts.

Boardman was intrigued when Merriam proposed that Oregon create a giant park extending roughly from Dayville to Kimberly, a park that
would include the magnificent fossil beds where Thomas Condon had pioneered and Merriam himself had worked, as well as the Indian pictographs
at Picture Gorge. Such a park was beyond the reach of Boardman, but in
1931 he arranged for purchase of 1,361 acres from the federal government
for $1.25 an acre. Additions followed. Boardman's view of what was worth
saving was clearly broadening.[7]

In the 1940s, pushed by Merriam, Sawyer, and Phil Brogan—rapidly
becoming Oregon's leading popularizer of geology—Boardman also
acquired a site at The Cove, located on Crooked River just above its confluence with the Deschutes. The deep canyon with massive rimrocks of
columnar basalt above, layered outcroppings of sedimentary rocks below,
and the tumbling waters of the river itself was a stunning acquisition,
one that revealed, as few other places did, the great Miocene lava flows
that had shaped the region. Boardman also acquired Painted Hills, near
Mitchell, another paleontological site; historical Battle Mountain State
Park on the northern edge of the Blue Mountains; and a park at pristine, glacier-formed Wallowa Lake, gateway to the rugged Wallowa high
country. Yet the focus of Boardman's activity continued to be west of the
Cascades, especially along the Pacific Coast, where costs were rising and
sites were in more imminent danger than those east of the Cascades.
When he retired in 1950, many of Eastern Oregon's best potential park
sites—Smith Rock, Picture Rock Pass, Succor Creek Canyon, Newberry
Crater, Fort Rock, Jordan Craters, the head of the Metolius—remained
outside the system. Still, Boardman had come a long way, and his views
were continuing to evolve. From retirement he urged Governor Douglas
McKay to make an area on Owyhee Reservoir a park; there is, he told
the governor, "only one volcanic scenic attraction superior to it in the
state . . . Crater lake."[8]

What happened to Sam Boardman was happening to others: across
America, appreciation of arid environments was growing. Joseph Wood
Krutch, a New York literary and theater critic, moved to Arizona in 1952,
fell in love with the desert, and launched a new career as its champion.

Krutch wrote about the issues of ecology, the southwestern desert environment, and the natural history of the Grand Canyon, and in the process won renown as a naturalist and conservationist. Krutch urged a simpler, more contemplative life in touch with the land. Although primarily about the Southwest, his writings found an audience in Eastern Oregon. So too did Walt Disney's movie *The Living Desert*, released in 1953 and shown widely.[9]

More was involved than the growing interest in arid lands that Krutch and Disney reflected and nurtured. As historian Earl Pomeroy argued in 1955, the West was never as different as popular views and many earlier historians had made it out to be. Settlers brought a full complement of cultural baggage and erected things that reflected and supported it—newspapers, schools, opera houses, churches, governmental institutions, and more.[10] The interpretation is fine as far as it goes, but incomplete. People gain their identity not just from received institutions, but also from the places they sink their roots. This is especially true in Eastern Oregon, where settlements tend to be small and scattered, their influence muted by their very newness, and where the land is too open, too demanding, and too dominant to be ignored.

From an early date, and to a degree less evident west of the Cascades, people in Eastern Oregon displayed a fascination with what had gone on in the area before their arrival. Not just Thomas Condon and Luther Cressman, but everyday people sought out evidence of the area's prehistory. Visitors gathered so many specimens at Fossil Lake it would have been stripped had it not been for winds that regularly blew away the playa's sands to reveal yet more remains. Residents of the John Day area searched for fossils and led Condon, Merriam, and others to the places where they could be found. Similarly, the town of Fossil got its name from exposed fossil-bearing strata within its boundaries. The founding generation set aside those beds as a place where the public could search for specimens; to this day it remains open to anyone with the strength and curiosity to labor on its slopes.[11] Responding to this longtime interest—and in an effort to educate so as to reduce the destructive practices of some collectors—in 1951 the Oregon Museum of Science and Industry launched a summer camp program on federal land near Clarno where students participated in directed digs. OMSI was based in Portland, and its camp drew people from well outside Eastern Oregon, but it is unlikely the program would have come into being if Eastern Oregonians had not had a long-term interest in the area's past and brought it to the attention of generations of scientists. The area was made a state park in 1965.

There were those who decried collectors as vandals, but the story is not so simple; they were not the "pothunters" of the Southwest who sought items for profit—the market for arrowheads and similar finds was too limited for that—nor were they people with desecration on their minds; the vast majority were simply looking for relics for themselves and, in the process, identifying with the area's pre-settlement past. At times they actually contributed to the advancement of scientific knowledge. In the 1930s, Luther Cressman learned of the wife of a former governor (probably Jay Bowerman) who journeyed by buckboard to the Burns area "to buy up for preservation authentic Indian wares from remnant Indian families."[12]

Carrol Howe reflected—and furthered—this interest in the area's past. As a teacher in Klamath County, Howe was appalled when one of his students, a Klamath, found some artifacts, but neither he nor Howe knew what they represented. Howe could find ample information on Southwestern and Great Plains cultures, but nothing on the Klamaths. He set about to find out. Turning to Cressman and other specialists for help, he began doing fieldwork. He was aided in his search by the draining of Lower Klamath Lake, which exposed vast stretches of light soil rich in artifacts and fossils. Howe's discoveries indicated Native American settlement in the basin, as at Fort Rock, was far older than was generally assumed, predating the eruption of Mount Mazama that created Crater Lake, and that some Pleistocene megafauna remained in the area much longer than had previously been realized—being present as recently as ten thousand years ago and thus overlapping human presence. His early books—*The Ancient Tribes of the Klamath Country* and *Ancient Modocs of California and Oregon*—as well as his finds, helped tie his student and others to the area's past.[13]

Phil Brogan's interests were similar, but he ranged more widely. Born in The Dalles, Brogan grew up on a ranch near Ashwood, attended the University of Oregon, and in 1923 was hired by Robert Sawyer as a science writer for the *Bend Bulletin*. He would remain with the paper for forty-four years, during which time he turned out a steady stream of articles on the history and geology of lands east of the Cascades. He also wrote a weekly feature for the *Oregonian*. In spite of an odd, truncated writing style, Brogan became widely popular and won numerous awards. His *East of the Cascades* and Howe's *Ancient Tribes of the Klamath Country*, both published in the mid-1960s, sold well and went through repeated printings. For decades he publicized the Newberry Crater complex and campaigned for its preservation. Finally set aside in 1990, seven years after Brogan's death, Newberry National Volcanic Monument stands as a monument to his long career.[14]

Brogan did more than write. He did extensive fieldwork, interviewed many old-timers, and called finds to the attention of Cressman and other specialists, often leading them to sites in person. Cressman valued such help. "Cooperation between different fields of knowledge had always been a cardinal point in my teaching and research," he later recalled, "The help . . . people gave, from the simplest ranch hand reporting a site to the internationally known scientists contributing their expertise toward a problem's solution, was basic to my . . . success." His autobiography abounds in examples of amateurs leading him to new sites. Helen Marie Worthington and Arnold Shotwell were other professionals who recognized the value of such support. And well they should have; as Carrol Howe observed, "I'll bet you 90 percent of the information archaeologists have accumulated has been a result of some amateur somewhere."[15]

Not everyone was as appreciative. Howe put it bluntly: many "archeologists probably would consider me as a vandal for having salvaged all this stuff." He worked cooperatively with the Forest Service and National Park Service, but found the Bureau of Land Management "so nasty in their description of anyone who hunts stuff or preserves it" that many collectors "who have important information . . . [won't] give them the time of day."[16] Eventually even that agency came around. Collecting for commercial purposes is banned at Fossil Lake, which is under BLM management, but private collecting is now allowed.

Rockhounds represent a different side of the broadening interest in the Eastern Oregon scene. From an early date, one Jefferson County resident recalls, "Every child and many adults collected what they called 'pretty rocks' as a hobby. They were almost everywhere."[17] Over time, enthusiasm for collecting grew, attracting people from well outside the region. Rasmus Petersen was the most noted of the growing body of collectors. A Danish immigrant who settled in Central Oregon in the early 1900s, Petersen began collecting obsidian, thunder eggs, agates, crystals, and other specimens. Using his finds, in 1935 he began constructing a rock garden featuring miniature castles, churches, and other buildings and monuments on his farm near Redmond; year by year he built ever more elaborate additions, including bridges, water features, and landscaped picnic facilities. In time he also added a small museum. Petersen worked on the project until his death in 1952.[18]

Petersen Rock Garden became an offbeat tourist attraction, but its larger importance stems from the impetus it gave to rockhounding. By the 1960s the recreational collecting of rocks and mineral specimens was growing apace and drew not only locals but also people from well outside the region. There were at least fourteen rockhound clubs in the state, many of which made annual treks to collecting sites. Reflecting the rising interest, in 1965 the thunder egg was declared Oregon's state rock. The area around Madras and Prineville offered some of the best collecting, but sites were also found near Mitchell, Burns, Lakeview, and Jordan Valley. Many were on land administered by the Forest Service or Bureau of Land Management, but privately owned locations were opened too—for a price. The Richardson Rock Ranch near Madras became a popular location. In 2012 its owner noted with pride that the rock shop on the site had not been closed a day in the thirty-eight years since the family turned from cattle ranching to the rockhound business.[19]

Rockhounding slowly changed, in part because many sites passed into private ownership and were closed to public access and in part because some sites were so picked over that quality finds became infrequent. Whereas Glass Butte, located between Bend and Burns, had once been "covered with obsidian" of various colors, by the early twenty-first century its more accessible areas were nearly picked clean in spite of limits placed on collectors by the BLM; by then collecting often required considerable digging. After his death, Rasmus Petersen's rock garden fell into decay, but it and the rockhounds it helped inspire had played a role—however intangible—in broadening the connection of Eastern Oregonians to their lands.[20]

So too did the recreational gold panning that came in the wake of rockhounding, and rock climbers lured by the challenges of Smith Rock, especially after it finally became a state park in 1960. Smith Rock, aficionados claim, was where sport climbing was introduced to the United States.[21] Thus, with decades of drought, depression, and war behind them, a variety of forces, not just Brogan and Howe, were broadening Eastern Oregonians and increasingly turning their attention to their surroundings.

As views of the physical environment took on more appreciative forms, so too did those regarding flora and fauna. Naturalists had collected botanical specimens in Eastern Oregon since the days of Lewis and Clark, and some—such as William Cusick and Louis F. Henderson—were major contributors to herbaria.[22] By the 1920s the Oregon Roadside Council was campaigning for the protection of roadside beauty, but their focus was west of the Cascades, where flora was more lush and spectacular plants like rhododendrons were being grubbed up for home gardens. East of the Cascades Robert Sawyer, Sam Boardman, and others pushed for the protection of timber along highways, but public attention largely focused on other issues. Still, action was not entirely absent. In 1945 Boardman acquired the Redmond-Bend Juniper Wayside to protect stands of western juniper between the two towns. It was an odd addition to the state park system, for the wayside consisted of several separated tracts along Highway 97, with no public access to any except for one small, unmarked dirt road. Boardman also toyed with the idea of an Artemisia Wayside near Painted Hills State Park, but protecting sagebrush, even an impressive stand like the one Boardman was eyeing, generated little enthusiasm. The idea went nowhere.[23]

Interest in Oregon's flora was growing, encouraged by publication of Helen Gilkey's *Handbook of Northwest Flowering Plants* (1936) and Morton E. Peck's *Manual of the Higher Plants of Oregon* (1940). Charles G. Hansen's doctoral dissertation (1956) was the first complete study of Steens Mountain's flora—and perhaps the most thorough for any area east of the Cascades. Yet, when the Native Plant Society of Oregon, formed in Portland in 1961, spun off thirteen chapters around the state, the one in Eastern Oregon—the High Desert Native Plant Society—struggled to survive. In 1967 John Scharff included an illustrated section on the flora of Steens Mountain in the work he coauthored with E. R. Jackman, but birds, not plants continued to be the main focus of visitors to Malheur Wildlife Refuge, as were geology, animals, and scenery for those visiting Steens Mountain proper.[24]

There were limits to the broadening in the attitudes of Eastern Oregonians toward their environment, but they applied less to animals than

Controlling "the plague": jackrabbit drive near Burns, 1912. Credit: OSU Libraries Special Collections & Archives Research Center.

to plants. Questions surrounding game management continued to draw attention, but new issues and fresh concerns emerged during and after the 1950s. Until then, efforts at predator control through government trappers, bounties, and the use of poisons on "undesirable" species dominated. When Floyd Capps died in 1946, his obituary in the Burns newspaper noted he had been a well-known airplane coyote hunter.[25] Only financial limitations kept such efforts within bounds. Typically, in 1929 a government trapper announced he was declaring war on the lone remaining wolf in Klamath County's Sycan area. Ere long wolves had been eliminated not only there, but throughout the state—as were grizzly bears.[26] Rabbit drives—seeking to reduce crop damage done by the exploding population of jackrabbits as the number of predators fell and new sources of food (read alfalfa and clover) appeared on irrigated farmland—became common.[27] Aside from attempts at restoring healthy populations of elk, bighorn sheep, and prong-horns, most game animals got little attention. Officials established closed seasons, limits on take, and refuges (actually merely areas closed to hunt-ing), but beyond that the animals essentially managed themselves. And the take by hunters was heavy. Near the beginning of the twentieth century, George Cecil estimated there were one hundred thousand deer in the Blue Mountain Forest Reserve, and hunters took fourteen thousand annually.[28]

Refuges provided breeding grounds and rest stops for migratory waterfowl, and their self-evident value contributed to the idea that big game would benefit from similar sanctuaries. Those established were only marginally successful. Driving to Newberry Crater in the 1940s and 1950s, my parents and I often saw large herds of mule deer gathered on the refuge south of the road; away from there, deer were scarce. The animals had learned where they were safe and gathered there, even though browse on the protected area was stripped while elsewhere food was abundant. Moreover, thanks to years of rules against shooting does, the ratio of males to females was unbalanced, keeping annual production of fawns low. Under such circumstances the State Game Commission began to look for new, better ways of managing deer.

The commission's concern was well founded. Sport hunting burgeoned after World War II, and Central Oregon became a prime destination for hordes of hunters from Portland and the Willamette Valley. A day or two before the opening of deer season, the highway through Sisters was crowded with the vehicles of hunters headed to favored areas south and east of Bend. They were a major source of income for motels, restaurants, and other area businesses. Locals hunted too. Students at Sisters High School, where I was teaching at the time, received an excused tardy if they shot a deer before class; staying and properly caring for a kill was deemed more important than getting to school on time. The increase in the number of deer hunters and their annual take made reexamination of management practices timely.[29]

A public outcry erupted when game managers proposed doing away with closed areas, as a way to disperse herds, and allowing the hunting of does to help correct the sex ratio. To many, the utility of refuges seemed self-evident, and the idea of shooting does generally repugnant. State law had banned shooting does since 1923; the sport hunter's ethic had long held against it, and Walt Disney's extraordinarily popular movie *Bambi*, released in 1942, had spread the idea well beyond hunters' circles. The general anti-hunting message of the film—in which hunters were depicted as little more than bloodthirsty, armed thugs—may not have won many converts in Eastern Oregon, where too many hunted for the depiction to ring true even to the area's nonhunters, but the emotional depiction of poor Bambi and her mother surely had a subliminal influence on reactions to the proposed changes.[30] The game commission launched a major campaign to win people over; it held public meetings, provided speakers, and sent explanatory pieces to newspapers. From this distance, it is difficult to appreciate the extent and fervor of the debates, but a national commentator caught the importance of deer hunting in Oregon when he observed of Douglas McKay, President Eisenhower's appointee as secretary of the interior, that the biggest decisions he had to make while Oregon's governor "were whether to proclaim daylight saving time (thus annoying farmers) and whether to ban hunting when forests were tinder dry (thus annoying Oregon's legions of deerslayers)."[31] Surely intended as a put-down, the comment revealed more than its author probably realized. But in the end, in spite of the emotional and political pitfalls surrounding the new game regulations, the commission prevailed.

Attention to the policies surrounding deer hunting soon waned. Devastating drought commenced in the 1970s, and winterkill rose sharply as poorly conditioned animals were unable to find sufficient food to make it through the winter months. Changing land-use patterns reduced the browse available, while new roads and developments fragmented what range remained. In 1961, the peak year, 265,326 hunters harvested 163,939 mule deer, a 68 percent success rate—staggering figures for an area as lightly populated as Eastern Oregon. Thereafter the success rate fell, but the number of hunters stayed high. A temporary rebound in take occurred from 1977 to 1981, but after that the downward trend resumed, continuing into the twenty-first century. In the process, deer hunting gradually ceased to be a major concern other than for wildlife managers and the hunters themselves.

While deer declined as a public issue in the 1970s, other creatures took their place. Sage grouse were one of the first—although concern could hardly be described as widespread. These large gallinaceous birds, with their impressive displays during breeding season, were a popular sight on the Malheur refuge, but for whatever reason their numbers became small. In 1935 Stanley Jewett noted, "Twenty odd years ago they were found by tens of thousands on all the bench lands of the Steens Mountains and adjacent sage-covered hills. In 1920 some disaster, possibly Tularemia, killed them off and they never fully recovered." Nor have they to this day. Jewett's guess that the culprit was tularemia may well have been correct; sage grouse are susceptible to the disease, and at the time of the crash tularemia had been introduced into Eastern Oregon in an effort to reduce the hordes of crop-ravaging jackrabbits. The crash may have been triggered by a population density that made transmission of the disease easy. However, the number of sage grouse had apparently begun to fall even before the 1920s; the causes of sage grouse decline remain unclear. Currently popular explanations—the loss of sagebrush habitat in particular—seem questionable; on Steens Mountain in the 1920s overgrazing seems to have led to an expansion of sagebrush, not its disappearance, and, in any case, if they suffered from a decline in sagebrush that would hardly explain the suddenness of the crash Jewett reported. The rush of homesteaders into sage grouse country on the eve of the population drop-off may have been a factor; many destitute settlers depended on them as a food source, but sport hunting can hardly be blamed; sage grouse were game birds, but—barely edible—they never became a popular one.[32]

Other game birds earned awareness in less mysterious ways. Ring-necked pheasants, an East Asian native imported and released in Western Oregon in 1881 and 1882, were introduced east of the Cascades later. They prospered, especially in the Columbia and Klamath Basins and in northern Malheur County, competing aggressively with sharp-tailed grouse and taking over much of their range. The shift was little noted and hardly regretted—sharp-tails were little valued, while pheasants became a favorite game bird.[33] But like all creatures, the fortunes of pheasants were affected by changes in their habitat. As farms grew larger and more efficient, the weedy fencerows and odd corners of small farms where pheasants flourished slowly disappeared. The Soil Bank, which went into operation in 1958 and continued to 1963, brought a resurgence, but when soaring international grain prices led to the Soil Bank's cancellation, pheasants struggled until the Conservation Reserve Program (CRP) commenced in 1985, taking large acreages out of production and sparking a rebound—although the effect was less than it might have been, for much of the retired cropland was planted to crested wheatgrass which, with its tiny seeds, provided cover but little food.

Other Old World introductions followed the pheasant: the gray or Hungarian partridge in 1907 and the chukar partridge in 1951. "Huns" never became a major game bird, but chukars, one of the few birds that do well on a diet of cheatgrass seeds, flourished—and with less effect on native species than pheasants. Oregon established an open season on chukars in 1956. Adapted to the rugged canyons and escarpments of Eastern Oregon, they were a welcome addition and soon became the most-harvested game bird in the state (between 1956 and 1967, more than 1.2 million were taken). Juntura was among the communities benefiting; chukars attracted hunters (and their money) to the isolated little community and spurred the building of Chukar Park Campground to serve them.[34]

However slowly, views of wildlife took on less utilitarian aspects. As the environmental revolution ushered in by Rachel Carson and others spread across the land, its impact was felt in Eastern Oregon. The Endangered Species Act (ESA), revised in 1973 to include not just species but individual populations, drove events. Decades before, John C. Fremont had recognized the endorheic nature of the Great Basin, but the implications of his insight were slow to be recognized. During the Paiute war, troops took time to go fishing near the Nevada-Oregon border and on occasion happened upon Native fishing weirs and equipment. No one seems to have asked how fish got to these isolated desert locations.[35]

In the late Pleistocene the basin had been well-watered, its huge lakes—Chewaucan, Lahontan, Modoc, Bonneville, and others—frequently connected both to one another and to the sea by way of the Snake, Pit, Deschutes, and Klamath Rivers. As the climate grew drier, water levels fell, the lakes shrank, and remnant aquatic populations, now separated from one another, gradually diverged. The ranges of these relict populations were severely limited; one species of chub is found only in the arsenic-laden waters of little Borax Lake, isolated near the Oregon-Nevada border.[36] Falling water levels left even the upper Deschutes and Klamath Rivers, although outside the Great Basin proper, sufficiently isolated by falls and distance to support the rise of genetically distinct populations. Under the circumstances, it is hardly surprising that nine of Oregon's ten fishes designated as endangered or threatened under the ESA are from east of the Cascades.[37] For years protecting these fishes was not a concern. Speaking of the Warner Lake sucker, William Kittredge remembered it as "a creature we would not have valued at all, slippery and useless, and thus valueless." Many another species was also dismissed as "trash" fish, a pejorative term applied to anything not a game fish—and in much of Eastern Oregon this meant anything not a trout.[38]

Trout were another matter altogether. By the late nineteenth century, sportsmen were increasingly concerned over declining stocks. In the

1870s the federal government established its first salmon and trout hatcheries on northern California's pristine McCloud River. Oregon followed. The earliest hatchery in Eastern Oregon (and one of the first in the state) was built on the Wallowa River near Minam after the state appropriated $15,000 in 1905. In 1907 it was moved upstream to take advantage of a dam formed during railroad building; when the dam became a problem, the hatchery was moved to a site near Enterprise. For years, fish from the hatchery stocked lakes and streams in the Wallowas and eastern Blue Mountains—and occasionally farther afield. An egg-collecting station began operating in Klamath County in 1913, and a year later Dallas Lore Sharp joined state officials and the Harney County Rod and Gun Club in bringing a truckload of rainbow fingerlings from a hatchery near The Dalles for release near Burns. The community turned out to welcome the new arrivals, but nearly all had died in transit; the community tried again the following year, bringing in eyed eggs that were then hatched in local facilities under the direction of a state employee "to start it off right." Just how successful this second effort was is not clear. But there were spots in Eastern Oregon where fishing was better than one might have anticipated. William Kittredge recalls that, in the 1940s, "some Sundays in the summer my family would spread blankets by Deep Creek or Twenty-Mile Creek [in the Warner Valley], and even us kids would catch all the rainbow trout we could stand." Still, public concern for fisheries—and a demand for more hatcheries—was growing; by themselves, newly imposed fishing regulations were proving an inadequate solution.[39]

After building dams on the Klamath River, the California-Oregon Power Company (COPCO) added fish ladders and opened hatcheries to ameliorate their impact. Other hatcheries followed, funded largely by newly required fishing license fees. In time there would be several hatcheries in Eastern Oregon—but none in the huge southeastern quadrant, which was served largely from the state's hatchery near Fort Klamath, officially established in 1929 and sometimes called the area's first—although a decade earlier a state game official said the whole state depended on its Spencer Creek (i.e., Klamath) hatchery, and in 1921 the Klamath Falls *Evening Herald* announced that a hatchery on Crooked Creek had doubled its capacity. There had been others in operation as well. In 1911 Oregon raised and released 323,700 trout, a year later more than 4.6 million; and the number kept rising: by 1937 it stood at 31.6 million. By 1929 Fish and

Game was making a list of stocked streams available; that year it sent a crew to Diamond Lake that collected over a million eggs.[40] Subsequent plantings in the Blitzen, Silvies, and elsewhere (reportedly carried on until 1993) were more successful than the initial effort by Sharp and his cohorts. In place after place, this affected the genetic purity of the relict redband and Lahontan cutthroat strains, but modern systems of DNA analysis eventually provided tools to evaluate the situation and develop effective management strategies. Knowledge and concerns had clearly broadened.[41]

Even after establishment of the Fort Klamath hatchery, the state did little planting in the Great Basin, concentrating on places like Paulina, East, and Diamond Lakes instead. All three became superb fisheries, especially Diamond Lake, located just west of the Cascade summit but more tied to Eastern than Western Oregon as a result of the ease of access from the former and long-standing ties to Bend and Central Oregon. For these lakes fisheries, experts sought out fast-growing strains, which often meant rainbows from northern Idaho and Montana, rather than local varieties. To further serve sportsmen, the agency also planted brook and brown trout in waters suited for them—an approach that severely affected the rainbow population in the Deschutes below Bend, for so much water was diverted for irrigation that the river became warmer in summer months, thus favoring browns over rainbows.[42]

To many people, the species that were enumerated as endangered or threatened were little more than biological curiosities, but for people directly affected it was a different story. In 1992 the Snake River Chinook salmon, hard hit by Idaho Power's Hells Canyon dams, was listed as endangered. Wallowa County ranchers and the Nez Perce tribe were affected, for the Grande Ronde River, which entered the Snake below the dams, was one of the few remaining tributaries with significant runs. Efforts to ensure a continued presence of salmon would inevitably affect Native fishermen, ranchers, and other land users along the river. In 1992 the tribe and Wallowa County joined in drafting a salmon recovery plan for the drainage and, in 1996, created the Natural Resource Advisory Committee to implement it.[43]

Bull trout (long known as Dolly Varden) faced similar, if less publicized, problems. Once abundant, their numbers declined sharply as the result of habitat change. By 1930 many riparian areas were badly degraded; limited corrective efforts began, and by 1959 some areas had shown significant improvement, although not enough to halt the decline of bull trout. Few cared. Bull trout, barely edible, were not an important game species and had a reputation as voracious predators that gobbled rainbow trout endlessly. Still, once listed, steps had to be taken to improve chances of their survival; among other things, this meant new restrictions on grazing in riparian areas.[44]

Solutions were especially difficult to come by in the Klamath Basin. Fishes of the basin, especially the Lost River and short-nose suckers—once a major food source for Klamath and Modoc peoples, as well as a sportfish for whites—were in extreme danger, and restrictions on irrigation seemed the only way of ensuring their survival. For area farmers, this was a direct threat to their livelihood and hardly seemed justified in view of the limited economic importance of the fish and of water rights that, because of past promises, they considered inviolate. The heated, ongoing struggle verged on violence; it led to vigilante action, forcing open closed head gates; a welter of studies; and lawsuits, one of which eventually reached the Supreme Court (*Dept. of the Interior v. Klamath Water Users Protective Assoc.*, Jan. 2001 #99-1871). The complexities became even more evident as restricted diversions led to growing desiccation of the Lower Klamath Wildlife Refuge that William Finley and others had fought so hard to preserve.[45]

Just beneath the surface of the environmental contests of the 1950s and after were differences between preservationists and sportsmen, as well as between preservationists and farmers and ranchers. But to paint the preservationists as do-gooders from the outside—with an idealized view of the land and a lack of concern, if not contempt, for those who made a living on it—is wide of the mark. Nor was it simply a struggle between government agencies empowered by the ESA and local residents dependent on the land. Support for husbanding the land and its creatures was growing east of the Cascades, and less exploitive systems of land use were emerging. Eastern Oregonians were no more immune to the wave of change that came with the environmental revolution than were people elsewhere—and, being more intimately affected by the changes taking place than most urbanites, they were both knowledgeable and involved.

15

A Broadening World

The people of Eastern Oregon were never a homogeneous whole. Attitudes toward environmental issues, and much else, varied widely. To be sure, the population was largely Caucasian, native-born, and nonurban. Basque and Irish immigrants, Native Americans, and in time a smattering of black railroad workers and loggers and Mexican farm workers leavened the general ethnic pattern slightly.[1] But the façade of uniformity masked differences of other sorts.

Alongside the middle- and working-class folk who dominated early settlement was a significant minority of those well-to-do. Henry McCall, son of a former Massachusetts governor, was noticeable among them. McCall and his wife Dorothy, herself extremely wealthy, moved to Central Oregon early in the twentieth century and built a home on Crooked River a few miles downstream from Prineville. They were something of an anomaly. Bemused neighbors did not know quite what to make of them, but the McCalls persevered in relative isolation from the world of privilege from which they sprang. Their son Tom, still sporting a patrician accent that revealed the family's Massachusetts origins, would in time become governor of the state.[2]

Other affluent, well-connected residents arrived from an early date. Clarence Bishop in Pendleton, David Baldwin on Trout Creek, Samuel O. Johnson in Klamath Falls, and George Palmer Putnam, Robert W. Sawyer, Dwight Brooks, and Alexander M. Drake in Bend. They networked with one another, with the educated middle class in their towns, and with people in Portland, San Francisco, and eastern cities but had relatively little social intercourse with the working class of their communities. Sawmill and woods workers, railroad and irrigation construction crews, penniless homesteaders, and ranch hands moved in circles of their own. Later, Dust Bowl refugees, former CCC enrollees, and sawmill workers brought out from the South to places like Kinzua and Gilchrist added to the mix of poorer folk. With typical teenage thoughtlessness, in high school some of us used to joke, "We are bilingual, we can speak both English and Okie." World War II brought a further influx. Military air bases outside Redmond and Madras, Camp Abbot (south of Bend), the ordnance depot near Boardman, and lesser military facilities brought thousands; some stayed—or, after discharge, returned. They were joined by others as new land was brought under irrigation by the North Unit in Jefferson County and the Owyhee project in Malheur. Population growth was especially noticeable in Jefferson County, where the population more than doubled between 1940 and 1950; by 1960 its population was more than triple what it had been in 1940.

As communities developed, an upper-middle-class element of merchants and professionals was added to the mix—people like Bernard Daly in Lakeview, J. R. Roberts in Redmond, Jay Bowerman in Condon, Elmo Smith in Ontario, and Earl Snell in Arlington. They became arbiters of community taste and had a more lasting influence than the elites who had preceded them. One mark of their rise was the number of upscale hostelries that emerged: places like the Geiser Grand Hotel (originally the Warshauer) in Baker City (1889), the Bowman Hotel in Pendleton (1906), the Ochoco Inn in Prineville (1923), and the New Hotel Redmond (1928). Such hotels were too costly for working-class people, but prospered nonetheless. Even smaller communities added hotels, although not ones as grand as those in the larger towns. These included the Balch Hotel in Dufur (1908), the Hotel St. Patrick in Heppner (1919), the Hotel Condon (1920), and the Union Hotel (1921).[3]

Tourism was long beyond the reach of the working class, but the well-to-do traveled to resorts in favored locations. Eastern Oregon had its share. Encouraged by E. H. Harriman and San Francisco's Herbert Fleishacker, in the early twentieth century a series of Craftsman-style resorts sprang up by Pelican Bay on the west side of Upper Klamath Lake—Point Comfort, Eagle Ridge, Odessa, and Harriman Springs lodges. They long remained favorite summer retreats for California's Bay Area wealthy, who traveled the twenty-nine miles from Klamath Falls to the resorts by steamboats—and, if they wished, could go on by stage to Crater Lake Lodge, built in 1915.[4] Pilot Butte Inn in Bend followed in 1917 and, by 1930, had expanded to 160 rooms. Pilot Butte Inn stood at the forefront of such hostelries in

Steamer *Winema* off-loading passengers at Pelican Bay on Upper Klamath Lake. Credit: OSU Libraries Special Collections & Archives Research Center.

Eastern Oregon, drawing an impressive array of visitors: Eleanor Roosevelt, Herbert Hoover, various Hollywood actors and actresses, and sportsmen attracted by the famed trout of the Deschutes. Long before fly-fishing became something of a national outdoor craze, Central Oregon was a mecca for it and, by the 1930s, Evans Fly Company a fixture supplying those who pursued it. Ted Trueblood, *Field & Stream*'s renowned fishing editor, was among the visitors—but to the amusement of locals had little success on crystalline Fall River, a Deschutes tributary upstream from Bend. Wallowa Lake Lodge, built in 1923, was more isolated, but it too drew an affluent, if more limited, clientele.[5]

Gradually tourism became democratized. Automobiles played a major role, making travel to outdoor destinations possible for more and more people. Money saved during World War II—when employment was high but rationing and scarcities kept consumption low—added to the flood of tourists that descended on the outdoors in the 1950s. Oregon never had more than eight hundred thousand tourists a year before the war; in 1946 it had 1.2 million and the number continued to rise thereafter. Many a community undertook projects designed to attract them. In 1966, John Day commenced restoration of the Kam Wah Chung building, onetime center of the local Chinese community, and developing a park to house it. The motivation was clear: with the once-despised Chinese gone, evidence of their former presence could be turned to advantage; the *Blue Mountain Eagle* predicted it could become "a major tourist attraction." Eastern Oregon got its share of tourists, but not everywhere benefited. The Winnemucca-to-the-Sea highway, constructed through far southeastern Oregon in the 1950s in hopes of attracting tourist traffic, remained virtually unused; tourists had better places to go.[6]

For Eastern Oregon as a whole, the number of residents who traveled, camped, fished, and hunted after the war probably was more important than the number of tourists. Modest resorts at places like Suttle, Elk, and Diamond Lakes, on the Minam, and at Camp Sherman on the Metolius, served them—and uses were broadening. In the late 1950s, seeing a large number of boats on Cultus Lake, I innocently commented to an acquaintance who ran the resort there that the fishing must be good. "Oh, they don't come to fish," he replied, "They come to play." White-water rafting on the Deschutes and Grande Ronde and windsurfing on the Columbia were still largely in the future, but the way had been pointed.

For all the ethnic and social continuities, the population of Eastern Oregon had clearly changed by the end of the 1950s. The desperate focus on commodity exports that consumed—and restricted—early settlers was being moderated by service employment less tied to the land; the boom-and-bust cycles of early years were giving way to increased stability. Eastern Oregon became a place dominated more than ever by a stable middle class made up of people who had the time and money to engage in the outdoor activities the region offered, to appreciate as well as exploit the land and its physical resources.

The development of modest skiing facilities across the region illustrated the trend. Residents of Bend formed the Skyliners Club in 1927 "to promote winter recreation in the central Oregon Cascades." Their efforts were crowned in 1936 when the New Deal's WPA completed Skyliners Lodge, Central Oregon's first downhill ski lodge. Similar facilities followed (with or without lodges): Warner Canyon outside of Lakeview, Spout Springs near Weston, Anthony Lakes northwest of Baker, Ferguson Ridge a short distance south of Joseph, and—most modest of all—Dixie Summit, with its single rope tow above Prairie City. All were funded locally, depended heavily on volunteer support, and served primarily area residents—although in the 1950s and 1960s Spout Springs did serve as a Winter Olympics training site for various Norwegian and American competitors. Also reflecting the growing interest in winter sports, from 1927 to 1938 residents of Klamath County sponsored a Fort Klamath–Crater Lake ski race (initially forty-two miles round trip) and an accompanying winter carnival. Central Oregon's Rim Rock Riders, founded in 1937 to provide affordable family fun with horses, focused on the non-winter seasons but reflected the same growing middle-class influences.[7]

The career of Les Schwab illustrates middle-class ascendancy in a very different way. While circulation manager for the *Bend Bulletin*, Schwab longed for a business of his own. In 1952 he purchased OK Rubber Welders, a tire business in Prineville, and within a year increased its sales fivefold. The warm personality that had made him a successful circulation manager for the *Bulletin*—and popular with those of us who had paper routes under his direction—worked to his advantage. So did the explosive growth of automobile ownership. He soon opened branches elsewhere—first in Redmond in 1953, then in Bend in 1955. By 1971 he had dropped the OK Rubber Welders title and had thirty-four branches in Oregon, Washington, and Idaho under his own name. Eventually Les Schwab had more than four hundred outlets scattered across the western United States, making it the third-largest retail tire outlet in the nation and a Fortune 500 company, described in an industry journal as "arguably the most respected independent tire chain in the United States." Through it all, Schwab maintained his common touch and remained tied to Central Oregon, where he had grown up.[8]

Less heralded, George Dukek, Wheeler County's district attorney, developed his own ties to the outside world. Retriever field trial competition had emerged in the early twentieth century as an activity for the wealthy upper class. Initially concentrated in the Northeast and Midwest, participation gradually spread, and in 1959 Dukek's Labrador retriever, Bracken's High Flyer, won the National Amateur Retriever Championship in weeklong competition in St. Louis, Missouri. Although it was small and physically isolated, Fossil and other such places were becoming increasingly tied to the outside world in a variety of ways, many of them noneconomic. Along with others in the area, Dukek had a private airplane that helped him overcome the problems of distance from major centers.[9]

Commercial air service was more problematic. In the 1950s passenger flights were added out of Klamath Falls, Redmond, and elsewhere. One could fly from Klamath to Portland on West Coast Airlines for a mere

$16.45 (plus tax), but most people continued to travel by car. Air service never became more than limited and spotty.[10]

Even as new attitudes toward the land were developing, so too were those toward the area's oldest residents—Native Americans. Once viewed as hostiles to be removed or corralled, and then as nuisances, anachronisms paraded at the Pendleton Round-Up and elsewhere, or seasonal workers who showed up in Central Oregon to aid in the fall potato harvest and then disappeared back onto the Warm Springs Reservation, they gradually began to be viewed as people with real needs, concerns, and rights. But progress was uneven.

From its beginning in 1910, tribesmen from the Umatilla Reservation participated in the Pendleton Round-Up. The Happy Canyon events that accompanied the rodeo proper from 1913 on had Native input from the first and avoided the sort of battle scenes, pitting brave settlers and the cavalry against "savages," that were featured in earlier Wild West shows. At the Indian encampment, Native arts and crafts, foods, horsemanship, and dancing were on display. With two hundred or more teepees—located on individual sites handed down from generation to generation—Happy Canyon became the largest annual Indian encampment in North America. But even when modified over the years to present less stereotyped images, Happy Canyon offered a romanticized vision of the "vanishing American," a view that did little to advance the place of Natives in the larger society. Sculptor James Earle Fraser's *The End of the Trail* (1915), Joseph K. Dixon's *The Vanishing Race* (1913), and Zane Grey's *The Vanishing American* (1925) presented the dominant melancholic image. Chief Umapine had been one of those involved in early planning of the roundup and was presented as a regal figure in Pendleton Woolen Mills advertising, but Bill Hanley, who knew him, was unable to see in him anything other than a sad, defeated relic of past events. The nearby Umatilla reservation remained isolated from the American mainstream, a place of widespread poverty where leaseholders like Walter Pierce paid a pittance to farm tribal land, while others simply trespassed—and both groups justified their actions by saying the Indians were not using the land anyway. Still, the Confederated Tribes of the Umatilla *were* recognized by the federal government, had a reservation that was relatively productive, and could turn the nearby Pendleton Round-Up to their advantage each year.[11]

However slowly, things changed. Thousands of Native Americans fought in World War I and in the process gained citizenship for themselves and helped spur passage of the Indian Citizenship Act of 1924. Charles Dawes, a quarter-blood Kaw, won election as vice president the following year (admittedly his reputation was as a financier; few realized his ethnic background). But, while these developments suggested the Indian was not going to "vanish," they offered mixed blessings. Assimilation had been a goal of federal policy since the Dawes Act of 1887, and that approach long continued. A new direction was launched with the Indian Reorganization (Wheeler-Howard) Act of 1934, which recognized the importance of the heritage of Native Americans and the value of self-determination; it sought policies that would build on these. Reflecting the improved confidence that came with this, by the 1960s the Umatilla tribes were emboldened to push for better treatment and less stereotyping at the annual Round-Up, and in 1998 they opened the Tamástslikt Cultural Institute to chronicle the tribes' culture, history, and vision. It was followed in 2005 by Nixyaawii Public Charter School, which provided quality high school education focusing on Native culture and languages as well as the usual academics.[12]

Paiutes around Burns were considerably less fortunate; their situation illustrated how far Native Americans still had to go to reach an honored position in American society. After the Bannock-Paiute War, the Malheur Indian Reservation was terminated and most of its Paiutes dispersed to the Yakama and other reservations. A few stayed on in the Burns area, refusing to go to reservations dominated by rival tribes, and some who left sneaked back. In 1897 the government granted 115 allotments east of Burns (by 2010 only seventy-one remained), but even recipients struggled. Poor, despised, largely landless, and deemed ineligible for further federal aid, they lived on the margins of white society, scavenging and picking up occasional work as laborers, washerwomen, or ranch hands. Easy access to liquor exacerbated problems. Lacking a recognized government to speak for them, their future seemed bleak indeed.[13]

The door to change opened in 1925 with the arrival of Father Peter Heuel, a fiery Catholic priest who had previously served a parish in Joseph and took care of missions in Wallowa and Union Counties. Father Heuel was shocked by the "demeaning and unspeakable wretchedness" of the Burns Paiutes; he quickly became their advocate, a "stormy petrel" urging efforts to address the situation and writing a "persistent and unending" stream of letters calling for action. Progress came slowly. In 1928, Father Heuel persuaded lumberman Edward Hines, a fellow Catholic, to donate ten acres of marginal land near the old city dump to the Paiutes (who had already been pitching tents in the vicinity). He also acquired surplus army tents and persuaded the Bureau of Indian Affairs to build some small, unheated houses on the acreage, known thereafter as Old Camp.[14]

Father Heuel enjoyed other small successes. The BIA responded to his pleas by underwriting minimal health care and providing a teacher for a simple school at Old Camp. These were but partial victories. Heuel criticized the doctor and his teacher wife for their lax efforts and racist attitudes. He was not alone. In 1929 Chief Johnny Capp wrote,

> The Doctor here is not doing his duty toward us Indians. Every Indian when bad sick dies and goes to the graveyard. Not one has been saved for many years. We want a Doctor who takes care of our sick Indians. The teacher, who has care of the medicines, does not give medicines to the Indians. His wife is matron, paid by the Government, but she does nothing for us Indians. Our sick die without help. A few weeks ago 3 died of the same family, but they gave us no care. The teacher does not want his wife, the matron, to tend to the sick Indians. She has never been in any of the Indian houses.

Others had similar complaints. In response, the BIA closed the school, but distant boarding schools proved an unacceptable alternative, and the day school in Burns reopened in 1931.[15]

Many in Burns saw things differently than Father Heuel. When a report on the local situation was prepared in response to a request from the chamber of commerce, town leaders insisted sections of the report dealing with the Indians' ease of access to liquor be eliminated, arguing those portions reflected badly on the white community. And when Heuel welcomed the Paiutes to the Holy Family Church in Burns, white parishioners objected and began a campaign to have their priest removed. Heuel responded by offering services at Old Camp. Similarly, arguing that their presence would be a health risk for white students—tuberculosis, trachoma, impetigo, and lice were common at Old Camp—school officials barred Indians from Burns's public schools. There was justification for their fears. Heuel admitted, "They sleep in rags, they are crowded. . . . There is no chance for sanitary conditions," but he stubbornly continued to agitate for change.[16]

Opposition to Father Heuel's efforts grew. The local Kiwanis Club complained he was stirring insubordination toward Indian Department officials. The chamber of commerce added its voice, as did W. M. Bennett, the principal of Burns High School. Indeed, the chairman of the chamber of commerce's investigative committee believed its underlying purpose was to get rid of Father Heuel. Finally, in 1929, his bishop, located in Baker, suspended Heuel. Apparently the bishop's ecclesiastical superiors had directed him not only to suspend Heuel, but also not to appoint him to serve elsewhere in the archdiocese. Looking back, a former parishioner argued that Heuel was "a stubborn man with a vicious temper who could not abide opposition," but had been treated unjustly in his conflicts with authority.[17]

Suspended, but not defrocked, Heuel stayed on in Burns and continued to work in behalf of area Indians; for fifteen years he maintained an annex to his home from which he dispensed food and clothing. Details of this later work are obscured by the loss or destruction of key records, but clearly he began to get results. In 1934 the Burns Paiutes named him to serve as their agent in pursuing a claim for payment for lands taken when the Malheur Reservation was unilaterally terminated. To further their efforts, in 1936 they formed the Federation of Snake and Piute [sic] Indians—complete with constitution, bylaws, and officers. The case went nowhere until 1941, when Congress granted authority to sue for redress through the Indian Claims Commission; in 1964 a settlement was won; and in 1969 repayment finally made. By then Peter Heuel was long dead, but he *had* lived to see the government purchase land for the Burns Paiutes in 1935 and, three years later, build New Village on it, replacing wretched Old Camp. In 1947, two years after Heuel's death, Indian students were admitted to Burns' public schools.[18]

Finally, in 1972, the federal government recognized the Burns Paiutes as a tribe and established a 750-acre reservation for it by executive order. Together with earlier allotments held in trust and further acquisitions, this brought tribal holdings to 13,736 acres. Annual powwows in celebration of tribal recognition gradually became popular well beyond the membership. Acceptance grew. When the tribe opened the Old Camp Casino and restaurant in 1998, they became popular with locals (although a fire and mismanagement soon led to their closure). And when the remains of Chief Egan were finally returned the following year for a solemn reburial ceremony (in a secret location), the local reaction was sympathetic. Subsequent efforts to reintroduce traditional salmon fishing on the Malheur also earned considerable applause, as did use of a $1.7 million payment from the Bonneville Power Administration (in compensation for its impact on the tribe's traditional fisheries) to buy a 6,450-acre cattle ranch on the Malheur, which was managed for fish and wildlife restoration while local ranchers bought grazing rights on it and adjoining allotments.[19]

Conditions were less extreme and such progress as occurred more subtle on the Klamath Reservation. Tribal officials had resisted termination, recognizing that many members were ill-prepared and that it would eliminate the land base that made the tribe one of the nation's more affluent, but their objections were brushed aside. Ignoring testimony from officials from the Bureau of Indian Affairs and the tribe itself, Senator Arthur V. Watkins of Utah, driven by Mormon religious convictions about Indians as well as his own conservative political views, led the effort that rammed through the Klamath Termination Act of 1954.[20]

When implemented in 1961, termination proved a disaster.[21] Previously the average income of tribal members had been 93 percent of the area's majority population; after termination it plummeted and attendant problems rose. Between 1966 and 1980 28 percent of tribesmen died by age twenty-five, 52 percent by age forty; 40 percent of deaths were alcohol-related; infant mortality was two and a half times the state average. Gerald Skelton, a tribal member who grew up during the period, put it poignantly: "What I remember growing up was going to a lot of funerals." The poverty level among Klamaths reached three and half times that of non-Indians in the county; 70 percent did not have a high school education.[22]

Termination resulted in each tribal member receiving a lump sum of $43,000. Over half were deemed unqualified to handle such a large payout without a legal guardian. Even among those who received their money directly, few were prepared to handle it wisely. Unscrupulous lawyers, automobile dealers, and others moved in. The pages of the Klamath Falls *Herald and News* were replete with stories of profligate expenditures by drunken Indians, but much of the fault lay elsewhere. Treated with contempt and exploited by opportunists, Klamaths took a psychological as well as monetary battering. They bought consumer goods they thought heralded their move into mainstream society, but as a tribal spokesman put it, "No amount of money could purchase a non-racist community willing to deal honorably with them." The psychological damage was as destructive as the economic. Dispirited young people drifted away; tribal leader Lynn Schonchin put it succinctly: as a result of termination, "we lost a whole generation."[23]

Termination was not the end. Soon tribal members were agitating for redress. Their struggle—and the well-publicized ill effects of government actions—earned sympathy from a wide circle of whites. Supporters emerged even in Klamath Falls—and as the tribe persevered, sympathy slowly turned to admiration. The tribe regained federal recognition in 1986, providing a vehicle for progress through a variety of services to its members. But reservation lands were not restored. Lacking that economic base, improvements came slowly. In 1997 the tribe opened Kla-Mo-Ya Casino, providing employment for 150 and speeding change. The worst may have been over, but problems remained. As recently as 2015, some 80 percent of the students at Chiloquin High School, which served much of the reservation, were economically disadvantaged; mathematics proficiency scores were only 22 percent of the norm and English proficiency 39 percent.[24]

Not all of Eastern Oregon's tribes were as despised as the Burns Paiutes, nor as ill-served by the federal government as the Klamaths. The struggle of the Wallowa band of Nez Perce had elicited sympathy during and after the Nez Perce War of 1877. The work of C. E. S. Wood popularized their plight, and subsequent generations of scholars kept alive the story of the injustices heaped upon them. Robert Sawyer's precocious daughter Grace married a member of the tribe and was thus able to tell elements of the story from the Nez Perce point of view. When Chief Joseph returned to the Wallowa Valley in 1903, settlers welcomed him as a guest—one offered his entourage all the apples they could eat—and in 1926 when Old Joseph was reburied in an Indian cemetery at the foot of Wallowa Lake (the original burial site having been desecrated by souvenir hunters), hundreds of locals turned out but, not wanting to detract from the solemnity of the Native ceremony, stayed out of the way. Eventually a number of Nez Perce moved back to the valley where, among other things, they cooperated with whites in efforts to protect the Grand Ronde's salmon runs.[25]

The Nez Perce were not alone in cooperative efforts. The Umatilla, Warm Springs, and other tribes were active—and respected—participants in efforts to protect and restore salmon runs not only in their own waters but also in others nearby. The Columbia River Inter-Tribal Fish Commission, founded in 1977, was an integral part of the efforts. A year later, the Warm Springs tribes joined with the United States Fish and Wildlife Service to build and manage a hatchery on the Warm Springs River. Tribal efforts extended beyond cooperation to unilateral action. The Warm Springs tribes did extensive work on the John Day, seeking to make it a more significant contributor to Columbia River runs; meanwhile, the Umatilla tribes worked to restore runs on the Walla Walla and nearby streams and employed fisheries biologists to direct the process. Following restoration in 1987, the Klamath tribe became an active participant in efforts to find solutions to the many-sided struggle over the waters of the Klamath River and upper Klamath Basin and in efforts to restore salmon and sucker runs. It built and operated a tribal research station and hatchery on Sprague River as a part of the process. Such efforts were welcomed. Rather than being viewed as a nuisance or as hapless dependents, the tribes had become partners and, in the process, helped to erode prejudices in the larger population.[26]

Education was broadening too. In the forefront was Bernard Daly, who emigrated in 1864 from Ireland and, after attending medical school, joined the US Army. In 1887 he left the army and joined the Irish migration to Lake County, where he took up medical practice. The young bachelor prospered mightily in his new home. When he died in 1920, he had business interests throughout Lake County. He was the largest stockholder in the Bank of Lakeview as well as a number of other businesses, operated the biggest ranch in south-central Oregon, and owned fourteen or more buildings in downtown Lakeview. He served for years on the local school board, on the county court, in the state legislature, and as a regent of what would become Oregon State University. He accomplished all this while pursuing his medical career and earning a reputation as something of a sharp dealer. On his death, Daly left an estate worth nearly $1 million. With no children of his own, Daly directed that his estate be used to establish a scholarship program for students from Lake County's high schools who wanted to go on to higher education. Since its establishment in 1922, the Bernard Daly Educational Foundation has provided funds to more than two thousand students, some 40 percent of those who graduated from the county's three small high schools. In practice, just about any Lake County graduate who wished to go on for higher education could get a Daly scholarship. Hazel Stingley, a graduate of tiny Silver Lake High School, was an early recipient. Her homesteader parents were unable to provide financial support, but with the $600 annual stipend the Daly Fund supplied, she was able to cover her expenses at the state university.[27]

Daly's legacy is more complex than one might assume. Shortly before his death, he said Lakeview was "in desperate need of the kind of refinement that only educated men and women could bring," while in his will he declared, "It is my earnest desire to help . . . worthy and ambitious young men and women of my beloved county of Lake, to acquire a good education, so that they may be better fitted and qualified to appreciate and help to preserve the laws and constitution of this free country . . . and by their conduct . . . reflect honor on Lake county and the state of Oregon." On the one hand he seems to have hoped to improve Lakeview, on the other to prepare its young people to go out into the wider world from which he himself had emerged. He may well have accomplished both. Ted Conn, longtime community leader and head of the fund's board of trustees, commented in the 1960s, "There's no doubt that the Daly Fund is taking away some of our best people." But they might have left anyway. William Kittredge, who grew up in Lake County, remembers, "In my boyhood we all dreamed of going away." The education that drew talented young people away from Lakeview did so by opening the doors to fresh opportunities. Yet not all the best and brightest left. Lakeview has a vital chapter of the American Association of University Women, which on one occasion drew an audience of more than 150 to a presentation by Paul Dull, professor of East Asian history at the University of Oregon. As for Daly, his views were decidedly progressive—his faith in public education was intense, his view that women as well as men should receive higher education was not yet widely shared, and over time Lakeview's residents came to see him as a kindhearted, farsighted benefactor rather than a businessman whose practices were hardly above reproach.[28]

Other developments in education also furthered the broadening of Eastern Oregon's citizenry. From its beginning, Eastern Oregon University in La Grande, founded as a teacher's training institution in 1929, had a special regional role. Today its mission statement describes the school as "an educational, cultural and scholarly center . . . [that] connects the rural regions of Oregon to a wider world. . . . EOU guides student inquiry through integrated, high-quality liberal arts and professional programs that lead to responsible and reflective action in a diverse and interconnected world." Reflecting this, in 2018 the Oregon legislature recognized it as "Oregon's Rural University," a position Oregon State had long considered its own. Bernard Daly would surely have endorsed such a mission—and it is nothing new. Friends who taught there in the 1960s, when it was still Eastern Oregon College, described it in terms similar to its current mission statement and spoke of the special responsibility faculty felt for students with the limited backgrounds provided by the small towns from which much of the student body came. Appropriately, in 1952 when the Shriners inaugurated a high school all-star football game between players from smaller schools east and west of the Cascades, the East team held its training camp at Eastern Oregon College.[29]

Other forces were at work tying students in Eastern Oregon to the wider world. Bill Edwards, a twenty-four-year-old navy veteran, arrived to teach at Sisters High School in 1949 and within a year was named school principal. Working with a small, dedicated faculty and "talking Navy" to unruly students and parents, he turned around the hardscrabble community's high school, which state officials had been threatening to close. The tiny school—it enrolled only some seventy students—soon became a focus of community pride and was winning accolades around the state. As Edwards later explained, the students were basically "good kids," but lacked experience, role models, and direction; an atmosphere had developed that made them pariahs with whom other schools in the area did not want to associate: "We did everything we could think of, interest broadening activities because they were so limited in their lives here." Participation in statewide one-act play competitions and a broadened—and successful—sports program were integral parts of the new order. The most notable—and noted—innovation was a conservation class Edwards instituted. He was "a naturalist before it was fashionable," but in a community where livelihoods were rooted in the land, the idea quickly caught on. State fish and game officials provided aid, the Forest Service leased a ninety-acre tract on Indian Ford Creek to the school for field study, and the county agent and others stepped forward to offer assistance. Well before Rachel Carson's *Silent Sprint* (1962), Sisters students found themselves actively involved in analyzing and addressing the environmental problems that were beginning to engage national and international attention. The number of Sisters High School graduates going on to college burgeoned.[30]

Although not with the same fanfare, change was under way at other small high schools: Crane, Mitchell, Fossil, Condon, Dayville, Ukiah, and elsewhere. All benefited from limited enrollment, which kept teacher-student ratios low, and from a shift away from the standard one-size-fits-all educational philosophy and toward a flexible curriculum encouraging approaches tailored to local needs and opportunities. In the early 1940s, when Eileen McVicker was ready to enter high school, her parents considered the boarding school at Crane "a little too wild" and shipped their children to Burns to live alone in a rented house while the parents tended their ranch near Fields; nothing in Cactus Smyth's experience at Crane during that period suggests the school was more than minimally passable. But by the 1960s things were changing. In 1963 Quentin Wright took over as principal. A native of the area who had broad experience in California and in overseas schools for military dependents, Wright brought vision and imagination to the job. By 1999 the Oregon Department of Education was rating Crane High one of the ten best schools in Eastern Oregon. One teacher who went to Crane thinking it might be an interesting short-term experience found himself staying on for years. Among other innovations, students were allowed to get work-study credit for breaking horses after regular school hours. By 2004, one parent noted, former Crane students were "working as teachers, nurses, research biologists, and [in] numerous other professions, so coming from a small rural school has not limited students' career pursuits." To her, the key was the camaraderie among staff, students, and parents. Similar cooperation developed at Dayville, where local foresters, fish and game managers, and the Grant County Stockmen's Association joined in supporting field trips that broadened students' outlook and experience.[31]

Small schools continued to face problems. High among them were inadequate funding—which forced some districts to cut back to four-day-a-week schedules—and great distances.[32] Still, there were positives. The advent of the internet opened fresh possibilities for educational improvement. Condon and Fossil combined forces to develop a broader, stronger curriculum than either could manage alone. So did Merrill and Malin, which in 1970 merged their tiny high schools to form Lost River High School, located halfway between the two communities. Nearby Bly simply closed its high school and began bussing students to Bonanza; the result was a school large enough to provide essential services (but with an attendance area of 950 square miles and some students living as many as fifty-five miles from the school). Cooperation came on other fronts too. Prairie City and Burnt River combined to field eight-man football teams, as did Monument and Dayville, and Harper and Huntington. Even so, it was often difficult to field teams; in 2016, Monument-Dayville played with a single substitute. Intercommunity cooperation also made it possible for Prairie City, Monument, Dayville, Long Creek, Burnt River, Spray, Mitchell, and Ukiah high schools—none with more than ten or so seniors a year—to host a joint prom to see graduates off in style. Reflecting such achievements, in 2009 when *U.S. News & World Report* published its rankings of America's best high schools, fourteen of the thirty-one from Oregon were small schools east of the Cascades.[33]

Schools were an indication of broader developments. Although its regional identity remained, Eastern Oregon was increasingly tied to the outside world by more than exported commodities. As a resident said in response to the view that Lakeview was a provincial community isolated behind a "sagebrush curtain" (a view presented by Ken Metzler in an essay in *Old Oregon*), "The people aren't isolated, the land is."[34] In an effort to breach that curtain, Unity's Burnt River School, with a total enrollment of thirty-four in kindergarten through twelfth grade, instituted a program in which Portland high school students studied for a semester in Burnt River School, learning in class and from friends and host families about ranching and the environment as they never could in the city. At the same time, the program broadened the perspectives of the Unity area's residents, students and adults alike.[35]

Throughout Eastern Oregon, young people were finding increased opportunities, albeit ones that often led them far afield. Bernard Daly would have been pleased that they had such options, even if what resulted may not have been as dramatic as what followed when Vernon Jackson and Kenneth Smith left the Warm Springs Reservation for the University of Oregon.

16

Invasion

Tom McCall came to public notice through radio and television work in Portland, but his roots ran deep in Central Oregon. He spent his youth on the family ranch on Crooked River, was student body president of Redmond Union High School, worked for time for the *Bend Bulletin* after graduating from the University of Oregon, and in the end chose to be buried next to his parents in the Redmond cemetery. A progressive Republican, McCall fought against the rise of Barry Goldwater, Richard Nixon, and Ronald Reagan until, despairing of the direction the GOP was taking, abandoned the party to become an Independent.[1]

His years as governor (1967–1975) were active ones, and the outspoken McCall earned a nationwide reputation for actions protecting Oregon's beaches, battling for a bottle bill to curb roadside litter, cleaning up pollution in the Willamette River, pushing for a massive greenway along it, and initiating stringent land-use planning to halt suburban sprawl and the destruction of productive farmland. But nothing caught the public fancy so much as his attack on uncontrolled growth threatening the quality of life in Oregon. In 1971 McCall announced on national television, "Come visit us again and again. This is a state of excitement. But for heaven's sake, don't come here to live!" The statement spawned a wave of Oregon "ungreeting cards" that announced, among other things, "People don't tan in Oregon, they rust."[2]

McCall's concern was not development but runaway growth and new industries that would pollute the state's air, water, and land. Such concerns focused more on problems west of the Cascades than east, but were relevant even there. With Bend's sawmills closing, its leaders were eager to attract new sources of employment. Numerous developments followed. Bachelor Butte (renamed Mount Bachelor to give it more appeal) became the site of a major ski resort. Sunriver, an upscale development of retirement and recreational homes, emerged on the upper Deschutes. Century Drive, a largely unpaved forest road looping roughly one hundred miles through the high country west of Bend, was paved and renamed the Cascade Lakes Highway. Farther afield, Black Butte Ranch, sitting at the foot of the huge, forest-covered, conical butte from which it took its name, was converted into an expensive planned community. Eagle Crest Resort, a 1,700-acre complex on the Deschutes west of Redmond, followed. South of Bend, the High Desert Museum opened in 1982. It drew visitors interested in the outdoors and the romance of the range country rather than those who made their living from the land. More active adventurers turned downstream portions of the Deschutes into a major white-water rafting destination.

Less noted, many Central Oregon ranches and farms were sold off and subdivided. In the Tumalo Irrigation District, the average farm had 120 irrigated acres in 1913, 72 in 1955, and only 11 by 2012. Working farms were replaced by hobby farms, cattle by llamas and riding horses. In Redmond, the seed-cleaning plant, turkey processing plant, and Hodecker's potato packing plant all closed. The owner of the last of these explained succinctly, "No spuds!"—not even from the Powell Butte area, which once produced many tons. Deschutes Grain & Feed's buildings were turned into an antique mall. Redmond was no longer the agricultural center it had once been. Its sawmills closed too. Housing there was less expensive, and Redmond was slowly morphing into a bedroom community for Bend.[3]

For decades *Bend Bulletin* editor Robert Sawyer had championed the scenic and recreational wonders of Central Oregon, but nothing in his voluminous papers suggests he expected its economy ever to rest on anything other than commodity production. Tourism was to be an add-on, as it had been from the beginning.[4] But by McCall's day, things were changing. Central Oregon had gained attention far and wide. Outsiders poured in. Deschutes County became the fastest growing county in the state, growing 104 percent between 1960 and 1970 and continuing to add population thereafter (although the growth rate slowed during Oregon's economically depressed 1970s). Deschutes County had a population of 23,100 in 1960; by 2000 it had ballooned to 115,367. In 1950 it had the fourth-largest population east of the Cascades; by 1990 it was the largest, well ahead of Klamath County, which in 1960 had possessed more than twice its population. Bend was the sixth-fastest-growing city in the United States.

Spillover effects pulled along neighboring Jefferson and Crook Counties. Between 1960 and 1990, Jefferson grew some 60 percent, Crook almost 40 percent. Rather than discouraging people from moving to Oregon, Tom McCall's visit-but-don't-stay mantra helped create an image of the state as a place where the good life was still possible; Central Oregon, with its sunshine, forests, mountains, sparkling rivers, and numerous recreational opportunities, fit the image perfectly. Ernest Callenbach's *Ecotopia*, a novel based in the Northwest and briefly popular after its publication in 1975, did nothing to undermine the view.

More than a growth of population was taking place. The shipment of commodities from the region—lumber, cattle, agricultural products—had from the first supported the economy. Now tourists and escapees from other places brought the dollars, and service employment circulated and recirculated it. Central Oregon had moved into the postindustrial, post-agrarian, post-pastoral world. As Oregon's timber industry collapsed and the state faced budget crises, Governor Victor Atiyeh (1979–1987) casti-gated McCall for having made Oregon unattractive to new industries, but Atiyeh's scapegoating overlooked the basic transformation taking place. McCall may have had a limited vision of what Oregon would become, but he was certainly closer to the mark than Atiyeh.[5]

What was occurring in Central Oregon was happening elsewhere in the West—and not without problems. The quest for tourism and recreational dollars was, as the late historian Hal Rothman put it, a "devil's bargain." Not only is tourism "the most colonial of colonial economies," he wrote, it "triggers a contest for the very soul of a place." As a rule, Rothman noted, "tourism served as a replacement economy; it was added on, sometimes with embarrassment, after the demise or decline of another economy, usu-ally by someone from elsewhere who could redefine the place in national or at least extralocal terms. . . . By the way it drew people to visit or live, it altered the meaning of local life."[6] The case studies he presented began at Lahaina, Maui, and ranged across the Mountain West. Bend and Central Oregon do not appear in his pages, but well they might have. With local variations, what Rothman detailed at Jackson Hole, Aspen, Sun Valley, Santa Fe, and Las Vegas was happening in Oregon too. As native son Jarold Ramsey looked forward to returning, he could not help but wonder (with apologies to Gertrude Stein), would there be a "there" there?[7]

The changes generated disquiet. In Central Oregon many older residents came to feel the place they knew and loved was slipping away in the face of incoming people and values. Those who worked hardest to introduce the new order were those who stood to benefit from it—real estate developers, businessmen, tourist facility operators—themselves often relative newcomers. Many of Bend's old elite decamped with the lumber industry or simply died or retired; those who remained active either came to terms with the new order or were increasingly marginalized. Meanwhile, those not near the heart of new developments found their work no longer held up as valuable or worth emulating. What they had built was now judged a mere foundation for change or, worse, to have been inexcusably destructive. Working-class residents found themselves increasingly ignored, a less and less visible underclass. Across the West, William Kittredge observed, "Native Americans are being joined in their disfranchisement by loggers and miners and ranchers."[8]

Citizens long present could make a living off the tourist trade, but in effect were reduced to the servant class, "not so much fearing the [new arrivals] . . . as despising them." In a joint study released in 1993, the Bend Chamber of Commerce and City of Bend found part-time and seasonal employment accounted for 49 percent of jobs, their combined payroll a mere $33 million compared with $74.7 million for the same number of jobs in the timber industry. By the first decade of the twenty-first century, 30 percent of real estate mortgages in Deschutes County were for second homes for people whose primary residence was elsewhere, and land prices had escalated dramatically.[9] When those of us who have left return for class reunions or familial visits, we share the disquiet that has developed. What happened to the place we once knew? We grieve over the unfamiliar place Central Oregon has become.

The problem was not just that a new economy was swamping the old. Incomers brought values and attitudes at odds with those already in place. They came seeking the natural rather than the social environment; indeed, they tended to look down on, when they did not ignore, what was already in place, and in due course Central Oregon's social and built environments were transformed beyond recognition. In Bend, William Robbins has observed, "new people, new homes, new wealth, and very different cultural tastes" took hold; the "new monied classes have introduced social and cultural changes. . . . . [and] the community has become increasingly layered and polarized." Incomers erected a built environment in the name of back to nature, but one could hardly call it tied to the land; nature was simply the setting. Ellen Waterston caught the resulting clash in a poignant essay, "What One Thing?" Something of a new arrival herself, she appreciated what had been lost yet recognized that old lifeways could not be recaptured, only a sort of balance between old and new could be achieved. And the changes were not taking place just in Bend. Handsome estates popped up across rural Central Oregon, even in such isolated places as the Fly Lake area north of Grandview; flying in to Sisters for a reunion, a former resident saw million-dollar homes (many with their own landing strips) scattered across that rugged, isolated landscape.[10]

Christmas Valley provided an extreme example of the changes. In 1961, California developer M. Penn Phillips bought seventy-two thousand desert acres east of Fort Rock, laid out a townsite with fanciful holiday street names (Candy Lane, Mistletoe Road, Comet Street, Vixen Street, and so on), an airstrip, a golf course, a lodge, rodeo grounds, and an artificial lake. Phillips aggressively promoted the development in California, often providing free bus tours and flights, and marketed the land as potentially green and arable. The parcels quickly sold out. Many bought sight unseen, and those arriving by air often had no idea how isolated the valley was. Despite claims the community would soon have more than five thousand residents, few actually moved to Christmas Valley, and many of those who did soon left. In 1966, Judge Edward Howell of the Oregon Tax Court ruled "the land . . . is arid, dusty, windy, isolated, [and] subject to temperature extremes." Tom McCall, a champion of careful land-use planning, opposed leapfrog developments miles from support facilities and labeled Phillips and other such developers "sagebrush saboteurs." By the early 1970s, Phillips's company faced lawsuits for misrepresentation, and in 1973 the development, by then widely recognized for the scam it was, came to an end. Today only sad remnants of Phillips's grand scheme remain, but somehow scattered landowners hold on and occasional land sales occur.[11]

Oregonians uncomfortable with developments found a ready scapegoat: California. Long both resented and envied, Californians provided an easy target—and not just for residents of Central Oregon. Jackson County residents were equally vocal. One complained Californians "move in here and the first thing they'll want to do is start changing things." His wife added, "There's a lot of them moving in here . . . [and] they talk about, you know—the low-life Oregonians. . . . Like we're all backwards . . . [and live] in Oregon where nothing's happening like in the Bay Area." Not surprisingly, Tom McCall joined the chorus. While pushing for a ballot measure to revise Oregon's arcane and ineffectual system for funding schools, he overheard a recent arrival at a neighboring restaurant table complaining about the proposal, which he claimed would cost him an extra $800 a year in taxes. Doing a quick mental calculation, McCall realized the man was making over $60,000 a year; he jumped up and, towering over the man, shouted, "You son of a bitch, if you don't care any more than that about the schools in Oregon, why don't you go back to California?" In Bend, bumper stickers appeared reading "Don't Californicate Oregon," and complaints about the overbearing behavior and gross materialism of those arriving from the Golden State became more and more common.[12]

Gradually these attitudes spread to areas less immediately threatened. In the 1990s ranchers, federal authorities, and environmentalists agreed on a plan to protect Steens Mountain. As Nancy Langston noted, although deeply suspicious of one another, they feared the development and subdivision that Californians—already buying up inholdings on the mountain's slopes—might bring. Looking west to Bend, they could see auguries of what might happen if they did not cooperate. Somewhat later, voters in Union County, fearing Californization of the Grande Ronde Valley, voted in support of developmental limitations.[13]

Even some of Central Oregon's new arrivals became disenchanted. Jane Kirkpatrick moved to Bend in the mid-1970s and rose to become director of mental health services for Deschutes County, but she soon tired of empty social activities, weekly manicures and hair appointments, and a life bereft of meaning. She departed with her husband to build a homestead on the lower John Day. They struggled but prospered spiritually, if not financially. Employment as a social worker on the Warm Springs Reservation followed. Except for occasional visits from friends, their lives were divorced from what they had experienced in Bend; they embraced the change eagerly and stayed on the banks of the John Day for over a quarter of a century.[14]

For all the paranoia about incoming Californians, that state's citizens were not alone in reshaping Eastern Oregon. Strangest of all the incomers were the followers of the Bhagwan Shree Rajneesh, who bought the seventy-thousand-acre Big Muddy Ranch near Antelope for $5.75 million and built a commune there. Rajneeshpuram grew to some two thousand residents during the early 1980s. As it grew, so did friction with neighboring ranchers; Rajneeshee leaders also clashed repeatedly with local and state authorities. In 1983 commune members moved in to Antelope and, outvoting the handful of prior residents, changed the community's name to Rajneesh. Attempts to poison local officials and to control county elections were the last straws. Charged with visa violations, the Bhagwan fled the United States, and Antelope returned to its old name and something approximating its former norm.[15]

Much of what was happening was less bizarre than that and the product of Oregonians rather than of Californians or Rajneeshees. The Dalles was becoming almost a Portland exurb; increasing numbers relocated there to commute to the city, while river sports and restaurants drew others for weekends. Wasco County's voting patterns reflected the change, shifting to a closer approximation of Multnomah County's and away from patterns of counties farther east.

The development of Sunriver, more than anything around The Dalles, demonstrated the home-grown forces at work. In 1965 Portlanders John D. Gray and Donald V. McCallum announced plans for a private residential and resort community fifteen miles south of Bend on ranchland once the site of the World War II training facilities known as Camp Abbot. Gray, the head of Omark Industries, was the prime mover.[16] Already involved in developing Salishan, an upscale resort on the Oregon Coast, Gray moved deliberately. As the Architectural Foundation of Oregon put it in honoring Gray in 2008, he had a "passion for Oregon's beauty" and a "respect for how we develop our state to accommodate those of us who choose to live here alongside the creatures who came before us." His daughter recalls that he was a strong supporter of land-use planning. Thus at both Salishan and Sunriver, Gray sought to build facilities that sat lightly on the land. Sunriver's lodge and first condominiums were completed in 1968 and a master plan adopted a year later. Eventually it would include four thousand private residences along the Deschutes and a permanent population of 1,700.[17]

Black Butte Ranch was similar. Located a few miles northwest of Sisters, the property was a working ranch until the 1930s when Stewart S.

Lowery, a wealthy San Franciscan, acquired it. The ranch changed little under Lowery. His family used it as a summer retreat, while manager Carl Campbell continued to operate it as a cattle, sheep, and horse operation— "Nine months of the year we thought we owned the place," one of Campbell's daughters recalls. Following Lowery's death in 1957, Portlander Howard Morgan—long a power in Oregon politics—acquired the ranch and continued to run it as a working ranch, but things changed when Morgan sold out in 1969. The buyer was Brooks Resources, a subsidiary of Brooks-Scanlon Lumber Company created after Brooks acquired rival Shevlin-Hixon and came to realize it was "not just in the timber business, but in the land business." Brooks turned Black Butte Ranch into a carefully planned community of residential and summer homes with limited commercial activity. Most tracts sold in its first three months. Black Butte Ranch was the firm's first major development; others would follow, including the Mount Bachelor Village Resort. Portlanders as well as Californians were major buyers.[18]

For some years Brooks-Scanlon had centered much of its logging in the Sisters area, so Black Butte Ranch was hardly a leap into unfamiliar territory. Since little commercial activity was planned at the resort, Sisters became its business center, but as area sawmills closed, the little town had fallen on hard times. Businesses closed, population dropped. In an effort to make its main street more attractive—the street that would serve as the primary service center for their resort—Brooks Resources offered $5,000 and free architectural advice to businesses that adopted a "Western" theme for their architecture; eager for anything that would halt the town's economic slide, many accepted the offer, and the newly established Sisters Planning Commission had an 1880s theme written into the town's zoning code. Business from residents of Black Butte Ranch as well as from tourists soon rejuvenated the town's economy—and gave fresh life to the Sisters Rodeo, which moved to spacious new facilities east of town. It might be argued that through the "Western" theme, Sisters was returning to its roots, but what developed was—like Sunriver—actually new, tied to an emerging postindustrial economy.[19]

Differences of income as well as lifestyle were involved. Deschutes County's older economy—based primarily on agriculture, lumbering, and service employment—had been dominated by a stable middle class that set the tone of life. But the new order brought disquieting change. The

Pew Research Center found that from 2000 to 2014, the county's middle class fell by over 8 percent. Nationwide, the much-commented-upon decline of the middle class reflected a drop in industrial employment and the results thereof in metropolitan areas. This was not the case in Central Oregon. A population influx, not urban flight, was at work. And the new arrivals tended to be sufficiently affluent to pick where they wanted to live and how. They had a lifestyle—and demands—sharply at odds with the old order, and they both reshaped and replaced what had gone before. Rim Rock Riders, established as a middle-class recreational outlet by ranchers Reub Long and Dean Hollingshead, was transformed; its new multimillion-dollar facilities catered to those with a much higher level of affluence than its original members—as the addition of that most elitist of equestrian activities, dressage competitions and training, illustrated. Such changes reinforced the feeling of many longtime residents that the world they knew and loved was slipping away.[20]

Developments seen so dramatically at Sunriver and Black Butte Ranch were present in more muted forms elsewhere. Lacking the dramatic settings of the projects in Deschutes County, most areas adjusted to the new realities in modest ways. Burns introduced an annual birders' festival at nearby Malheur National Wildlife Refuge and Steens Mountain. At Wallowa Lake, a four-thousand-foot-long tramway, advertised as the steepest in the country, climbed up Mount Howard. Nearby, boat tours on the wild waters in Hells Canyon gained popularity, as did white-water rafting on the Grande Ronde and bicycle touring on little-traveled highways out of Heppner and La Grande. Dayton Hyde converted a portion of his Yamsi Ranch on the upper Sprague to a fishing resort. Meanwhile, residents of Paisley introduced a "redband" trout tournament on the Chewaucan River in an attempt to draw outsiders to their isolated little community. Music festivals, brewfests, and art fairs sprang up, especially in the area of Enterprise, Wallowa, Lostine, and Joseph.[21] Even Milton-Freewater, hardly in a location apt to draw tourists, joined in: for some years it has offered a Muddy Frogwater Country Classic Festival—which plays on the community's unusual name but hardly recalls scenic wonders. Meanwhile, La Grande offers its Eastern Oregon Beer Festival. Such efforts have drawn visitors, especially from Portland, and helped sustain communities that otherwise would have been in decline—or dying. At the same time, they draw new residents who differ sharply from the miners, loggers, farmers, and ranchers that preceded them. In Union County the population rose sharply between 1970 and 1980; many newcomers were retirees. The development was reflected in employment figures. In 1940 farming generated 27 percent of the county's jobs; by 1990 agriculture's role had dwindled to 6.3 percent, and La Grande, its least rural center, claimed some 50 percent of the county's population.[22]

Many new developments played on Eastern Oregon's history. Older rodeos continued to flourish and new ones appeared. In Harney County state park officials cooperated in making Peter French's unusual round barn and the hotel at Frenchglen into tourist attractions.[23] Nearby, the main buildings at White Horse Ranch were converted (for a time at least) into a bed and breakfast inn, as were those at the Wilson Ranch near Fossil. Historic preservation efforts in places like Echo, Condon, and Lakeview and attempts to capitalize on the Chinese heritage in John Day and Pendleton probably interrupted through traffic more than they drew new visitors; but however brief stays might be, they contributed to the local economies. And in 1965, at the urging of Congressman Al Ullman, three of Oregon's state parks were combined to form the John Day Fossil Beds National Monument, thus increasing funding and publicity for the area.[24] Meanwhile, the National Historic Oregon Trail Interpretive Center near Baker City, combined with historic preservation efforts in the community's center—some one hundred of its structures, capped by the Geiser Grand Hotel, were placed on the National Register of Historic Places—and nearby attractions, such as the old Sumpter Valley Railroad, operated as tourist attractions that sought to make Baker City a destination rather than a place for brief stopovers.

In northeastern Oregon friction occurred between longtime residents and newcomers with decidedly different lifestyles, but to a lesser degree than in Central Oregon, where the influx of outsiders seemed to sweep everything before it. It was not just a matter of numbers. Ranching, farming, and logging continued to be significant elements in its local economies, and many new arrivals shared a love of the outdoors—of hunting, fishing, and camping—that old-timers cherished. Indeed, old ways remained sufficiently strong to draw newcomers. After retirement, Bill Bowerman, the University of Oregon's famed track coach, moved back to Fossil, where he had spent a portion of his childhood. F. Smith Fussner, a history professor at Reed College, moved to Wheeler County to pursue his dream of becoming a cattle rancher and became so entranced with the area he wound up compiling a history of it. Les Zaitz retired from the *Oregonian* to a ranch near Bates. And Larry McGraw, a Portland horticulturist of note, spent his retirement years at Kimberly, where he purchased a pioneer orchard along the John Day and continued his work with heritage apple varieties.[25]

Not all who came to Eastern Oregon as part of the influx of outsiders during and after the 1960s came as would-be residents or tourists. Activists came too—and as often as not they continued to live outside the region. Impatient with the approach of leaders like Tom McCall, Robert Straub, and John Kitzhaber,[26] they soon launched a variety of aggressive proposals, many of which required federal action. One of their first salvos was fired in 1991 when a consortium of environmental groups led by Oregon Natural Resources Council stepped forward with an ambitious proposal for southeastern Oregon: national park status for Steens Mountain, three new national monuments, forty-seven wilderness areas covering some five million acres, a National Wildlife Refuge at Lake Abert, and wild and scenic river status for fifty-four streams (mostly small creeks draining the Steens and Pueblo Mountains). The proposal called for phasing out grazing on all these properties over a ten-year period. Immediate results were few, but clearly war on the status quo had been declared.[27]

Others soon added their voices, most notably Bill Marlett, who arrived in Bend in 1984, hired by the county help halt proposed new hydroelectric projects on the Deschutes. A soil scientist educated at the University of Wisconsin—where, as one website put it, he "solidified his aversion for the bovine species"—Marlett soon turned his attention to grazing on Eastern Oregon's public lands. In 1987 he was a founder of the Oregon Natural Desert Association (ONDA), self-described as a "hodgepodge group, including teachers, housewives, doctors, students, naturalists, and retirees." From the first, Marlett was a member of the board and then, in 1993, became its first executive director. Under his leadership, the organization took extreme positions. For the health of the land, Marlett insisted, all grazing on public lands had to be halted: "We want a date-certain phaseout of grazing. We just don't think that cattle grazing is compatible with the desert environment." Revealingly, when Bill Robbins, an environmental historian of note, addressed an ONDA meeting, he was booed. Taken aback, Robbins asked his host what he had done wrong. The reply: "You didn't say you hate cows enough."[28]

Under Marlett's leadership, ONDA became a force to be reckoned with. In 1994 it joined the National Wildlife Federation in bringing suit to halt grazing along the Donner und Blitzen River, the upper reaches of which had gained Wild and Scenic River status in 1988 and were allegedly being degraded by grazing. Then, in 1996, ONDA got the Clean Stream Initiative on the statewide ballot. Designed to protect against the polluting effects of livestock, the measure put the until-then-obscure organization in the public eye. In an effort to elicit support, ONDA distributed bumper stickers proclaiming "Cows Kill Salmon." The slogan seemed absurd in Eastern Oregon, for salmon had never been present in much of it—and even where present had been affected more by dams than cows—but the Clean Water Initiative was a statewide issue, and ONDA was seeking votes west as well as east of the Cascades. In the end, however, many viewed their proposal as a blatant attack on property rights, and it went down to defeat.[29]

Relations between ONDA and local interests—including ranchers and range managers—remained frosty. And for good reason. Viewing the Bureau of Land Management as a kept agency dominated by ranching interests, ONDA took legal action time and again to force modification of the agency's land-use plans—this in spite of Marlett's conviction that the agency would "never give us what we want."[30]

Environmentalist views of the BLM also played a major role in debates over the management of wild horses on Great Basin rangelands. Feral horses—"mustangs"—had long been an iconic presence in Eastern Oregon, reflecting wild nature and cowboy culture as did few other things. William Kittredge and Cactus Smyth remembered them fondly. Kittredge recalled his first effort at rounding up mustangs: "I learned something that day . . . the splendor of running with the wind." During World War II, with young cowboys—their natural predators—away on the battlefronts, the number of wild horses skyrocketed. After the war, they were "cleared out . . . run with airplanes and rounded up in great swirling herds." Mustangers, one of their number noted, "managed the wild horse population and made a profit doing it," selling the animals they captured to slaughterhouses in Redmond and elsewhere to be turned into pet or chicken food.[31]

Nevadan Velma Bronn Johnston—known far and wide as "Wild Horse Annie"—was shocked by inhumane practices involved in the roundups and launched a campaign to regulate (or halt) them. Horse lovers, the Animal Welfare Institute, and a variety of others provided support, and in 1959 Congress passed legislation banning the poisoning of waterholes to kill wild horses and the use of aircraft and motorized vehicles to round them up. More seemed needed, and when additional legislation was proposed in 1971, Congress was flooded with letters from mothers and children—more letters, wild horse advocates claimed, than on any other non-war issue in American history; one Congressman reported receiving fourteen thousand such letters. Out of this came the Wild and Free-Roaming Horses and Burros Act, signed into law by President Richard Nixon in 1971.[32]

Responsibility for managing mustangs fell to the Bureau of Land Management. The bureau claimed there were ten thousand more horses on land it administered than the land could support. For a time a program of capture and adoption successfully reduced the population—from 1998 to 2007 it fell from forty-five thousand to thirty thousand—but the number of potential adoptees slowly fell (and many horses proved unadoptable). The bureau housed the excess in large "sanctuaries," but the facilities were soon overflowing and budgeted funds stretched to their limits. Debates over how to proceed swirled. There were no easy solutions; indeed, environmental historian Dan Flores observed, wild horse management was "one of the most contentious and vexing of all modern natural resource issues" faced by the Bureau of Land Management.[33]

Vast tracts in southeastern Oregon—and some 4,300 horses—were involved.[34] The bureau established a holding facility outside of Burns to house captured animals, but like other such facilities it was soon full. In 2015 matters came to a head when the bureau announced a plan to round up some 1,500 horses in the isolated Beatys Butte Management Area sixty-five miles east of Lakeview, an undertaking that would reduce its mustang population to roughly one hundred. To help ensure local support, BLM's Lakeview office launched an educational and outreach program in the community.[35]

Still, protests erupted. Laura Leigh, another Nevadan, was one of those attacking the proposal. She had founded Wild Horse Education "to inform the public of the unreported, hidden holocaust that is taking place

Beatys Butte horse gather. Credit: Lisa Bogardus, Bureau of Land Management.

on our public ranges with our heritage animals," and she brought to bear arguments inherent in such a view. Others saw the conflict as over the use of rangeland: one protester proclaimed it was "ranchers versus the wild horses. The horses eat the same food as cows," an argument that rested in part on the belief that the Bureau of Land Management was a tool of the ranching industry. The agency replied it was simply thinking of what was good for the range—a concern many ranchers shared, for they had voluntarily reduced grazing in the area by almost 70 percent.[36] Moreover, the health of the range was tied to concerns other than grazing. The area was sagebrush steppe and a prime habitat for endangered sage grouse. Todd Forbes, field manager for the BLM's Lakeview Resource Area, believes a key factor in gaining funds for such a large roundup was concern for the sage grouse population.[37]

The Beatys Butte gather will probably never be repeated. Over a month of activity, the BLM captured 1,070 horses, reducing the population to just over a hundred, a figure well within the carrying capacity of the range. In subsequent years, the bureau planned to capture a few each year to stabilize numbers at that level. Small-scale captures would be easier to manage, less costly, and should keep the horse population at healthy levels. Moreover, on September 16, 2016, the Beatys Butte Wild Horse Gather, Fertility Control, and Training Center—a private, nonprofit body operating out of Adel—entered into a contract to work with the BLM to make captured horses tamer, even saddle-ready, and thus more adoptable, and to work with the BLM in future captures and related activities.[38]

Ranchers were sometimes critical of how the BLM managed the wild horse problem, but most of the debate was driven by outsiders whose concern was tied more to an emotional attachment to horses than concern for the environment. However, the sixty or more observers who arrived to monitor the Beatys Butte gather found little to complain about; the worst of the abuses that had driven "Wild Horse Annie" and others to action were a thing of the past, and the BLM had handled the situation with an eye to public opinion. In the end no significant local opposition developed, although many outside activists remained unswayed.[39]

Conditions were different in Grant County, where forests not rangelands were the primary source of controversy. National forests made up almost 40 percent of the county, and the Forest Service's management rankled locals. Grumbling about the agency had a long history in John Day. While Fred Herrick was building his sawmill near Burns in the 1920s, the *Blue Mountain Eagle* groused that timber from the sale would be shipped south to Harney County rather than milled in the John Day area, which was closer to the stands, and complained that the Forest Service was far too lenient when Herrick failed to meet contract obligations.

By the 1990s, criticism had turned in new directions. Across the country, some people had come to see the Forest Service as a "shill" for the lumber industry—and political pressure during the 1960s and 1970s to "get out the cut" gave some credence to the charge. Critics of the resulting overcutting slowly emerged, urged on both by environmentalists and by many within the ranks of professional forestry.[40]

The appointment of Jack Ward Thomas as chief of the Forest Service in 1993 reflected the changes. Thomas represented a sharp shift away from the silvicultural emphasis of previous chiefs. He was a wildlife biologist who had worked for the Forest Service in the La Grande area for twenty years, was the editor and moving force behind a much-lauded study of wildlife habitat in the Blue Mountains, and had headed the task force appointed to develop strategies for managing forest habitat for endangered spotted owls. His appointment as chief represented a shift that many in and out of the agency viewed with disquiet; his widely quoted statement that "ecosystems are not only more complex than we know, they are more complex than we can know"—smacking as it did of concerns long obscured in the production-oriented Forest Service—did nothing to lessen their unease.[41]

In response to the conviction that environmentalists had taken control of the Forest Service, in 1995 Grant County voters passed by a three-to-one margin an initiative measure refusing to recognize federal control over public lands in the county. No ordinance was involved, but the vote reflected deep-seated feelings. Angst continued, and in 2002 voters passed a follow-up measure declaring the "right of citizens to participate in stewardship of natural resources on public lands." Proponents pushed for transfer of federally owned lands within Grant County to county control and the creation of a local board to oversee their management—action that would have reduced the Forest Service to an advisory role. They argued the Forest Service was so hamstrung by environmentalists, it "hasn't been able to work as it should." Logging, thinning, and controlled burns had been so restricted in response to pressure from environmentalists that forests had grown overly dense, their fuel loads so heavy that devastating fires were a constant threat. Passage of the measure led to no immediate changes but clearly revealed the distrust of outside control that had developed in the isolated county—as did a companion measure declaring Grant County a United Nations–free zone. Suspicion of outsiders had joined concern for private property rights and hostility to environmentalists in a muddled mix that grew apace.[42]

In 1996 activist Patrick Shipsey, a recent arrival in the John Day area, shot a neighbor's cows that "trespassed" on his property to eat grass on land he was trying to restore to health after years of overgrazing. Grant County operated under open-range laws that required people to fence out cattle if they did not want them on their land, but that made no difference to Shipsey. He believed he had a right to protect the land, *his* land. Reactions to Shipsey's actions were so harsh he soon decamped for California— where he soon got himself into other difficulties. The incident was widely publicized, and perhaps not coincidentally, a clean waters bill Shipsey was actively supporting went down to crushing defeat.[43]

In a somewhat similar situation, the owners of GI Ranch prosecuted a party of hunters from the Willamette Valley who killed an elk on BLM land enclosed within their holdings. The hunters had crossed ranch land— unfenced and unsigned—to get to the public land. Elsewhere the ranch posted "No Trespassing" signs along county roads and then added in small print at the bottom "except for BLM access." Even earlier, armed employ-ees of the Hudspeth Land Company patrolled the firm's holdings near Antone—not always making a distinction between company property and BLM land on which it had only grazing rights. And when ONDA proposed a High Desert Trail running from near Bend to Owyhee Reservoir, the question of its impact on property rights (and the impact hikers, presum-ably mostly outsiders, might have on private holdings) was raised repeat-edly. Clearly, the welcome mat was no longer out, and in a variety of ways, freedom to roam the outback was being eroded, at least for outsiders.[44]

In Harney, Grant, Lake, and Crook Counties, developments took a dif-ferent form than in Deschutes: environmentalists and outsiders in general, rather than Californians, were cast as the threat, but there was a common thread. Across Eastern Oregon a widespread fear had developed that life as residents had long known it was slipping from their grasp, changed irrepa-rably by outside forces. David Carkhuff, editor of the *Blue Mountain Eagle*, summarized the situation: people "feel they no longer control their lives, livelihoods or the land." It was a malaise shared by the generally irrepress-ible Tom McCall who, late in life and dying of cancer, wandered the halls of his boyhood home on Crooked River musing on things that were no more.[45]

17
Accommodation

Commodity exports long undergirded the economy of Eastern Oregon, but at unsustainable levels. They brought in money that built communities and supported the population, however unevenly, yet gradually the source of economic support shifted. During the late twentieth century tourists, recreational development, retirees from elsewhere, and increased government services brought in funds that replaced the dwindling income from commodity exports. Baker City (long known simply as Baker), La Grande, Burns, and Lakeview continued to be nearly as large as in their heyday as centers of ranching and lumber manufacture, while Redmond grew as a satellite community for Bend even as the agricultural production that once supported it dried up.

Some towns held on to their past better than others. As the twenty-first century began, an area resident observed, "Prineville remains true to its redneck roots." It hosts the annual state high school rodeo championships and the Crooked River Roundup, begun in 1945 "to celebrate the cultural heritage of the 'Cowboy Capitol of Oregon' . . . [and provide] a unique glimpse into the area's wild-west heritage." From the first, organizers saw the roundup as a "real" rodeo, unlike the glamorized events at Pendleton, and it attracted elite participants including Casey Tibbs, Slim Pickens, and Ross Dollarhide—all eventually in the ProRodeo Hall of Fame. Yet even in Prineville the forces that remade Bend began to intrude. Ellen Waterston, surveying changes taking place in Central Oregon, wrote, "For a dose of what's left of the real, go to Madras," not Prineville. Not everywhere has been so fortunate, if that is the correct word. Many a modest little community shriveled and some vanished: a listing would include Kinzua, Izee, Post, Paulina, Lonerock, Adel, Blitzen, Brogan, Crane, Durkee, and more.[1]

As social, economic, and environmental circumstances changed, the attitudes of many who lived on the land adjusted accordingly. A society

that had initially been exploitive, and then confrontational, was gradually
moving toward custodianship and cooperation.

Doug McDaniel was among those coping with the new realities while
continuing to pursue a rural livelihood some would dismiss as passé.
McDaniel, born and raised in Wallowa County, had forebears among its
first white settlers. He grew up hunting and fishing in nearby valleys and
mountains. After working at the Bates Mill, he left to study at Oregon State
University and returned to start and manage companies involved with logging, construction, and ranching. Through it all, McDaniel developed a
respect for the restorative power of nature and a growing concern over the
environmental degradation going on around him.

The Wallowa River runs through McDaniel's ranch east of Lostine, but
by the 1980s it was a far cry from what it once had been. The river had been
damaged by unrestricted livestock grazing, diverted eastward in 1908 to
accommodate railroad construction, and channelized in the name of flood
control. Through much of the valley the river was confined to a twenty- to
thirty-foot-wide channel with a steep gradient and was useless as a spawning site for anadromous fishes—and nearly as valueless for trout.

McDaniel determined to do something about it. Knowing correctives
were beyond the capacity of individuals, in 1996 he helped found Wallowa Resources, a nonprofit community-based organization. Wallowa
Resources describes itself as seeking to further "sustainable land management, ecosystem health, family-wage jobs, and community well-being,
and preserving Wallowa County's rural way of life . . . [and] to blend the
ecological needs of the land with the economic needs of the community."
McDaniel served on its board from the first, and it was on his ranch
that in 1999 the organization launched its first major project, restoring
McDaniel's portion of the Wallowa into a meandering stream with riparian
vegetation and gravel bars for spawning salmon and steelhead. The Oregon
Department of Fish and Wildlife, Oregon Watershed Enhancement Board,
National Resource Conservation Service, Nez Perce Tribe, and Bonneville
Power Administration all contributed support.

What had worked on his land was needed on other stretches of the
river too, and McDaniel pushed for further restoration. James Nash and
others soon followed McDaniel's lead on another section of the Wallowa.
Wallowa Resources was becoming a model for those in rural areas seeking

to bring long-term economic and ecological health to their environs. None of this came easily. Frustrated with the impediments of bureaucracy, McDaniel urged policy makers to trust the creativity of individual land-owners and leave space in regulations for grassroots contributions.

McDaniel's concerns were justified. In 1995 the Wallowa-Whitman National Forest instituted a Grande Ronde River Fish Habitat Restoration Project on that steam's upper reaches. Private inholdings and grazing leaseholds were scattered throughout the area, but project planners proceeded as if they alone had the expertise and wherewithal to carry out the project. Vestiges of the technological hubris that had long afflicted the Forest Service clearly remained.[2]

Initially some locals were wary of Wallowa Resources, concerned that it was the instrument of outsiders and might threaten local property rights. The fact that so many of its staff were from elsewhere—four of the ten from Portland—added to suspicions, but gradually the organization won over doubters. Its claim that it valued "making a living from the land" and to that end sought "to invest in people and businesses that take care of the land" had proved more than window dressing.[3]

The Wallowa Land Trust was a key ally in Wallowa Resources' efforts to restore rivers and improve fisheries while protecting the rural lifestyle. In 2001 the success of a Land Trust chapter in Walla Walla led to formation of the Blue Mountain Trust centered in La Grande; in 2005 James Monteith and others followed suit, creating the Wallowa Land Trust. In the years that followed, the organization pursued its goal of "protecting the rural nature of Wallowa County" by purchasing conservation easements on private properties using grants and donated funds. Title remained with private owners, but development rights rested with the trust, guaranteeing the tracts would remain working land and helping keep farms and ranches intact.

The trust's first major acquisition was a 197-acre easement near the confluence of the Lostine and the Wallowa Rivers. The tract was ideal for subdividing for trophy homes, but ranch owner Woody Wolfe wanted none of that. He had seen what had happened to property values elsewhere when such development took place. "If the place turned into a Sunriver or a Jackson Hole, my net value would go through the roof, but then where would I live? If enough people buy land over here because of the way it is, it won't be the way it is."[4] Wolfe's fears were more than justified. One

Wallowa Lake and its moraines, a major target of the Wallowa Land Trust. Credit: Leon Werdinger.

local asked why conservation easements were necessary, since Oregon's Land Conservation and Development Commission, established during Tom McCall's governorship, already provided protection;[5] but LCDC was hardly foolproof. As Meta Loftsgaarden, executive director of the Oregon Watershed Enhancement Board, noted, "This system alone isn't enough to prevent fragmentation of working lands." In Wallowa County, where 60 percent of privately held land belonged to absentee owners, the problem was especially complex. Still, the trust was able to preserve from development a number of areas, including the moraines overlooking Wallowa Lake, one of North America's most perfectly formed and best-preserved glacial landscapes, which included sacred Nez Perce lands (a special concern to Monteith as his Nez Perce great-grandmother had resided in the area).[6]

But easements raised concerns. Grant County rancher Roger Ediger supported them. He told a reporter, "If we don't look farther than our own lifespan, then we'll have nothing," yet he questioned the "environmental agenda" of some organizations behind easements and the resulting potential for interference in land use.[7]

Concerns such as those that drove McDaniel, Monteith, and Wolfe existed in other corners of Eastern Oregon too. A proposal to build a destination resort near the headwaters of the Metolius was especially contentious. The huge spring where the river emerged full-blown from the foot of Black Butte had long been cherished by locals. A microclimate that resulted from moisture-blocking Green Ridge kept the area green and lush even in summer. In the 1930s Sam Boardman had sought to acquire the river's headwaters for a state park, but landowner S. O. Johnson claimed to be planning a sawmill there and wanted the water for a mill pond. Johnson used his supposed plans to demand a large tract of timber in exchange for the site. Lacking the wherewithal to complete the transaction, Boardman had to back off. Perhaps Johnson had been dissembling; no sawmill was ever built there, but in time he fenced off the springs and built a summer home nearby. Years later, after Johnson's son took over family interests, the area was opened to the public and quickly became a popular destination.[8]

Early in the twenty-first century, the upper Metolius again became a center of contention. A group of developers proposed a major new destination resort, dubbed the Metolian, nearby. "Unlike most destination resorts," they proclaimed, "the Metolian is thoughtfully considered and designed to have minimum impact on the land and . . . will set the standard for sustainable and stewardship-based development." For years there had been modest development at Camp Sherman, but the scale of the proposed project was unprecedented. As early as 1974, Tom McCall had singled out the river as a site of special environmental concern, and in 1988 it had been granted national Wild and Scenic Rivers status. The Salem *Statesman-Journal* argued that, like the Oregon Coast and Columbia Gorge, the upper Metolius was an area valued by all Oregonians, not just residents of Central Oregon. Recognizing its vulnerability, in 2003 the Deschutes Land Trust acquired 1,240 acres near the river's headwaters, but other prime locations remained. A proposal for resort development in the basin was guaranteed to be controversial.[9]

Under LCDC rules, the Jefferson County Commission was responsible for reviewing the proposal and, swayed by the developers' claims and eager for the increased tax base, approved the project. But others had doubts. Crook County had already taken steps to put the brakes on new resort projects, and Jerry Andres, a leading Klamath County businessman, proclaimed, "Destination resorts are done in Oregon." Protests to the Metolian soon echoed. In 2008, pushed by Governor Ted Kulongoski, the state took steps to block it. The LCDC drew on previously unused authority to declare the Metolius Basin an Area of Critical Concern. Jefferson

County officials objected, maintaining the local control central to LCDC procedures should be honored. Conservatives, never enamored of centralized control and intent on protecting private property rights, added their voices. Editorials, petitions, and letters to editors followed. The Sisters City Council voted support for locally controlled land-use planning, but like much of the rest of Central Oregon, it was deeply divided on the issue.[10]

Debate soon focused on two proposals in the state legislature. The first would codify the LCDC's designation of the Metolius Basin as an Area of Critical Concern. The second, something of a sop to Metolian's would-be developers, offered approval of a similar project outside the basin if it met environmental guidelines. The votes were close, but supporters of the proposals carried the day. Still, a national economic downturn had already set in that might have doomed the Metolian in any case; some developments in neighboring Deschutes and Crook Counties had already gone under; reportedly there had been some six thousand foreclosures of destination resort properties in Deschutes County alone. But this hardly proved permanent. As the economy recovered from the Great Recession, new resort developments appeared in Central Oregon once again—and elsewhere as well.[11]

Complex though the story was, in the end at least one thing was clear: those who desired to develop holdings now had to accommodate their proposals to the views of those who lived on and with the land and to others who sought to protect it—mere assurances that projects were environmentally sensitive would no longer suffice.

Creeping development was a more insidious threat than destination resorts, and 1000 Friends of Oregon, a statewide watchdog group that Tom McCall helped launch in 1975, set about to ensure that the type of runaway exurban development that plagued Colorado would not occur in Oregon.[12] To that end, it sought strict enforcement of the rules and the spirit of the LCDC.

Much of the work of 1000 Friends focused on blocking unwarranted expansion of urban development boundaries west of the Cascades, especially in the upper Willamette Valley, but it saw problems in Eastern Oregon, too, and laid out the perceived threats in a powerful booklet, *Too Many Homes on the Range*. In 2004, funded by a grant from the William and Flora Hewlett Foundation, 1000 Friends undertook a major study seeking "practical solutions to . . . [the] common threat to viability of both ranching and habitat—rural sprawl." Central to the study was dialogue between ranchers and environmentalists, dialogue based on rejection of "the common assumption that ranchers and environmentalists are at odds." *Too Many Homes on the Range* was one result. Summing up the project, a 1000 Friends spokesman wrote, "Although we heard many opinions on a variety of topics, one thing was eminently clear: by and large, Oregon farmers and ranchers do not see the land-use system itself as an impediment to their success."[13]

Lucky Creek Ranch near Prineville provided an example of what could happen without LCDC. The Riverside Ranch subdivision, approved before the law establishing the commission went into effect, resulted in a busy road through the property, troublesome neighbors with no concept of ranching, and harassment and sabotage in a variety of forms. After coping for years, the owners put their ranch up for sale—even though they feared doing so would lead to a new subdivision. Beverly Wolverton, whose grandfather had homesteaded the ranch, lamented, "It's hard to think of leaving this land after 90 years, but I don't see if we have any choice."[14]

Yet the overall picture was positive. A study by the Oregon Department of Forestry found that 98 percent of the nonfederal farm, range, and forestland in Oregon remained undeveloped in 2009. A follow-up study comparing developments in Oregon and Washington showed that the former had a considerably better record both east and west of the Cascades than its northern neighbor, largely because it had passed stronger land-use regulations at an earlier date.[15]

The reports seem to give undue credit to the LCDC. Land trust conservation easements, which had been so successful in the Wallowa Valley, were utilized elsewhere as well. Jack Sparrowk's Drew's Valley Ranch, west of Lakeview, used a conservation easement to keep his land intact—and in the process protected eight creeks, a considerable body of wetland, a lake, and over eight miles of riparian corridor. LCDC regulations had been designed to protect such property, but without the easement there was no guarantee it would have remained a working ranch. Projects such as Sparrowk's developed from the actions of concerned individuals, not from legal mandates.[16]

In the same period, long-contentious issues were moving toward settlement in the Klamath Basin, but nowhere was accommodation harder to come by.

On February 18, 2010, after years of negotiations, Governor Kulongoski, California governor Arnold Schwarzenegger, Secretary of the Interior Ken Salazar, the National Oceanic and Atmospheric Administration fisheries administrator Jane Lubchenko, Pacific Power and Light's Greg Abel, agricultural and tribal leaders, assorted conservation and fishing groups, and commissioners of the affected counties signed an agreement calling for removal of COPCO's four hydroelectric dams on the Klamath River by 2020—the nation's largest dam removal and river restoration project to that time. With the dams gone, salmon, steelhead, and trout populations were expected to return to healthy levels and water quality in the river to rise. An associated Klamath Basin Restoration Agreement promised to provide certainty for water users in the Klamath Basin while continuing to protect endangered species. For the moment, decades of disputes seemed to be settled. No one was completely pleased, but accommodations had been reached that it seemed all could live with. However, Congress refused to endorse the settlement until dam removals were eliminated from the formula, and in 2013 new water shutoffs reopened old wounds. Thus by 2016 the agreement was unravelling, although the goal of a shared settlement, mutually agreed-on, remained, and progress continued, however slowly.[17] Still, with water inadequate for all the desired uses, the issue is certain to remain contentious.

Problems in the Steens Mountain country were nearly as intractable. Critics of grazing practices became increasingly active in the 1990s. Together with the Wilderness Society, the Oregon Natural Desert Association (ONDA) sponsored a conference at Malheur Field Station in 1991, where they unveiled a proposed Oregon High Desert Protection Act. The *Burns Times-Herald* covered the conference in what it considered an "objective and comprehensive" manner, but when another conference was convened the following year, the newspaper was not invited. Even mild critics were clearly not welcome; apparently only one local was admitted. A silent protest soon developed in the community, and Fred Otley, a fourth-generation Harney County rancher, mounted a counterattack. Speaking to the local chamber of commerce, he argued land managers needed to avoid politics "and concentrate on doing the job on the land." To counter ONDA's claims, he showed slides illustrating grazing was not necessarily bad, indeed that some ungrazed stream banks in the area were in worse shape than those grazed carefully. As he put it later, "We've worked really hard to manage the area in a progressive manner. Our land is in good and excellent condition. . . . It makes sense to continue the public-private partnership." But the Oregon Natural Desert Association gradually gained strength outside of Harney County, if not within, as it attacked what it claimed were the prevailing practices of ranchers and the policies of the BLM, which it viewed as beholden to them. When the bureau proposed building a 3.5-mile-long fence to keep cattle out of an ecologically sensitive area, ONDA challenged the plan: "Today it's a fence, tomorrow it's a feedlot. This goes to the heart of why we want the National Park Service to manage the Steens and get the BLM out of there."[18]

When the BLM failed to prepare an environmental impact statement regarding its management plan for the Blitzen-Steens area, ONDA took it to court. In the decision that followed, Judge Ancer Haggerty found the BLM had failed to meet the requirements of existing laws, but he had no solution other than to order the agency to meet with the plaintiffs to work out an agreement on grazing allotments. Should the parties be unable to come to an understanding, Judge Haggerty threatened a court-ordered plan. Faced with this possibility, intractable, long-hostile adversaries were soon sitting together at the negotiating table.[19]

There were precedents. In 1988, Whitehorse Ranch, located south of the Steens in the Trout Creek-Pueblo Mountain country, had joined the Bureau of Land Management, United States Fish and Wildlife Service, Oregon Department of Fish and Wildlife, Oregon Environmental Council, Oregon Cattlemen's Association, Oregon Trout, and the Izaak Walton League to form the Trout Creek Mountain Working Group to review, discuss, and resolve land-use conflicts in the area. As the group's work proceeded, the owners of Whitehorse Ranch voluntarily removed livestock from fifty thousand acres of its Whitehorse Butte grazing allotment and two other mountain pastures for a period of three years to prevent further overgrazing and allow watershed and riparian areas to recover. Finally, in 1992, the working group agreed on a long-term plan. As part of that agreement, Whitehorse Ranch agreed to reduce the number of its cattle on public lands from 3,500 to 800.[20]

Progress came more slowly on the Steens. Advocates on both sides had strongly entrenched views. ONDA executive director Bill Marlett was blunt: "Livestock grazing is responsible for more habitat destruction than all other human activities combined," and he called for an end to grazing on public lands. Faced with such views, ranchers worried about their future. Among them was Stacy Davies, manager of the huge Roaring Springs Ranch. Davies feared area ranchers were within a year of losing everything; if they were kicked off the Steens, he told one reporter, "I'd probably go to law school and [learn how to] give Bill Marlett hell."[21] Boiling just below the surface was fear that, without some form of action, landowners might sell their property to developers, opening the door for such changes as had happened around Bend.[22]

The issue became even more complex when activists sought endangered species status for the area's redband trout populations. The Roaring Springs Ranch, federal Fish and Wildlife Service, and Oregon Department of Fish and Wildlife soon entered into the Catlow Valley Fish Conservation Agreement to help ensure a future for redbands and the tui chub even if the petition for endangered species protection failed—which it did. The agreement was lauded by the American Fisheries Society, Monty Montgomery of the Isaak Walton League, Doug Young of the Oregon Fish and Wildlife Department, Governor John Kitzhaber, and Environmental Stewardship (which named Roaring Springs its regional Environmental Stewardship winner in 2007). But ONDA's leadership was unimpressed. Roaring Springs was able to do things small ranchers could not, it argued, and in any case the agreement "really begs the question whether we should be grazing those areas at all." The *Oregonian's* Richard Cockle noted Roaring Springs was "a livestock operation . . . that some environmentalists would say attempts the impossible. It focuses on the health of the rangeland and wildlife." In any case, the introduction into the equation of the Endangered Species Act (and the Blitzen's protection as a Wild and Scenic River) made a workable compromise on the Steens, let alone consensus, seem less likely than ever.[23]

Bruce Babbitt, secretary of the interior under President Bill Clinton, broke the impasse. Babbitt had been responsible for a number of new national monuments—most notably the Grand Staircase-Escalante National Monument in southern Utah, created in 1996 to the applause of environmentalists and the chagrin of both ranchers and the State of Utah. In a meeting in Burns in August 1999, Babbitt floated the idea of making the Steens Mountain area another such monument (or possibly a national park), but such designation, he added, could be avoided if the BLM, environmentalists, and ranchers could craft a workable alternative. Frightened by the prospect of a national monument instituted by executive fiat—and by their fear that it would bring hordes of tourists whose very presence would destroy the wildness of the mountain that they cherished—ranching interests entered into serious negotiations. Fred Otley, who referred to Steens Mountain affectionately as "the Old Girl," put it bluntly: "We've worked really hard to manage the area in a progressive manner. . . . We're concerned that the wrong type of designation or wrong language could screw that up."[24]

Bill Marlett saw Babbitt's action as pivotal; as he put it, "President Clinton and Secretary Babbitt's willingness to protect the Steens through national monument designation was an essential ingredient" in driving antagonists to the bargaining table. But just how serious Babbitt had been is unclear. A westerner himself, Babbitt preferred solutions hammered out by locals to ones imposed from Washington.[25]

Eventually, negotiators were able to craft an agreement creating Steens Mountain Cooperative Management and Protection Area (CMPA). The agreement required an act of Congress to formalize it, and Babbitt insisted that before submission it needed the support of the entire Oregon congressional delegation and incoming Governor John Kitzhaber. Marlett opposed the agreement—which ONDA had not been a participant in crafting—for grazing would not be eliminated. But gradually requisite support was garnered, and the Steens Mountain CMPA came into being. The use of the lands on the mountain would now include "grazing, recreation, historic, and other uses that are sustainable." It guaranteed "traditional access to cultural, gathering, religious, and archaeological sites," a concern of area Paiutes, and the conservation and protection of "geological, biological, wildlife, riparian, and scenic resources." No industrial activity would be allowed, and development would be limited to private ranches and primitive campgrounds and recreation facilities. Part of the mountain was set aside as a wilderness area.[26]

Accommodation had not come easily. Under its new executive director, Brent Fenty, ONDA boasted of its role in bringing the Steens agreement into being, claiming it had "worked for decades to protect, defend, and restore the natural character of the mountain" and "was instrumental in the passage of the Steens Mountain Cooperative Management and Protection Act that designated the first 'livestock-free' Wilderness Area in the country." The claim was a stretch; under Marlett, ONDA had opposed such a unit, had not been a party to its crafting, and on various legal grounds had challenged the compromises that were at its core. In 2010 roughly a quarter of ONDA's budget was still going for legal expenses. Even when it proposed ambitious new projects like the Oregon Desert Trail—undertakings offering little threat to vested livestock interests—locals remained suspicious. As one put it, "I think ONDA is taking on this whole [desert trail] project to recruit people to its legal work." A Burns resident was blunt: "Why do you think the community should support an effort by ONDA? I see your [entire] history as obstructionist."[27]

The BLM had problems of its own with the agreement. Cooperation restricted its freedom of action, and the agreement included fencing requirements that BLM's budget was inadequate to meet. Congressman Greg Walden was among those who had helped craft the agreement, but he was chagrined when "little by little the [federal] agencies decided to reinterpret it at their own convenience or ignore it altogether." He complained to BLM officials and, getting no satisfaction, got congressional reassertion of the act's intent. Unwilling to openly admit errors, BLM officials simply said they would "revisit" the issue. Walden asked pointedly, "How can people be expected to have faith in a public process when they see outcomes like this?"[28]

The settlement may not have been what Bill Marlett or the BLM wanted, but it represented a new, though fragile, spirit of accommodation and a framework within which differences could be worked out. Ellen Waterston and Nancy Langston, both of whom thought land-use policies ought to emerge from give-and-take among local interests, shared Bruce Babbitt's view that the best land-use policies resulted from compromises among contending interests at the local level. Such settlements were difficult for the BLM, whose land managers disliked having their decisions questioned, and were equally challenging for true believers such as Bill Marlett, but by the turn of the century they were becoming more and more common. Under Bruce Fenty, even ONDA grudgingly moved in that direction. It remained to be seen whether the BLM would follow suit.[29]

Not all accommodations were as difficult to come by as those involving Klamath Basin and Steens Mountain; indeed, in forests south of Bend it came with remarkable ease. Originally owned by the Gilchrist interests, what would become the Gilchrist State Forest was sold to Crown Pacific

Partners in 1991. Crown Pacific struggled under the large debt load of its heavily leveraged buyout. Abandoning Gilchrist's careful sustained-yield management, the new owners cut with abandon, trying to generate funds to stay afloat. The strategy failed, and in June 2003, Crown Pacific filed for bankruptcy. Creditors took over the remaining assets, the forestlands going to Cascade Timberlands LLC. Two years later, Fidelity National Timber Resources, a subsidiary of Fidelity National Financial, purchased them.[30]

The forest had been heavily cut—stripped—by Crown Pacific; remaining timber values were slight, but it was traversed by the Little Deschutes. Coupled with the fact Fidelity's CEO was developer Bill Foley, whose holdings included Whitefish Mountain Resort in Montana, the sale seemed ominous. It did not take much imagination to foresee another resort development like nearby Sunriver. Even without a major resort, another threat remained: fragmentation. If steps were not taken to keep the forest intact, leaders of environmental nonprofit The Conservation Fund believed, the forest would likely be sold in small parcels, and the opportunity for multiple-use forest management lost.[31]

To head off such developments, Governor Kulongoski encouraged the Oregon State Board of Forestry to purchase the land. The state lacked discretionary funds with which to make the purchase, but a strategy soon emerged. Using bonds secured by money from the state lottery, it purchased forty-three thousand acres from Fidelity National for $15 million. Even in their depleted state, the former Gilchrist holdings were too valuable for the state to purchase the whole, so The Conservation Fund bought an additional twenty-five thousand adjacent acres with the intent of holding title until funds became available for the state to purchase them. In the interim, both the state-owned lands and those of the nonprofit were to be managed as a single unit by the state. In June 2010 Kulongski dedicated Gilchrist State Forest, Oregon's first new state-owned forest in six decades. As he observed at the dedication, "Forests are a part of Oregon's identity and essential to Oregon's economy and well-being. Even during challenging times . . . we need to make investments in our state's economic and environmental future, and that is what we are doing . . . [with] this new forest."[32]

Surrounded by three national forests, BLM land, and other state property, Gilchrist Forest seemed well insulated against developers. But

debate soon developed over its management. Kulongoski believed decisions should be made by experts rather than shaped by political pressure.
He rejected legislation dictating that forest harvests be kept at sustainable
and responsible levels, the sort of practices the Gilchrists had followed.
Instead Kulongoski wanted experts of the State Department of Forestry
and Board of Forestry to make determinations based on facts, not politics
or inflexible legislative directives. In a period when there was considerable
public hostility to government resource agencies and plans, he opposed
ballot measures prescribing forest policy and harvest levels. His desire to
keep decision making with professionals in the state's forestry agency was
not an easy sell in the face of the belief of many that it was a "kept" organization beholden to industry, and of others that they were overly influenced
by environmentalist pressures that damaged local economies by keeping
harvests unnecessarily low. But in the end Kulongoski prevailed.[33]

Forest officials—and Kulongoski—anticipated Gilchrist Forest would
bring both sustainable forestry and public recreation, each of which would
provide increased revenue for Klamath County, where income had fallen well
below the state median. John Pelliser, in charge of the forest, put it plainly:
this "is not a park. It is not a conservation area. It is a working forest." But
he did not expect it to be ready for timber harvests for thirty years. In the
meantime, Interfor, the new owners of the Gilchrist sawmill, would have to
obtain logs elsewhere—and it was feasible to do so since, with the exception
of the sawmill at Warm Springs, most mills in Central Oregon and the Klamath Basin had closed and no longer competed at private or federal timber
sales—and within a year the Warm Springs sawmill would close too.[34]

The creation of Gilchrist State Forest could serve as an object lesson.
It showed that such diverse groups as environmentalists, professional land
managers, developers, recreationists, and champions of local control could
work together without being threatened by the sort of heavy club Babbitt
had wielded to force a settlement on Steens Mountain. Interfor's sawmill at
Gilchrist continued to operate, and—although no longer a company town—
the Gilchrist community (and its satellite, Crescent) continued to prosper.

Tensions surrounding forestlands were more evident elsewhere. Years
of low rainfall during the early twenty-first century exacerbated problems in the Blue Mountains. Drought weakened trees even when it did
not kill them and opened the way for pine bark beetles to complete the

job: by 2007, more than five hundred thousand acres were infested. One researcher noted that whereas fire had once been the main thinning agent keeping forests healthy, insects had now assumed that role. But in fact the two worked together. Tinder-dry fuel loads resulting from beetle kills led to devastating wildfires year after year; by 2008 over 40 percent of the Forest Service's budget was going to fire control, leaving less and less for silviculture and other needs.[35]

Meanwhile Oregon's lumber industry was in free fall. Structural changes in the lumber industry made small mills less profitable; many closed. Statewide the number of sawmills plummeted from 405 in 1980 to 106 in 2010; during the same period timber harvests fell from 3 billion board feet per year to 510 million. Baker County, once a major lumber producer, saw its last sawmill close in 1996. The situation was even worse in the Ochocos, where output dropped from 120 million board feet a year to five million. Payments from timber sales for local schools and roads fell accordingly. The Great Recession that commenced in 2008 led to even more sawmill closures; by 2015 only fifteen mills remained in Eastern Oregon. Some 1,200 jobs vanished with the closures. In the 1970s, Grant and Harney Counties had boasted some of the highest per capita income levels in the state, but as the lumber industry imploded they plummeted. Remaining mills often had difficulty getting an adequate supply of sawlogs, since an estimated 9.5 million acres of eastside forests were in at least a moderately unhealthy condition and many had been badly overcut. A lack of sufficient funds to manage Forest Service lands exacerbated problems. Inevitably, the agency's timber management policies came in for sharp criticism.[36]

Friction had grown following the appointment of Jack Ward Thomas as chief of the Forest Service in 1993. Under Thomas's leadership, the agency shifted from an emphasis on silviculture to environmental protection. He announced that the Forest Service "is going to be a leader in ecosystem management." As a result, one congressman complained, the agency's personnel "became park rangers instead of silviculturists." Environmentalists, spurred on by the well-publicized plight of the spotted owl and rising concern for watershed protection, were vocal in their criticism of earlier practices and lent support to the policy shift.

But many thought progress was coming too slowly; lawsuits became a primary weapon in the quest for speedier change. Groups like the Western

Environmental Law Center forced review after review of Forest Service management decisions and led to many being put on hold, thus exacerbating the problems that structural changes in the lumber industry already posed for sawmill operators. In Grant County, local issues added to the volatile mix when supervisors on the Malheur National Forest took a variety of steps—road closures, limits on access for off-road vehicles, and restrictions on the long-established practice of firewood gathering—that angered many.[37]

Things only got worse. Many critics—not just those in Grant County—blamed regulatory overreach, while Republican congressman Greg Walden argued the "crux of the problem is the need to reduce the regulatory gridlock." He argued, "We're creating through federal policies and litigation impoverished communities and impoverished people." Democrat Ron Wyden was more succinct: "Under the current system, we end up suing the dickens out of each other." A district ranger in the Wallowa-Whitman National Forest agreed: "This country is so polarized we can't get on the same page to make a decision."[38]

Aware of the impasse, Governors Kitzhaber and Kulongoski encouraged a fresh approach. In 2000 Kitzhaber issued an executive order creating a Sustainability Workgroup tasked with developing fresh approaches to resource use that would enable "people to meet their current needs while allowing future generations to meet their needs." The group was formalized (and funded) by the legislature as the Oregon Sustainability Board; and in 2006, with key portions of the act about to expire, Kulongoski continued the agency through an executive order. Out of this emerged a program known as Oregon Solutions, initially operated out of the governor's office and, after 2002, out of Portland State University. The program developed more than sixty community-based projects in which government and private organizations, together with interested individuals, worked on projects directed at specific local needs. Only a few of these focused on forests or sites east of the Cascades, but they offered hope that groups with widely differing priorities could work together to address Eastern Oregon's forest problems.[39]

Pushing further, in 2004 Kulongoski asked the State Board of Forestry for "recommendations to restore healthy, productive forests" through "a unified vision of how federal forests should be managed to restore a sustainable blend of social, environmental and economic benefits of the forests." After two years of work by its Federal Forestland Advisory Committee, which represented a wide range of interests, and with the aid of Oregon Consensus, which provided "neutral facilitation and process assistance," the board presented its study, *Achieving Oregon's Vision for Federal Forestlands*. In sum it recommended a collaborative approach to managing federal forests. As the report put it, "Strategic goals [should be] developed and implemented through a collaborative partnership with national, state, local, and tribal governments, and public involvement." Under such an approach the Forest Service, long accustomed to charting its own course, would have to work closely with others and adjust its policies to their desires as never before. Whether it would or not remained to be seen.[40]

Senator Ron Wyden pushed in the same direction. In 2009 he introduced S.2895, his Eastside Forest Plan, designed to bring a significant increase in logging in Oregon's forests (including some west of the Cascades), while incorporating environmental protections and setting limits on legal challenges. It was a proposal with which no one was entirely happy. The *Baker City Herald* put it bluntly: "We don't believe Wyden's bill would change in any meaningful way how the Forest Service manages those 8.3 million acres" it controls. The *Herald* was correct. Wyden's bill eventually passed (as S.2895), but the Forest Service gave ground grudgingly as management proposals and counterproposals were floated and numerous hearings held in an effort to make a reality of the approach Wyden championed.[41]

Government agencies and individuals met, studied, and made reports, but little changed on the ground. Then, in 2005, Grant County judge Mark Webb took a first step toward turning calls for cooperation into reality. He reached out to Western Environmental Law Center's Susan Jane Brown, proposing they form a group of varied stakeholders to evaluate the forest situation in the southern Blues and make recommendations thereon. With the aid of County Commissioner Boyd Britton, they gradually brought others into a strange marriage of environmentalists, forest managers, and locals that would emerge in 2006 as the Blue Mountain Forest Partners. At first participants eyed one another with suspicion, but gradually they came to see they shared a concern for the long-term health of the forest.[42]

Matters came to a head in August 2012. Malheur Lumber Company, the county's largest private employer and its lone remaining sawmill (there once had been five), announced it was unable to obtain an adequate log supply and would cease operations in November. Locals were stunned.

Scotta Callister, editor of the *Blue Mountain Eagle*, noted closure would be "a huge hit for a county already beleaguered by unemployment, poverty and remoteness. Ah, yes, remoteness. That translates . . . as 'easy to forget.'" Perhaps Malheur Lumber "could be revived," she wrote, "but we haven't had much experience with that kind of phenomenon here in Grant County in recent years."[43]

Callister's fears proved unwarranted. A multifaceted scramble to keep the mill open soon developed. Timberland owners who had been holding trees off the market because of low prices offered to make additional stumpage available, thus providing an extra month or two to seek more permanent answers to the mill's problems. Mark Webb took the issue to Portland, where he met with Oregon's congressional delegation, Governor Kitzhaber, and state legislators. Solutions did not appear at once. Bruce Daucsavage, president of the Ochoco Lumber Company (of which Malheur Lumber was a subsidiary), was heartened by the leadership of the Malheur National Forest and state and county officials, but chafed at the "lack of support by others in the national forest system" and complained that under current circumstances Malheur Lumber had to go 250 miles to obtain logs.[44]

Gradually things turned in the mill's favor. Besieged from all sides, the Forest Service bent to pressure. It announced eleven million board feet of already prepared timber sales would be offered at once and the dates of other timber sales moved up. For fiscal year 2013, the agency promised fifty to sixty million board feet, a significant increase over recent years, and planned for a similar level in 2014. In addition, it announced that $5 million appropriated for forest restoration would be used on the Malheur, treating twenty thousand acres and producing forty million board feet of timber a year. Finally, the agency's regional forester, Kent Connaughton, promised to "move more swiftly to increase our restoration work, which will increase timber supply in eastern Oregon." To aid in turning the promises into reality, in the fall of 2013 the Forest Service signed a ten-year stewardship contract with Iron Triangle, a respected logging firm based in John Day. As Scotta Callister observed, the contract gave Malheur Lumber—and the community—"a fighting chance."[45]

More than desperation drove the settlement. Prior to 2006, the Malheur National Forest had the dubious distinction of being "one of the most litigated units in the entire national forest system." Nearly every proposal that incorporated "any form of timber harvest was met with a lawsuit." One participant summed it up neatly: "Litigation was paralyzing forest management, the local industry, and forest restoration." But with Blue Mountain Forest Partners in place, a new order gradually emerged. Working within the legal system, members developed a common vision, a vision that grew out of give-and-take and substituted compromise for confrontation. It "may not be perfect," one member commented, "but it has given the community a voice in the [decision-making] process."[46]

Collaboration had not come about easily; looking back, the Western Environmental Law Center's Susan Brown commented that if someone had told her ten years before that by 2012 she would be working with others to ensure timber harvests on the Malheur, she would not have believed them. But she was; indeed, she became a key member of the group. Regional Forester Connaughton, who might well have tried to claim credit for himself and his agency, was forthright: the settlement that saved Malheur Lumber rested on gains made through the Blue Mountain Forest Partners. Moreover, Senator Jeff Merkley noted, by 2016, not one of the Blue Mountain Cooperative's projects had been tied up in court.[47]

It is clear the cooperative approach that saved Malheur Lumber did not spring solely from a concern for jobs. Although participants started with differing concerns and priorities, a shared love of the land and concern for its health drove events, bringing former opponents into a cooperative designed to improve forest management and bring improved health to the pineries of the southern Blues. So successful was the approach that numerous similar partnerships soon emerged in Eastern Oregon.[48]

Accommodation did not always involve reconciling groups with differing ideas of proper land management. In some cases it developed when individuals simply came to view things in new ways. No one illustrated this better than Patrick Dale "Doc" Hatfield and his wife Connie, who in 1986 founded the fourteen-member cooperative Oregon Natural Beef.[49] The organization took a revolutionary approach to marketing and, at the same time, was a trailblazer in sustainable land management.

In 1976 Hatfield sold his veterinary practice and small ranch in Montana and bought the thirty-two-thousand-acre High Desert Ranch near the tiny community of Brothers, miles east of Bend. Things started well enough, but conditions were changing. During the 1980s, interest rates skyrocketed, land values plummeted, and some consumers were shying away from beef because of health concerns. For many cattlemen it was one of the toughest periods they ever experienced. As Hatfield's wife Connie later remembered, they were running their herds more efficiently than ever, "but we were slowly going broke."[50]

In the mid-1980s, Connie had a chance meeting with a fitness trainer in Bend. He argued there was an unserved market for quality natural beef that was grass-fed and free of antibiotics and added growth hormones. Once home, Connie and Doc discussed the conversation and decided to act on the information. "We'd always sold our calves and then took whatever the market would give us. We'd never thought about holding our yearlings and going all the way through, but this man had given us an idea for a market," she recalled. Meetings with other ranchers followed, and Oregon Natural Beef was soon born.

The group's organizational goal, set down in 1986, was "to provide a sustainable means for a group to profitably market the quality beef products desired by discriminating consumers while retaining every possible bit of independence." Within six months, ONB's product was available in two stores. Rapid expansion followed, spurred on by concerted efforts to keep the ranchers in touch with their customers. Each member was required to spend two days a year at urban sales outlets, explaining their product and getting feedback. Hatfield and his associates had created a marketing cooperative without bricks, mortar, employees, or debt. "If we were to close down," Hatfield noted, "together our total capital assets in . . . [the co-op] would be less than $30,000."[51]

More was involved than a Spartan organization and imaginative marketing. A writer for *High Country News* observed that the Hatfields "hated the fact that cattle often beat up the land." They and the other members of ONB dedicated themselves to sustainable land management and every year opened their ranches to visitations designed to showcase their practices.[52]

The Hatfields also initiated consensus groups made up of ranchers and environmentalists—groups that, as ONDA's Craig Miller put it, "helped conservationists understand that there were some ranchers that actually cared for the land . . . [and] helped the ranchers to understand that the environmentalists' primary goal isn't to destroy the ranching community." A writer in *High Country News* put it simply: "The Hatfields changed the face of public-land ranching in the West."[53] In short, they and ONB took steps to bridge the urban-rural divide. No one was more eloquent about it than Doc Hatfield himself. He explained,

> Our product is more than just beef. It's the smell of sage after a summer thunderstorm, the cool shade of a Ponderosa forest. It's 80-year-old weathered hands saddling a horse in the Blue Mountains, the future of a six-year-old in a one-room school on the high desert. It's trout in a beaver-built pond, hay stacks in an aspen-framed meadow. It's the hardy quail running to join the cattle for a meal, the welcoming ring of a dinner bell. All of these pictures are real. That's not just a story. That's who and what we are. That's what sustainability looks and feels like.

A writer for the *Capital Press*, an agricultural publication from Salem, applauded: "Hatfield got it. He got what makes men and women so passionate about life in the country, raising livestock and making a living a hundred miles from the nearest town."[54]

Many other ranchers were turning to a new land-use ethos too. Among them was Jack Southworth of Seneca, who explained his undergirding land-use philosophy in terms that echoed Aldo Leopold. When he took over the family ranch, in operation since 1885, he repeatedly clashed with his father over fencing off streams, the restoration of riparian strips, and similar practices that in time led to the return of beaver and healthy trout populations to the section of the Sylvies that crossed their land. In contrast, his father wanted grass right to streamside and dumped old automobiles into the river to counter erosion of its banks. "Maybe," the younger Southworth opined, "it was a generational thing. Dad tried to control the land, my approach is to go with what nature gives you." That may have been, but in any case Southworth's approach was not something learned while studying at Oregon State University. He led, more than followed what was taught there, and in time the university would induct him into its Agricultural Hall of Fame. In 2016 he also received a range management award from the Forest Service for his practices on twenty-five thousand acres of grazing allotments.[55]

Hatfield and Southworth were far from alone. Other members of ONB, ranchers who entered into land trust agreements, and numerous other landowners, large and small, were crafting a land-use ethic based on the concept that working with nature rather than simply mining it was the only feasible route forward. Environmentalists like Bruce Marlett seldom gave them credit for having moved beyond the long-dominant ethos of the West, and the Oregon Natural Desert Association and its many allies continued to see the creation of areas protected from commercial use— and ranching in particular—as necessary to prevent despoliation. However artificially, the lines for conflict that had been drawn earlier still remained.

18
Testing

The sort of accommodation represented by the comfortable relationship Southworth and the Hatfields developed with their land, their neighbors, and changing circumstances—or by the more problematic relationship between the members of the Blue Mountain Forest Partners and the larger forest-dependent community—was soon tested on a variety of fronts. Perhaps the greatest challenge to the often-grudging open-mindedness underlying accommodation involved Malheur National Wildlife Refuge south of Burns. Early in 2016, armed protesters seized the headquarters of the refuge. News media from across the country pounced on the story, and crosscurrents aplenty swirled amid claims and counterclaims.

The arrest and conviction of Dwight and Steven Hammond for arson of federal property triggered the occupation, but the roots ran deeper. Thanks to the Steens Mountain CMPA, by the mid-1990s local concern over the conflict between ONDA and the BLM had declined, and actions of the Fish and Wildlife Service on the Malheur refuge moved to center stage. Former refuge manager John Scharff, who knew the ranching community and its needs, had perfected a nonconfrontational approach with the refuge's neighbors, but he had been replaced by a new generation of personnel less sensitive to local concerns and more in tune with the environmentalism of the period. Conflict with the Hammonds was soon aborning. In 1988 the Hammonds filed on 4.5 cfs of water from Krumbo Creek, arguing the Malheur refuge had forfeited its claim by failing to use it for more than five years. To the Hammonds, "use" meant diversion for irrigation. Refuge authorities noted the average flow in the creek was only 5 cfs, and that the diversion planned by the Hammonds would wipe out the redband trout in Krumbo Creek, which had the highest number per mile in Eastern Oregon.[1]

The Hammonds had a number of subsequent confrontations with refuge personnel and reputedly refused to sell their ranch for enlargement of
the Malheur refuge (in all probability not just an effort by FWS to enlarge
the refuge, but also to get rid of these difficult neighbors). Things came
to a head early in 1995. In June, refuge manager Forrest Cameron told
Dwight Hammond his right to graze cattle and grow hay on the refuge
had been revoked. Then in August refuge personnel began erecting a fence
between two pieces of Hammond property that were separated by a strip
of refuge land; Hammond argued the fence would deny his cattle access to
a vital waterhole, which he had gained the right to use through an earlier
exchange of Steens Mountain property for land near his ranch. Moreover,
he proclaimed the fence illegal, since it blocked a traditionally established right-of-way. Ever feisty, he took physical action to stop the fence's
construction, and the FWS responded by filing charges for "disturbing
and interfering with federal officers and contractors." One observer proclaimed, "Access and water, that's what this is all about," but fellow rancher
Brent Otley suspected more was involved, that the government was after
Hammond's land. Others viewed the problems as stemming from the
Hammonds' confrontational approach.[2]

Social media picked up the story, and a firestorm erupted. Chuck
Cushman, executive director of the American Land Rights Association,
came to Burns to help organize a protest meeting. Nearly five hundred
people showed up. Organizers distributed bumper stickers reading "Save
Our Community from the FWS Eco-Cops," and Cushman urged supporters to "flood refuge employees with protest calls"—which they did. Congressman Bob Smith (R–OR) weighed in, writing Secretary of the Interior
Bruce Babbitt on Hammond's behalf. Four days later, the felony charges
were reduced to misdemeanors, and Hammond was released after two
days in jail.[3]

Friction continued, and in 2012 Dwight and Steve Hammond were
arrested again, this time for arson of federal property. Officials claimed
that, since 2001, the Hammonds had illegally set at least eight range fires.
The Hammonds claimed they set them to control invasive sagebrush and
juniper and to reduce the threat of wildfire. Federal attorneys claimed the
Hammonds set at least one of the fires to cover up evidence of illegal deer
hunting. Whether they set them on their own property and they spread to
BLM land or set them on the twenty-six thousand acres of BLM land on

Before the takeover: Hammond supporters in Burns. Credit: Amelia Thompson, Oregon Public Broadcasting.

which they had grazing rights is not clear; in any case, fires got out of control. Some 139 acres of federal land were burned. Prosecution followed, and government attorneys called for the mandatory five-year sentences for violating a federal law against the intentional destruction of government property. They were found guilty, but the federal district court judge hearing the case considered such sentences excessive (and therefore unconstitutional) and reduced them to less than a year apiece. On appeal the Ninth Circuit Court ruled the mandatory sentences should be applied, and the Hammonds, who by then had served their shorter sentences, returned to federal prison.[4]

Cries of protest followed. The Hammonds were well known in the Burns area and were viewed as outspoken but hardly criminals. Five years for such a crime seemed excessive, and many thought having to go back to prison after serving the sentence of the district court smacked of double jeopardy. Indeed, there did seem to be an element of vindictiveness by prosecutors—sympathetic fellow rancher Fred Otley called it "an act of revenge."[5]

Use of the law under which the Hammonds were prosecuted added to the conviction that government operatives were involved in payback.

Rather than the law that was usually applied in such cases, prosecutors turned to one designed for the intentional destruction of federal facilities, legislation passed following Timothy McVeigh's bombing of the federal building in Oklahoma City. The sentence was, the Oregon Farm Bureau declared, "a gross injustice," and Greg Walden, who by then represented Eastern Oregon in Congress, observed that "the government set fires to reduce fire danger that crossed onto private lands. They [those responsible] did not go to federal prison," but the Hammonds did.[6]

The situation quickly became complicated. Right-wing antigovernment activists, enflamed by social media, seized on the issue to further their efforts to obtain transfer of federal land in the West (including the Malheur refuge) to local control. A variety of protesters poured into Burns. Foremost among them was Ammon Bundy, whose family had a long-running conflict with the Bureau of Land Management in Nevada. In late 2015, he appeared at the home of Susan Hammond and spent some hours trying to persuade her to join his fight against federal land ownership in the West. She declined, for although she had a strong distaste for the area's federal authorities, her family had "their own troubles to handle without picking a fight with the very people who controlled their future."[7]

Some two months later, at a meeting in Burns attended by a variety of protesters, Bundy proclaimed it was time to take action and proceeded to lead a contingent of supporters to seize the headquarters of the Malheur Wildlife Refuge as a step toward ending federal land ownership in the West. As Harney County sheriff David Ward put it, "There are people here who tried to do a peaceful rally [in support of the Hammonds] and that got hijacked."[8]

Nearly all the "patriots" who took over the refuge—including their main spokesmen—were from out of state.[9] In many ways, the group, the self-styled Citizens for Constitutional Freedom, was an outgrowth of the Sagebrush Rebellion of the 1970s and 1980s and drew on widespread displeasure with federal land management and alleged government overreach. Their platform was based not on state's rights arguments as much as semi-anarchist, power-to-the-people ideas. Ammon Bundy explained that he opposed transfer of federal lands to the states, for then "the state becomes the new master." For most, the underlying ideas were more nebulous. Although more evident in other parts of the West, the La Grande *Observer* found "an awful lot of angst" in Eastern Oregon.[10]

There was another, less noticed, element. The leadership and many of the members of the takeover were from a strain of right-wing Mormonism that burgeoned after World War II and that had lent strength to organizations like the John Birch Society. They saw their actions as preludes to millennial change, and thus they were done with God's blessing. As Ammon Bundy, the primary spokesman of the group, explained, "I began to understand how the Lord felt about Harney County and about this country, and I clearly understood that the Lord was not pleased with what was happening to the Hammonds." Bundy believed he had to act. Leaders of the Church of Jesus Christ of Latter Day Saints feared that fallout from the takeover would pose a threat to acceptance of mainstream Mormonism in the larger society and were quick to "strongly condemn" it; the occupation was not a church matter, they proclaimed, nor did it represent the will of God— Bundy would later respond that the church had been infiltrated by socialists and environmentalists. But perhaps LDS leaders worried too much: like other papers outside the church's heartland, the Portland *Oregonian* failed to make the connection between the "delusional behavior" of the protesters and Mormonism. It simply denounced the takeover as "hapless play-acting" and expressed the hope that "the anarchy [would] die of its own cluelessness."[11]

Initially authorities took a cautious approach. Harney County sheriff David Ward was in the forefront. He met with protest leaders, who were allowed to come and go freely, hosted public meetings open to the protesters, and at one point offered them safe conduct out of state if they would end the occupation.[12] Most Burns residents seem to have opposed the takeover and simply wanted the protesters to leave. At one community meeting of some three hundred people, the chant arose "Go! Go! Go!" and billboards sprouted on the edge of town espousing the same view. One read, "We Are Harney County. We Have Our Own Voice."[13]

Among the most outspoken opponents of the occupation were spokesmen for the Burns Paiutes. Tribal council member Jarvis Kennedy was blunt: "We don't need some clown to come in here and stand up for us. We survived without them before, and we'll survive without them when they're gone. So they should get the hell out of here. We didn't ask them here. We don't want them here." Tribal chair Charlotte Rodrique went further; noting Bundy's expressed desire to return federal land to the people, she declared, "The protesters have no claims to this land. It belongs to the native people who still live here." The Paiutes never ceded title to the land, she argued, for the supposed treaty of 1868 was never ratified, and her people were simply "dragged out" of the area. If refuge land were to be "returned" to anyone, it should be to Burns Paiutes: "[We still] view this as our land, no matter who is living on it." Reports that the occupiers were trampling tribal burial sites and pawing through artifacts stored at the refuge headquarters added to Paiute concerns.[14]

One observer noted that although the residents of Harney County were "poor, white, and conservative, . . . [not] one of them has joined the Bundy militia." Nonetheless, sympathy for the Hammonds and frustration with federal land management spurred divisions in the community. The Harney County Chamber of Commerce placed orange ribbons around town in an effort to promote unity; many were torn down. Death threats were made against Sheriff Ward and his family; others reported having their vehicles followed and tires slashed. Whether the perpetrators were outsiders was unclear, but County Judge Steve Grasty, concerned about the potential for violence, refused to approve use of a building on the county fairgrounds for a meeting in which Bundy and gun-toting followers would participate. Supporters of the occupation responded with a drive to recall Grasty from office.[15]

Meanwhile, the *Burns Times-Herald*, made a surprising editorial decision: it refused to send Samantha White, its sole reporter, to the refuge. She later explained: "We did not want to go out there and give this guy [Bundy] any more attention or leverage. We were absolutely not going to give him a platform." Instead, the paper focused on local voices and reactions. White, a fourth-generation Burns resident, explained that the paper did not want to be the voice of the community, but its reflection. Letters to the editor flooded in from both sides.[16]

Divisions grew. As a reporter for the *Los Angeles Times* put it, the people of Burns did not rise up against the federal government, but "against one another, in cafes, on Facebook, in their places of worship. . . . The protest's primary casualties are the emotionally wounded residents of Harney County." John Day's *Blue Mountain Eagle* considered the occupation "the cry of the fearful, the pessimistic, and the proud. . . . At times . . . scary . . . and at times farcical." Danger came not from weapons openly carried, it argued, but from "the seeds of distrust of neighbors and animosity to government" that the occupation generated. Just how accurate this was is unclear. While visiting Burns some five months later, the author was told repeatedly, "You can't believe everything [about the occupation] that you read in newspapers."[17]

Gradually authorities took a firmer stance, limiting the ability of Bundy and his cohorts at the refuge to come and go, reducing access from outside, and cutting off supplies. Pushed by Governor Kate Brown and others, the FBI and state police began taking a more conspicuous role. As the screws tightened, occupation leaders desperately sought allies in Grant County, where anti-federal sentiments had long simmered. En route to a public meeting in John Day, their vehicles were stopped at a roadblock just south of the county line; the situation quickly deteriorated, and Robert "LaVoy" Finicum—a Mormon from Kanab, Utah, and one of the takeover's key leaders—was shot and killed. The end was now in sight, and ere long the occupation came to an end.[18]

But damage remained. In the immediate aftermath of the occupation, the Fish and Wildlife Service spent $4.3 million in cleanup and repairs on the refuge (it had spent another million on temporary law enforcement). Its annual carp removal program, designed to protect the native trout population, had to be suspended in 2016. More important, the imbroglio turned "Burns from a place where residents felt comfortable and unified into a nightmare of discontent and fear," an overstatement, but one containing a seed of truth. And Judge Grasty's attempts at maintaining peaceful discourse while blocking extremist demands earned him enmity among those angered by government policies and actions—even if they were not supporters of the takeover itself. For his part, Grasty made no secret of his opinions, at one point describing the refuge occupiers as "thugs, criminals, [and] militia. . . . I don't know what they're capable of. No one does. . . . Bundy just put us back a decade or two" in terms of cooperation. Grasty's decision to block use of county facilities for a public meeting that Bundy's supporters desired was denounced as an infringement on freedom of speech and triggered a movement to recall him from office. It was, one reporter observed, a referendum on the handling of the armed occupation.[19]

The primary election in May and the recall vote that followed brought a kind of closure. In the primary, 72 percent of the county's registered voters cast ballots, and candidates opposed to the occupation carried the day. Four candidates were on the ballot to replace Judge Grasty, and Pete

Runnels, an outspoken Grasty supporter, won 53 percent of the votes, a margin large enough to negate the need for a runoff. In the recall election that followed, the turnout was again huge and the results clear. Over 70 percent voted against recalling Grasty. It was, he observed, "an affirmation that we did a lot of things right, and I mean the community when I say 'we.'"[20]

In the general election that followed, Sheriff David Ward was opposed by Alan Johnson, an experienced lawman who had announced his candidacy before the takeover and had not been at the forefront when it began. But Johnson was sympathetic to the occupiers and received the endorsement of the Constitutional Sheriffs and Police Officers Association, a bulwark of support for Bundy and his cohorts. Johnson had predicted the election might turn into a referendum on Ward's handling of events, and as one outside observer put it, the election was likely to keep alive "the bitter divisiveness" in Burns. In fact it *was* a referendum of sorts, one in which Ward was vindicated; he received overwhelming support for his candidacy and—by implication—his actions. Analyzing the takeover, Peter Walker concluded that, in spite of divisions, the collaborative approach developed in solving land-use issues on Steens Mountain and elsewhere undercut the Bundys' approach and doomed the takeover to failure.[21]

Events in Grant County were less noticed by the outside world, but in their own way equally revealing. In spite its cooperation in saving the Malheur Lumber Company, the Forest Service continued to be a target of criticism. Grumbling about the agency had begun in the 1920s, and the Forest Service earned even more critics as years passed. In 1995, by a three-to-one margin, Grant County voters supported an initiative measure refusing to recognize federal control over public lands within the county. Although no ordinance was involved, the vote reflected deep-seated feelings among voters.[22]

Devastating wildfires during the first years of the new century joined with increasing environmentalist influence and frequent sawmill closures to add to discontent over the agency's forest management. In 2002, residents of Grant County turned to the ballot box in an effort to gain transfer of the county's public forests from federal to local control and created a Grant County Public Forest Commission to manage the forests once transferred. Although the measure passed, the forests remained in federal hands. With nothing to manage, the forest commission soon became little more than a vehicle for conspiracy theorists and attacks on federal authority. Further reflecting their hostility to outside control, in the same election voters passed a measure declaring Grant County a United Nations–free zone.[23]

Forest Service actions fed the growing discontent. Periodically the agency developed long-range management plans for its lands. In 2013 it rolled out a new plan to replace one in force for the Blue Mountains since 1990. A period of public hearings and comment followed, but the time for response to the 1,200-page document was limited to ninety days, and there was no requirement that revisions based on objections be made. Steve Beverlin, supervisor of the Malheur National Forest, admitted that in Grant County the reaction to the first draft was "less than stellar." It could have been worse. The Grant County Public Forest Commission was still finalizing its response when the public meeting was held in John Day, and no one doubted that it would have been sharply critical. But even without that commission's input, the atmosphere was poisonous. As one Grant County resident put it, the Forest Service's response to complaints had always been to stall and ignore. Similar views were reported at meetings elsewhere in the Blues. Indeed, the Eastern Oregon Counties Association labeled the entire plan "a step backward from recent gains made through collaboration." Republican congressman Greg Walden joined in urging changes to the plan and once again noted that federal agencies needed to do a better job of listening to local communities.[24]

But the Forest Service did not prove as intransigent as Walden and other critics feared it would be. During the year following the plan's unveiling, Forest Service representatives met with some seven hundred people in twenty-four "listening sessions." They then revised the original plan in response to concerns raised and scheduled a second round of public hearings. At one follow-up meeting, Beverlin asked how many thought the Forest Service just planned to go ahead and do whatever it wanted; a majority raised their hands. Considering the widespread view within the agency that it was the guardian against exploiters and knew best what was good for forests, an attitude present since the days of Gifford Pinchot, such suspicion was hardly surprising—but it was unwarranted. Beverlin responded, "I don't believe that's true. Otherwise why are we [here] listening again?" To find something workable, he added, "It's going to take compromise from everyone." Further revisions followed, yielding a plan the *Blue Mountain Eagle* labeled "A Forest Plan We Can Live With." Zach Williams of Blue Mountain Forest Partners agreed; as he put it, the plan "may not be perfect . . . but it has given the community a voice in the process." Once again objections were raised, and planning resumed. More than a hundred people were present at one public meeting (which was also broadcast over Oregon Public Broadcasting). Responding to the fresh input, the Forest Service went into "deliberation mode" and, in due course, came forth with two alternative revisions.[25]

The process continued. To speed things along, the Forest Service decided to postpone changes to its travel management portion until the overall management plan had been approved. With the thorny issue of travel management temporarily set aside, the agency anticipated the larger document could be implemented in December 2017—but that was overly optimistic. It remained to be seen whether, without the threat of the Malheur Lumber Company's closure hanging over them, give-and-take—accommodation—could lead to mutually acceptable decisions. Still, the mere fact that a wide range of interest groups could engage in policy debates showed that the idea of jointly searching for acceptable compromises had come a long way—whether it could in fact lead to a workable solution in the face of society's increasing polarization remains to be seen.[26]

Confrontation took other forms as Sheriff Glenn E. Palmer came to the fore in Grant County. First elected to office in 2000, Palmer had strong views about local control of public lands—and they grew stronger over time, especially after he was taken under the wing of Richard Mack, a former Arizona sheriff and founder of the Constitutional Sheriffs and Peace Officers Association, a body that challenged federal authority on a number of fronts. Palmer informed the Malheur National Forest's then-supervisor, Teresa Raaf, that he saw no constitutional authority for Forest Service law enforcement in Grant County: "Forest Service jurisdiction as I see it is limited to the federal building in John Day." Raaf's successor, Steve Beverlin, found working with Palmer impossible; the sheriff, he said, "has refused to work with me at all." His actions quickly made Palmer the poster boy for the Constitutional Sheriffs and Peace Officers Association, and they honored him as their first sheriff of the year.[27] Seeking to give teeth to the public will expressed in earlier ballot measures, in 2012 Palmer deputized eleven citizens to draw up a forest management plan for the county. The group included members of the Grant County Public Forest Commission plus others, but it is unclear whether they were operating under that body's authority or Palmer's. In any case, the County Commission refused to endorse the work of the group as it had dubious authority, operated largely in secret, and had no control over the lands it sought to manage.[28]

The *Oregonian* described what was developing in Grant County as having roots similar to those undergirding the occupation of Malheur refuge, but noted it was "A Quieter Battle over Federal Land."[29] Similar roots, perhaps, but what was developing in Grant County manifested earlier and was less influenced by outsiders. Locals had long found various Forest Service regulations galling, especially those regarding the closure of roads across public land, closures that, critics charged, were done unilaterally. Reflecting public attitudes, the Grant County Commission passed an ordinance early in 2013 requiring agencies wishing to close roads "over and across public land" to first consult with the county sheriff and county court. The Forest Service ignored the ordinance, seeing it as clearly invalid and insisting, as Malheur National Forest Supervisor Steve Beverlin later put it, that the actual process regarding closures was "real open, transparent" and, in any case, the agency valued public opinion. Without power to enforce its ordinance, county officials turned to other matters.[30]

Dissatisfaction with the County Commission's nonconfrontational stance, including its failure to take on the Forest Service over handling of the devastating Canyon Creek fire complex of 2015, led to an effort to recall Commissioner Boyd Britton, an outspoken Palmer critic. Britton had been a key figure in getting the increased timber harvests that saved the Malheur Lumber Company, but to some his history of cooperation with the Forest Service was unforgivable. Yet when the recall election was held, over 60 percent of voters cast ballots, and 65.3 percent voted against recall. Britton held on to his office, but the recall effort deepened divisions in the county.[31]

Meanwhile, the Grant County Public Forest Commission was increasingly a mouthpiece for far-right, antigovernment activists. Campaigning for a position on the commission in 2012, Nicky Sprauve ran ads declaring "Let's put the BLM and US Forest Service on notice. This is OUR COUNTY! . . . I guarantee you, no one is going to shut the door on me!"[32]

Sprauve was elected—but it was a Pyrrhic victory. In 2016, Circuit Court Judge William D. Cramer Jr. blocked inclusion on the ballot of candidates for positions on the commission. The legislation creating it was, he wrote, null and void, for it clearly conflicted with paramount federal and state laws and with the United States Constitution.[33]

The anti-UN vote, the election (and reelection) of Sheriff Palmer, and the attacks on federal authority in the relatively isolated county gained attention beyond its borders, created an image attractive to the marginalized, and "encouraged militia groups across the nation to see Grant County as a friendly haven" where they could "work to build their base by spreading misinformation and making unsubstantiated allegations." In 2010 organizers for the Aryan Nation arrived from northern Idaho, hoping to make John Day their new headquarters; but racism, so central to the group's neo-Nazi agenda, was not a huge issue in Grant County, where the minority population was tiny. A well-attended public meeting, organized by the *Blue Mountain Eagle*, made clear that these white supremacists were not welcome, and they soon decamped. Then, in the wake of the take-over of Malheur Wildlife Refuge, Michael Emry arrived, also from Idaho, with an arsenal of weapons (including a stolen fifty-caliber machine gun with identification numbers removed) and glowing praise for Palmer. He had been, he claimed, invited by locals. Emry and his wife arrived intent on aiding Bundy and were soon serving as hosts of a conspiracy-minded online website, *The Voice of Grant County: Defenders of the Constitution*. Reacting to these developments, a critic wrote that Palmer's actions had invited "lawless loons into an otherwise peaceful community." Emry was soon arrested (by authorities other than Palmer), convicted on weapons charges, and, in due course, left.[34]

As views grew increasingly polarized, a group called Grant County Positive Action emerged. In a lengthy statement published in the *Blue Mountain Eagle*, it proclaimed,

> A community thrives when people work together and can express their opinions without fear of threat, intimidation and retaliation. . . . We are local residents with a wide range of political opinions, but all of us share a belief that problems need to be settled peacefully, respectfully and lawfully. We believe that incivility, intimidation, undemocratic tactics and hidden agendas damage

our community. . . . The solution to the division in our community rests with all of us.

The committee decried the "militia presence" in the county and groups seeking to advance their agendas by "misinformation and making unsubstantiated allegations," charges clearly aimed at Palmer and his allies. The appeal seems to have built few bridges. Divisions continued to grow.[35]

Bit by bit Palmer, rather than the Forest Service, became the focal point of events. He openly sympathized with the occupiers of the Malheur Wildlife Refuge, calling them "patriots," and invited Bundy and supporters to John Day to present their views; he refused to work with Harney County sheriff David Ward in his efforts to get the occupiers to stand down. So suspect had Palmer become that when authorities decided to intercept the caravan of militiamen headed for John Day for an "informational" public meeting, they kept Palmer in the dark and placed their blockade just south of the Grant-Harney county line, where he would have no authority. Following this, Palmer clashed with the Grant County dispatcher who, he charged, had intentionally failed to keep him informed, with the County Commission, and with the Portland *Oregonian*, which sought to obtain copies of Palmer's records dealing with the matter through a freedom of information request.[36]

In the midst of this tangle of events, Todd McKinley—a former deputy who had previously clashed with Palmer over his refusal to cooperate with the Forest Service—announced he would run for sheriff in the upcoming election. He was convinced Palmer's actions demonstrated he was incapable of providing fair, evenhanded law enforcement and that his political views overrode his judgment. McKinley was blunt. In the county *Voters' Guide*, he decried the "sheer audacity of individuals that think they can dictate the course of Grant County without the input of all," and promised, "I will mend some broken fences as I believe we as a county have more than a few." The campaign soon turned ugly, deeply dividing the community. Letters to the editor flooded the pages of the *Blue Mountain Eagle*, and long lists of people supporting one candidate or the other appeared in its pages. In the end, in spite of McKinley's pleas for peacemaking, Palmer was reelected by a narrow margin.[37]

Palmer may have been a bit chastened by the closeness of the election, but he did not change his basic positions. He continued to clash with the

Oregonian, with Les Zaitz (its main investigative reporter for the area), and with the County Commission; but with the occupation of the Malheur refuge over and the Forest Service engaged in efforts to reach out to the community, he felt less need to fulminate against those who opposed him—and they felt less need to counterattack. Even Nicky Sprauve, a longtime Palmer supporter, moderated his stance: "We need to all come together to work for the good of our neighbors and friends. . . . Let's all citizens and agencies come to the table and leave our egos at home. This includes me." Judy Schuette, who had been an outspoken opponent of Palmer's (and a member of Grant County Positive Action), also reflected the changing atmosphere. In a letter to the editor, she asked "Are things in Grant County really as bad as some would have you think?" She went on to provide a long list of things accomplished in recent years "by varied groups working hard together." Included in her list was the work of the Blue Mountain Forest Partners, which had helped ensure increased timber harvests and jobs. Which message about Grant County do you want to send, she wondered, conflict or cooperation? Others took a similar tack.[38]

Yet sharp divisions remained. Letters to the editor continued to arrive at the *Blue Mountain Eagle*, castigating the County Commission for not appealing Judge Cramer's decision invalidating the measure creating the Grant County Public Forest Commission, repeating timeworn charges of federal overreach, attacking those who had cooperated in crafting the solution to the Malheur Lumber Company's problems, and deriding the principals in Iron Triangle (recipients of the forest stewardship contract that helped save Malheur Lumber) as "boot lickers" and beneficiaries of "crony capitalism." Frances Preston of Prairie City exemplified the critics' position when she told the County Court that the "way of life in Grant County is threatened . . . [by] a systematic attempt to control the people by controlling the land." It was the same argument Sheriff Palmer had voiced repeatedly. But bit by bit an exchange of ideas seemed to be replacing intimidation and threats of violence. When a public meeting was held early in 2017—a meeting intended as a replacement for "the meeting that never was" on the night LaVoy Finicum was killed—old charges were leveled, but the atmosphere was relatively calm and peaceful. Kay Steele of Ritter applauded: we need to "work cooperatively to improve our government—not destroy it," and she saw this as a step in that direction.[39]

Old ideas died hard. In the fall of 2017, Dave Traylor and eight others who had been highly critical of the Blue Mountain Forest Partners sought to join the group. Several were former members of the now-defunct Grant County Public Forest Commission, and social media posts suggested some wanted to infiltrate and undermine the cooperative's efforts. John D. George expressed a view others no doubt shared: "The environmental community . . . now get to drive their message through these collaboratives." But the applicants insisted they wanted to join in the give-and-take that was central to the cooperative's approach. Perhaps they themselves were not entirely clear on what they desired. The same could be said of ONDA, which continued its litigious approach, but at the same time began working cooperatively at the local level on projects such as stream habitat improvement.[40]

For all the continuing differences, it is clear that residents of Grant County, like those in other parts of Eastern Oregon, shared a love of the land. Or, if love is not quite the right word, a strong attachment to it, a feeling that the land was central to their lives and self-identities. They might disagree strongly on how best to manage and use it, but they shared an appreciation of it—an appreciation not always recognized by outsiders, even outsiders who have moved into the area to enjoy its outdoor amenities but have never had to make a living from the land. This deeply felt connection has been in place for decades, it has helped the people develop a shared identity, an identity decidedly different from that of those surrounded by built environments and whose ties are more to family and groups than to place. It is the strength of this connection that has made recent events in Grant and Harney Counties—and, less dramatically, elsewhere in Eastern Oregon—incomprehensible to many who live elsewhere. However, Native Americans—Cayuse, Paiute, Wasco, Klamath, and others—understand this connection. To them the land is and always has been more than a source of sustenance. It lies at the heart of their identity.

Epilogue: Quo Vadis?

Spring winds still blow across Oregon's interior, parching lands south of the Blue Mountains and everywhere carrying cold reminders from the remaining snows in the high country of the winter just past. The range and forestland is depleted of its onetime cover; cheatgrass, Russian thistle ("tumbleweeds" to most folk), and a variety of noxious weeds have invaded, dense stands of western juniper and sagebrush have encroached where once they were scattered, and fir has replaced Ponderosa pine in large areas of the Blues. Streams that once ran free have been dammed, their waters often diverted to irrigate introduced crops. In the wheat counties, the vast fields of grain that replaced native bunchgrass still stretch toward the horizon, but wheat ranches have been increasingly mechanized, reducing the need for laborers and the small towns that supported them. Yet not all has changed. The age-old dance of residents with the land continues. The history of Eastern Oregon has ever been defined by the interaction between people and their environment, an interaction that brought prosperity to some, poverty and disillusionment to others. The dance continues amid conflicts and fresh challenges. But a paradigm shift can be noted. More and more whites are learning what Native peoples knew before them: people must live with the land on its own terms, not on theirs.

But is this land moving, as some scholars have proposed, in directions that will create "One Oregon"? The argument seems badly flawed, resting as it does on selected statistical measures while downplaying or ignoring social and psychological indicators.[1] Even many statistical measures fail to support the idea. Levels of economic interdependency have always existed between areas east and west of the Cascades, between the Portland metropolitan core and its periphery. This is neither new nor, if one is to judge from recent election results, increasing.

Since 1988, Democrats have carried Oregon in every presidential election, while Republicans have consistently won in Eastern Oregon. In 2000, *every* Eastern Oregon county voted for George W. Bush, who got 80 percent of the vote in Grant County and over 70 percent in Harney, Lake, Malheur and Wallowa. The pattern repeated time and again. In the election of 2016, Donald Trump carried every county in Eastern Oregon, as did Republican gubernatorial candidate Bud Pierce; Republican Greg Walden was reelected to Congress with 71.9 percent of the vote.[2]

Contests for the state legislature follow a similar pattern. The four Senate districts largely or entirely in Eastern Oregon have consistently gone Republican. In 2004, and again in 2008, no Democrats even filed to run in Senate Districts 28, 29, and 30, but Democrats maintained their statewide senatorial majority. David Nelson represented District 29 from 1996 until his retirement in 2013, when he was replaced by another Republican. Ted Ferrioli of John Day, first elected in 1996 to represent District 30, continued in office to 2017. He ran unopposed in the elections of 2008 and 2012. He left office as the longest-serving member of Oregon's senate and its Republican caucus chair. Clearly, the political pattern east of the Cascades remained a far cry from that of the state as a whole.[3]

Hardly the ideologue many Republicans have become, Ferrioli had long been interested in land-use issues. As executive director of Malheur Timber Operators, he was cognizant of forest issues, and criticized federal management—"I don't see how the state could do worse than the feds in land management." But this was not what he was proposing. His basic approach was to push for dialogue between the public and private, federal and state sectors. He decried the occupation of the Malheur Wildlife Refuge.[4]

Ferrioli recognized the inherent differences between Oregon's metropolitan core and its rural areas, differences that made Tom McCall's signature LCDC a poor fit in much of the area east of the mountains—and in southwestern Oregon as well. Responding to this, in 2017 Ferrioli proposed SB432, a bill designed to bring sweeping revision to Oregon's regulations on land use. Under it, counties with minimal (or no) population growth could opt out of the LCDC and implement their own plans. In effect, he was opposing one-size-fits-all legislation and attacking the notion that those unable to find work in rural counties should simply move to where the jobs were, what he called the "move or starve model." He argued that some simply "don't want to live in the city and shouldn't be forced to by economic pressure." But Ferrioli's efforts were for naught. The state's League of Women Voters, 1000 Friends of Oregon, and a variety of environmental organizations opposed the bill, and the legislature closed its contentious 2017 session with SB432 still in committee. A majority of Oregonians, if not of those east of the Cascades, were clearly in no mood to abandon Tom McCall's landmark land-use policies.[5]

Meanwhile, east-west and rural-urban differences continued to fester. In 2015, Ken Parsons of La Grande proposed Eastern Oregon should secede and join Idaho. Few took the idea seriously, but it gained press while generating a modicum of the ridicule it deserved: one reader of the Ontario *Argus Observer* suggested Parsons "just needs to move to Idaho. This would solve his problem and not create one for me. I don't want to live in Idaho." Another labeled his proposal a great idea: it would save a lot of money to lower Eastern Oregon's educational support to that of Idaho's notoriously impoverished system. For his part, Parsons conceded it "all comes back to Malheur County. If they don't want to move into Idaho I don't see any other counties having the economic and political incentive" to do so. And there it rests.[6]

Gradually Oregon's economy recovered from the Great Recession. By 2016 the state had one of the healthiest in the nation. Still, in much of the area east of the Cascades, post-recession unemployment rates remained high.[7] Nowhere was harder hit than the little Klamath County community of Bly. In the mid-1980s, its sawmill closed and out-migration began. Enrollment in Bly's elementary school plummeted from one hundred in 1988 to eleven in 2015. Meanwhile, in Malheur County, two of every five children lived in poverty. Analysts expect difficulties to continue, projecting that, from 2014 to 2024, Oregon's economy will grow 14 percent, more than double the national average, whereas Eastern Oregon will lag—Harney and Malheur Counties economies are expected to increase only 3 percent and their population growth to stagnate.[8]

In Crook County unemployment reached a staggering 19.6 percent in 2009, but by 2017 it had dropped to "only" 7.3 (still the highest of any county in the state). Save for expansion of Les Schwab's regional distribution center and new Facebook and Apple facilities, little happened in Crook County to explain the improvement; much of it could be attributed to the growing economy of Deschutes County, especially Bend, to which many Crook County residents commuted for work.[9] Indeed, the influx of people and money into Deschutes County so changed it that, to many, it no longer seemed part of Eastern Oregon. Ellen Waterston catches the new spirit of the place:

> Start and finish strong, right here in Bend.
> A newly branded land rush is on! Now
> houses, now condos, now centers of learning,
> now land trust, now music, now film and writing.
> Celebrate invention, amazement, and derring-do.
> Harvest sun, snow and all things virtual. Bend
> beckons us to regale on a cornucopia sublime
> during this our allotted capsule of time.

Such lines could hardly have been written about any other place east of the Cascades (even though similar factors were at work in muted form around The Dalles). The Oregon Employment Department put it simply: unlike other Eastern Oregon counties, Deschutes was no longer statistically rural (or non-metro).[10]

Education showed a similar duality. In Oregon as a whole, 89.8 percent of the population had at least a high school education and 30.8 percent a bachelor's degree. Most Eastern Oregon counties trailed. Only Wallowa, Sherman, and Gilliam exceeded the statewide average for high school graduation, and none came close to that for a college degree. Morrow County was the state's least educated: 23.6 percent lacked a high school diploma and only 10.2 percent had a bachelor's degree.[11]

The apparent weakness in educational achievement stems in part from the fact that to grasp opportunities, many high school and college graduates move to urban centers beyond the boundaries of Eastern Oregon for employment. This is hardly new. Community leaders in Lakeview long knew Daly Fund scholarships opened the doors to opportunities well beyond Lake County, and William Kittredge remembers he and his peers looking forward to getting away: "What all of us young boys wanted was escape and connection with the Great World we had just begun hearing about." And much of my own generation in Redmond—and many of the students I taught in Sisters in the 1950s—shared the outlook and built lives far from where they had grown up. Veterinarian Scott Campbell shared the experience. He grew up in Burns, but left because few opportunities existed for him or his wife, a registered nurse. It was the sad side of the long-present and often romanticized American dream of finding a better future in places just over the horizon—or perhaps farther away. Still, even after they had departed, many expatriates—Kittredge among them—continued to express affection for the places they left behind. From her new home in Portland, Eileen McVicker gave voice to the feeling: "I loved Steens Mountain. I love it today and as a little child I loved it. . . . I used to wonder if heaven could be like the Steens." She confessed, "Now and then I can still get awfully lonesome for the Steens."[12]

In spite of high rates of unemployment, stagnant income levels, an ongoing brain drain, and divisive issues such as those that have troubled Burns and John Day, analysts consider Eastern Oregon "a good place to raise a family and have one's children be successful." Measured thus, Burns, John Day, Condon, Enterprise, and Lakeview all rank in the top third of the nation's community zones. La Grande and Ontario are not far behind. Good schools, adequate housing, safe communities, and ample recreational opportunities help make this possible. Colby Marshall, who had grown up in Burns, was explicit: he moved back because he and his wife wanted to raise their children in the area.[13]

Old issues continue to plague Eastern Oregon. In 2015, ONDA proposed protecting Oregon's Owyhee Canyonlands through a combination of national monument, wilderness, wild and scenic river, and conservation area designations. Their Owyhee Canyonlands Conservation Area would encompass 2.5 million acres, some 40 percent, of Malheur County. ONDA claimed polling showed 70 percent of Oregonians favored protection for the area. The Pew Charitable Trusts rallied to the cause—pointing out that it was "the largest intact unprotected natural expanse in the lower 48 states." Together with other groups, it joined ONDA in forming the Wild Owyhee Coalition to champion the cause.[14]

A firestorm of opposition quickly developed. Public meetings in the tiny communities of Adrian and Jordan Valley drew six hundred and three hundred people, respectively. The Malheur County Commission formed a task force to work against the proposal, and correspondents flooded the Ontario *Argus Observer* with opinion pieces and letters to the editor.

Ranchers expressed fear for their grazing rights and argued—as had those on Steens Mountain before them—that their practices necessarily involved care of the land, for their futures depended on its continuing health. One pointed out that ONDA's proposal did not consider protections already in place; another was more caustic: the proposal was being justified with "falsely presented idealistic hype." A large sign on the outskirts of Nyssa summed up the overall reaction: "No Monument, No Way!"[15] Responding to the uproar, the Malheur County Commission called for an advisory vote. The result was overwhelming. Every precinct in the county voted against the proposal. In Ontario, 83 percent opposed, in the county as a whole, 90 percent. Hoping to persuade outgoing President Barack Obama against last-minute action creating an Owyhee reserve, Congressman Greg Walden hastened the results of Malheur County's advisory vote to the president and Secretary of the Interior Sally Jewell. In the end, Obama did not move on the reserve (although he did on similar land in Utah). Supporters of a Canyonlands reserve were left to bide their time until changed circumstances might offer renewed hope of success.[16]

In the final analysis, one is left with the question: Is there still an Eastern Oregon, a self-defined land with its own pride of identity? Or is what remains a mere residue of leftovers from an earlier age? Inevitably, the answers to these questions will vary from person to person, area to area. Certainly, resorting to unemployment and income figures, education levels, election results, and the like fails to provide a solid answer. These figures reflect the realities of life in Eastern Oregon, but only hint at the attitudes essential for regional identity. Yet however elusive and inconclusive the evidence may be, to me it seems clear there was and *is* an Eastern Oregon, a place shaped by both what it has been and what it is, a place self-consciously distinct from the rest of the state.

From the first, the relationship between people and the land has been at the core of the identity of Eastern Oregonians. Whites—miners, cattlemen, sheepherders, wheat ranchers, timbermen, even settlers who took up claims on the High Desert—initially came to the region to exploit opportunities the land offered (or seemed to offer). In their efforts to tap the area's productive potential, they depended on the outside world for capital, markets, and additional settlers intent on joining the harvest. Over time, less exploitive approaches and attitudes emerged—working with the land replaced merely taking from it. Reliance on commodity production declined, replaced in part by noneconomic ties to the land, but the land was still a central part of regional identity. Yet in spite of this continuity amid change, a perceived lack of fresh opportunities undermined the social optimism that had once been so strong.

A new dynamic has gradually emerged, one pitting those who see themselves as defenders of private property rights against those who view themselves as defenders of the land itself. Not infrequently, this involves a contest between those who live on the land and those who do not—and who often are from outside the area. The fact that the larger society has moved into a postindustrial (and post agrarian-pastoral) age distances them from those who still earn a living working on and with the land. Where once the course of events had been defined by competition for use of the land and where once commodity production was viewed as a valuable goal, new views emerged that attacked commodity-production practices as destructive rather than productive. Increasingly, the relationship between Eastern Oregonians and outsiders was marked by conflict and controversy, not mutual dependence.

Perhaps no one illustrates this distance as well as George Wuerthner, who arrived in Bend from Pennsylvania by way of Montana, Eugene, and Santa Cruz and launched a career as a prolific writer on environmental topics. In his flood of newspaper essays and books, Wuerthner proved himself an environmental purist. He has argued that ruralites do not pay their fair share of taxes to support the outdoor amenities they enjoy, that payments to rural entities in lieu of taxes on federal lands were unwarranted subsidies, that sparsely populated rural Montana ought to be returned to open space (the so-called Buffalo Commons), that ranching is the most pervasively destructive force on public land, that "logging is forest devastation," that wolves destroying livestock should not be killed, and that the Deschutes River should be managed for the public interest—which to him meant ending or at least greatly reducing diversions for irrigation. In all this there was no hint of the necessity of working with locals to find mutually acceptable solutions. Indeed, his approach is so out of touch with political and social realities that it has little chance of winning widespread acceptance.[17]

Grasslands have presented a different scenario. Although some have advocated taking wheatlands north of the Blues out of production and returning them to their original state as bunchgrass steppe—views that tend to equate the area's wheat production with mining the soil—such views are rare. Rather than setting wheat ranchers against environmentalists, a pattern has emerged in which the two groups work together. The owners of Lightning Creek Ranch near Enterprise joined the Nature Conservancy, the Land Trust, and others to create the Zumwalt Prairie Preserve. It eventually grew to encompass thirty-three thousand acres and earn National Park Service designation as a National Historic Landmark: "The best example of bunchgrass prairie that still exists." The Crooked River National Grassland is larger, but less pristine.[18]

Smaller preserves have also emerged, including the Lindsay Prairie Preserve in Morrow County (a tract marginal for wheat and thus apparently never tilled) and the Lawrence Memorial Grassland Preserve south of Shaniko. Other proposals to set aside grasslands that had not been converted to wheat production also emerged from time to time. For more than fifteen years a group based in Santa Barbara, California, has managed a thousand-acre tract on the headwaters of the Grande Ronde. They explained why they and others have enjoyed success (and limited opposition) in putting together such preserves: they built a diverse group of stakeholders rather than setting one group against another.[19]

Government agencies also sought to harness the power of cooperation. The United States Department of Agriculture worked in a nonconfrontational way through its Grassland Reserve Program (and the Agricultural Conservation Easement Program that replaced it in 2014), providing help and financial incentives to landowners wanting to protect farm and rangeland from degradation. Oregon followed suit with its State Wildlife Action Plan, in which it identified Conservation Opportunity Areas (COAs) to help focus efforts and thereby increase chances of long-range success. It noted that 77 percent of the Palouse grassland ecosystem had been converted to dryland agriculture, primarily wheat, and many of the remaining grasslands were badly degraded by invasive species and poorly managed grazing. The situation was also dire in lower elevations of the Blue Mountains, but restoration efforts were proceeding. The largest of the protected areas there, the Rock Creek-Butter Creek COA, encompassed 809 square miles and "significant intact foothill grasslands." Unlike so many other issues in recent decades, none of these efforts set locals against outsiders to a significant degree.[20]

One may be tempted to view differences over land use not only as between those from within the region and those from outside, but also as between those who work on and with the land and those who do not. But such contrasts overlook a basic fact: even those who use land for recreational purposes or nature appreciation are "using" the land. And they can despoil it in any number of ways. Land has a limited carrying capacity for people and off-road vehicles as surely as for cattle, lumbermen, and the like.

Withal, it seems clear that today there are those who love and identify with Eastern Oregon's often-harsh lands, people who recognize it as a special place and are tied to it emotionally to one degree or another. Historical museums in Prineville, Burns, Klamath Falls, Pendleton, and elsewhere—entities largely aimed at and supported by locals rather than tourists—reflect the connection. Reub Long shared the view: "Why should I travel?" he once asked, "I'm already here."[21] Long was reflecting the simple fact that there is, as there always has been, an Eastern Oregon separate and distinct from the lands that surround it. It is a construct not only of physical reality, but also of human perception and emotion. And it is a land dear to the hearts of many who live there.

Notes

CHAPTER 1

1 Robert D. Clark, *The Odyssey of Thomas Condon: Irish Immigrant, Frontier Missionary, Oregon Geologist* (Portland: Oregon Historical Society Press, 1971), 171–174 (quotes).

2 Clark, *Condon*, 175–176.

3 Clark, *Condon*, 359, 426–430, and passim; Charles H. Sternberg, *Life of a Fossil Hunter* (1909; reprint, Lafayette: Indiana University Press, 1990), 119–142; Thomas Condon, *The Two Islands and What Came of Them* (Portland: J. K. Gill, 1902); Stephen Dow Beckham and Florence K. Lentz, *John Day Fossil Beds National Monument: Rocks and Hard Places, A Historical Resources Summary* (Seattle: National Park Service, 2000), 167–171. Condon called the area that would become the Blue Mountains "Shoshone Island." Today it is understood to have been a peninsular extension from the ocean shoreline to the east, rather than an island.

4 Ellen Morris Bishop, *In Search of Ancient Oregon: A Geological and Natural History* (Portland: Timber Press, 2010), provides a good summary of today's more complex understanding. See also, Alan D. St. John, *Oregon's Dry Side: Exploring East of the Cascade Crest* (Portland: Timber Press, 2007), 27–42.

5 As William Kittredge notes, "That huge drift of country is pretty much nonexistent in the American imagination. The whole of it . . . is still populated by no more than a few thousand people." Kittredge, *Hole in the Sky: A Memoir* (New York: Knopf, 1992), 19. As if to prove his point, bibliographers providing the cataloging information for his memoir listed it as dealing with Montana, not Oregon.

6 Robert Bunting, "Introduction," in Urling C. Coe, *Frontier Doctor: Observations on Central Oregon and the Changing West* (reprint, Corvallis: Oregon State University Press, 1996), xv; John Caughey, "Toward an Understanding of the West," *Utah Historical Quarterly* 27 (1959): 11.

7 Scharff, quoted in William O. Douglas, *Of Men and Mountains* (1950; reprint, San Francisco: Chronicle Books, 1990), 36. Sagebrush is *Artemisia tridentata*.

8 On her views, see Judith Austin, "Desert, Sagebrush, and the Pacific Northwest," in William G. Robbins, Robert J. Frank, and Richard E. Ross,

eds., *Regionalism in the Pacific Northwest* (Corvallis: Oregon State University Press, 1983), 129–147.

9   Silver Lake was reported to be six feet deep in 1886, but "had only dust, sagebrush, and tumbleweed in 1938." Luther S. Cressman, *A Golden Journey: Memoirs of an Archeologist* (Salt Lake City: University of Utah Press, 1988), 417 (quote). Condon was not the first to collect at Fossil Lake. Ex-governor John Whiteaker collected there in 1875. See Eugene *Guard*, November 6, 1875; and September 29, 1877; *New York Times*, June 4, 1877.

10 Clark, *Condon*, 303–305 (quote, p. 304); Kittredge, *Hole in the Sky*, 18, 42–43; Barbara Allen, *Homesteading the High Desert* (Salt Lake City: University of Utah Press, 1987), 11; Klamath Falls *Herald and News*, April 12, 1951. In the late Pleistocene, Warner Lakes had been a single entity two hundred feet deep.

11 The "desert" appellation is misleading. Actually, the area is largely sagebrush-bunchgrass steppe.

12 Isaiah Bowman, *The Pioneer Fringe* (New York: American Geographical Society, 1931), 93–94.

13 The photos were collected by Professor Kenneth Gordon of what was then Oregon State College for use in his natural history classes to illustrate what he called simply "the changing scene" of Oregon. They were housed in the school's Horner Museum until it closed; their current location is unknown to this author.

14 Cheatgrass is a term used for a variety of grasses of little value, but in the Interior West it is reserved for nonnative *Bromus tectorum*, a shallow-rooted, briefly edible annual native to Eurasia.

15 James A. Young and B. Abbott Sparks, *Cattle in the Cold Desert* (Logan: Utah State University Press, 1985), 3–37; Aldo Leopold, *A Sand County Almanac and Sketches Here and There* (New York: Oxford University Press, 1949), 154–158 (quote, p. 158); Eileen O'Keeffe McVicker, with Barbara Scott, *Child of Steens Mountain* (Corvallis: Oregon State University Press, 2008), 82. Leopold's observations were first published as "Cheat Takes Over," in *The Land* 1 (Autumn 1941): 310–313.

16 Henry P. Hansen, "Postglacial Forest Succession, Climate Change, and Chronology in the Pacific Northwest," *Transactions of the American Philosophical Society* n.s. 60 (1947): 114–115; Nancy Langston, *Forest Dreams, Forest Nightmares: The Paradox of Old Growth in the Inland West* (Seattle: University of Washington Press, 1995), 16, 38–39; Emily K. Heyerdahl, "Spatial and Temporal Variation in Historical Fire Regimes of the Blue Mountains, Oregon and Washington: The Influence of Climate" (PhD diss., University of Washington, 1997). Similar patterns have been found in the pine country of Central Oregon. See Kelly A. Pohl, Keith S. Hadley, and Karen B. Arabas, "A 545-Year Drought Reconstruction for Central Oregon," *Tree-Ring Research* 62 (2006): 37–50.

17 On such changes, see Jon M. Skovlin, *Interpreting Long-Term Trends in Blue Mountain Ecosystems from Repeat Photography*, General Technical Report

PNW 315 (Portland: Forest Service, Pacific Northwest Research Station, 1995).

18 Within these longer periods of drought, NOAA's records show a number of especially severe individual drought years. In addition to NOAA's online records, see P. A. Knapp, H. D. Gressino-Meyer, and P. T. Soule, "Climatic Regionalization and the Spatial-Temporal Occurrence of Extreme Single-Year Drought Events (1500–1998)," *Quaternary Research* 58 (2002): 226–233.

19 Douglas, *Of Men and Mountains*, 39–40.

20 Kenneth Gordon, *The Natural Areas of Oregon* (Corvallis: Oregon State College, 1953); Donald H. Mansfield, *Flora of Steens Mountain* (Corvallis: Oregon State University Press, 2000), 4–13; Charles Goodman Hansen, "An Ecological Survey of the Vertebrate Animals on Steens Mountain, Harney County, Oregon" (PhD diss., Oregon State College, 1956). Hansen was a Gordon protégé.

21 Lost Forest, located in the midst of sagebrush steppe well east of Central Oregon's pine country, is an anomaly; it exists thanks to a clay substrate that holds the limited precipitation near the surface, where it supports Ponderosa pines.

22 Langston, *Forest Dreams, Forest Nightmares*, 15–20, 27–28; Jack Ward Thomas, ed., *Wildlife Habitat in Managed Forests: The Blue Mountains of Oregon and Washington*, Agricultural Handbook No. 553 (Washington, DC: USDA, Forest Service, 1979), 20, 44, 134, and passim; Richard W. Highsmith Jr., *Atlas of the Pacific Northwest: Resources and Development* (4th ed.; Corvallis: Oregon State University Press, 1968), 28–29, 162, 164–166; D. W. Meinig, *The Great Columbia Plain: A Historical Geography, 1805–1910* (Seattle: University of Washington Press, 1968), 4–16.

CHAPTER 2

1 Cressman, *Golden Journey*, 337, 341–343, 364–380, 383.

2 Cressman, *Golden Journey*, 337, 352–353 (quote), 374, 380, 388; Dennis L. Jenkins, "Introduction to the 2005 Edition," in Luther S. Cressman, *The Sandal and the Cave: The Indians of Oregon* (reprint ed.; Corvallis: Oregon State University Press, 2005), viii.

3 Native American folklore provides evidence that ancestral Klamaths were present when Mount Mazama blew. See Jarold Ramsey, comp. and ed., *Coyote Was Going There: Indian Literature of the Oregon Country* (Seattle: University of Washington Press, 1977), 202–205; Ella E. Clark, *Indian Legends of the Pacific Northwest* (Berkeley: University of California Press, 1958), 53–60.

4 Cressman, *Golden Journey*, 378–379, 422–424; Jenkins, "Introduction," vi–xxxiii; C. Melvin Aikens and Dennis L. Jenkins, eds., *Archaeological Researches in the Northern Great Basin: Fort Rock Archaeology since Cressman*, University of Oregon Anthropological Papers 50 (Eugene: University of Oregon, 1994); Dennis L. Jenkins, Thomas J. Connolly, and C. Melvin Aikens, *Early and Middle Holocene Archaeology of the Northern*

Great Basin, University of Oregon Anthropological Papers 62 (Eugene: University of Oregon, 2004); Dennis L. Jenkins et al., "Clovis Age Western Stemmed Projectile Points and Human Coprolites at Paisley Cave," *Science* 13 (2012): 223–228.

5   James C. Chatters, "The Recovery and First Analysis of an Early Holocene Human," *American Antiquity* 65 (2002): 291–316; interview with James C. Chatters, "Last Word on Kennewick Man?" *Archeology* 55 (2002): 17; James C. Chatters, *Ancient Encounters: Kennewick Man and the First Americans* (New York: Simon and Schuster, 2002); J. R. Nelson et al., "Mitochondrial Population Genomics Supports a Single Pre-Clovis Origin for the Peopling of the Americas," *American Journal of Human Genetics* 82 (2008): 583–592; Lynda V. Mapes, "Kennewick Man Bones Not from Columbia Valley Scientist Tells Tribes," *Seattle Times*, October 10, 2012; Douglas W. Owsley and Richard L. Jantz, *Kennewick Man: The Scientific Investigation of an Ancient American Skeleton* (Lubbock: Texas A&M University Press, 2014); Morton Rasmussen et al., "The Ancestry and Affiliations of Kennewick Man," *Nature* 523 (2015): 455–458; Ewen Callaway, "Ancient American Genome Rekindles Legal Row," *Nature* 522 (2015): 404–405.

6   Bernard DeVoto, ed., *The Journals of Lewis and Clark* (Cambridge, MA: Riverside Press, 1953), 246, 250, 255, 268.

7   DeVoto, *Journals*, 248.

8   Some Native Americans argue that horses were always present in North America, that cayuses were descended from prehistoric American horses, and that mustangs were descended from horses introduced from Europe. See Edward Kowrach and Thomas E. Connolly, eds., *Saga of the Coeur d'Alene Indians: An Account of Chief Joseph Seltice* (Fairfield, WA: Ye Galleon Press, 1990), 179–181; *Coeur d'Alene Press*, March 27, 2016; William O. Douglas, *Go East, Young Man: The Early Years* (New York: Dell, 1974), 74–75.

9   Northern Paiute traditions maintain they got horses before the Umatillas, who then stole so many the Paiutes soon had few (or none), and that horses then spread to the Tenino, Klamaths, and others. Robert F. Heizer and Thomas R. Hester, eds., *Notes on Northern Paiute Ethnography: Kroeber and Marsden Records* (Berkeley: University of California Archeological Facility, 1972), 10–11. See also, H. M. Painter, "The Coming of the Horse," *Pacific Northwest Quarterly* (hereafter *PNQ*) 2 (1946): 155–157; Eugene S. Hunn, "Mobility as a Factor Limiting Resource Use in the Columbia Plateau of North America," in Nancy M. Williams and Eugene S. Hunn, eds., *Resource Managers: North American and Australian Hunter-Gatherers* (Boulder, CO: Westview Press, 1982), 23–33.

10   Francis D. Haines, "The Northward Spread of Horses among the Plains Indians," *American Anthropologist* 40 (1938): 429–437; Meinig, *Great Columbia Plain*, 24–25; Robert H. Ruby and John A. Brown, *The Cayuse Indians: Imperial Tribesmen of Old Oregon* (Norman: University of Oklahoma Press, 1972), 3–4, 7–20 (quote, p. 18); James A. Teit, "The Salishan Tribes of the Western Plateaus," *Annual Report of the Bureau of American Ethnology* 45 (1927–1928): 109–110.

11   Meinig, *Great Columbia Plain,* 23–25.

12   Langston, *Forest Dreams, Forest Nightmares,* 46–49, 248–251, 259–260;
     Stephen J. Pyne, *Fire in America: A Cultural History of Wild Land and Rural
     Fire* (Princeton, NJ: Princeton University Press, 1982), 71–83. See also,
     Harold Weaver, "Ecological Changes in the Ponderosa Pine Forests of the
     Warm Springs Indian Reservation in Oregon," *Journal of Forestry* 57 (1959):
     15–20. Weaver spent much of his career studying the impact of fire on pine
     forests, especially those on Indian lands. His papers are at the Forest History
     Society, Durham, NC.

13   Erna Gunther, "The Westward Movement of Some Plains Traits," *American
     Anthropologist* n.s. 52 (1950): 176–177; Meinig, *Great Columbia Plain,* 25
     (quotes).

14   James A. Goss, "Culture-Historical Inference from Utaztekan Linguistic
     Evidence," in Earl H. Swanson Jr., ed., *Utaztekan Prehistory, Occasional
     Papers of the Idaho State University Museum* 22 (1968): 1–42; Catherine L. S.
     Fowler, "Comparative Numic Ethnobiology" (PhD diss., University of
     Pittsburgh, 1972); David B. Madsen and David Rhode, eds., *Across the West:
     Human Population Movement and the Expansion of the Numa* (Salt Lake
     City: University of Utah Press, 1994). Recent DNA studies lend strength to
     this view. See Frederika A. Kaestle and David Glenn Smith, "Ancient
     Mitochondrial DNA Evidence for Prehistoric Population Movement,"
     American Journal of Anthropology 115 (2001): 1–12.

15   Ramsey, *Coyote Was Going There,* 232–236 (quote, p. 233), 248–250; Heizer
     and Hester, *Northern Paiute Ethnography,* 37, 54; Wilson Wewa, *Legends of
     the Northern Paiute,* ed. by James A. Gardner (Corvallis: Oregon State
     University Press, 2017), 33–42. It seems likely the reference in Ramsey is not
     to grinding and cooking in a kettle, but in a hollowed stone container; one
     suspects a typographical or transcription error, "or rock" should perhaps be
     "of rock." For a brief review of the theories on origins, see Susan Jane Stowell,
     "The Wada-Tika of the Former Malheur Indian Reservation" (PhD diss.,
     University of California, Davis, 2008), 22–24.

16   Stowell, "Wada-Tika," 40–47, 58–60; Omer C. Stewart, "The Northern Paiute
     Bands," *Anthropological Records* 2 (1939): 127–149; Kittredge, *Hole in the
     Sky,* 17 (quote); Beckham and Lentz, *Rocks and Hard Places,* 6, 14–15.

17   Stowell, "Wada-Tika," 120. Tribal accounts describe the role of Weahwewah
     in bringing horses to the Paiutes.

18   Carrol B. Howe, *Ancient Tribes of the Klamath Country* (Portland: Binford
     and Mort, 1969), 101–102. Although not a professionally trained ethnologist,
     Howe rests his work on solid primary and secondary sources, fieldwork, and
     tribal informants.

19   Robert H. Ruby, John A. Brown, and Cary C. Collins, *A Guide to the Indian
     Tribes of the Pacific Northwest* (3rd ed.; Norman: University of Oklahoma
     Press, 2010), 343–345; Robert H. Ruby and John A. Brown, *Indians of the
     Pacific Northwest* (Norman: University of Oklahoma Press, 1981), 201–204;
     Gregory Michno, *The Deadliest Indian War in the West: The Snake Conflict,
     1864–1868* (Caldwell, ID: Caxton, 2007), 26; Donald P. Hines, *Forgotten*

Tribes: Oral Tales of the Teninos and Adjacent Mid-Columbia River Indian Nations (Issaquah, WA: Great Eagle, 1991), 21–24, 27–28. There is debate over whether the Paiute or Tenino were expanding in the pre-reservation era. Since the Redmond Caves were badly disturbed before archeologists were able to examine them, information on them rests on an imperfect base of evidence; the artifacts found there *may* have in fact been Paiute.

20 W. A. Ferris, *Life in the Rocky Mountains: A Diary . . .*, ed. by Paul C. Phillips (Denver, CO: Old West Publishing, 1940), 99, 299–300 (quotes, p. 300), 310. Peter Skene Ogden's journals, cited below (n21), are replete with references to raids by mounted Nez Perce, Piegan, and others into Paiute territory. Howe notes that the Paiutes in turn frequently raided the Klamaths. Howe, *Ancient Tribes*, 101–103.

21 T. C. Elliott, ed., "Peter Skene Ogden's Snake Country Journal, 1825–1826," *Quarterly of the Oregon Historical Society* 10 (1909): 331–365 (quote, pp. 354–355). For a more careful edition, see E. E. Rich, ed., *Peter Skene Ogden's Snake Country Journals* (London: Hudson's Bay Record Society, 1950), vol. 13.

22 The most thorough study of Astor remains Kenneth Wiggins Porter, *John Jacob Astor, Businessman* (2 vols.; Cambridge, MA: Harvard University Press, 1931). There have been reprint editions.

23 Quotations are from the online English translation accompanying Hunt's journal, published as "Voyage de M. Hunt et de ses compagnons de Saint-Louis a l'embrochure de la Columbia par au nouvelle route a traverse les Rocky-Mountains," in *Nouvelles Annales des Voyages . . .* (Paris: J. B. Eyries and Malte-Brun, 1821), vol. 10: 31–88. Location of original unknown.

24 The Malheur, from the French for misfortune, received its name after the loss of a sizable cache of furs to Indians; the Owyhee (a then-common way of spelling Hawai'i) was named after Hawaiians, dispatched to trap and trade on the river in 1819 and killed by Indians. T. C. Elliott, ed., "The Peter Skene Ogden Journals: Journal of Expedition of 1825–1826," *Oregon Historical Quarterly* (hereafter *OHQ*) 10 (1909): 353–354. Ironically, John Day never visited the upstream area known today as the John Day country.

25 Philip Ashton Rollins, ed., *The Discovery of the Oregon Trail: Robert Stuart's Narratives . . .* (New York: Charles Scribner's Sons, 1935), 84 (quote), 156, 158–163. Stuart's discovery would not become widely known until Jedediah Smith and Thomas Fitzpatrick rediscovered it in 1824.

26 Jennifer Ott, "'Ruining' the Rivers of the Snake Country: The Hudson's Bay Company's Fur Desert Policy," *OHQ* 104 (2003): 166–195. For a full study of Ogden, see Gloria Giffen Cline, *Peter Skene Ogden and the Hudson's Bay Company* (Norman: University of Oklahoma Press, 1974).

27 All quotes are from Elliott, "Journal of Expedition of 1825–26."

28 Elliott, "Journal of Expedition of 1825–26" (entry of February 21), 354; T. C. Elliott, ed., "Journal of Peter Skene Ogden: Snake Expedition, 1826–7," *Quarterly Journal of the Oregon Historical Society* 11 (1910): 201–226 (entries

of October 8 and 11, and November 1, 3, and 4, pp. 206, 207, 208). The Indian structure was apparently near where Sherar's Bridge would later be located.

29 Elliott, "Journal of Expedition" (entry of November 23), 336; Elliott, "Snake Expedition, 1826–7" (entry of November 3; quote, p. 208).

30 Elliott, "Snake Expedition, 1826–7" (entries for November 3 and 4), 208–209. While traveling west, Ogden crossed the Paulina Mountains and, on November 16, discovered East and Paulina Lakes, which he called "a God-send," for by then the party was in desperate need of water.

31 Rachel Applegate Good, *History of Klamath County, Oregon: Its Resources and Its People* (Klamath Falls, OR: no pub., 1941), 6–8. There may have been a white presence earlier. A large rock found near Bend, carved with the date 1813 and some initials (largely illegible), is on display in the Deschutes County Historical Museum.

32 Ogden's route from the Klamath country to Harney Basin is unclear, but his journal seems to indicate he reached the Chewaucan River, Lake Abert (which he called Salt Lake, a name he also applied to Harney Lake), and perhaps the Warner lakes before turning north to Wagontire Mountain. He seems to have just missed Summer Lake, located west of Lake Abert. Elliott, "Snake Expedition, 1826–7" (entries of May 14–24, 30, and June 4), 218–220. Warner Lakes are shown on Arrowsmith's map of 1832 (which was based on information from the Hudson's Bay Company) and on Robert Greenhow's map of 1839; one can only assume knowledge of the lakes was the result of information obtained from Ogden, the only known explorer of the area until then. Derek Hayes, *Historical Atlas of the Pacific Northwest: Maps of Exploration and Discovery* (Seattle: Sasquatch Books, 1999), 114.

33 Ogden, "Snake Expedition, 1826–7" (entries for November 17, 1826, p. 210; July 18, 1827, p. 222).

34 John C. Frémont, *Report of the Exploring Expedition to the Rocky Mountains* (Washington, DC: GPO, 1845), 200.

35 John Charles Fremont, *Memoirs of My Life . . .* (Chicago: Belford, Clarke, 1886), 301. See also, Allen Nevins, *Fremont, Pathmarker of the West* (Lincoln: University of Nebraska Press, 1992), 149, and passim.

36 Fremont, *Memoirs*, 459.

37 Fremont, *Memoirs*, 487–490 (quote, p. 490). Fremont called the tribe and lake "Tlamath," a not unreasonable rendering of how the name was pronounced by resident tribes.

38 Fremont, *Memoirs*, 490–496; Good, *History of Klamath County*, 11–18.

39 Some sources suggest Meek intended to cross to the Deschutes and then find a pass over the Cascades, thus bringing the party into the Willamette Valley well south of Oregon City. See Fred Lockley, *Captain Sol. Tetherow, Wagon Train Master . . .* (Portland: Fred Lockley, n.d.), 4; Fred Lockley, *Conversations with Pioneer Women* (Eugene, OR: Rainy Day Press, 1981), 238, 241–243; Keith Clark and Lowell Tiller, *Terrible Trail: The Meek Cutoff, 1845* (1966; rev. ed., Bend, OR: Maverick, 1993), 60. Meek himself left no record that would clarify the matter.

40 Anonymous, *An Illustrated History of Baker, Grant, Malheur, and Harney Counties* ... (Spokane, WA: Western Historical Publishing, 1902), 138–141; Hubert Howe Bancroft, *History of Oregon* (2 vols.; San Francisco: History Co., 1888), vol. 1: 509, 512–516. See Clark and Tiller for the fullest account. Meek may have been encouraged by a map of 1841 that showed a Sylvies (i.e., Harney) Lake (misspelled) and the river flowing into it from the north.

41 The 2010 movie "Meek's Cutoff" badly represents what followed. The film reflects the monotony, frustration, and anguish of those who took the route and struggled to survive, but makes it appear that only a handful of wagons were involved. In fact, Meek led a major train.

42 W. A. Goulder, *Reminiscences: Incidents in the Life of a Pioneer in Oregon and Idaho* (Boise, ID: Timothy Regan, 1909; reprint ed., Moscow: University of Idaho Press, 1989), 126.

43 Samuel Parker, "Diary, 1845" (ms 1508, Oregon Historical Society, Portland), entries for August 24, August 30, and September 21.

44 A small body of water a short distance west of Harney Lake, not to be confused with the larger—and better known—Silver Lake to the southwest.

45 Clark and Tiller, *Terrible Trail* (quote, pp. 66–68); James H. and Theona J. Hambleton, *Wood, Water, and Grass: Meek Cutoff of 1845* (Caldwell, ID: Caxton, 2014), 76, 87. The route Meek had proposed would have led the party to the upper reaches of Crooked River and thence to the Deschutes. If taken, much suffering would have been avoided.

46 James Field Jr., "The Diary of James Field" (published in Salem *Willamette Farmer*, April 1–Aug. 18, 1879), entry for October 17, 1845. Paiute accounts argue there was plenty of food—the immigrants simply did not know where to look. Wewa, *Legends of the Northern Paiute*, xxxiii–xxxiv.

47 Some sources have Elliott leading a party over Meek Cutoff in 1851 as well as 1853, but this apparently stems from a misreading of the sources. In 1851, Elliott probably followed the regular Oregon Trail route.

48 For a detailed account, see Leah Collins Menefee and Lowell Tiller, "Cutoff Fever," *OHQ* 77 (1976): 308–340; *OHQ* 78 (1977): 121–157, 207–250, 293–331.

49 Quoted in Menefee and Tiller, "Cutoff Fever," 241. McClure's remark may seem odd, but there is considerable evidence sagebrush was initially less ubiquitous and grass more plentiful than they later became.

50 Gale Ontko, *Thunder over the Ochoco* (5 vols.; Bend, OR: Maverick, 1993–1999), vol. 2: 236–238. See also, John E. Simon, "Wilhelm Keil and Communist Colonies," *OHQ* 35 (1934): 128–130.

51 Devere Helfrich, "The Applegate Trail," *Klamath Echoes* 9 (1971). See also, Lindsay Applegate, "Notes and Reminiscences of Laying Out and Establishing the Old Immigrant Road into Southern Oregon in the Year 1846," *Quarterly of the Oregon Historical Society* 22 (1921): 12–45.

52 The nature of Modoc Plateau is indicated by the fact that today a considerable portion is known as Devil's Garden, but it was traversed because

NOTES TO PAGES 28–31

staying north of the Oregon border would have required crossing demanding mountain terrain.

53 Good, *History of Klamath County*, 19–27; Klamath County Historical Society, *The History of Klamath Country, Oregon* (Portland: Taylor Publishing, 1984), 171; Ananias Rogers Pond, "Journal," vol. 1 (mss HM 19383, Henry L. Huntington Library, San Marino, CA), entries for September 3, 8–9, 1849 (quote, September 8). Pond was bound for California, so he left Applegate's route at Goose Lake to travel down the Lassen Cutoff to near present-day Chico. His entries from August 24 to September 9, 1849, cover the portion of the route included in the Applegate Trail.

54 When a trans-Cascade rail line was finally built in Oregon in 1928, it followed this route.

55 Robert W. Sawyer, "Abbot Railroad Surveys, 1855," *OHQ* 33 (1932): 1–24, 115–135 (1st quote, p. 19); US War Department, *Explorations and Surveys for a Railroad Route from the Mississippi River to the Pacific Ocean*, vol. 6, pt. 1: *Report of Lieut. Henry L. Abbot . . .* (Washington, DC: GPO, 1857), 26–29, 37–38, 41–46 (2nd quote, p. 46). The two separated from time to time to investigate various optional routes; observations from the upper Deschutes to The Dalles are Abbot's. See also, Jarold Ramsey, "Henry Larcom Abbot in Central Oregon," *The Agate* n.s. 5 (2016): 3–14.

56 John Minto, "From Youth to Age as an American," *Quarterly of the Oregon Historical Society* 9 (1908): 157; Clark and Clark, "Pioneers of Deschutes Country," in Thomas Vaughan, ed., *High and Mighty: Selected Sketches about the Deschutes Country* (Portland: Oregon Historical Society, 1981), 17. Others located the route in 1859, and a wagon road was built over Santiam Pass to Central Oregon in 1861–1868. Subsequent efforts to build a railroad over Santiam Pass failed, more for financial than geographical reasons.

57 War Department, *Abbot Report*, 41 (quote); discussions with Richard Gervais, Corvallis, Oregon, September–October 1952.

58 George Gibbs to Captain George B. McClellan, March 4, 1854, in Isaac Ingalls Stevens, *Reports of Explorations and Surveys . . . for a Railroad from the Mississippi River to the Pacific Ocean* (Washington, DC: GPO, 1855), 422; Ruby and Brown, *Cayuse*, 7–8, 94–95; Harold E. Driver and William C. Massey, "Comparative Studies of North American Indians," *Transactions of the American Philosophical Society*, n.s. 47 (1957): 284–287.

59 Pond, "Journal," vol. 1: entries of September 3 and 8, 1849; Wewa, *Legends of the Northern Paiute*, xxxiii.

60 With extensive timber and grazing resources, it was a reservation better suited for tribal needs than many. See A. B. Meacham, *Wigwam and War-Path* (2nd ed.; Boston: John P. Dale, 1875), 52–54.

61 *Bend Bulletin*, April 3, 1978; *Redmond Spokesman*, June 1, 2010; Ontko, *Thunder over the Ochoco*, vol. 2: 204; vol. 4: 3–21, 29; Cactus Smyth, *Sunshine, Shadows and Sagebrush*, ed. by Carol Smyth Sawyer (Elgin, AZ: Desert Graphics, 1996), 3–4, 7.

62 Ruby City (Idaho) *Owyhee Avalanche*, June 2, 1866; Mike Hanley with Ellis Lucia, *Owyhee Trails: The West's Forgotten Corner* (Caldwell, ID: Caxton, 1975), 16–17. See also, Susan M. Colby, *Sacagawea's Child: The Life and Times of Jean Baptiste (Pomp) Charbonneau* (Norman: University of Oklahoma Press, 2009).

CHAPTER 3

1 Secretary of War, *Annual Report, 1856–57*, Senate Exec. Docs., *Records of the 34th Cong.*, 3rd sess., vol. 1, pt. 2: pp. 166–169.

2 *Records of the 33rd Cong.*, 2nd sess., Sen. Exec. Docs. (1855), and 2nd sess., Sen. Exec. Docs. (1854), 486–493.

3 Charles Henry Carey, *History of Oregon* (3 vols.; Chicago: Pioneer Historical Publishing, 1922), vol. 1: 767. Eventually eight Oregon counties would be carved from Wasco's original territory.

4 Meinig, *Great Columbia Plain*, 156–157; Bancroft, *History of Oregon*, vol. 2: 252–253, 345, 478–482; Ruby and Brown, *Cayuse*, 255–256.

5 Ruby and Brown, *Cayuse*, 234–240; Anon., *History of Baker, Grant, Malheur, and Harney Counties*, 103–105; John W. Evans, *Powerful Rockey: The Blue Mountains and the Oregon Trail, 1811–1883* (La Grande: Eastern Oregon State College, 1991), 256; Portland *Oregonian* quoted in Ruby and Brown, *Indians of the Pacific Northwest*, 157.

6 Wool to John Cunningham, April 4, 1852 (Frederick Collection of Western Americana, Beinecke Library, Yale University); Ruby and Brown, *Cayuse* (2nd quote, p. 240); Wool to Stevens, February 12, 1856; *Records of the 34th Cong.*, 1st sess., House exec. doc. 93 (1856), 47.

7 Governor Isaac Stevens, "Message to the Third Annual Session of the Legislative Assembly, January 21, 1856," in Charles M. Gates, ed., *Messages of the Governors of the Territory of Washington to the Legislative Assembly, 1854–1889* (Seattle: University of Washington Press, 1940), 23–47; Kent Richards, *Isaac I. Stevens, Young Man in a Hurry* (Pullman: Washington State University Press, 1993), 289, and passim.

8 Thirty-Fifth Congress, 1st sess., *U.S. Executive Documents, No. 2*, vol. 2: 78. Closer to the scene than Wool, Wright realized the untenable position in which the order left The Dalles and modified it by making the Deschutes River the western boundary of the area of exclusion.

9 Miles F. Potter, *Oregon's Golden Years: Bonanza of the West* (Caldwell, ID: Caxton, 1976), 13–31. See also, Leslie M. Scott, "The Pioneer Stimulus of Gold," *Quarterly of the Oregon Historical Society* 18 (1917): 147–166.

10 Anon., *History of Baker, Grant, Malheur, and Harney Counties*, 139–141, 152, 640; Fred Lockley, *Voices of the Oregon Territory . . .* comp. and ed. by Mike Helm (Eugene, OR: Rainy Day Press, 1981), 40, 71–72, 279–281; Potter, *Oregon's Golden Years*, 6–8; Ontko, *Thunder over the Ochoco*, vol. 2: 155–158; Herman Oliver, *Gold and Cattle Country* (Portland: Binford and Mort), 31–34.

11 Portland *Oregonian,* May 9, June 8, and October 7, 1863; April 29, 1864; Bancroft, *History of Oregon,* vol. 2: 479; Meinig, *Great Columbia Plain,* 154–156, 208–211; Arthur L. Throckmorton, *Oregon Argonauts: Merchant Adventurers on the Western Frontier* (Portland: Oregon Historical Society, 1961), 247–250.

12 Bancroft, *History of Oregon,* vol. 2: 478–482; Potter, *Oregon's Golden Years,* 37–41, 95; Verne Bright, "Blue Mountain Eldorados: Auburn, 1861," *OHQ* 62 (1961): 213–356; Barbara Ruth Bailey, *Main Street, Northeastern Oregon: The Founding and Development of Small Towns* (Portland: Oregon Historical Society, 1982), 43.

13 Anon., *History of Baker, Grant, Malheur, and Harney Counties,* 382, 755–767; Potter, *Oregon's Golden Years,* 61, 69, 73–77; Mrs. J. S. Doane, interview by Manly M. Bannister, "The Ghost Town of Auburn," Oregon Folklore Studies, WPA, Federal Writers Project, February 28, 1939; Oliver, *Gold and Cattle,* 17–39.

14 Potter, *Oregon's Golden Years,* 61–65; H. C. Thompson, "Reminiscences of Joaquin Miller and Canyon City," *OHQ* 45 (1944): 326–336; John Day *Blue Mountain Eagle,* October 19, 2016.

15 George S. Trumbull, *History of Oregon Newspapers* (Portland: Binford and Mort, 1939), 274–276; William C. Haight, interview. Grant County was created in October 1864, but its election returns that year are included in those for Wasco County, which McClellan carried with over 51 percent of the vote. Indeed, although Lincoln carried the state as a whole, McClellan prevailed in every county east of the Cascades (including Jackson, which at that time included land on both sides of the range). See Burton W. Onstine, *Oregon Votes: 1858–1972 . . .* (Portland: Oregon Historical Society, 1973), 6, 12, 34, 40, 70, 74, 78.

16 Glenn Thomas Edwards Jr., "Oregon Regiments in the Civil War Years: Duty on the Indian Frontier" (MA thesis, University of Oregon, 1960), 81, 123–124; Lockley, *Voices of Oregon Territory,* 251–252; Joseph Gaston, *Centennial History of Oregon, 1811–1911* (3 vols.; Chicago: S. J. Clarke, 1911), vol. 1: 654; US War Department, *War of the Rebellion . . . Official Records of the Union and Confederate Armies* (Washington, DC: GPO, 1880–1901), series I, vol. 50, pt. 2: 1003, 1012–1013, 1035; F. Smith Fussner, ed., *Glimpses of Wheeler County's Past: An Early History of North Central Oregon* (Portland: Binford and Mort, 1975), 38–39.

17 David Newsom, *David Newsom, The Western Observer, 1805–1882* (Portland: Oregon Historical Society, 1972), 121–126 (emphasis original).

18 Meinig, *Great Columbia Plain,* 212–214; Potter, *Oregon's Golden Years,* 42–48; Throckmorton, *Oregon Argonauts,* 247–267; Gaston, *Centennial History of Oregon,* vol. 1: 497–498; F. A. Shaver, *An Illustrated History of Central Oregon . . .* (Spokane, WA: Western Historical Publishing Co., 1905), 117, 127.

19 Anon., *History of Baker, Grant, Malheur, and Harney Counties,* 388; Michno, *Deadliest Indian War,* 169–172, 217; Ruby and Brown, *Indians of the Pacific Northwest,* 201–202; Ontko, *Thunder over the Ochoco,* vol. 3: 280, 334; Potter, *Oregon's Golden Years,* 57–59; Stowell, "Wada-Tika," 108–111; Janet L.

Stinchfield and McLaren E. Stinchfield, *History of Wheeler County, Oregon* (Dallas: Taylor, 1983), 11; Fussner, *Glimpses of Wheeler County's Past*, 23–25; Beckham and Lentz, *Rocks and Hard Places*, 103–106; Dan Chamness, "The Dalles-Canyon City Wagon Road," *The Agate* n.s. 7 (2017): 9–13.

20 Potter, *Oregon's Golden Years*, 54–56, 61–63; Bancroft, *History of Oregon*, vol. 2: 485–487; Anon., *An Illustrated History of Union and Wallowa Counties . . .* (Spokane, WA: Western Historical Publishing, 1902), 137–139, 141–142, 221–222 (2nd quote, p. 142), 260–261; Evans, *Powerful Rockey*, 311 (1st quote), 314 (3rd quote); George R. Mead, *A History of Union County . . .* (La Grande, OR: E-Cat Worlds, 2006), 112–116.

21 Anon., *History of Baker, Grant, Malheur, and Harney Counties*, 519–522; Julie Welch, "Hill Beachy," *Owyhee Outpost* 20 (1989): 71–75. Mike Hanley, *Owyhee Trails: The West's Forgotten Corner* (Caldwell, ID: Caxton, 1973), 22–77, provides a view of developments as seen by a scion of a pioneer ranching family.

22 Hines, *Forgotten Tribes*, 20, 24, 27–28; Beckham and Lentz, *Rocks and Hard Places*, 52. Hines claims Tenino territory extended south to an east-west line running roughly from Simnasho to Shaniko, thus making the reservation only partially on Paiute land. See also, George P. Murdoch, "The Tenino Indians," *Ethnology* 19 (1990): 129–149.

23 Ruby and Brown, *Indians of the Pacific Northwest*, 201 (Fitch quote); Wewa, *Legends of the Northern Paiute*, xxxiv, xxxvi; Ontko, *Thunder over the Ochoco*, vol. 2: 247–250.

24 Michno, *The Deadliest Indian War*, is the most complete account. See also, Stowell, "Wada-Tika," 114–123; Martin F. Schmitt, ed., *General George Crook: His Autobiography* (2nd ed.; Norman: University of Oklahoma Press, 1960), 142–159; Wewa, *Legends of the Northern Paiute*, xxxv–xxxvi; Ruby and Brown, *Indians of the Pacific Northwest*, 200–210; Anon., *History of Baker, Grant, Malheur, and Harney Counties*, 743–754, 777–782. Ontko, *Thunder over the Ochoco*, has interesting details, many based on native sources, but his claim of a Paviotso Confederacy suggests more formal inter-band cooperation than existed. Michno simply uses Paviotso to indicate the Northern Paiutes as a whole (thus making it nearly synonymous with "Snakes," but less pejorative). Weahwewah was, however, recognized as the preeminent chief. See Ontko, *Thunder over the Ochoco*, vol. 2: 181–182; Michno, *Deadliest Indian War*, 8–9; Wewa, *Legends of the Northern Paiute*, xx, xxxii, xxxvii–xxxiii.

25 Just how useful the scouts were is problematic. The Tenino and Wasco did not have a strong military tradition, but, as one of Weahwewah's descendants observed, when given rifles by the military they believed themselves great warriors. Wewa, *Legends of the Northern Paiute*, xxxiv.

26 Michno, *Deadliest Indian War*, 55–57 (quote, p. 56); Ontko, *Thunder over the Ochoco*, vol. 2: 303–310.

27 Michno, *Deadliest Indian War*, 156–161; Hanley, *Owyhee Trails*, 60–65, 68–77.

28 Michno, *Deadliest Indian War*, xiii–xvii, 34–37, 153–155, 195–197, 254–268, 351–357; Hanley, *Owyhee Trails*, 50–77.

29 Ruby and Brown, *Indians of the Pacific Northwest*, 209; Ontko, *Thunder over the Ochoco*, vol. 3: 377–381; Dorsey Griffin, *Who Really Killed Chief Paulina?* (Netarts, OR: Self-published, 1991).

30 Schmitt, *Crook*, 307–309. Schmitt's account of the parlay is from Crook's longtime associate, Azor H. Nickerson, whose report is appended at the end of Crook's autobiography. For a Paiute account, see Wewa, *Legends of the Northern Paiute*, xxxvii–xxxiii.

31 Stowell, "Wada-Tika," 150–151; Minerva T. Soucie, "Burns Paiute Tribe," in Laura Berg, ed., *The First Oregonians* (Portland: Oregon Council for the Humanities, 2006), 46; Wewa, *Legends of the Northern Paiute*, xxxvii–xxxviii. Various secondary sources say Grant's order created the reservation for "all the roving and straggling bands of eastern and southeastern Oregon." Their source is unclear; the order as published said only "Snake or Piute Indians." See Charles J. Kappler, ed., *Indian Affairs: Laws and Treaties* (7 vols.; Washington, DC: GPO, 1904), vol. 1: 887–888.

32 Tom Marsh, *To the Promised Land: A History of Government and Politics in Oregon* (Corvallis: Oregon State University Press, 2012), 80–82; Anon., *History of Baker, Grant, Malheur, and Harney Counties*, 443, 445; Potter, *Oregon's Golden Years*, 66–68; Hanley, *Owyhee Trails*, 211–215; Beckham and Lentz, *Rocks and Hard Places*, 54–55. For a survey of Chinese activities, see Laban R. Steeves, "Chinese Gold Miners in Northeastern Oregon, 1862–1900" (MA thesis, University of Oregon, 1984).

33 Anon., *History of Baker, Grant, Malheur, and Harney Counties*, 531–532; Canyon City *Grant County News*, October 15, 1885 (quote); November 12, 1898.

34 Michno, *Deadliest Indian War*, 152–153; Hanley, *Owyhee Trails*, 15, 53, 68; Bancroft, *History of Oregon*, vol. 2: 521–522.

35 Union *Oregon Scout*, April 20, 1888; David H. Stratton, "The Snake River Massacre of Chinese Miners, 1887," in Duane A. Smith, ed., *A Taste of the West: Essays in Honor of Robert G. Athearn* (Boulder, CO: Pruett Publishing, 1983); R. Gregory Nokes, *Massacred for Gold: The Chinese in Hell's Canyon* (Corvallis: Oregon State University Press, 2009).

36 Ashwood, Redmond, and elsewhere had minor gold rushes in the early twentieth century, and a brief boom of cinnabar mining centered in the Ochocos. Shaver, *History of Central Oregon*, 741; *Redmond Spokesman*, January 28 and February 18, 1915; March 1, 1917; Portland *Oregonian*, June 28, 1931; Keith Clark, *Redmond: Where the Desert Blooms* (Portland: Oregon Historical Society, 1985), 20–21; B. Elizabeth Ward, *Redmond, Rose of the Desert* (Redmond, OR: Self-published, 1975), 41; Potter, *Oregon's Golden Years*, 158–164.

37 Potter, *Oregon's Golden Years*, 168–169.

CHAPTER 4

1   On these early developments, see J. Orin Oliphant, *On the Cattle Ranges of
    the Oregon Country* (Seattle: University of Washington Press, 1968), 39–74,
    77–78.

2   Peter K. Simpson, *The Community of Cattlemen: A Social History of the
    Cattle Industry in Southeastern Oregon, 1869–1912* (Moscow: University of
    Idaho Press, 1987), 6–7, 23, 224–225; Oliphant, *Cattle Ranges*, 88, 95–96,
    190; George Francis Brimlow, *Harney County, Oregon, and Its Range Land*
    (Portland: Binford and Mort, 1951), 40–44, 55; Anon., *History of Baker,
    Grant, Malheur, and Harney Counties*, 401, 625, 637, 739. Eventually
    Whitehorse Ranch came to include 63,222 acres of deeded land and
    controlled another 287,205 acres of public domain.

3   Young and Sparks, *Cattle in the Cold Desert*, 48–80, 95; Oliphant, *Cattle
    Ranges*, 137–141; Simpson, *Community of Cattlemen*, 27; Brimlow, *Harney
    County*, 42–43. The Central Pacific enlarged its facilities in Winnemucca in
    1874, and it quickly became "the cow center of the region to an even greater
    degree than before." Many animals were driven to Cheyenne as well. George
    E. Carter, "The Cattle Industry of Eastern Oregon, 1880–1890," *OHQ* 67
    (1966): 146; Margaret J. LoPiccolo, "Some Aspects of the Range Cattle
    Industry of Harney County, Oregon, 1870–1900" (MA thesis, University of
    Oregon, 1962), 83–85.

4   Victor Goodwin, "William C. (Hill) Beachey, Nevada-California-Idaho
    Stagecoach King," *Nevada Historical Society Quarterly* 10 (1967): 17–24;
    Welch, "Hill Beachey," 71–75.

5   Hanley, *Owyhee Trails*, 112–114; Simpson, *Community of Cattlemen*, 6–7;
    Brimlow, *Harney County*, 54–57, 174–176; Anne Shannon Monroe, ed.,
    Feelin' Fine!: Bill Hanley's Book (Garden City, NY: Doubleday, Doran, 1931),
    72–75, 107–111; Kittredge, *Hole in the Sky*, 21–22; E. R. Jackman and John
    Scharff, *Steens Mountain in Oregon's High Desert Country* (Caldwell, ID:
    Caxton, 1996), 168–169.

6   Brimlow, *Harney County*, 60, 173–176; Simpson, *Community of Cattlemen*,
    13, 27, 33 (quotes), 58–60; Oliphant, *Cattle Ranges*, 190–192.

7   Brimlow, *Harney County*, 170–178; Hanley, *Owyhee Trails*, 112–114;
    Oliphant, *Cattle Ranges*, 95–96.

8   Kittredge, *Hole in the Sky* (quote, p. 25); Linda McCarthy, *History of Oregon
    Sheriffs, 1841–1991* (Salem: Oregon State Sheriffs Assoc., 1992), 87–88;
    Hanley, *Owyhee Trails*, 88–100; Jackman and Scharff, *Steens Mountain*, 174.
    See also, Martin F. Schmitt, ed., *The Cattle Drives of David Shirk: From Texas
    to the Idaho Mines, 1871 and 1873* (Portland: Champoeg Press, 1956), 131–
    140; Giles French, *Cattle Country of Peter French* (Portland: Binford and
    Mort, 1972), 144–156.

9   Brimlow, *Harney County*, 176, 212, 214; Simpson, *Community of Cattlemen*,
    32–35; French, *Peter French*, 94–97, 115, 117; Kittredge, *Hole in the Sky*
    (quote, p. 22); Monroe, *Feelin' Fine*, 104–108, 128–131, 136–141; Oliphant,

Cattle Ranges, 146; Anon., *History of Baker, Grant, Malheur, and Harney Counties*, 524, 541, 636–637, 732–733.

10 Johnie Cactus Smyth, *Footloose and Ahorseback: Memories of a Buckaroo on Steens Mountain, Oregon* (Bend, OR: Maverick, 1984), 23–24, 36, 98–99; Smyth, *Sunshine, Shadows, and Sagebrush*, 3–7.

11 Irene Locke Barklow, *Gateway to the Wallowas* (Wallowa, OR: Enchantment Publishing, 2003), 35, 45–48; Phil F. Brogan, *East of the Cascades* (Portland: Binford and Mort, 1964), 64–65, 171–174; Clark and Clark, "Pioneers of Deschutes Country," 23; Fred Lockley, "Impressions and Observations of the Journal Man," Portland *Oregon Journal*, November 30, 1938; Tillie Wilson and Alice Scott, *That Was Yesterday: A History of Sisters, Oregon, and the Surrounding Area* (Redmond, OR: Self-published, 1974), 28–29. Todd's son claimed the bridge his father built "opened up Central Oregon," but the Santiam Wagon Road, completed in 1868 to Camp Polk (near present-day Sisters), did its part too, serving as a major route for getting Willamette Valley cattle to Central Oregon's rich summer range. Lewis A. McArthur, ed., "Reminiscences of John Y. Todd [Jr.]," *OHQ* 30 (1929): 71–73.

12 Clark and Clark, " Pioneers of Deschutes Country," 22–25; Ontko, *Thunder over the Ochoco*, vol. 3: 260–261, 269–270; *Bend Bulletin*, July 8, August 5, and October 12, 1922; George L. Green, *Soil Survey of Trout Creek-Shaniko Area, Oregon* . . . (Washington, DC: Soil Conservation Service, 1975), 74 (Steen quote); Brogan, *East of the Cascades*, 105; Many Hands (pseud.), *Jefferson County Reminiscences* (Portland: Binford and Mort, 1957), 21–22.

13 Brogan, *East of the Cascades*, 149–152; Clark and Clark, "Pioneers of Deschutes Country," 34–36; Shaver, *History of Central Oregon*, 704 (1st Barnes quote), 761, 781; Ontko, *Thunder over the Ochoco*, vol. 4: 3 (2nd Barnes quote), 17–28. Crook was not Oregon's first "cow county"; that honor goes to Lake County, created in 1874 (and then including Klamath County, which would be separated from it in 1882).

14 Shaver, *History of Central Oregon*, 824, 843–844, 905, 910, 915, and passim; Allen, *Homesteading the High Desert*, 10–11, 15–16; Ward Tonsfeldt, "Historical Resources Survey, Lakeview, Oregon" (typescript report, Lake County Historical Society library, Lakeview, Oregon, July 1969), 7–12.

15 William Kittredge, *Restoring the Klamath Basin* (Berkeley: University of California Press, 2000), 9–12; Melany Tupper, *The Sandy Knoll Murder: Legacy of the Sheepshooters* (Christmas Valley, OR: Central Oregon Books, 2010), 264; C. J. Hadley, "Mr. Spud," *Range Magazine* 6 (Summer 1998): 30 (quote). On Haggin and his contests with Miller and Lux, see Wallace M. Morgan, *History of Kern County, California* . . . (Los Angeles: Historic Record Co., 1914), 80–81, 85–88, 98–100, 102–104, 109–110; and M. Catherine Miller, *Flooding the Courtrooms: Law and Water in the Far West* (Lincoln: University of Nebraska Press, 1993).

16 Shaver, *History of Central Oregon*, 117; Nard Jones, *Oregon Detour* (reprint ed.; Corvallis: Oregon State University Press, 1990), 107 (quote). Jones called the town Acme, but it was probably Adams. See also Jon M. Skovlin and Donna McDaniel Skovlin, *Hank Vaughan (1849–1893): A Hell-Raising Horse*

Trader of the Bunchgrass Country (Cove, OR: Reflections, 1996), 92–100, 147–150.

17 Marion T. Weatherford, *Arlington: Child of the Columbia* (Portland: Oregon Historical Society, 1977), 2–4 (quote, p. 4), 19.

18 Meinig, *Great Columbia Plain*, 220–223, 232, 235–237, 248, 285–293; Oliphant, *Cattle Ranges*, 77–80, 85–87, 89–90; Shaver, *History of Central Oregon*, 426–427; William G. Robbins, *Landscapes of Promise: The Oregon Story 1800–1940* (Seattle: University of Washington Press, 1997), 145–146 (quote, p. 146).

19 Kappler, *Laws and Treaties*, vol. 1: 798–799; 59th Cong., 1st sess., 1906, 23 Stat., 342, vol. 1, 226; J. Orin Oliphant, "Encroachments of Cattlemen on Indian Reservations of the Pacific Northwest, 1870–1890," *Agricultural History* 24 (1950): 42–58; Oliphant, *Cattle Ranges*, 293–294; Ruby and Brown, *Cayuse*, 287–288; Meinig, *Great Columbia Plain*, 235; John J. Minto, "Sheep Husbandry in Oregon: The Pioneer Era of Domestic Sheep Husbandry," *Quarterly of the Oregon Historical Society* 3 (1902): 235–236.

20 A. B. Guthrie Jr., *These Thousand Hills* (Boston: Houghton-Mifflin, 1956), 3–7 (quote, p. 3).

21 Monroe, *Feelin' Fine*, 47, 63–75 (quote, p. 63), and passim; Hanley, *Owyhee Trails*, 112–114.

22 Monroe, *Feelin' Fine*, 75, 78 (quote), 125. The Supreme Court legalized such practices in 1890 when it ruled an "implied license" existed whereby people were free to use unenclosed public land. Brimlow, *Harney County*, 55.

23 Oliphant, *Cattle Ranges*, 137–138, 296–304; Simpson, *Community of Cattlemen*, 29–30; Stowell, "Wada-Tika," 112–118; Ruby and Brown, *Indians of the Pacific Northwest*, 249.

24 Sarah Winnemucca Hopkins, *Life among the Piutes: Their Wrongs and Claims* (reprint; Reno: University of Nevada Press, 1994), 133–134 (quotes; Hopkins's translation).

25 Stowell, "Wada-Tika," 150–155; Ruby and Brown, *Indians of the Pacific Northwest*, 249–250; Monroe, *Feelin' Fine*, 22–34; Smyth, *Footloose and Ahorseback*, 98–99, 103, 186–189; Smyth, *Sunshine, Shadows and Sagebrush*, 4–6; Lockley, *Conversations with Pioneer Women*, 13–14 (quote, p. 13); J. F. Santee, "Egan of the Paiutes," *Washington Historical Quarterly* 25 (1934): 16–25. For fuller accounts, see George Francis Brimlow, *The Bannock Indian War of 1878* (Caldwell, ID: Caxton, 1938); Mark V. Weatherford, *Bannack-Piute War: The Campaign and Battles* (Corvallis, OR: Lehnert Printing, 1957); Ontko, *Thunder over the Ochoco*, vol. 4: 159–213; Hopkins, *Life among the Piutes*, 106–239; Joseph Wasson, "Colonel Crook's Campaign," reprinted from *Owyhee Avalanche*, various dates, 1867, in Peter Cozzens, ed., *Eyewitnesses to the Indian Wars, 1865–1890* (5 vols.; Mechanicsburg, PA: Stackpole Press, 2001–2005), vol. 2: 33–83; Oliver O. Howard, "Causes of the Bannock War," in Cozzens, *Eyewitnesses*, 604–664. Hopkins, Wasson, and Howard were highly partisan; their works should be used with caution. However, to label the conflict the Bannock War, as Howard and others have done, obscures the degree to which Northern Paiute were involved.

26 Hopkins, *Life among the Piutes*, 133–134; Jarvis Kennedy, Burns Paiute tribe press conference, January 6, 2016 (Portland *Oregonian/Oregon Live*); Kittredge, *Hole in the Sky* (quote, p. 23). Adding to Paiute angst, it would be well over a century before Egan's remains would be returned from the Smithsonian Institution in Washington, DC, for a solemn tribal burial ceremony. *Burns Times-Herald*, April 28, May 5, 1999.

27 Monroe, *Feelin' Fine*, 71 (1st quote), 78 (2nd quote); Simpson, *Community of Cattlemen*, 33–37, 41–46, 56–60.

28 Seasonally flooded swamplands were especially vexing. Legal title could be obtained, but just what qualified was unclear. In 1881 a sand barrier between Malheur and Harney Lakes was breached (with a bit of human help); the resulting flow filled nearly dry Harney Lake and lowered the level of Malheur, transforming a considerable acreage formerly underwater into land that could be claimed under the swamp land act.

29 Monroe, *Feelin' Fine*, 124–126, 129–131 (2nd quote, p. 130), 135 (1st quote); Margaret L. Sullivan, "Conflict on the Frontier: The Case of Harney County, Oregon, 1870–1900," *PNQ* 66 (1975): 174–181 (3rd quote, p. 174).

30 Richard White, *"It's Your Misfortune and None of My Own": A New History of the American West* (Norman: University of Oklahoma Press, 1991), 344.

31 Simpson, *Community of Cattlemen*, 25 (1st quote); Smyth, *Footloose and Ahorseback*, 78, 138, 171; Monroe, *Feelin' Fine*, 99 (2nd quote); Kittredge, *Hole in the Sky*, 26 (3rd quote), 39–40; Alice Day Pratt, *A Homesteader's Portfolio* (New York: Macmillan, 1922), 43–44, 87 (4th quote); Lee Juillerat, "A Conversation with Bill Kittredge," *Range Magazine* 6 (Summer 1998): 28. See also Oliphant, *Cattle Ranges*, 319–337.

32 Monroe, *Feelin' Fine*, 62–63, 101–102, 139–142; Brimlow, *Harney County*, 170–171, 214; Simpson, *Community of Cattlemen*, 27–29; Clark and Clark, "Pioneers of Deschutes Country," 27–28; Edward Gray, *William "Bill" Brown, 1855–1941: Legend of Oregon's High Desert* (Salem, OR: Your Town Press, 1993), 34–49.

33 Monroe, *Feelin' Fine*, 131.

34 Monroe, *Feelin' Fine*, 132; *Burns Times-Herald*, August 1, 1930. Hanley estimated that the worst of these winters killed 80 to 90 percent of the cattle in the valley. Others put the figure somewhat lower, but in any case the losses were huge. See Simpson, *Community of Cattlemen*, 53–54; Oliphant, *Cattle Ranges*, 261–262; Brimlow, *Harney County*, 176. Otley's diaries, located in the Harney County Library in Burns, provide insights into his efforts to protect riparian rights for many nearby ranchers who turned to hay-raising in this period.

35 Monroe, *Feelin' Fine*, 51–52, 78–79, 83–90, 132; Simpson, *Community of Cattlemen*, 51–52; Walter M. Pierce, *Oregon Cattleman/Governor Congressman: Memoirs and Times of Walter M. Pierce*, ed. and expanded by Arthur H. Bone (Portland: Oregon Historical Society, 1981), 71–72.

36 Monroe, *Feelin' Fine*, 135–142 (1st quote, p. 136; 2nd quote p. 137; 3rd quote, p. 139); Simpson, *Community of Cattlemen*, 137–139, 130; Oliphant, *Cattle*

Ranges, 179–180; Carter, "Cattle Industry of Eastern Oregon," 150–151, and passim. See also Gene M. Gressley, *Bankers and Cattlemen* (New York: Knopf, 1966), 89–212.

37 Jackman and Scharff, *Steens Mountain*, 149–156; Crook County Historical Society, *A Historical Tour of Bear Creek* (Prineville, OR: Crook County Historical Society, 2000); Jack Southworth, "The Pioneers of Izee," in www.izranch.com; Clark and Clark, "Pioneers of Deschutes Country," 28–31; Shaver, *History of Central Oregon*, 710–712; Ellen Waterston, *Where the Crooked River Rises: A High Desert Home* (Corvallis: Oregon State University Press, 2010), 115–118; Gray, *Bill Brown*, 83–99, 109, 113, 158–198.

38 Monroe, *Feelin' Fine*, 108 (1st quote), 134; Kittredge, *Hole in the Sky*, 27 (2nd quote), 153 (3rd quote); David Igler, *Industrial Cowboys: Miller & Lux and the Transformation of the American West, 1850–1920* (Berkeley: University of California Press, 2001), esp. 179–184. Igler's focus is primarily on Miller & Lux's California operations, but his study fits what was taking place on their Oregon holdings as well.

39 Bernard Augustine DeVoto, "The West: A Plundered Province," *Harper's Magazine* 183 (1934): 355–364; William G. Robbins, *Colony and Empire: The Capitalist Transformation of the American West* (Lawrence: University Press of Kansas, 1994), esp. 162–184; Gressley, *Bankers and Cattlemen*, 296–297. There is considerable literature on the subject, and on Fernand Braudel, who provides its larger context.

40 Richard White, "Americans Didn't Always Yearn for Riches," *Boston Review*, February 1, 2013; White to the author, August 24, 2013. The outlook was hardly new. See Alan Taylor, *Liberty Men and Great Proprietors: The Revolutionary Settlement of the Maine Frontier* (Chapel Hill: University of North Carolina Press, 1990), 1–9, 73–77, and passim.

CHAPTER 5

1 Alfred L. Lomax, *Later Woolen Mills in Oregon: A History of the Woolen Mills That Followed the Pioneer Mills* (Portland: Binford and Mort, 1974), 257–301.

2 Minto, "Sheep Husbandry in Oregon" (1st quote, p. 242), 244; Edward Norris Wentworth, *America's Sheep Trails: History, Personalities* (Ames: Iowa State College Press, 1948), 399 (2nd quote); *West Shore* 13 (1887): 773–774.

3 Alexander Campbell McGregor, *Counting Sheep: From Open Range to Agri-Business on the Columbia Plateau* (Seattle: University of Washington Press, 1982), 108–153; Meinig, *Great Columbia Plain*, 274, 293, 348–349, 442–443; John F. Kilkenny, *Shamrocks and Shepherds: The Irish of Morrow County* (rev. ed.; Portland: Oregon Historical Society, 1981), 9 (Minto quote), 11–13.

4 Alfred L. Lomax, "Thomas Kay Woolen Mill Co.: A Family Enterprise," *OHQ* 54 (1953): 102–106, 114–115; Lomax, *Later Woolen Mills*, 18–64; "Thomas Kay," Salem Online History website, www.salemhistory.net.

5 Lomax, *Later Woolen Mills*, 260–265, 267–268, 275–276; Pendleton Woolen Mills, "Indian Trading Blanket History," www.pendleton-usa.com website; Robert W. Kapoun and Charles J. Lohrman, *Language of the Robe: American*

Indian Trade Blankets (Layton, UT: Gibbs Smith, 1992), 121–152. Lomax renders the name as Rownsley.

6 Michael Bales and Ann Terry Hill, *Pendleton Round-Up at 100: Oregon's Legendary Rodeo* (Pendleton: East Oregonian Publishing, 2009), 22, 53, 54, 61, 246, 250–254; Pendleton *East Oregonian*, September 30, 1912; Lockley, *Voices of the Oregon Territory*, 126.

7 Wentworth, *America's Sheep Trails*, 176–180; Gaston, *Centennial History of Oregon*, vol. 1: 327; Minto, "Sheep Husbandry in Oregon," 219–229; Throckmorton, *Oregon Argonauts*, 221–222; Brogan, *East of the Cascades*, 106. Brogan has the 1842 flock brought from California by Joseph Gale.

8 Minto, "Sheep Husbandry in Oregon," 230, 232–234; Lomax, *Later Woolen Mills*, 199, 205; Weatherford, *Arlington*, 15, 19; Wentworth, *America's Sheep Trails*, 206–210; Meinig, *Great Columbia Plain*, 222–223; Barklow, *Gateway to the Wallowas*, 53, 124–127; Peter A. Shroyer, "Oregon Sheep, Wool, and Woolen Industries," *OHQ* 67 (1966): 128–135; Hands, *Jefferson County Reminiscences*, 96–104; Bancroft, *History of Oregon*, vol. 2: 758.

9 Lawrence Rakestraw, "A History of Forest Conservation in the Pacific Northwest, 1891–1913" (PhD diss., University of Washington, 1955), 25–26.

10 McArthur, "Reminiscences of John Y. Todd," 71.

11 Minto, "Sheep Husbandry in Oregon," 241–242 (quote, p. 242); Weatherford, *Arlington*, 210–211; Lomax, *Later Woolen Mills*, 255; Wentworth, *America's Sheep Trails*, 212–213; Clark and Clark, "Pioneers of Deschutes Country," 26; Brogan, *East of the Cascades*, 111–112; Shaver, *History of Central Oregon*, 701, 736, 739–740; Hands, *Jefferson County Reminiscences*, 10–30. During the winter of 1883–1884, A. W. Boyce lost all but 400 of his band of 2,600 sheep on Agency Plains. Minto, "Sheep Husbandry in Oregon," 234; Prineville *Crook County News*, August 4, 1939.

12 Minto, "Sheep Husbandry in Oregon," 242–243; Lomax, *Later Woolen Mills*, 255; *The Oregonian Handbook of the Pacific Northwest* (Portland: Oregonian Publishing, 1894), 279.

13 Waterston, *Where the Crooked River Rises*, 115–124; Gray, *Bill Brown*, 55–81, 113.

14 "History," www.imperialstockranch.com. Other spreads, some nearly as large, appeared elsewhere in the area. See Clark and Clark, "Pioneers of Central Oregon," 25–26.

15 Brimlow, *Harney County*, 43–44, 170–171, 214; Oliver, *Gold and Cattle Country*, 59–60 (quote); Brogan, *East of the Cascades*, 122–127; Ontko, *Thunder over the Ochoco*, vol. 5: 245–251; McVicker, *Child of Steens Mountain*, 80–81; E. R. Jackman and R. A. Long, *The Oregon Desert* (Caldwell, ID: Caxton, 1973), 138–148.

16 McGregor, *Counting Sheep*, 108–153.

17 Shaver, *History of Central Oregon*, 169–170; The Dalles *Times-Mountaineer*, September 20, 1899. See also, Helen Guyton Rees, *Shaniko: From Wool Capital to Ghost Town* (Portland: Binford and Mort, 1982).

18 Shaver, *History of Central Oregon*, 170–171; Lomax, *Later Woolen Mills*, 206, 255; Beckham and Lentz, *Rocks and Hard Places*, 114–116. The railroad did not completely replace teamsters; some big horse- and mule-team wagons hauled wool to Arlington until 1923. See Weatherford, *Arlington*, 73–74.

19 Jon M. Skovlin, *Fifty Years of Research Progress: A Historical Document on the Starkey Experimental Forest* (Portland: Forest Service, PNW Research Station, 1991), 8 (1st quote); Mary Austin, *The Flock* (Boston: Houghton, Mifflin, 1906), 55–56 (2nd quote); Pierce, *Memoirs*, 72–73 (3rd quote, p. 73); Jackman and Scharff, *Steens Mountain*, 136.

20 Richard W. Etulain, "Foreword," in McVicker, *Child of Steens Mountain*, xi; Minto, "Sheep Husbandry in Oregon," 231; Clark and Clark, "Pioneers of Deschutes Country," 26–27, 31; Brimlow, *Harney County*, 142; Shaver, *History of Central Oregon*, 120–121, 124; Wentworth, *America's Sheep Trails*, 213–214, 260–265; Potter, *Oregon's Golden Years*, 133; Rakestraw, "Forest Conservation in the Pacific Northwest," 175–176; Jackman and Scharff, *Steens Mountain*, 136. The Portland *Oregonian*, September 19, 1902, provides figures for Morrow, Umatilla, Union, Wasco, Wheeler, Crook, and Grant Counties, but they were merely rough estimates.

21 Portland *Oregonian*, May 23, 1897; Lawrence Rakestraw, "Sheep Grazing in the Cascade Range: John Minto vs. John Muir," *Pacific Historical Review* (hereafter *PHR*) 27 (1958): 371–382; Stephen R. Mark, "Closing Down the Commons: Conflict between Sheep Grazing and Forestry in Oregon's Cascade Range, 1865–1915," *Journal of the Shaw Historical Library* (hereafter *JSHL*) 18 (2004): 63–74; Rakestraw, "Forest Conservation in the Pacific Northwest," 121–123, 175–176; Frederick V. Coville, *Forest Growth and Sheep Grazing in the Cascade Mountains of Oregon*, USDA Division of Forestry Bulletin no. 15 (Washington, DC: GPO, 1898); Harold D. Langille, "Mostly Division 'R' Days: Reminiscences of the Stormy, Pioneering Days of the Forest Service," *OHQ* 57 (1956): 302–305. The vast Cascade Forest Reserve incorporated forestland on both sides of Oregon's Cascade Range. It was later divided into a number of national forests.

22 McGregor, *Counting Sheep*, 29; Oliver, *Gold and Cattle Country*, 59; *West Shore* 13 (1883): 773; Portland Board of Trade, *Annual Report, 1888*, 86; Brimlow, *Harney County*, 171–172 (Miller quote).

23 Langille, "Mostly Division 'R' Days," 308; Stephen A. D. Puter, *Looters of the Public Domain* (Portland: Portland Printing House, 1908), 347–356. Butte Creek's actions led to company owners being indicted in the Oregon timber fraud trials of 1905, but they had been motivated by different concerns than the other defendants. See Jerry A. O'Callaghan, "Senator Mitchell and the Oregon Land Frauds, 1905," *PHR* 21 (1952): 255–261; John Messing, "Public Lands, Politics, and Progressives: The Oregon Land Fraud Trials, 1903–1910," *PHR* 35 (1966): 35–66.

24 Portland *Oregonian*, September 9, 1902; Prineville *Crook County Journal*, March 3 and December 4, 1902; May 5, July 21, and October 20, 1904; Oliver, *Gold and Cattle Country*, 60–61; Anon., *History of Union and Wallowa Counties*, 175; Mead, *History of Union County*, 63–65; Lois Blackstone

Mitchell and Corrine Blackstone Neeley, *Edge of the Desert: A Saga of the Percy Blackstone Family, 1915–1945* (Prineville, OR: Bowman Museum, 1988), 47–48; Southworth, "Pioneers of Izee," 2–3; Brogan, *East of the Cascades*, 114–121; Clark and Clark, "Pioneers of Deschutes Country," 31–33; Fussner, *Glimpses of Wheeler County's Past*, 83–96; Ontko, *Thunder over the Ochoco*, vol. 5: 195–200, 233–238, 245–252; Gray, *Bill Brown*, 76–81; Tupper, *Sandy Knoll*, 55–84 (quote, p. 56). For the broader context, see Bill O'Neal, *Cattlemen vs. Sheepherders: Five Decades of Violence in the West* (rev. ed.; Austin, TX: Eakin Press, 2004).

25 Prineville *Crook County Journal*, February 5, 1903; Lakeview *Lake County Examiner*, April 30, 1903; Tupper, *Sandy Knoll*, 62–63; Waterston, *Where the Crooked River Rises*, 118.

26 *Heppner Gazette*, January 19, 1904; Lakeview *Lake County Examiner*, February 11, 1904; *Prineville Review*, February 11, 1904; Portland *Oregonian*, June 9, 1904; Tupper, *Sandy Knoll*, 29, 31–36, 64–65, 70–74; Shaver, *History of Central Oregon*, 718–721, 827; Brogan, *East of the Cascades*, 116–119; Allen, *Homesteading the High Desert*, 23–25; Jeffrey Ostler, "The Origins of Central Oregon's Range War of 1904," *PNQ* 79 (1988): 2–9; Bill Johnson, "The Central Oregon Range War, 1896–1906," *JSHL* 18 (2004): 75–84.

27 Tupper, *Sandy Knoll*, 73, 108–109; Lakeview *Lake County Examiner*, May 5 and 26, 1904; Portland *Oregonian*, May 13, 1904; Roseburg *Plaindealer*, May 16, 1904; *Burns Times-Herald*, May 28, 1904; "Message of George E. Chamberlain, Governor of Oregon to the Twenty-third Legislative Assembly," *Messages and Documents, 1905, Governor's Regular Session Message* (Salem: State Printer, 1905), 37–38.

28 Brogan, *East of the Cascades*, 120–121; Charles Congleton, "Forest Service Reminiscences" (Crook County Historical Society, Bowman Library, Prineville), 374 (1st quote), 375 (2nd quote); Langille, "Mostly Division 'R' Days," 309 (3rd quote); Anon., *History of Baker, Grant, Malheur, and Harney Counties*, 529; Rakestraw, "Forest Conservation in the Pacific Northwest," 166, 174–176, 178–180, 196–199, 201–208; Barry Greenslate, "The Role of Culture in the History of the Sheep Industry in the Inter-Mountain West," *JSHL* 18 (2004): 10–11; Klamath Falls *Evening Herald*, January 3, April 5 and 22, 1918; February 15 and 17, 1919; Stephen Dow Beckham, *The Gerber Block: Historical Developments on the Public Rangelands in Klamath County, Oregon* (Klamath Falls, OR: Bureau of Land Management, 2000), 38–41.

29 Marion Clawson and Burnell Held, *The Federal Lands: Their Use and Management* (Baltimore, MD: Johns Hopkins University Press, 1957), 85; William A. Douglass and Jon Bilbao, *Amerikanuak: Basques in the New World* (Reno: University of Nevada Press, 1975), 291.

30 Brogan, *East of the Cascades*, 119; Clark and Clark, "Pioneers of Deschutes Country," 33; Tupper, *Sandy Knoll*, 70. See also, Klamath Falls *Evening Herald*, February 17, 1919; January 30, 1920; Jon M. and Donna McDaniel Skovlin, *Into the Minam: A History of a River and Its People* (Cove, OR: Reflections, 2006), 30–31.

31 Jackman and Scharff, *Steens Mountain* (quote, p. 136); Douglass and Bilbao, *Amerikanuak*, 282–291.

32 Marie Kelleher, *Duhallow to Oregon, 1880–1960* (Lakeview, OR: Duhallow Development, 1985). Oddly, David Emmons ignores sheepherding and the Irish presence in Oregon's outback. See Emmons, *Beyond the Pale: The Irish in the American West, 1845–1910* (Norman: University of Oklahoma Press, 2010).

33 Minto, "Sheep Husbandry in Oregon," 231; Klamath Falls *Herald and News*, March 15, 2004 (1st quote); Lakeview *Lake County Examiner*, January 2, 2005; and July 17, 2013 (2nd quote); irishsheepherders.com website; McVicker, *Child of Steens Mountain*, 6–9; Kilkenny, *Shamrocks and Shepherds*, 8–16; Greenslate, "The Role of Culture," 8–9; Lee Juillerat, "Voices: Early Sheepmen Recount Times Past," *JSHL* 18 (2004): 101–110, 113–115; Beckham, *Gerber Block*, 109–110.

34 Written as a poem by Jerry C. Murphy of Klamath Falls, and apparently privately circulated, this work was set to music by folksinger Corey Murphy, whose version is the most readily available source. Jerry Murphy, www. irishfolksinger.com. Dog Mountain and Dog Lake are west of Lakeview.

35 Clawson and Held, *Federal Lands*, 85–88; Clark and Clark, "Pioneers of Deschutes Country," 33; Hanley, *Owyhee Trails*, 176–178; Jackman and Scharff, *Steens Mountain*, 136. Dog Mountain and Dog Lake are west of Lakeview.

36 Douglass and Bilbao, *Amerikanuak*, 252–297; Hanley, *Owyhee Trails*, 183–197; Greenslate, "The Role of Culture," 11–13; Wentworth, *America's Sheep Trails*, 222; Ione B. Harkness, "Basque Settlement in Oregon," *OHQ* 34 (1933): 273–275; Joseph Harold Gaiser, "The Basques of the Jordan Valley Area: A Study in Social Progress and Social Change" (PhD diss., University of Southern California, 1944). See also, Richard H. Lane and William A. Douglass, *Basque Sheep Herders of the American West* (Reno: University of Nevada Press, 1985).

37 Greenslate, "The Role of Culture," 11–13 (1st quote, p. 11); Juillerat, "Voices," 111–113 (2nd quote, p. 113). See also, Carrol B. Howe, "Life in a Sheep Camp," *JSHL* 18 (2004): 121–125.

38 Douglass and Bilbao, *Amerikanuak*, 284–297 (3rd quote, p. 295); Langille, "Mostly Division 'R' Days" (2nd quote, p. 312); Hanley, *Owyhee Trails*, 179–180, 185, 187 (4th quote), 195 (1st quote); Young and Sparks, *Cattle in the Cold Desert*, 226; Kevin Dean Hatfield, "'We Were Not Tramp Sheepmen': Resistance and Identity in the Oregon Basque Community, Accustomed Range Rights, and the Taylor Grazing Act, 1890–1955" (PhD diss., University of Oregon, 2003).

39 Hanley, *Owyhee Trails*, 186, 193–197 (1st quote, p. 193; 2nd quote, p. 197); Douglass and Bilbao, *Amerikanuak*, 367–370.

40 Tupper, *Sandy Knoll*, 31, 33, 37, 65; Shroyer, "Oregon Sheep, Wool, and Woolen Industries," 130–131; Oliver, *Gold and Cattle Country*, 58–63, 214–215, 221; McGregor, *Counting Sheep*, 50–74.

41 Larry L. Irwin et al., *Effects of Long-Term Grazing by Big Game and Livestock*, General Technical Report 325 (Portland: Forest Service, Pacific Northwest Experiment Station, 1994), 5.

CHAPTER 6

1 John C. Ainsworth, "Autobiography of John C. Ainsworth, Oregon Capitalist," MS, Ainsworth Papers (Knight Library, University of Oregon, Eugene), box 1; Throckmorton, *Oregon Argonauts*, 119–123, 206, 250–252; Johansen and Gates, *Empire of the Columbia: A History of the Pacific Northwest* (New York: Harpers, 1957), 338–341.

2 Dorothy O. Johansen, "The Oregon Steam Navigation Company, 1860–1880: An Example of Capitalism on the Frontier," *PHR* 10 (1941): 179–188; Ainsworth, "Autobiography," entry of February 9, 1881 (quote).

3 *Walla Walla Statesman*, February 3, 1865; Meinig, *Great Columbia Plain*, 225–226; F. A. Shaver et al., *Illustrated History of Southeastern Washington* (Spokane, WA: Western Historical Publishing, 1906), 94, 111; John B. Watkins, *Wheat Exporting from the Pacific Northwest*, Bulletin 201 (Pullman: Washington Agricultural Experiment Station, 1915), 10; Donald W. Meinig, "Wheat Sacks Out to Sea: The Early Export Trade from the Walla Walla Country," *PNQ* 45 (1954): 13–18. The date of the first shipment to Liverpool is unclear, but it was before 1870.

4 Meinig, *Great Columbia Plain*, 223–226, 231–234; Carrie Adell Strahorn, *Fifteen Thousand Miles by Stage* (new ed.; 2 vols.; Lincoln, NE: Bison Books, 1988), vol. 1: 303–304 (1st quote); Gordon Macnab, *A Century of News and People in the East Oregonian, 1875–1975* (Pendleton: East Oregonian, 1975), 25, 28 (2nd quote); John H. Garland, "The Columbia Plateau Region of Commercial Grain Farming," *Geographical Review* 24 (1934): 371–379.

5 It cost roughly as much to haul wheat fifteen miles by wagon as it did five hundred miles by railroad or three thousand miles by ocean transportation. Clarence Fielden Jones and Gordon Gerald Darkenwald, *Economic Geography* (rev. ed.; New York: Macmillan, 1954), 261.

6 John Fahey, *The Inland Empire: Unfolding Years, 1879–1929* (Seattle: University of Washington Press, 1986), 56; Robbins, *Landscapes of Promise*, 147–148. For analyses of the impact of the OR&N's connections to the east, see the series of articles in *OHQ* 67 (June 1966) and 71 (March 1970).

7 The literature is extensive, but mostly focused on political economy. On implications for trade, see Jeffrey G. Williamson, "The Impact of the Corn Laws Just Prior to Repeal," *Explorations in Economic History* 27 (1990): 123–156; Kevin H. O'Rourke, "The European Grain Invasion, 1870–1913," *Journal of Economic History* 31 (1997): 773–801. In years when grain prices and demand fell in Europe, shipments of flour to East Asia took up the slack. Johansen and Gates, *Empire of the Columbia*, 450; Thomas R. Cox, "The Passage to India Revisited: Asian Trade and the Development of the Far West, 1850–1900," in John A. Carroll, ed., *Reflections of Western Historians* (Tucson: University of Arizona Press, 1969), 89–91.

8   K. S. Quisenberry and L. F. Reitz, "Turkey Wheat: Cornerstone of an Empire,"
    Agricultural History 48 (1974): 98–110.

9   J. Allen Clark and B. B. Bayles, *Varieties of Club Wheat*, USDA Farmers
    Bulletin 1708 (Washington, DC: GPO, 1940), 3; Meinig, *Great Columbia
    Plain*, 305, 406; Giles French, *The Golden Land: A History of Sherman
    County, Oregon* (Portland: Oregon Historical Society, 1958), 175. In the
    twentieth century, smut made a belated appearance in the interior, adding
    impetus to the search for new varieties. Fahey, *Inland Empire*, 55.

10 *Dry Farming: Bulletin of the International Dry-Farming Congress* 5, no. 2
    (1911): 236; Macnab, *News and People*, 213, 262–263. Bluestem also did well
    in the Klamath Basin; wheat from there won first prize in international
    competition in Omaha in 1909. Klamath Falls *Evening Herald*, December 13,
    1909.

11 Pierce, *Memoirs*, 9–10 (1st quotes); Hayes Perkins, "Here and There: An
    Itinerant Worker in the Pacific Northwest," *OHQ* 102 (2001): 352–376 (last
    quote, p. 358). See also, Gerald Schwartz, "Walter M. Pierce and the
    Tradition of Progressive Reform: A Study of Eastern Oregon's Great
    Democrat" (PhD diss., Washington State University, 1969), 1–3, 42–47, 50;
    Robert R. McCoy, "The Paradox of Oregon's Progressive Politics: The Political
    Career of Walter Marcus Pierce," *OHQ* 110 (2009): 390–419; Carlos A.
    Schwantes, *Hard Travelling: A Portrait of Work Life in the New Northwest*
    (Lincoln: University of Nebraska Press, 1994). Milton (not yet combined with
    neighboring Freewater) was eight miles south of Walla Walla on the Oregon
    side of the border.

12 Meinig, *Great Columbia Plain*, 404–405, 411–412, 420, 500; Shaver et al.,
    History of Southeastern Washington, 93, 109.

13 Fahey, *Inland Empire*, 60–64; Pierce, *Memoirs* (quote, p. 68); Macnab, *News
    and People*, 80, 97–98, 175; Douglas, *Go East, Young Man*, 75–76. As one
    historian put it, "Pierce was primarily a farmer, imbued with agricultural
    values." Schwartz, "Walter M. Pierce," 25–26 (quote, p. 25).

14 Jones, *Oregon Detour* (quote, p. 132). Jones's *Wheat Women* (New York:
    Duffield and Green, 1933) is a more fugitive work, but provides many of the
    same insights.

15 Pierce, *Memoirs*, 68–69 (quotes). The first combine did not arrive in the
    Klamath Basin, with its more diversified agriculture, until 1920. Klamath
    Falls *Evening Herald*, July 30, 1920.

16 Meinig, *Great Columbia Plain*, 430–432, 499–500. See also, Earl Pomeroy,
    The American Far West in the Twentieth Century (New Haven, CT: Yale
    University Press, 2008), 53–59; Fred A. Shannon, *The Farmer's Last Frontier:
    Agriculture, 1860–1897* (New York: Harper, 1945), 125–147.

17 Jones, *Oregon Detour*, 65, 132, 136 (1st quote); Pratt, *Homesteader's Portfolio*,
    15 (2nd quote). In Jones's novel, Weston was thinly disguised as Creston.

18 Juxtaposition of sheepmen and wheat growers generated relatively little
    friction, for the two did not utilize the same lands.

19 John F. Due and Giles French, *Rails to the Mid-Columbia Wheatlands: The Columbia Southern and Great Southern Railroads and the Development of Sherman and Wasco Counties, Oregon* (Washington, DC: University Press of America, 1982); John F. Due and Frances Juris Ray, *Roads and Rails South from the Columbia: Transportation and Economic Development in the Mid-Columbia and Central Oregon* (Bend, OR: Maverick, 1991); Shaver, *History of Central Oregon*, 117, 443, 454, 574.

20 Pierce, *Memoirs*, 28, 67–68 (quotes, p. 68). Low land rent was a key element in Pierce's success. Exploitative leaseholds on reservations would become a huge issue in subsequent years and the cause of major tribal lawsuits against the Bureau of Indian Affairs. Until the Indian Self-Determination and Education Act of 1975, tribes had little say in the use of their land.

21 Pendleton *East Oregonian*, September 1, 1910 (quote, p. 10), and 22; Macnab, *News and People*, 104, 174.

22 Virgil Rupp, *PGG: The Growth of a Cooperative* (Pendleton, OR: Pacific Grain Growers, 1996); Macnab, *News and People*, 207; Jones, *Oregon Detour*, 137–138.

23 For indications of this, see Jones, *Oregon Detour*, 107–108, 130–131; Shaver et al., *History of Southeastern Washington*, xv–xviii, xxiv–xxvi, 112, 114, 124.

24 Jones, *Oregon Detour*, xxv–xxvi, 244–245 (1st quote, p. 245); Meinig, *Great Columbia Plain*, 511 (2nd quote).

25 The Dalles *Weekly Times*, May 4, 1880 (1st quote); The Dalles *Times-Mountaineer*, January 1, 1898; Shaver, *History of Central Oregon*, 117, 164, 430, 431 (2nd and 3rd quotes), 443, 454, 574; Earl Pomeroy, *The Pacific Slope: A History of California, Oregon, Washington, Idaho, Utah, and Nevada* (New York: Knopf, 1965), 98–99; Robbins, *Landscapes of Promise*, 146–147, 149–153.

26 Shaver, *History of Central Oregon*, 163–164, 429–430, 455–456, 559, 568, 574. In the twentieth century, two Nobel Laureates would emerge from Condon.

27 Weatherford, *Arlington*, 11. Arlington was not alone in having uninviting surroundings. George Putnam wrote, "Biggs, under the grassless hills beside the Columbia, baked by the sun, lashed by the wind and blinded with sand, was impossible; and had it not been for the existence of Biggs, one might truthfully call Shaniko the least attractive spot in the universe." George Palmer Putnam, *In the Oregon Country* (New York: G. P. Putnam's Sons, 1915), 44.

28 Fred Lockley, interview with Owen Ebi, Portland *Oregon Journal*, October 8, 1913. See also, Shaver, *History of Central Oregon*, 571–572.

29 Onstine, *Oregon Votes*, 12–79.

30 Strahorn, *Fifteen Thousand Miles*, vol. 1: 304–308 (quote, p. 304); Meinig, *Great Columbia Plain*, 323–324. Nard Jones attributes Walla Walla's character to the influence of Whitman College, from which he had graduated with honors, but much more was involved. See Jones, *Oregon Detour*, 110.

31 Meinig, *Great Columbia Plain*, 348–349 (quote, p. 348); Strahorn, *Fifteen Thousand Miles*, vol. 1: 303–304; Pratt, *Homesteader's Portfolio*, 7–14. The

booster-dominated view pervades the pages of Bales and Hill, *Pendleton Round-Up.*

32   Jones, *Oregon Detour*, 109 (1st quote), 110 (2nd quote).

33   Macnab, *News and People*, 53, 58–62, 72–73, 86, 151 (Jackson quote), 153–155, 161; Jones, *Oregon Detour*, 110; Pratt, *Homesteader's Portfolio*, 6–14 (quotes, pp. 6, 14). George Venn did a reading from *Oregon Detour* for Weston High School students in 1983, a reading focused on graduation night; he learned that Jones's image of Pendleton and the behavior of high school students who went there for a fling were still the same. Jones, *Oregon Detour*, x.

34   Meinig, *Great Columbia Plain*, 235–236; Strahorn, *Fifteen Thousand Miles*, vol. 1: 120 (quote).

35   Fahey, *Inland Empire*, 64–65, 69; Greg Hall, *Harvest Wobblies: The Industrial Workers of the World and Agricultural Laborers in the American West* (Corvallis: Oregon State University Press, 2001); Macnab, *News and People*, 176, 179–180; Carlos A. Schwantes, *The Pacific Northwest: An Interpretive History* (Lincoln: University of Nebraska Press, 1996), 334–335, 339, 341–343, 355.

36   Early in the twenty-first century, Hermiston would pass Pendleton in population, but the latter continued its sociopolitical predominance.

CHAPTER 7

1   Leonard Arrington, *David Eccles, Pioneer Western Industrialist* (Logan: Utah State University Press, 1975), 27–59 (quote, p. 59).

2   Arrington, *Eccles*, 83–89; *Timberman* 34 (September 1933): 48–49. Initially called Baker City, the town's name was changed to Baker in 1911 and back to Baker City in 1989. In an obvious typographical error, The *Timberman* called it Barker.

3   Arrington, *Eccles*, 85 (quotes). See also, Christopher Merritt, "'Wooden Beds for Wooden Heads': Railroad Tie Cutting in the Uinta Mountains, 1867–1938," *Utah Historical Quarterly* 84 (2016): 102–117.

4   Arrington, *Eccles*, 89–94, 216–221; Strahorn, *Fifteen Thousand Miles*, vol. 2: 300–301 (quote); Robbins, *Landscapes of Promise*, 171–172.

5   Anon., *History of Baker, Grant, Malheur, and Harney Counties*, 172–173, 180; Arrington, *Eccles*, 228–230; Potter, *Oregon's Golden Years*, 99, 116, 129–137; Mallory H. Ferrell, *Rails, Sagebrush, and Pine: A Garland of Railroad and Logging Days in Oregon's Sumpter Valley* (San Marino, CA: Golden West Books, 1967); Anon., *History of Union and Wallowa Counties*, 399–400; Bailey, *Main Street*, 21, 32, 51; Skovlin, *Fifty Years of Research*, 11–12. Like the OLC, the Grande Ronde Lumber Co. was created by outside investors, in this case from Wisconsin (and perhaps the Booth-Kelley interests from Eugene).

6   Arrington, *Eccles*, 86, 94–95, 218. Church authorities had not yet banned polygamy. Eccles himself had two wives (or perhaps three).

7 Langston, *Forest Dreams, Forest Nightmares*, 80–83; Rakestraw, "Forest Conservation in the Pacific Northwest," 174–203 (Langille quoted, p. 194); Don E. Norton, ed., *The Collected Works of Hugh Nibley: Approaching Zion* (Salt Lake City: Deseret Book Co., 1989), 469; Langille, "Mostly Division 'R' Days," 306–309.

8 Sally Campbell, Dave Azuma, and Dale Weyermann, *Forests of Eastern Oregon: An Overview*, PNW-GTR 578 (Portland: Forest Service, Pacific Northwest Research Station, 2003), 1–2, 6–8. Ponderosa pine was more valuable than the Douglas-fir found west of the Cascades and, with the exception of sugar pine, more valuable than its intermingled species.

9 For further discussions, see Thomas R. Cox, *Lumberman's Frontier: Three Centuries of Land Use, Society, and Change in America's Forests* (Corvallis: Oregon State University Press, 2010), 331–338; Michael Williams, *Americans and Their Forests: A Historical Geography* (Cambridge, UK: Cambridge University Press, 1989), 291–304.

10 Rakestraw, "Forest Conservation in the Pacific Northwest," 1–6; Roy Robins, *Our Landed Heritage* (New York: Peter Smith, 1950), 119–245; Benjamin Horace Hibbard, *A History of Public Land Policies* (New York: Peter Smith, 1939), 228–472. See also, Thomas R. Cox, "The Conservationist as Reactionary: John Minto and American Forest Policy," *PNQ* 74 (1983): 146–153.

11 There is a considerable literature on the subject. For a solid introduction, see Harold K. Steen, *The U.S. Forest Service: A Centennial History* (Seattle: University of Washington Press, 2004). See also, Elmo R. Richardson, *The Politics of Conservation: Crusades and Controversies, 1897–1913* (Berkeley: University of California Press, 1962).

12 Rakestraw, "Forest Conservation in the Pacific Northwest," 27–34, 45–47, 90–91, 166–167, 176, 193, 195–206; Mead, *History of Union County*, 147, 149; Allen, *Homesteading the High Desert*, 24.

13 Rakestraw, "Forest Conservation in the Pacific Northwest," 53–66. The so-called Forest Reserve Act of 1891 was part of the General Revision Act (26 Stat. 1095), the Forest Management Act and Forest Lieu acts of 1897, which were portions of that year's Sundry Civil Appropriations (30 Stat. 11, 34–36).

14 Under the terms of Oregon's admission to the Union, Sections 16 and 36 of each township of public domain were reserved to provide an endowment for the state's schools, but bit by bit Oregon sold these off and these sales often opened the door for fraud.

15 Eccles and the Oregon Lumber Company were indicted for fraud just days before the statute of limitations would have taken effect. The case ground on for years and was finally dismissed by the Supreme Court on a technicality. Arrington, *Eccles*, 94. Federal surveyors found almost no evidence of valid settlement in the Cascades, and the Blues were much the same. Cox, *Lumberman's Frontier*, 298–299, 334.

16 Puter, *Looters of the Public Domain*, 81–85 (1st quote, p. 82; 2nd quote, p. 84); Jerry A. O'Callaghan, *The Disposition of the Public Domain in Oregon* (Washington, DC: GPO, 1960), 13–15, 61–66, 71–80, 92; Ronald L. Gregory,

"Life in Railroad Logging Camps of the Shevlin-Hixon Company, 1916–1950," *Anthropology Northwest* 12 (2001): 16–22; Philip Cogswell Jr., "Deschutes Country Pine Logging," in Vaughan, *High and Mighty*, 236–238; Coe, *Frontier Doctor*, 2–4, 164. The accounts of Shevlin's use of Minnesotans as claimants agree with stories I heard as a boy from my stepfather and an uncle, both of whom had worked for the company.

17 Rakestraw, "Forest Conservation in the Pacific Northwest," 47–53, 159–161, 206–208; Oswald West, "Reminiscences and Anecdotes of Oregon History," *OHQ* 50 (1949): 107–110; Langille, "Mostly Division 'R' Days," 306; "Message of George E. Chamberlain" (1905), 26–31.

18 Langille, "Mostly Division 'R' Days," 308; Puter, *Looters of the Public Domain*, 347–356 (quote, p. 356); Rakestraw, "Forest Conservation in the Pacific Northwest," 174–195 (quote, p. 175); Tupper, *Sandy Knoll*, 80–83, 142–148, 162–163, 172–174. See also, O'Callaghan, "Senator Mitchell," 255–261; Messing, "Public Lands, Politics, and Progressives," 35–66; Marsh, *To the Promised Land*, 66–69, 108–112.

19 *New York Times*, March 21, 1888 (quote); O'Callaghan, *Disposition of the Public Domain*, 50–52, 80–82.

20 148 U.S. Stat. 31. In 1902, in a second suit, federal authorities charged the government had no authority to offer a land grant through the Klamath Reservation, for that land had already been reserved for the Indians; it also failed. 192 U.S. Stat. 355.

21 Jerry A. O'Callaghan, "Klamath Indians and the Oregon Wagon Road Grant, 1864–1938," *OHQ* 53 (1952): 21–28.

22 Kinzua Lumber Co. to W. S. Jackson, July 31, 1909; Kinzua Lumber Co. to W. N. Jones, April 8, 1913; Wetmore, report to stockholders, October 21, 1916; all in Kinzua Lumber Co., outgoing corres., 1909–1918 file, Wetmore Papers (Warren County Historical Society Archives, Warren, PA), box 97. While their investment increased in value, the partners worried about the danger of forest fires, which had ravaged large parts of western Pennsylvania. To keep down highly flammable grass and provide someone on the ground to keep an eye out for fire, they leased grazing rights to a leading local sheep operation. See Butte Creek Land, Lumber & Livestock Co. to W. C. Calder, February 14 and 28, and March 5, 1918; Calder to Butte Creek, February 18, and March 2, 1918; Calder to Wetmore, March 2 and 28, 1918; all in Kinzua Lumber Co., outgoing corres., 1909–1918 file, Wetmore Papers, box 97.

23 The Timber and Stone Act was repealed in 1903 and the lieu land provisions in 1905, so thereafter acquisition became more aboveboard than previously, thus perhaps explaining the relatively restrained approach of Wetmore and his partners, who began their purchases in 1909.

24 John C. Driscoll, *Gilchrist, Oregon: The Model Company Town* (Bend, OR: Self-published, 2012), 14, 17, 31. See also, Driscoll, "Gilchrist, Oregon: A Company Town," *OHQ* 85 (1984): 135–153.

25 Cox, *Lumbermen's Frontier*, 346–347, 350–352.

26   Numerous works cover these events, but Gifford Pinchot's autobiography catches the spirit of the times better than most. See Pinchot, *Breaking New Ground* (New York: Harcourt Brace, 1947), 235–276.

27   Gardinier Lumber Co., minutes of annual stockholders meeting, October 26, 1925, Wetmore incoming corres., 1915–26 file, Wetmore Papers, box 3; Langston, *Forest Dreams, Forest Nightmares*, 159–161; Barklow, *Gateway to the Wallowas*, 64, 110, 114, 192–196.

28   Henry S. Graves, "Report of the Forester," *Annual Reports of the Department of Agriculture, 1919* (Washington, DC: GPO, 1920), 10.

29   Barrington Moore, "Working Plans: Past History, Present Situation, and Future Developments," *Proceedings of the Society of American Foresters*, 10 (1915): 217–258; Cox, *Lumberman's Frontier*, 353, 355, 357–361; Langston, *Forest Dreams, Forest Nightmares*, 167–175, 183–187; Jay P Kinney, *Indian Forest and Range: A History* . . . (Washington, DC: Forestry Enterprises, 1950), 183–216; Good, *History of Klamath County*, 116–121. See also, Klamath County Historical Society, *Klamath Country History*, 25–29; Jack Bowden, "Land, Lumber Companies, and Mills in the Klamath Basin, 1864–1950," *JSHL* 16 (2002): 5–41; Ward Tonsfeldt, "Selling Klamath Reservation Timber, 1910–1935," *JSHL* 16 (2002): 66, 69–70.

30   E. J. Hanzlik, "Working Plan Report for the Burns Working Circle," July 6, 1922; B. E. Hoffman, "Report Concerning Plan of Management of Timber Tributary to Burns," February 1, 1926; Walt L. Dutton, "Management Plan, Silvies [Burns] Working Circle, Malheur National Forest," May 1928; S-Plans, Timber Management, Malheur, Burns W.C.(1922–1950) file, Forest Service, Pacific Northwest Regional Office Records (National Archives & Records Service, Seattle); Langston, *Forest Dreams, Forest Nightmares*, 167–168, 172–173, 185–187.

31   Klamath Falls *Evening Herald*, October 8 and 9, 1918; July 18 and 31, and August 23, 1919; April 23, 1920.

32   Klamath County Historical Society, *The History of Klamath Country, Oregon* (Dallas: Taylor Publishing, 1984), 55–56; Good, *History of Klamath County*, 79–86; Beckham, *Gerber Block*, 34–38, 42–43, 46 (DuVaul quote); Klamath Falls *Evening Herald*, September 4 and 21, December 30, 1912; October 12 and November 20, 1917; September 27 and November 26, 1918; June 30, July 3, and December 5, 1919; August 8, 13, and 20, 1920; January 2, 1929; Merrill Centennial Committee, *Merrill Centennial, 1894–1994* (Merrill, OR: Merrill Centennial Committee, 1994), 256, 284–287.

33   Inaction was justifiable. A number of sawmills were built after the area was reached by a railroad from California in 1909, but some timberland owners hesitated, since box shooks, the primary item in demand in California at the time, was a less-than-optimum use of their timber. W. E. Lamm, *Lumbering in Klamath* (Klamath Falls, OR: Lamm Lumber Co., n.d.), 13–17.

34   Cox, *Lumberman's Frontier*, 355–356.

35   Cox, *Lumberman's Frontier*, 341–343; Langston, *Forest Dreams, Forest Nightmares*, 178, 182–183; Simpson, *Community of Cattlemen*, 152, 154–155.

I shared an office with Simpson in the 1960s, and discussions of the situation in and around Burns ranged well beyond what is reported in his study.

36 Ron Aeschbacher, conversation with the author, Medford, Oregon, June 6, 1998; David Zalunardo, conversation with the author, Payette, Idaho, September 8, 2012 (quote).

37 Cogswell, "Deschutes Country Pine Logging," 241, 246–247; Gregory, "Life in Railroad Logging Camps," 33–39.

38 George Palmer Putman, *In the Oregon Country* (New York: G. P. Putnam's Sons, 1915), 50 (quote).

39 Stewart Holbrook, *The American Lumberjack* (enlarged ed.; New York: Colliers, 1962), 215–224.

40 Gregory, "Life in Railroad Logging Camps," 41–53; Dixie Caverhill Weberg, "Growing Up in [Brooks-Scanlon's] Railroad Logging Camps," reminiscences, December 16, 2016 (A. R. Bowman Museum, Prineville). "Sam Johnson," Elizabeth H. Johnson, oral history interview by Maret Pajutee, May 29, 1998 (Sisters Country Historical Society website, 2006) (quote). See also, Cogswell, "Deschutes Country Pine Logging," 251–252, a more sedate image of the Shevlin camp that notes it largely served families rather than single men.

41 Bill Edwards, oral history interview by Maret Pajutee, June 10, 1998 (Sisters Country Historical Society website, 2006); personal observations, 1957, 1958; Sisters *Nugget*, May 3, 2015. See also, Wilson and Scott, *That Was Yesterday*, 37–43, 65–70; and Raymond R. Hatton, Lawrence A. Chitwood, and Stuart G. Garrett, *Oregon's Sisters Country: A Portrait of Its Lands, Water, and People* (n.p.: Self-published, 1996). Hatton, Chitwood, and Garrett lauded Tillie Wilson, a longtime elementary teacher in the community, for being "actively involved with the growth and 'civilizing' of this rough logging/farming community" (p. 12).

42 *Bend Bulletin*, August 28, 1923. See also, Gregory, "Life in Railroad Logging Camps," 61–63.

43 Information on Kinzua is based on my own reminiscences and those of John Shaw, Larry Clark, Mary Hall, Michael Tierney, and Robert Detweiler (all of whom once lived there or nearby). See also, *Fossil Journal*, April 8 and October 23, 1927; Wetmore to R. G. Chapel, July 18, 1930, WP, incoming corres., box 4; Stinchfield and Stinchfield, *History of Wheeler County*, 7, 30, 256; Fussner, *Glimpses of Wheeler County's Past*, 38.

44 Driscoll, *Gilchrist*, 33–34, 43–46, 101–102.

45 Cox, *Lumberman's Frontier*, 255–259; Thad Sitton and James H. Conrad, *Nameless Towns: Texas Sawmill Communities, 1880–1942* (Austin: University of Texas Press, 1998), 79–126.

46 Driscoll, *Gilchrist*, 112–114.

47 Pearl Alice Marsh, "A Black Logger's Journey: Jackson Parish, Louisiana, to Wallowa County, Oregon," *OHQ* 116 (2015): 500–503, 509–521 (quote, p. 511). In time a number of these workers moved to La Grande and Pendleton, increasing the towns' admittedly slight ethnic diversity.

48   Charlotte James-Duguid, *Work as Art: Idaho Logging as an Aesthetic Moment* (Moscow: University of Idaho Press, 1996), 9 (quote), 15, 36, 45–46, 59, 70, 103–106, 130; Edwards, oral history interview; Gregory, "Life in Railroad Logging Camps," 77–80; *Bend Bulletin*, March 4, 1954.

CHAPTER 8

1   Cleon L. Clark, *History of the Willamette Valley and Cascade Mountain Wagon Road* (Bend, OR: Deschutes County Historical Society, 1987), 5–7; *Bend Bulletin*, June 16, 1953; January 12, 2000. Through much of its history, the Santiam Wagon Road was officially the Willamette Valley and Cascade Mountain Wagon Road.

2   Charles F. Query, *A History of Oregon Ferries since 1826* (n.p.: Self-published, 2008), 12; Lawrence Nielsen, Doug Newman, and George McCart, *Pioneer Roads in Central Oregon* (Redmond, OR: Self-published, 1985), 70. In the telescoped historical time east of the Cascades, Jesse was still active when I grew up nearby. Tetherow's house, the oldest in Deschutes County, still stands.

3   After Hill's railroad reached Redmond in 1911, Jesse and a partner continued the Tetherow family connection to transportation services by establishing a stage line to Prineville, which had been bypassed by the line.

4   *Bend Bulletin*, April 3, 1978; February 18, 2002; *Redmond Spokesman*, August 22, 1955; June 1, 2010. In 1963 the venerable *Bend Bulletin* became simply the *Bulletin*.

5   Kittredge, *Hole in the Sky*, 24 (1st quote); Hanley, *Feelin' Fine*, 133 (2nd quote).

6   Ivan Doig, *Heart Earth: A Memoir* (New York: Atheneum, 1993), 17.

7   H. L. Davis, "Back to the Land—Oregon, 1907," *American Mercury* 16 (1929): 318, 320–321; *Pacific Monthly* 16 (July 1911): 115; George P. Putnam, "Opening Up Central Oregon," *Putnam's Magazine* 7 (1910): 387–396; Clark and Clark, "Pioneers of Deschutes Country," 55–56; *Burns Times-Herald*, July 13, 1901 (quote); and February 3, 1906; Coe, *Frontier Doctor*, 227; James L. Crowell, *Frontier Publisher: A Romantic Review of George Palmer Putnam's Career at the* Bend Bulletin, *1910–1914 . . .* (Bend, OR: Deschutes County Historical Society, 2008), 50–58, 60; Jackman and Long, *Oregon Desert*, 30–64.

8   Shaver, *History of Central Oregon*, 738 (1st quote); Carl S. Scoville, *Dry-Farming in the Great Basin*, USDA, Bureau of Plant Industry, Bulletin 103 (Washington, DC: GPO, 1907), 7, 12 (2nd quote).

9   Crowell, *Frontier Publisher*, 80; *Lakeview Examiner*, March 4, 1909 (quotes); Bowman, *Pioneer Fringe*, 98; Clark and Clark, "Pioneers of Deschutes Country," 54–56; Pomeroy, *American Far West*, 34; Allen, *Homesteading the High Desert*, 28–29.

10   Smyth, *Footloose and Ahorseback*, 111; *Bend Bulletin*, April 1, 1914 (1st quote); *Dry-Farming Bulletin* 5 (1911): 56 (3rd quote), 243 (2nd quote); Clark and Clark, "Pioneers of Deschutes Country," 56–57.

11 John A. Widtsoe, *Dry Farming: A System of Agriculture for Countries under Low Rainfall* (New York: Macmillan, 1920) was an informed assessment but came too late to affect the High Desert's flood of settlers.

12 Pomeroy, *American Far West*, 35; Wilson quoted in US Congress, *The Resources of the Semiarid Region*, 58th Cong., 3d sess., 105, p. 1; Paul W. Gates, with Robert W. Swenson, *History of Public Land Law Development* (Washington, DC: Public Land Law Review Commission, 1968), 503–504. See also, Willard Lee Hoing, "James Wilson as Secretary of Agriculture" (PhD diss., University of Wisconsin, 1964); Rodman W. Paul, *The Far West and the Great Plains in Transition, 1850–1900* (New York: Harper and Row, 1988), 220–251. The acreage allowed for claims under the Enlarged Homestead Act was subsequently reduced to 320.

13 Monroe, *Feelin' Fine*, 133–134, 171–172 (1st quote), 186 (2nd quote). See also, Jackman and Long, *Oregon Desert*, 26–29, 48; Simpson, *Community of Cattlemen*, 149.

14 Coe, *Frontier Doctor*, 226–227 (1st quote, p. 226), 236–237; Jackman and Long, *Oregon Desert*, 64 (2nd quote).

15 *Burns Times-Herald*, September 14, 1912 (quote); Helen Parks, ed., *Portraits: Fort Rock Valley Homestead Years* (Bend, OR: Fort Rock Valley Historical Society, 1989), 173.

16 Smyth, *Footloose and Ahorseback*, 179–181; Brimlow, *Harney County*, 228–229; Cressman, *Golden Journey*, 303–306, 344–346; Jackman and Long, *Oregon Desert*, 319–321, 397–398; Jackman and Scharff, *Steens Mountain*, 174–176, 180.

17 Seeking to answer more complex questions about population changes from 1898 to 1912, Peter Simpson makes clear the inadequacies of available data. See Simpson, *Community of Cattlemen*, 97–115.

18 Onstine, *Oregon Votes*, 36–37, 48–49.

19 Dorothy Lawson McCall, *Ranch under the Rimrock* (Portland: Binford and Mort, 1968), ix; Jarold Ramsey, "'New Era': Growing Up East of the Cascades, 1937–1950," in William G. Robbins, Robert J. Frank, and Richard E. Ross, *Regionalism and the Pacific Northwest* (Corvallis: Oregon State University Press, 1983), 175–176 (quotes); Hands, *Jefferson County Reminiscences*, 282–328. See also, Jarold Ramsey, *New Era: Reflections on the Human and Natural History of Central Oregon* (Corvallis: Oregon State University Press, 2003). Less arid than the High Desert, the area around Metolius and Culver successfully yielded dryland wheat crops until the drought years of the 1930s rendered even that area submarginal.

20 Charles H. Carey, *History of Oregon, Illustrated* (3 vols.; Chicago: Pioneer Historical Publishing, 1922), vol. 3: 717–718 (quote); Jo Smith Southworth, *Millican Memories* (Bend, OR:, Maverick, 1977), 1–3, 8–9; *New York Times*, May 24, 2004; *Bend Bulletin*, February 10, 2009. When the Bend-Burns highway was completed in 1930, Billy Rahn, the postmaster and new owner of Millican's store, moved it northward from the original site near Pine Mountain to a location on the highway. Today even that is abandoned.

21 Monroe, *Feelin' Fine*, 133–134 (quote).

22 Simpson, *Community of Cattlemen*, 106–109, 117–120 (quote, p. 118), 147, 149.

23 Pratt, *Homesteader's Portfolio*, 26–27, 66–67, 70, 86–87, 96, 146–147; Waterston, *Where the Crooked River Rises*, 106–111; Raymond R. Hatton, *Pioneer Homesteaders of the Fort Rock Valley* (Portland: Binford and Mort, 1982), 24, 54, 57–58, 93–106, 119, 129–131; Simpson, *Community of Cattlemen*, 114; Pomeroy, *American Far West*, 33–34.

24 Pratt, *Homesteader's Portfolio*, 178–179. My uncle filed on a 320-acre claim north of Three Creek in 1916, but when the United States entered World War I, he enlisted in the marines and was killed in the Battle of Belleau Wood. Irrigation water never reached the area, and the "fields where they tried to raise rye and other crops have all gone back to sagebrush." See Lola Blossom, "Three Creek, Idaho," *Owyhee Outpost* 9 (1978): 20, 23–24, 27–28 (quote, p. 28).

25 Charles Erskine Scott Wood, *The Poet in the Desert* (Portland: F. W. Baltes, 1915); Ada Hastings Hedges, *Desert Poems* (Portland: Metropolitan Press, 1930); Ulrich H. Hardt, "Ada Hastings Hedges (1884–1980)," *The Oregon Encyclopedia* (Portland: Portland State University and Oregon Historical Society, 2014), www.oregonencyclopedia.org.

26 *Dial* 61 (1916): 108; Smyth, *Sunshine, Shadows and Sagebrush*, 6–7. Monroe also wrote of Bill Hanley in *Behind the Ranges* (Garden City, NY: Doubleday, Page, 1926). Her accounts of him were idealized; locals interviewed by Peter Simpson for *A Community of Cattlemen* and by Alice Scott, with whom my wife once taught, presented more mixed evaluations. Karen Blair's introduction to the reprint edition of Monroe's *Happy Valley* (Corvallis: Oregon State University Press, 1990) is the most accessible source of biographical information on Monroe.

27 Monroe, *Happy Valley*, 316 (quote).

28 Applegate to Mrs. Lindsay Applegate, June 4, 1866 (O. C. Applegate Papers, Knight Library, University of Oregon, Eugene), box 2, folder 6.

29 Merrill Lewis, "Introduction," in H. L. Davis, *Honey in the Horn* (reprint ed.; Moscow: University of Idaho Press, 1992), vi, xi (quote; emphasis original).

30 Kittredge, *Hole in the Sky*, 24–25 (2nd quote, p. 25); Robbins, *Landscapes of Promise*, 19–10; Putnam, *In the Oregon Country*, 65–66 (1st quote). Putnam distinguished these "gypsies" from "the sincere home seeker," the sort of folk who dominate Monroe's pages.

31 Laura Cray, "High Desert Dreams: Arid Land Management Policy and Visions of a Western Landscape" (typescript draft; Corvallis, Oregon State University, 2012), 10–17, 20–31; Jerry Ramsey, "Some 'What Ifs?' in Jefferson County," *The Agate*, n.s. 8 (2017): 9–10; www.madras.net/newspapers/natgrass.

32 Parks, *Portraits*, 73, 127 (1st quote), 196 (2nd quote); cf. Allen, *Homesteading the High Desert*, 142–146.

CHAPTER 9

1   George Palmer Putnam, *Wide Margins* (New York: Harcourt, Brace, 1942), 52 (quote).

2   Palmer Bend (pseud.), *The Smiting of the Rock: A Tale of Oregon* (New York: G. P. Putnam's Sons, 1918), 2, 34 (1st quote), 318 (3rd quote); Putnam, *In the Oregon Country*, 39 (2nd quote), 48; Putnam, *Wide Margins*, 49; Crowell, *Frontier Publisher*, 1–2, 4–7, 215–224. The oft-repeated claim that southeastern Oregon was the largest railroad-free area in the United States is questionable. The vast area south of the Humboldt River and north of Flagstaff, Arizona, and Las Vegas, Nevada, was equally huge—although it probably seemed less promising.

3   David Kent, the protagonist in the story, is clearly Putnam himself, and the struggle depicted between the irrigation company and the farmers closely parallel actual events.

4   Michael Hall, *Irrigation Development in Oregon's Upper Deschutes River Basin, 1871–1957* (Bend, OR: Deschutes County Historical Landmarks Comm., 1998), 14–15; Brogan, *East of the Cascades*, 97–98, 176–177; Ward Tonsfeldt and Paul G. Claeyssens, "Pre-Industrial Period, 1870–1910: Irrigation" (Portland: Oregon Historical Society, 2004), www.ohs.org/education/oregonhistory. Squaw Creek heads up near the Three Sisters and flows eastward to the Deschutes. As a result of diversions, it has sometimes run dry in its lower reaches during summer months. It was renamed Whychus Creek in 2005.

5   This complicated story is traced in Crowell, *Frontier Publisher*, 135–158; Clark and Clark, "Pioneers of Deschutes Country," 44–54; Robert W. Sawyer, ed., "Watering of the Wilderness: A History of Central Oregon Irrigation Company," *Bend Bulletin*, January 23–March 21, 1931. See also, John H. Lewis and Percy A. Cupper, *Irrigation in Oregon*, US Office of Experiment Stations, Bulletin No. 209 (Washington, DC: GPO, 1909).

6   Crowell, *Frontier Publisher*, 89–94; *Bend Bulletin*, September 14 (1st quote), November 30, December 7, 1910; and July 10, 1912 (2nd quote).

7   *Bend Bulletin*, July 24, 1910; and February 26, April 23, June 11, and September 10, 1913; James Withycombe, "Message to the Twenty-Eighth Legislative Regular Assembly, 1915," sos.state.or.us/.../guides/state/withycombe/inaugural1915.

8   Tonsfeldt and Claeyssens, "Pre-Industrial Period."

9   Shaver, *History of Central Oregon*, 717–722 (quote, pp. 718–719), 728–729, 738–739.

10 The project's history is traced in Martin T. Winch, *Tumalo, Thirsty Land: History of Tumalo Irrigation District* (Portland: Oregon Historical Society, 1985). One authority has called it "the most seriously vexed Carey Act project in Oregon, and possibly the Nation." See Hall, *Irrigation Development*, 16.

11 Shaver, *History of Central Oregon*, 733–734. For a time Laidlaw was larger than Bend; its site was chosen because of both the prospect of irrigation and promoters' belief it would be the intersection of the Columbia Southern,

when it was built south from Shaniko, and a railroad projected to cross the Cascades and then proceed eastward to Burns and Ontario. Neither railroad ever materialized.

12 In 1907 the State Land Board found that project managers had contracted to reclaim twenty-seven thousand acres, but had sufficient water to irrigate ten thousand at most. Crowell, *Frontier Publisher*, 139; *Bend Bulletin*, March 22, 1907.

13 Oswald West to Desert Land Board, December 10, 1912, in H. C. Brodie, *History and Engineering Reports on the Columbia Southern Irrigation Project, Crook County* (Salem, OR: State Printer, 1912), 1–4; *Bend Bulletin*, July 24, 1910; and June 11 and September 10, 1913.

14 On the storage potential of Crescent Lake (and nearby Odell Lake), see Israel C. Russell, *Preliminary Report on the Geology and Water Resources of Central Oregon*, US Geological Survey Bulletin no. 252 (Washington, DC, 1905), 120–121, 118–120.

15 Brodie, *History and Engineering Reports*, 50; Clark and Clark, "Pioneers of Central Oregon," 50–53; Hall, *Irrigation Development*, 16–18; *Bend Bulletin*, January 11, 1914. For a fuller account, see Winch, *Tumalo*. Laurgaard served as project engineer during construction of the dam.

16 *Burns Times-Herald*, March 10 and 19, and April 28, 1906.

17 Schwartz, "Walter M. Pierce," 82–83.

18 The rocky land created problems for settlers too, fragmenting useable acreage and requiring many an hour spent clearing land. One new arrival, taken aback upon viewing the family claim near Terrebonne, asked her spouse, "What in the world are we going to feed the children—rocks?" *Redmond Spokesman* August 22, 1955 (quote); Keith Clark, *Redmond, Where the Desert Blooms* (Portland: Western Imprints, 1995), 8–9.

19 John Dubuis, *Report to Desert Land Board on Central Oregon Project . . .* (Salem, OR: State Printing Office, 1915), 5, 41–44, 57, 58.

20 Brogan, *East of the Cascades*, 268, 289.

21 Hall, *Irrigation Development*, 18–19; Robert Metcalf, "A Historical Look at La Pine, Oregon," 3, 5–7, www.lapine.org/documents/metcalf; Anon., *History of Baker, Grant, Malheur, and Harney Counties*, 648–649. William Smythe encouraged such projects. In his drumbeat for irrigation, Smythe suggested the climate was good and there were ample sources of water throughout Eastern Oregon, including low-lying lakes such as Abert, Summer, and Goose—although their waters actually were so alkaline they were useless for irrigation. See William E. Smythe, *The Conquest of Arid America* (New York: Harper, 1900), 192.

22 Guy Swanson, "A History of Grandview, Oregon," *The Agate* n.s. 8 (2017): 3–7; Hands, *Jefferson County Reminiscences*, 231.

23 Clark and Clark, "Pioneers of Deschutes Country," 53–54; Crowell, *Frontier Publisher*, 139–140; *Bend Bulletin*, September 8, 1915; Prineville *Central Oregonian*, February 16 and 23, and March 8 and 15, 1928; Dubuis, *Report*, 26–31; Wilson and Scott, *That Was Yesterday*, 32; Hands, *Jefferson County*

Reminiscences, 230–231; Steve Lent, *Islands in Time: People, Places, and Events That Shaped Central Oregon* (Prineville, OR: Crook County Historical Society, 2008), 151. Grandview was on a plateau between the Deschutes and lower Metolius Rivers.

24 *Redmond Spokesman*, August 22, 1955 (quotes); Clark, *Redmond*, 6.

25 Clark, *Redmond*, 10–11, 21, 101–103.

26 Clark, *Redmond*, 99; Ward, *Redmond*, 43. On Redmond, the best sources are the fifty-year anniversary issue of the *Redmond Spokesman*, August 22, 1955, and Clark, *Redmond*. For many years the high school closed for two weeks every fall so students could assist in the all-important potato harvest.

27 Clark, *Redmond*, 7–8, 12, 16–17, 97–98; *Redmond Spokesman*, July 25, August 29, 1912; and April 3, 1913.

28 There is extensive literature on the subject. See, especially, William E. Warne, *The Bureau of Reclamation* (New York: Praeger, 1973); Michael C. Robinson, *Water for the West: The Bureau of Reclamation, 1902–1977* (Chicago: Public Works Historical Society, 1979); and Donald J. Pisani, *Water and American Government: The Reclamation Bureau, National Water Policy, and the West, 1902–1935* (Berkeley: University of California Press, 2002).

29 See, for example, Russell, *Preliminary Report*, 34–67, 83–84, 92, 100–102, 122.

30 *Burns Times-Herald*, June 8, 1912; Allen, *Homesteading the High Desert*, 29–30; Brimlow, *Harney County*, 236–237. A modest project on Silver Creek developed following construction of Thompson Valley Reservoir in 1922. It irrigated a mere 2,616 acres and excluded the Fort Rock area contemplated for inclusion in the Bureau of Reclamation's original plans. Allen, *Homesteading the High Desert*, 96–97; Secretary of State, *State Water Records, District Directory*, arcweb.sos.state.or.us/doc/records/state/water/pdf, 42.

31 Eric A. Stene, *Umatilla Project* (n.p.: Bureau of Reclamation, 1993), 11, 13–14; Stene, *Klamath Project* (n.p.: Bureau of Reclamation, 1994), 7, 31–33; Shaver, *History of Central Oregon*, 972, 975, 980–981; Good, *History of Klamath County*, 103–110; Ochoco Irrigation District, "History," www.ochocoid.org/history. Initial reports on the Klamath project were even more sanguine. One contemporary source reported the government would spend $4.4 million on the project and irrigate 320,000 acres. Shaver, *History of Central Oregon*, 973–974. In the first decades of the twentieth century, nearly every issue of the Klamath Falls *Evening Herald* had reports related to the project.

32 Stene, *Umatilla Project*, 3; Pendleton *East Oregonian*, August 8 and 26, and September 7, 1910; and August 30, 1911; Thomas R. Cox, *The Park Builders: A History of State Parks in the Pacific Northwest* (Seattle: University of Washington Press, 1989), 80–81 (quote).

33 Pratt, *Homesteader's Portfolio*, 21, 23 (2nd quote), 29–38 (1st quote, p. 38; 3rd quote, pp. 35–36).

34   Lee Juillerat, "Malin's 100th Anniversary" (quote), Shaw Historical Library
     website, www.oit.edu/shaw/exhibits/stories/malin-100th-anniversary.

35   Stene, *Klamath Project*, 30–31; Shaver, *History of Central Oregon*, 980–981;
     Klamath Falls *Herald and News*, September 10, 1918; June 14, 1950; and
     August 1, 1951; Good, *History of Klamath County*, 175; Stan Turner, *The
     Years of Harvest: A History of the Tule Lake Basin* (3rd ed.; Eugene, OR:
     Spencer Creek Press, 2002).

36   Stene, *Klamath Project*, 5–6; Klamath Historical Society, *History of Klamath
     Country*, 19–25; Klamath Falls *Klamath Republican*, April 5 and May 6, 1906.

37   Stene, *Klamath Project*, 31–33; Klamath Falls *Evening Herald*, September 23
     and 29, 1909. When I lived in the area in the 1960s, Merrill, Malin, and
     Tulelake were still quiet agricultural communities that contrasted to Klamath
     Falls with its broader economic base and greater vitality. By then, however,
     they also had their share of migrant farm workers (and former migrant farm
     families that had taken up permanent residence), adding a degree of ethnic
     and socioeconomic diversity previously lacking. Cf. Merrill Centennial
     Committee, *Merrill Centennial*, 17–28, 284–287; Klamath County Historical
     Society, *Klamath Country History*, 77–79.

38   Anon., *History of Baker, Grant, Malheur, and Harney Counties*, 547–550
     (quote, p. 547); Daniel M. Johnson, *Atlas of Oregon Lakes* (Corvallis: Oregon
     State University Press, 1985), 293; John Day *Blue Mountain Eagle*, June 22,
     2016.

39   Timothy A. Dick, *Vale Project* (n.p.: Bureau of Reclamation, 1993), 3, 5–6,
     12–14.

40   Private projects had begun in the area as early as 1883. Anon., *History of
     Baker, Grant, Malheur, and Harney Counties*, 523–524, 733–735.

41   Eric A. Stene, *Owyhee Project* (n.p.: Bureau of Reclamation, 1996), 3–5, 12,
     17; *New York Times*, July 18, 1932. The dam's preeminence was short lived; it
     was soon surpassed by the Lac du Chambon dam in France and Hoover Dam
     on the Colorado. The area actually irrigated—some 120,000 acres—fell
     slightly below initial projections.

42   Stene, *Owyhee Project*, 2, 14–16.

43   Crane Prairie Reservoir had its beginnings in 1922, when an irrigation
     district, operating under terms of the Carey Act, built a rock-fill and log crib
     dam at the site. Problems plagued the undertaking, but it pointed the way. In
     the 1930s, the Bureau of Reclamation replaced and enlarged this pioneer
     facility. An additional benefit, not much considered during planning, was the
     creation of two major new trout fisheries.

44   Robert Autobee, *Deschutes Project* (n.p.: Bureau of Reclamation, 1996), 2–13
     (1st quote, p. 2; 2nd quote, p. 13); Clark, *Redmond*, 106–108; www.
     northunitid.com/history. See also, Scott Cohen, "Controlling the Crooked
     River: Changing Environments and Water Uses in Irrigated Oregon, 1913–
     1988," *OHQ* 109 (2008): 204–225.

45   Autobee, *Deschutes Project*, 16–19; Samuel N. Dicken, "Deschutes Country
     Geography," in Vaughan, *High and Mighty*, 127, 139, 142–143; Hands,

Jefferson County Reminiscences, 329–349; North Unit Irrigation District, "History," www.northunitid.com/history; Ramsey, "Some 'What Ifs?,'" 9. Completion of the A. R. Bowman Dam in 1968, upstream on Crooked River, stabilized water availability from that source.

46 Macnab, *News and People*, 221–223, 338–339; *Hermiston Herald*, March 30, 2016. After sixty-five years, my memory of the stench of fermenting pea vines while I was a student at Whitman College remains strong.

47 Hatton, *Pioneer Homesteaders*, 131–133; Jackman and Long, *Oregon Desert*, 351–355; www.midstateelectric.coop/contents/mec-facts; Emery Castle and Carroll Dwyer, *Irrigation Possibilities in the Fort Rock Area* (Corvallis: Oregon State College Agricultural Experiment Station, 1956); Parks, *Portraits*, 198–200; Portland *Willamette Week*, September 19, 1979. In time, falling water levels in the aquifers from which water is pumped would pose a threat of their own.

48 Pomeroy, *American Far West*, 58, and passim; Macnab, *News and People*, 339–340.

49 Boise *Idaho Statesman*, May 25 and 31, 2008; Paul Lukas, "Mr. Potato Head: A Dirt-Poor Farmer Turned Spud Scraps into Gold," *CNN Money*, November 1, 2003.

50 For an example of later critiques of the Bureau of Reclamation and its policies, see Cecil D. Andrus and Joel Connelly, *Cecil Andrus: Politics Western Style* (Seattle: Sasquatch Books, 1998), 5–6, 25–27, 47–49, 127–129.

51 Arturo Romo and Paul Gebhardt Jr., *Great and Growing: Jobs in Oregon's Agri-Cluster* (Portland: 1000 Friends of Oregon, 2013), 6, 9–10, 13–14; Vale *Malheur Enterprise*, November 30, 2016; Milton R. Copulos, "Enforcement of an Anachronism: The 160 Acre Limitation," *Heritage Foundation Backgrounder*, December 15, 1977; Paul Andrew Spies, "Evaluation of the Ownership, Leasing, and Residency Restrictions of Proposed Amendments to the Reclamation Laws: Three Federal Irrigation Districts in Oregon" (MS thesis, Oregon State University, 1979); Sheila Martin and Bruce Weber, "A Tale of Two Oregons: Common Aspirations, Different Contexts, and Critical Interdependence in Urban and Rural Oregon," *Toward One Oregon: Rural-Urban Interdependence in the Evolution of a State* (Corvallis: Oregon State University Press, 2011), 30, 32. See also, www.Oregon-demographics.com/ Malheur-county-demographics; http://quickfacts.census.gov/qfd/states/4100. html; www.msn.com/en-us/money/ savingandinvesting/ the-poorest-county-in-each-state.

52 Cox, *Park Builders*, 81–82, 95–97; R. Douglas Hirt, "The National Grasslands: Origin and Development in the Dust Bowl," *Agricultural History* 59 (1985): 246–259. On Finley, see chapter 13.

CHAPTER 10

1 The Bell A was Hanley's "home" ranch, but page after page of *Feelin' Fine* show him to have been most at peace at the OO.

2 Randall V. Mills, *Railroads Down the Valleys: Some Short Lines of the Oregon Country* (Palo Alto, CA: Pacific Books, 1950), 32–72; Leslie M. Scott, "The

Yaquina Railroad: The Tale of a Great Fiasco," *OHQ* 16 (1915): 228–245; Monroe, *Feelin' Fine*, 152–153. Hanley misremembered Hogg's name, rendering it J. Atchison Hogg. On the same page, Peter Skene Ogden became J. Ogden Skeen.

3 Monroe, *Feelin' Fine*, 37 (1st quote), 152, 155–160; Anon., *History of Baker, Grant, Malheur, and Harney Counties*, 642–643 (2nd quote, p. 642).

4 John R. Signor, *Rails in the Shadow of Mt. Shasta* (Berkeley, CA: Howell-North Books, 1982), 98–100, 110, 121; Donald B. Robertson, *Encyclopedia of Western Railroad History: Oregon, Washington* (Caldwell, ID: Caxton, 1986), 107. Harriman may have seen the Weed-Klamath Falls link as a way to tap the traffic new irrigation projects and rich timber stands offered, but the larger picture suggests he was also moving to protect his control of the vast Oregon outback.

5 Monroe, *Feelin Fine*, 156–160 (quote, p. 157); Crowell, *Frontier Editor*, 40–42; *Bend Bulletin*, December 30, 1908; *Burns Times-Herald*, January 13 and 31, 1914; and June 1 and 11, 1915; Putnam, "Opening Up Central Oregon," 389. See also, George Kennan, *E. H. Harriman, A Biography* (2 vols.; New York: Houghton, Mifflin, 1922), vol. 1: 139–183; Maria Novak-Cronin, "Poet and Pioneer: C. E. S. Wood and Bill Hanley in the Oregon Desert," *Table Rock Sentinel: Journal of the Southern Oregon Historical Society* 12 (1992): 2–11; *Burns Times-Herald*, January 13, 1914; and June 11, 1915. Novak-Cronin and Edwin R. Bingham, the primary Wood biographer, say nothing about work with Hanley for a state-aid railroad, focusing instead on his literary and political efforts. However, they each make clear his friendship with Hanley and his deep love of the desert country of southeastern Oregon.

6 Monroe, *Feelin' Fine*, 159–160 (quotes).

7 Anon., *History of Baker, Grant, Malheur, and Harney Counties*, 169–170. The settlement opened the way for OR&N to build a shortline from La Grande to Joseph in 1908. See Edward A. Lewis, *American Shortline Railway Guide* (5th ed.; Waukesha, WI: Kalmbach, 1966), 154; Dietrich Deumling, "The Roles of the Railroad in the Development of the Grande Ronde Valley" (MA thesis, Northern Arizona University, 1972).

8 The widely chronicled competition even spawned a sensationalized sagebrush Western—Dan J. Stevens (pseud.), *Oregon Trunk* (New York: Avalon, 1950). For the Central Oregon perspective, see Crowell, *Frontier Publisher*, 33–50; Jarold Ramsey, *Words Marked by a Place: Local Histories in Central Oregon* (Corvallis: Oregon State University Press, 2018), 60–66.

9 McCarthy, *History of Oregon Sheriffs*, 191–192.

10 Crowell, *Frontier Publisher*, 40, 42–43, 50; *Bend Bulletin*, June 26, 1908; and February 24, 1909.

11 Crowell, *Frontier Publisher*, 57–60; *Madras Pioneer*, January 5, 1911; and January 4, 1912. The highway bridge completed next to it in 1927 bypassed treacherous Trail Crossing used previously. Jerry Ramsey, "Remembering Trail Crossing," *The Agate*, n.s. 6 (2016): 14–15.

12 Ramsey, "Some 'What Ifs,'" 9; Ramsey, *Words Marked by a Place*, 64–65; *Madras Pioneer*, October 24, 1912.

13 Brogan, *East of the Cascades*, 245; Hanley, *Feelin' Fine*, 167–168; Crowell, *Frontier Publisher*, 62–65. Brogan and Hanley quote Hill slightly differently, but agree on his basic statement. The final links occurred when passenger service reached Bend a month after the dedication ceremonies and a bridge over the Columbia near Celilo Falls connected the Oregon Trunk to the SP&S north bank mainline the following year. *Bend Bulletin*, November 1, 1911; Portland *Oregonian*, January 6, 1912.

14 *Madras Pioneer*, January 12, November 9 and 16, and December 14, 1911; John F. Due and Francis Juris, *Rails to the Ochoco Country: The City of Prineville Railway* (San Marino, CA: Golden West, 1968); Randall V. Mills, "Prineville's Municipal Railroad," *OHQ* 42 (1941): 128–132.

15 Cox, *Lumberman's Frontier*, 347–349; *Madras Pioneer*, January 12 and December 14, 1911; David Myrick, "Nevada-California-Oregon Railway," *Western Railroader* 18 (June 1955): 2–20; Arrington, *Eccles*, 228–230; Potter, *Oregon's Golden Years*, 137; Ferrell, *Rails, Sagebrush, and Pine*. In NCO's pre-SP years, Lakeview locals suggested it stood for Narrow, Crooked, and Ornery.

16 *Timberman* 25 (October 1924): 50; Thomas R. Cox, "Frontier Enterprise vs. the Modern Age: Fred Herrick and the Closing of the Lumberman's Frontier," *PNQ* 84 (1993): 19–29; Langston, *Forest Dreams, Forest Nightmares*, 175–187; Jerry L. Mosgrove, *The Malheur National Forest: An Ethnographic History* (Portland: Forest Service, Pacific Northwest Region, 1980), 183–189.

17 Cox, *Lumberman's Frontier*, 336–338; Michael Tierney, interview with the author, Jackson, Wyoming, July 27, 2002.

18 The *Lake County Examiner* provided extensive coverage. From February 1924 through the first half of 1925, it was rare for an issue not to have one or more articles about the railroad schemes of Strahorn and others. On his multifaceted career, see Strahorn's unpublished autobiography, "Ninety Years of Boyhood" (photocopy; Terteling Library, College of Idaho, Caldwell).

19 Portland *Oregon Journal*, October 24, 1916; Klamath Falls *Evening Herald*, August 15, 1916; July 2, 6, and 17, August 1, and November 6, 1917; July 3, 1918; July 10 and October 13, 1919; January 10 and February 5, 1929; David F. Myrick, "Strahorn System: Oregon, California & Eastern," *Western Railroader* 21 (April 1958): 3–8; Good, *History of Klamath County*, 95–96 (quote); Tonsfeldt, "Selling Klamath Reservation Timber," 69; Anon., "The O C & E Railroad," *Timberman* 21 (August 1920): 43; Anon., "Oregon-California Pine Development," *Timberman* 26 (October 1925): 230–235; Lamm, *Lumbering in Klamath*, 20–21. At least six Klamath mills built logging railroads off the Sprague River line.

20 In 1918 the Hill interests strengthened their position in the Bend area by purchasing the land grant of the Willamette Valley and Cascade Mountain Wagon Road Company (which it subsequently sold to the Brooks-Scanlon lumber interests).

21 Cox, *Lumberman's Frontier*, 356–357 (extract, p. 357); Charles F. Twining,
    George S. Long, Timber Statesman (Seattle: University of Washington Press,
    1994), 313, 320–321, 364; Ralph W. Hidy, Frank Ernest Hill, and Allan
    Nevins, *Timber and Men: The Weyerhaeuser Story* (New York: Macmillan,
    1963), 403–405. As a sop to the Southern Pacific, its Oregon Short Line was
    given the right to use the trackage.

22 Jack Bowden and Tom Dill, *The Modoc, Southern Pacific's Back Door to
    Oregon* (Hamilton, MT: Oso Publishing, 2002). On eastbound shipments, the
    route through Alturas shaved off 210 miles and 5,168 feet in elevation over
    the previous route through California and over Donner Summit.

23 Carlos A. Schwantes, *Railroad Signatures across the Northwest* (Seattle:
    University of Washington Press, 1996), 160–161; Harry J. Drew,
    Weyerhaeuser Company: A History of People, Land, and Growth (Klamath
    Falls, OR: Weyerhaeuser, Eastern Oregon Region, 1979), 6–25; Twining,
    George S. Long, 313, 364; Good, *History of Klamath County*, 96–98.

24 Driscoll, *Gilchrist*, 32–37, 40–43, 46–47.

25 Portland *Oregon Journal*, April 24, 1919.

26 Johansen and Gates, *Empire of the Columbia*, 338, 372–381; Throckmorton,
    Oregon Argonauts, 118–120, 122, 205–207; Hugh Myron Hoyt Jr., "The Good
    Roads Movement in Oregon, 1900–1920" (PhD diss., University of Oregon,
    1966), 11–15, 170–171; Beckham and Lantz, *Rocks and Hard Places*, 121;
    Pierce, *Memoirs*, 239.

27 Bailey, *Main Street*, 41–43, 45–46. See also, Mead, *History of Union County*,
    161–174.

28 Bailey, *Main Street*, 46–48, 50, 53; Barklow, *Gateway to the Wallowas*, 183,
    222–226, 231–232; Evans, *Powerful Rockey*, 99–100; *Redmond Spokesman*,
    August 22, 1955.

29 For a map showing the routing of these roads, see Oregon Department of
    Transportation, *History of State Highways in Oregon*, ed. by Richard Nathe,
    Shannon Sudeman, and Paul Morin (Salem: Oregon Dept. of Transportation),
    8.

30 Barklow, *Gateway to the Wallowas*, 83; La Grande *Mountain Sentinel*, quoted
    in Anon., *History of Union and Wallowa Counties*, 149, 151 (quotes), 154–
    155; Anon., *History of Baker, Grant, Malheur and Harney Counties*, 168.

31 Ralph Watson, *Casual and Factual Glimpses of the Beginning and
    Development of Oregon's Roads and Highways* (Salem: Oregon State Highway
    Comm., [c. 1950]), 3, 19; Hoyt, "Good Roads Movement," 15–17, 20–24.

32 Anon., *History of Union and Wallowa Counties*, 482–483, 491 (1st quote);
    Barklow, *Gateway to the Wallowas*, 65–66, 77–84, 151–153; Strahorn,
    Fifteen-Thousand Miles, 480–483 (2nd quote, p. 480); Anon., *History of Baker,
    Grant, Malheur, and Harney Counties*, 737; Fred Lockley, *Conversations with
    Pioneer Men* (Eugene, OR: Rainy Day Press, 1996), 179, 184–186; Klamath
    Falls *Evening Herald*, February 11, 1909; John Day *Blue Mountain Eagle*,
    January 13, 1916; Fussner, *Glimpses of Wheeler County's Past*, 106–109;
    Beckham and Lentz, *Rocks and Hard Places*, 117–123.

33 Hoyt, "Good Roads Movement," 11, 42, 61–240; C. Lester Horn, "Oregon's
    Columbia River Highway," *OHQ* 66 (1965): 249–271; William G. Robbins,
    "Town and County in Oregon," in Michael Hibbard et al., *Toward One
    Oregon: Rural-Urban Interdependence and the Evolution of a State* (Corvallis:
    Oregon State University Press, 2011), 67, 70; Charles L. Dearing, *American
    Highway Policy* (Washington, DC: Brookings Institution, 1941), 46–47. See
    also, Lawrence M. Lipin, "'Cast Aside the Automobile Enthusiast': Class
    Conflict, Tax Policy, and the Preservation of Nature in Progressive–Era
    Oregon," *OHQ* 107 (2006): 166–195.

34 Portland *Oregonian*, November 8, 1899; and July 3, 1910; Hoyt, "Good Roads
    Movement," 106, 150–153; Bowman, *Pioneer Fringe*, 98; Barklow, *Gateway to
    the Wallowas*, 167–170; Dallas Lore Sharp, *Where Rolls the Oregon* (Boston:
    Houghton, Mifflin, 1914), 48–53. Revealingly, most of Oregon's early state
    parks were little more than roadside rest stops and picnic sites for leisure
    travelers. See Cox, *Park Builders*, 10–11, 166, 171–172.

35 Clackamas County Historical Society and Wasco County Historical Society,
    Barlow Road (6th ed.; Bend, OR: Maverick, 1998); Hoyt, "Good Roads
    Movement," 73, 123–124.

36 Hoyt, "Good Roads Movement," 246–249.

37 Watson, *Casual and Factual Glimpses* (quote, p. 6); Department of
    Transportation, *State Highways in Oregon*, 12, 19.

38 Pierce, *Memoirs*, 185, 237, 241, 280; Hoyt, "Good Roads Movement," 248–
    249, 252–256, 268–269; Department of Transportation, *State Highways in
    Oregon*, 15, 22; Watson, *Casual and Factual Glimpses*, 36; Herbert Nunn,
    Annual Report of the State Highway Engineer . . . (Salem, OR: State Printing
    Office, 1918), 36–37; Oregon State Highway Commission, *First Biennial
    Report* . . . (Salem, OR: State Printing Office, 1919), 66, 69–154; Good, *History
    of Klamath County*, 98; Klamath Falls *Klamath Republican*, November 23,
    1905; Klamath Falls *Evening Herald*, February 25, and March 3, 10, and 11,
    and June 16, 1919; September 1 and 29, 1920; September 14, 1921. See also,
    John C. Burnham, "Gasoline Tax and the Automobile Revolution," *Mississippi
    Valley Historical Review* (hereafter *MVHR*) 48 (1961): 435–459.

39 Klamath Falls *Evening Herald*, November 5 and 7, 1917; and January 5 and
    29, 1918.

40 Sharp, *Where Rolls the Oregon*, 49–50 (quote, p. 50); Pomeroy, *American Far
    West*, 173–175. For the national picture, see Wayne E. Fuller, *RFD, The
    Changing Face of America* (Bloomington: Indiana University Press, 1964).

41 *The Dalles Chronicle*, March 26, 1926; Portland *Oregonian*, June 13, 1926;
    Bend Bulletin, September 5, 1929; April 18, 1930; and April 21, 1936. In both
    Bowlby's and Nunn's plans, the only trans-Cascade routes were the Santiam
    highway from Central Oregon to Albany, the tortuous McKenzie Highway
    from Sisters to Eugene, and the Green Springs Highway from Klamath Falls
    to Ashland. Nunn's proposed highways to Crater Lake from each side joined
    but hardly qualified as a trans-Cascade route.

42 Mary Lauzon to Mary Warnicke, March 30, 2007, Oregon Dept. of
    Transportation, interoffice memo, in Patrick Cimiyotti to author, January 9,

2015 (Cox, personal correspondence); *Bend Bulletin*, August 14, 1943; Portland *Oregonian*, July 24, 1949; October 30 and November 6, 13, and 14, 1949; Confederated Tribes of the Warm Springs, Planning Committee, *The People's Plan: Executive Business of the Comprehensive Plan for the Year 2020* (Warm Springs, OR: Confederated Tribes of the Warm Springs, 1999), 61.

43 Pierce, *Memoirs*, 233–235 (quote, p. 234), 240–241; Schwartz, "Walter M. Pierce," 77–78.

44 Bailey, *Main Street*, 62–63; Smyth, *Footloose and Ahorseback*, 5, 12 (quote).

CHAPTER 11

1 Hubert Howe Bancroft, *Popular Tribunals* (2 vols.; San Francisco: History Co., 1887), vol. 1: 630–634 (quotes, pp. 631, 633); Anon., *History of Baker, Grant, Malheur, and Harney Counties*, 148–152; Lockley, *Conversations with Pioneer Men*, 251.

2 Anon., *History of Baker, Grant, Malheur, and Harney Counties*, 383.

3 Shaver, *History of Central Oregon*, 430; Lewis A. McArthur, *Oregon Geographic Names* (3rd ed.; Portland: Binford and Mort, 1965), 194, 647–648; Anon, *History of Union and Wallowa Counties*, 674. Postal authorities took a dim view of Robbins's choice, and the name was changed to Drewsey—but until recently the little community continued to sport a Gouge Eye Saloon.

4 Shaver, *History of Central Oregon*, 109, 112; Gaston, *Centennial History of Oregon*, vol. 1: 458; The Dalles *Times-Mountaineer*, October 17, 1855.

5 Shaver, *History of Central Oregon*, 110–112.

6 Shaver, *History of Central Oregon*, 112.

7 The Dalles *Times-Mountaineer*, quoted in Shaver, *History of Central Oregon*, 112–113; Potter, *Oregon's Golden Years*, 58–59; McCarthy, *History of Oregon Sheriffs*, 76–77. When Grant County was established the following year, responsibility for the John Day country was no longer the problem of authorities in The Dalles.

8 Shaver, *History of Central Oregon*, 724–725; The Dalles *Times-Mountaineer*, September 6, 1880.

9 Tupper, *Sandy Knoll*, 10–28, 43–54, 115–133, and 245–278.

10 McCarthy, *History of Oregon Sheriffs*, 223.

11 Shaver, *History of Central Oregon*, 127, 131–135 (1st quote, p. 131; 2nd and 3rd quotes, p. 134).

12 For examples, see Hanley, *Feelin' Fine*, 141–142; Clark, *Redmond*, 7–8, 14–17; Crowell, *Frontier Publisher*, 105–108, 110–112; Anon., *History of Baker, Grant, Malheur, and Harney Counties*, 384, 442, 524, 541.

13 Brogan, *East of the Cascades*, 154–161; Shaver, *History of Central Oregon*, 709–712; Clark and Clark, "Pioneers of Deschutes Country," 28–31 (quote, p. 30); Lockley, *Voices of Oregon Territory*, 252–255. For a more detailed account, see Ontko, *Thunder over the Ochoco*, vol. 5: 30–47, 65–104.

14 Ontko, *Thunder over the Ochoco*, vol. 5: 88–89; William Thompson, *Reminiscences of a Pioneer* (San Francisco: Self-published, 1912), 175–177.

15 Ontko, *Thunder over the Ochoco*, vol. 5: 98–101; Shaver, *History of Central Oregon*, 712. Vaughan was something of an outlaw himself. When conflict over cattle rustling developed in Umatilla County a bit later, he was among those suspected, although "outwardly busy raising wheat on the Umatilla reservation." Skovlin and Skovlin, *Hank Vaughan*, 92–100, 147–150.

16 Clark, *Redmond*, 16; *Bend Bulletin*, August 21, 1912; Marsh, *To the Promised Land*, 125.

17 Clark, *Redmond*, 16–17; *Redmond Spokesman*, August 29, 1912; April 3 and 10, and December 11, 1913.

18 Coe, *Frontier Doctor*, 244–246.

19 *Bend Bulletin*, June 5, 1912.

20 Crowell, *Frontier Publisher*, 105–106; Putnam, *Wide Margins*, 53–54; *New York Times*, January 6, 1914 (quotes).

21 Crowell, *Frontier Publisher*, 105–108; Putnam, *Wide Margins*, 55 (quote).

22 Crowell, *Frontier Publisher*, 109–110, 113–114; *Bend Bulletin*, April 9 and November 26, 1913.

23 Klamath Falls *Evening Herald*, September 21 and November 2, 1912; December 5, 1919; Macnab, *News and People*, 153–155.

24 Jim Reavis, "La Grande History, Union County, Oregon," Oregon Genealogy and History website, oregongenealogy.com/union/lagrande; Anon., *History of Union and Wallowa Counties*, 223–224 (quotes), 238.

25 Anon., *History of Union and Wallowa Counties* (quote, p. 221).

26 Anon., *History of Union and Wallowa Counties*, 183; Jim Reavis, "The Chinese Troubles, Union County, Oregon," Oregon Genealogy and History website, oregongenealogy.com/union/lagrande.

27 *Bend Bulletin*, October 3, 1928; January 3 and September 24, 1929; November 3, 5, and 13, and December 1 and 3, 1948. Reiter would subsequently serve as city manager of Coos Bay and then Albany. Additional information on Reiter, my uncle, comes from family sources; the Hoagland story comes from Ron Aeschbacher (who, together with Hoagland's son, would go on to play football for the San Francisco Forty-Niners).

28 Onstine, *Oregon Votes*, 4.

29 Clark, *Redmond*, 17–18, 21; Crowell, *Frontier Publisher*, 117–131; Ramsey, *Words Marked by a Place*, 76–84, 86–93.

30 Shaver, *History of Central Oregon*, 561–565 (quote, p. 562); Weatherford, *Arlington*, 35–36.

31 Shaver, *History of Central Oregon*, 433–436.

32 Shaver, *History of Central Oregon*, 817–823; McCarthy, *History of Oregon Sheriffs*, 126.

33 Shaver, *History of Central Oregon*, 642–646; Fussner, *Glimpses of Wheeler County's Past*, 15, 29–36, 57–59.

34 Ben W. Olcott, *A Pamphlet Containing a Copy of All Measures* ... (Salem, OR: State Printer, 1912), 163–166. Defeat of the proposal may have resulted more from it being joined with other changes that generated opposition than

the actual contents of Section IV, the portion dealing with the creation of new counties.

35 Richard L. Neuberger, "Are Seven Counties Enough?" *This Week*, March 1952 (published in a magazine insert in the Portland *Oregonian*, the article may also be found in Richard Neuberger Papers, box 53, folder 14, Knight Library, University of Oregon). See also, Neuberger, "Our Rotten Boroughs," *The Progressive*, December 1951 (copy in Neuberger Papers, box 41, folder 44); Marsh, *To the Promised Land*, 222–223.

36 McCarthy, *History of Oregon Sheriffs*, 237.

37 Cox, *Lumberman's Frontier*, 352, 355.

38 Secretary of State, *Oregon Blue Book: Almanac & Fact Book, 2011–2012* (Salem, OR: State Printer, 2012).

CHAPTER 12

1 The fullest account of the district's establishment is Beckham, *Gerber Block*, 95–111. See also, Brooke Brown, *The Gerber Family Legacy on Public Lands* (Klamath Falls, OR: Bureau of Land Management, 2012), 3–6.

2 Beckham, *Gerber Block*, 95–97, 104; Stephen Dow Beckham, "Twilight of the Open Range: The Taylor Grazing Act and Formation of the Bonanza Grazing District," *JSHL* 18 (2004): 85–100.

3 Beckham, *Gerber Block*, 101–103. For a similar view, see Dayton Hyde, *Yamsi: A Year in the Life of a Wilderness Ranch* (reprint; Corvallis: Oregon State University Press, 2001), 87–95, 213–214. There was a personal element in Gerber's hostility to expansion of the national forest. His family had ranched in the area for decades, and when the Forest Service instituted a system of grazing leases, the Gerbers, with ample range outside the national forest, opted against obtaining one. Some years later, with available public domain grazing land overtaxed, the family approached the Forest Service for an allotment and were told they "could have gotten a permit 10 years ago but did not, so it was 'too bad.'" Quoted in Brown, *Gerber Family*, 5.

4 The Geological Survey oversaw grazing districts until establishment of the Department of the Interior's Division of Grazing in 1935. The Division of Grazing became the Grazing Service in 1939; it was folded into the Bureau of Land Management a decade later.

5 Steen, *U.S. Forest Service*, 204–209 (1st quote, p. 206; 2nd and 3rd quotes, p. 207), 238–239, 272–273.

6 Beckham, *Gerber Block*, ii (1st quote), 84–85 (3rd quote, p. 85), 110–111, 115–116 (2nd quote).

7 Beckham, *Gerber Block*, 63–72; Good, *History of Klamath County*, 108.

8 Beckham, *Gerber Block*, 38–41, 48–51, 73–94, 100–101; Brown, *Gerber Family*, 4.

9 Beckham, *Gerber Block*, 111–114, 116, 126; Pinchot, *Breaking New Ground*, 260–262 (quote, p. 261). Secretary of Agriculture James Wilson signed the letter containing this famous quote, but the letter itself appears to have been penned by Pinchot.

10 Beckham, *Gerber Block*, 127; Brown, *Gerber Family*, 6–8.

11 John Day *Blue Mountain Eagle*, January 13, 1966.

12 Hanley, *Owyhee Trails*, 280–287 (1st quote, p. 280; 2nd quote, p. 282); William Kittredge, *Who Owns the West?* (San Francisco: Mercury, 1996), 27.

13 Smyth, *Footloose and Ahorseback*, 130–131.

14 Smyth, *Sunshine, Shadows, and Sagebrush*, 124, 138.

15 Smyth, *Sunshine, Shadows, and Sagebrush* (quote, p. 138). Acty Mountain is southeast of Frenchglen.

16 Smyth, *Sunshine, Shadows, and Sagebrush*, 78.

17 Smyth, *Footloose and Ahorseback*, 5, 65 (1st quote), 68 (2nd quote), 71 (3rd quote); Smyth, *Sunshine, Shadows, and Sagebrush*, 70, 171 (4th quote).

18 Leopold, *Sand County Almanac*, 154–158 (1st quote, p. 155; 2nd quote, p. 158); P. B. Kennedy, *Summer Ranges of Eastern Nevada Sheep*, Nevada Agricultural Experiment Station Bulletin no. 55 (Reno: University of Nevada, 1903). On cheatgrass and fire, see Young and Sparks, *Cattle in the Cold Desert*, 3–15.

19 McVicker, *Child of Steens Mountain* (quote, pp. 82–83); Jessica L. Deshazo and Zachary A. Smith, "The Fragile Desert: Managing the Great Basin's Environmental Crisis," in Dennis R. Judd and Stephanie L. Witt, eds., *Cities, Sagebrush, and Solitude: Urbanization and Cultural Conflict in the Great Basin* (Reno: University of Nevada Press, 2015), 114–115.

20 Vernon Bailey, *The Mammals and Life Zones of Oregon*, North American Fauna 55 (Washington, DC: Biological Survey, 1936), 16–17.

21 Israel C. Russell, *Notes on the Geology of Southwestern Idaho and Southeastern Oregon*, US Geological Survey Bulletin no. 217 (Washington, DC: GPO, 1903), 19–20 (1st quote, p. 19); Russell, *Preliminary Report on the Geology and Water Resources of Central Oregon*, 55, 62–63 (2nd quote, p. 63). See also, Geoffrey L. Buckley, "Desertification of the Camp Creek Drainage in Central Oregon," *Yearbook of the Association of Pacific Coast Geographers* 55 (1993): 98; David Griffiths, *Forage Conditions on the Northern Border of the Great Basin*, Bureau of Plant Industries Bulletin no. 15 (Washington, DC: GPO, 1902).

22 Summaries of the interviews are in Steve Lent, Bill McCormick, and M. B. Rollins, *A Historical Tour of Bear Creek, Southern Crook County* (Prineville, OR: Crook County Historical Society), 33–36 (quotes p. 36). In time, range managers would tackle the problem of junipers, but as fourth-generation Harney County rancher Fred Otley put it, "We feel like we're buying our land a second time due to the cost." Larry Swan, "Western Juniper Briefing Outline: Prepared for Oregon Senate Committee on Agriculture and Natural Resources," unpub. report, February 26, 1999, phpglhojg_BRFORLEG.pdf (Otley quote, p. 1).

23 *Heppner Gazette*, June 18, 1903; Bob DenOuden, "Without a Second's Warning: The Heppner Flood of 1903," *OHQ* 105 (2004): 108–119; Joann Byrd, *Calamity: The Heppner Flood of 1903* (Seattle: University of Washington Press, 2009).

24 Weatherford, *Arlington*, 41–42 (quote, p. 42), 46; Brogan, *East of the Cascades*, 136–137; Anon., *History of Baker, Grant, Malheur, and Harney Counties*, 215–216, 402–403; Lockley, *Conversations with Pioneer Women*, 109; Macnab, *News and People*, 74–75; Stinchfield and Stinchfield, *History of Wheeler County*, 9. With the construction of the John Day Dam, much of Arlington was moved to higher ground, coincidentally eliminating the danger of flash floods.

25 Rhoda M. Love, "Pioneer Botanist William Cusick: His Dark and Silent World," *Kalmiopsis* 14 (2007): 8–16 (quote, p. 12).

26 William O. Douglas, *My Wilderness* (Sacramento, CA: Comstock Publishing, 1989), 194, 196–197 (quote, p. 202); A. W. Sampson, *Natural Revegetation of Depleted Mountain Grazing Lands: Progress Report*, Forest Service Circular 169 (Washington, DC: Forest Service, 1909); Sampson, "Natural Vegetation of Rangelands Based upon Growth Requirements and Life History of the Vegetation," *Journal of Agricultural Research* 3 (1914) 93–147; On Douglas, see also, Adam M. Sowards, *The Environmental Justice: William O. Douglas and American Conservation* (Corvallis: Oregon State University Press, 2009).

27 Barklow, *Gateway to the Wallowas*, 32–33 (color plate 8), 186, 215–217.

28 Wayne E. Heimer, "Bighorn Pneumonia Die-Offs: An Outsider's History, Synthesis, and Suggestions," *Northern Wild Sheep and Goat Council, Proceedings of the Biennial Symposium* (2009): 154–164; George Post, "The Pneumonia Complex in Bighorn Sheep," *Northern Wild Sheep and Goat Council, Proceedings of the Biennial Symposium* (1971): 98–106; Skovlin and Skovlin, *Into the Minam*, 115–117; Klamath Falls *Evening Herald*, February 6, 1908.

29 Hansen, "An Ecological Survey of the Vertebrate Animals on Steens Mountain," 25–26, and passim; Bailey, *Mammals and Life Zones of Oregon*, 63–69; V. L. Coggins, P. E. Matthews, and W. Van Dyke, "History of Transplanting Mountain Goats and Mountain Sheep—Oregon," *Northern Wild Sheep and Goat Council, Proceedings of Biennial Symposium* (1996): 190–195; Oscar Deming, "1960 Desert Bighorn Transplants at Hart Mountain," *Desert Bighorn Council Transactions* 7 (1961): 56–57; Jim Yoakum, "Reestablishing Desert Bighorn Ranges," *Desert Bighorn Council Transactions* 9 (1963): 122–125; Desert Bighorn Council, "Award and Remembrance for Our Friend Chuck," *Desert Bighorn Council Transactions* 18 (1974): 2–3; Hansen, conversations with the author, Corvallis, Oregon, 1953–1954. According to at least one source, California bighorns were first reintroduced at Hart Mountain and from there to the Steens. Rocky Mountain goats were reintroduced in 1971. See Oregon Department of Fish and Wildlife website, dfw.state.or.us/agency/history.asp.

30 Gaston, *Centennial History of Oregon*, vol. 1: 478; Klamath Falls *Evening Herald*, November 7, 1919; Klamath Falls *Herald and News*, June 23, 1951; Skovlin, *Fifty Years of Research*, 14.

31 George Bird Grinnell, "Range of the Antelope in 1896," *Forest and Stream* 48 (1897): 5–6; Gaston, *Centennial History of Oregon*, vol. 1: 478; Douglas, *My Wilderness*, 72; Arthur S. Einarsen, *The Pronghorn Antelope and Its*

Management (Washington, DC: Wildlife Management Institute, 1948), 9–11, 58–59, 61, 66, 69, 70, 132; John D. Black, *Biological Conservation with Emphasis on Wildlife* (New York: Blakiston, 1954), 256.

32 Bailey, *Mammals and Life Zones of Oregon*, 74–76 (quote, p. 74), 78–80; Einarsen, *Pronghorn Antelope*, 148–203; Douglas, *My Wilderness*, 66–68; Gabrielson, *Wildlife Conservation* (2nd ed., New York: Macmillan, 1959), 102; Ira Gabrielson, *Wildlife Refuges* (New York: Macmillan, 1942), 94–95; Barklow, *Gateway to the Wallowas*, 249. Befitting their environmental interdependency, Sheldon and Hart Mountain refuges are managed from a joint office in Lakeview.

33 Gabrielson, *Wildlife Refuges*, 93; Hallie Hills Huntington, *History of the Order of the Antelope* (Lakeview, OR: Lake County Examiner, 1969); Douglas, *My Wilderness*, 71, 74; Lakeview *Lake County Examiner*, July 17, 2013; *Seattle Times*, April 30, 1992. The order's raucous gatherings on Hart Mountain became a problem, and beginning in 1978 refuge managers sought to ban them. The order, somewhat chastened, continued to work in behalf of pronghorns (and Hart Mountain in particular).

34 Bailey, *Mammals and Life Zones of Oregon*, 78–80 (quote, p. 80); Barklow, *Gateway to the Wallowas*, 239–240; Enterprise *Record-Chieftain*, February 8 and March 7 and 21, 1912; Worth Mathewson, *William L. Finley: Pioneer Wildlife Photographer* (Corvallis: Oregon State University Press, 1987), 9–10; Frank B. Wise, "A Brief History of the Oregon State Game Commission" (typescript, 1938) www.state.or.us/agency/docs, 3–4, 8. Encouraged by success with elk, authorities began reintroductions of mountain goats into the Wallowas in 1950 and later, the Cascades near Mount Jefferson.

35 Bailey, *Mammals and Life Zones of Oregon*, 9–10; Barklow, *Gateway to the Wallowas*, 141–142; Skovlin, *Fifty Years of Research*, 14–15.

36 Israel Cook Russell, *A Reconnaissance in Southeastern Washington*, Water Supply and Irrigation Paper 4 (Washington, DC: GPO, 1897), 68–69; Meinig, *Great Columbia Plain*, 421–443 (quote, p. 421).

37 Meinig, *Great Columbia Plain*, 422–427.

38 Pomeroy, *American Far West*, 141; US Department of Agriculture, *Wheat Acreage, Yield, Production by States, 1866–1943* . . . , Agricultural Marketing Service Statistical Bulletin no. 158 (Washington, DC: GPO, 1955); Macnab, *News and People*, 208–211, 213, 262. Macnab was mistaken in calling the Heppner district the nation's first (p. 262); that honor goes to the Browns Creek, North Carolina, district, founded in 1937.

39 Clawson and Held, *Federal Lands*, 258; Douglas Helms, "Conservation Districts: Getting to the Roots," in Douglas Helms, ed., *Readings in the History of the Soil Conservation Service*, Historical Notes 1 (Washington, DC: Soil Conservation Service, 1992), 25–30. See also, David Pimentel et al., "Environment and Economic Costs of Soil Erosion and Conservation Benefits," *Science* 267 (1967): 1117–1123.

40 James C. Ebert and R. Dennis Roe, *Soil Erosion in the Palouse River Basin: Indications of Improvement*, Geological Survey Fact Sheet FS-069-98 (Pullman, WA: USGS, 1998).

41 Langston, *Forest Dreams, Forest Nightmares*, 119–134; Skovlin, *Fifty Years of Research*, 20–23, 34, 37; Charles G. Johnson Jr., *Green Fescue Rangelands: Change Over Time in the Wallowa Mountains*, General Technical Report 569 (Portland: Pacific Northwest Research Station, 2003), 1, 2, 4, 8, 9, 10, 21, 36; Elbert H. Reid, Gerald S. Strickler, and Wade B. Hall, *Green Fescue Grassland: Fifty Years of Secondary Succession under Sheep Grazing* (Baker City, OR: Wallowa-Whitman National Forest, 1991).

42 In time, range managers would tackle the problem of junipers. See, for example, USDA Forest Service, *Proceedings of the Western Juniper Ecology and Management Workshop*, General Technical Report PNW-74 (Portland: Pacific Northwest Forest and Range Experiment Station, 1978).

43 Tony Svejar, *Management of Great Basin Rangelands: History and Mission of the Squaw Butte Experiment Station*, Field Day Special Report no. 935 (Corvallis: Oregon Agricultural Experiment Station, 1994), 11.

44 F. A. Sneva, L. R. Rittenhouse, and P. T. Tueller, *Research in Rangeland Management: Forty Years—Inside and Out*, 1980 Progress Report (Corvallis: Oregon Agricultural Experiment Station, 1980), 1, 11–12 (quote, p. 12); C. Leo Hitchcock, *A Key to the Grasses of Montana, Based upon Vegetative Characters* (St. Louis, MO: John S. Swift, 1937); Hitchcock, *Key to the Grasses of the Pacific Northwest, Based upon Vegetative Characters* (St. Louis, MO: John S. Swift, 1969); A. R. Kruckeberg, "C. Leo Hitchcock," *Madrono* 20 (1969): 387–390.

45 Sneva, Rittenhouse, and Tueller, *Forty Years* (quote, p. 12); Svejar, *History and Mission*, 1–11.

46 A. L. Hafenrichter et al., *Grasses and Legumes for Soil Conservation in the Pacific Northwest and Great Basin States*, Agriculture Handbook 339 (Washington, DC: Soil Conservation Service, 1968); Erik Bruce Godfrey, "An Economic Evaluation of the Range Improvements Administered by the Bureau of Land Management in the Vale District of Oregon" (PhD diss., Oregon State University, 1971), 15, 18, 20.

47 H. L. Westover and George A. Rogler, *Crested Wheatgrass*, leaflet 4 (rev. ed.; Washington, DC: USDA, 1941). In mountain areas other species, mostly natives, were used for reseeding, and the results were less fraught with problems. See Skovlin, *Fifty Years of Research*, 20–23, 34, 37, 57; Gerald D. Pickford and E. R. Jackman, *Reseeding Eastern Oregon Summer Ranges*, Circ. 159 (Corvallis: Oregon Agricultural Experiment Station, 1944); Charles G. Johnson, *Forest Health in the Blue Mountains: A Plant Ecologist's Perspective on Ecosystem Processes*, General Technical Report 339 (Portland: Forest Service, Pacific Northwest Experiment Station, 1994), 12, 15, 21.

CHAPTER 13

1 Meacham, *Wigwam and War-Path*, 150–151. Teninos were also referred to as Walla Wallas, a term I eschew as, on the reservation today, they are known as the Warm Springs tribe, which together with the Wasco and Paiute make up the Confederated Tribes of the Warm Springs.

2   Katrine Barber, *Death of Celilo Falls* (Seattle: University of Washington Press, 2005), 153 (Thompson quotes); Eugene S. Hunn, *Nch'i-Wana, The Big River: Mid-Columbia Indians and the Land* (Seattle: University of Washington Press, 1991), 153–157, 224–225, 272.

3   On life in the village in the twentieth century, see Martha Ferguson McKeown *Linda's Indian Home* (Portland: Binford and Mort, 1956).

4   Thompson to Elliott, October 31, 1946 (quote); Brophy, memorandum for chairman, Interior Coordinating Committee, October 11, 1946, www.ccrh. org/comm/river/docs/celilo.

5   Richard L. Neuberger, *Our Promised Land* (reprint ed.; Moscow: University of Idaho Press, 1989), 123–139; Anthony Netboy, *Salmon of the Pacific Northwest: Fish vs. Dams* (Portland: Binford and Mort, 1958), 15–19; Barber, *Death of Celilo Falls* (quote, p. 153). See also, Blaine Hardin, *A River Lost: The Life and Death of the Columbia* (New York: Norton, 1996); Joseph E. Taylor III, *Making Salmon: An Environmental History of the Northwest Fisheries Crisis* (Seattle: University of Washington Press, 2001); and Roberta Ulrich, *Empty Nets: Indians, Dams, and the Columbia River* (2nd ed.; Corvallis: Oregon State University Press, 2007).

6   Courtland Smith, *Salmon Fishers of the Columbia* (Corvallis: Oregon State University Press, 1979), 102.

7   Katie Archambault, "Rural Electrification in Oregon, 1930–1955" (Honors thesis, Linfield College, 2010), 7–15 (Meier quote, p. 8); Wesley Arden Dick, "When Dams Weren't Damned: The Public Power Crusade and Vision of the Good Life in the Pacific Northwest," *Environmental Review* 13 (1989): 113–153 (esp. 119–128, 138–139); Pierce, *Memoirs*, 358–362, 383–385; Craig Wollner, *Electrifying Eden: Portland General Electric, 1889–1965* (Portland: Oregon Historical Society, 1990), 245–262; Andrus and Connelly, *Cecil Andrus*, 25–26, 47–48, 127–129.

8   Karl Boyd Brooks, *Public Power, Private Dams: The Hells Canyon High Dam Controversy* (Seattle: University of Washington Press, 2009), 119–128, 138–139; Elmo Richardson, *Dams, Parks, and Politics: Resource Development and Preservation in the Truman-Eisenhower Era* (Lexington: University Press of Kentucky, 1973), 35, 72–75. See also, Franklyn Daniel Mahar, "Douglas McKay and the Issues of Power Development in Oregon, 1953–1956" (PhD diss., University of Oregon, 1968).

9   For an analysis of Neuberger's unexpected victory over incumbent Guy Cordon, see John M. Swarthout, "The 1954 Election in Oregon," *Western Political Quarterly* 7 (1954): 620–625.

10 Bert Swanson and Deborah Rosenfield, "The Coon-Neuberger Debates of 1955: Ten Dam Nights in Oregon," *PNQ* 55 (1964): 55–60; Neuberger, *Our Promised Land*, 61–122; William G. Robbins, *Landscapes of Conflict: The Oregon Story, 1940–2000* (Seattle: University of Washington Press, 2004), 222–223; Richardson, *Dams, Parks, and Politics*, 157–160, 163–164.

11 Swanson and Rosenfield, "Coon-Neuberger Debates," 64–66; Richardson, *Dams, Parks, and Politics*, 161, 179–182; Marsh, *To the Promised Land*, 244;

Brent Walth, *Fire at Eden's Gate: Tom McCall and the Oregon Story* (Portland: Oregon Historical Society, 2000), 87–90, 94, 109.

12 Brooks, *Public Power, Private Dams*, 17, 24–25, 46–47, 55; Richardson, *Dams, Parks, and Politics*, 161–164; Marsh, *To the Promised Land*, 219–220, 228, 230, 232.

13 Brooks, *Public Power, Private Dams*, 182–183, 217–220; Swarthout, "The 1954 Election in Oregon," 623. Election data is from Onstine, *Oregon Votes*. The Second Congressional District included Hood River County, not considered a part of Eastern Oregon for purposes of this study.

14 Brooks, *Public Power, Private Dams*, 144–146, 220; Dick, "When Dams Weren't Damned," 144–146; Andrus and Connelly, *Cecil Andrus*, 95–101. For the larger context, see Anthony Netboy, *The Salmon: Their Fight for Survival* (New York: Houghton, Mifflin, 1984).

15 Portland *Oregon Journal*, January 20, 1949; Wollner, *Electrifying Eden*, 220–236. The consortium was made up of Portland General Electric, Pacific Power and Light, and Washington Water Power.

16 Edwards, oral history interview.

17 For brief accounts, see Robbins, *Landscapes of Conflict*, 237–247; Wollner, *Electrifying Eden*, 235–245; Ramsey, "Some 'What Ifs?,'" 10–11. See also, Netboy, *Salmon of the Pacific Northwest*, 35, 83–86; William H. Veeder, "The Pelton Decision . . ." *Montana Law Review* 27 (1965): 27–45. In addition to Pelton Dam, the plan envisioned a larger dam downstream near Round Butte. These, together with a reregulating dam, constituted the Pelton Dam Complex.

18 Robin W. Doughty, *Feather Fashion and Bird Preservation, A Study in Nature Protection* (Berkeley: University of California Press, 1975). Cf. John F. Reiger, *American Sportsmen and the Origins of Conservation* (New York: Winchester Press, 1975); Richard W. Judd, *Common Lands, Common People: The Origins of Conservation in Northern New England* (Princeton, NJ: Princeton University Press, 1988).

19 Mathewson, *Finley*, 57, 106.

20 William M. Finley and Irene Finley, "Malheur, the Unfortunate," *Nature Magazine* 28 (1936): 73 (quote). See also, http://www.fws.gov/refuges/history/bio/finley.html.

21 William L. Finley, "The Trail of the Plume Hunter," *Atlantic Monthly* 106 (1910): 373–379; Nancy Langston, *Where Land and Water Meet: A Western Landscape Transformed* (Seattle: University of Washington Press, 2003), 63–64; Jackman and Scharff, *Steens Mountain* (quote, p. 50). On Bendire, see *The Auk* 15 (1898): 1–6; Erwin F. Lange, "Major Charles E. Bendire and the Birds of Oregon," *OHQ* 66 (1965): 233–239. Both Tule Lake and Lower Klamath were partially in California, but extended into Oregon (at least seasonally).

22 *Bird Lore* 7 (1905): 336–342; Klamath Falls *Evening Herald*, August 22, 1906; Klamath Falls *Klamath Republican*, August 27, 1906; Sharp, *Where Rolls the Oregon*, 93–116. Roosevelt's first withdrawal for a refuge was Pelican Island, Florida, in 1903.

23 Monroe, *Feelin' Fine*, 169–170, 172–174, 189; Langston, *Where Land and Water Meet*, 69–74.

24 Accomplished in public relations, Finley avoided mentioning that drought as well as diversions lay behind the drying of the Malheur. The film can be found at media.oregonstate.edu/media.

25 Ira Noel Gabrielson, *Wildlife Refuges* (New York: Macmillan, 1943), 4–5 (quote).

26 Ira N. Gabrielson, "In Memoriam—Stanley G. Jewett," *The Murrelet* 36 (1955): 32–34 (quote, p. 33); Jackman and Scharff, *Steens Mountain*, 57. Purchase of the OO Ranch affected Harney Lake, not Malheur; Silver Creek flowed through the OO Ranch into Harney. Aside from overflow from Malheur, it was Harney's only significant source of water.

27 Finley and Finley, "Malheur, the Unfortunate," 73; Langston, *Where Land and Water Meet*, 94–106; Jackman and Scharff, *Steens Mountain* (quote, p. 65). By 1944, Oregon had joined the preservation effort by creating refuges at Summer Lake and elsewhere.

28 Cox, *Lumberman's Frontier*, 352, 360–361; Langston, *Forest Dreams, Forest Nightmares*, 189–200.

29 For details of the policy and its adoption, see Kenneth R. Philp, ed., *Indian Self-Rule: First Hand Accounts of Indian-White Relations from Roosevelt to Reagan* (Salt Lake City, UT: Howe Bros., 1985), 114–149, 174–185; Donald Lee Fixico, *Termination and Relocation: Federal Indian Policy, 1945–1960* (Albuquerque: University of New Mexico Press, 1986); Roberta Ulrich, *American Indian Nations from Termination to Restoration* (Lincoln: University of Nebraska Press, 2010), xiii–xv, 45–67, 193–220, 235–246.

30 Cox, *Lumberman's Frontier*, 353; Jay P Kinney, *Indian Forest and Range: A History of the Administration and Conservation of the Redman's Heritage* (Washington, DC: Forestry Enterprises, 1950), 204–206, 211–212.

31 Ulrich, *American Indian Nations*, 49, 51, 56, 59.

32 Paul W. Hirt, *A Conspiracy of Optimism: Management of the National Forests since World War II* (Lincoln: University of Nebraska Press, 1994), 248–249; Langston, *Forest Dreams, Forest Nightmares*, 264–265; Miles Burnett and Charles Davis, "Getting Out the Cut: Politics and National Forest Timber Harvests, 1960–1995," *Administration and Society* 34 (2002): 220–228. See also, Char Miller, *American Forests: Nature, Culture, and Politics* (Lawrence: University Press of Kansas, 1997); Samuel P. Hays, *Wars in the Woods: The Rise of Ecological Forestry in America* (Pittsburgh, PA: University of Pittsburgh Press, 2006).

33 I resided in Sisters at the time and observed these events firsthand.

34 Hyde, *Yamsi*, 87–95 (quote, p. 87), 213–214.

35 Personal reminiscences. I later heard the Black Canyon fire was the most expensive dollar-per-acre the State of Oregon had had up to that time. I cannot vouch for the statement's accuracy, but later fires in the county (Grant) would prove far more destructive.

36 Douglas, *Of Men and Mountains*, 177; Douglas, *My Wilderness*, 196–197.

37 Skovlin and Skovlin, *Into the Minam*, 14–15, 144–151, 178; *High Country News*, September 29, 1972; Committee on Interior and Insular Affairs S. Report 92–138 (Washington, DC: GPO, 1971); Cong. Record, Senate, October 3, 1974, p. 33759–33760. See also, Derek R. Larson, "Preserving Eden: The Culture of Conservation in Oregon, 1960–1980" (PhD diss., Indiana University, 2001).

38 However, see Kevin Marsh, *Lines in the Forest: Creating Wilderness Areas in the Pacific Northwest* (Seattle: University of Washington Press, 2010).

39 Jane Kirkpatrick, *Homestead: A Memoir* (New Kensington, PA: Whitaker House, 2014).

40 Orin Fletcher Stafford, *The Mineral Resources and Mineral Industry of Oregon for 1903*, University of Oregon Bulletin, n.s. vol. 4 (Eugene: University of Oregon, 1904), 1, 21–22; Sumpter Valley Dredging, news file, Grant County; Timms Gold Dredging Co., news and reports files, Baker County; Porter and Company, reports file, Baker County (Oregon Department of Geology and Mineral Industries, Oregon Historical Mining Information, Mining Records); Norman Johnson, "Mining History of the Middle Fork of the John Day River," www.precious-testimonies.com/Bates/Docs/Njohnson.

41 Potter, *Oregon's Golden Years*, 126–127; Oregon Department of Geology and Mineral Industries, Oregon Historical Mining Information, Mining Records, Grant County; *Sumpter Miner*, September 11, 1899–April 5, 1905; Prairie City *Grant County Journal*, April 6, 1915.

42 Schwartz, "Walter M. Pierce," 25 (3rd quote); Prairie City *Grant County Journal*, April 6, 1915 (2nd quote); Oliver, *Gold and Cattle*, 28–30 (1st quote, pp. 29–30).

43 Oregon Department of Geology and Mineral Industries, Oregon Historical Mining Information, Mining Records, Baker County, Sumpter Valley Dredging, news file.

44 Oregon Department of Geology and Mineral Industries, Oregon Historical Mining Information, Mining Records, Grant County, Western Dredging Co, reports and news files; Baker *Eastern Oregon News*, November 5, 1937; Tucson *Arizona Mining Journal*, September 13, 1941; John T. Leethern, "The Western Gold Dredging Company of John Day, Oregon," *Oregon Geology* 41 (1979): 91–95.

45 James A. Cox to author, December 19, 2014 (Cox, personal corres.). Critiques had small audiences, such as those in F. W. Libbey, "Dredging of Farmlands in Oregon," Oregon Department of Geology and Mineral Industries, Bulletin 19 (Salem, OR: Department of GMI, 1939): 1–40.

46 Hopkins, *Life among the Piutes*, 13; Meacham, *Wigwam and War-Path*, 154–156.

47 Kinney, *Indian Forest and Range*, 178–179, 237, 245, 309–310; Ward Tonsfeldt, "Selling Klamath Reservation Timber, 1910–1935," *JSHL* 16 (2002): 72 (quote).

48 Meacham, *Wigwam and War-Path* (quote, p. 179).

49 In the 1950s, Klamaths considered building a sawmill, but with tribal members little interested in sawmill work they opted instead to increase the grazing fees charged outsiders. Their economic base thus remained narrow. Klamath Falls *Herald and News*, February 10, 1950; Tonsfeldt, "Selling Klamath Reservation Timber," 66–67; Lamm, *Lumbering in Klamath*, 3.

50 Ken Metzler, "The Restless Indian," *Old Oregon* 45 (January/February 1965): 8–13 (quotes, pp. 10, 12); Portland *Oregonian*, December 5, 1969; "Kenneth L. Smith," www.warmsprings.com/warmsprings/Tribal_Community/ Tribal_ Investments/Ken_Smith.

51 Waldage Tunner, "Oregon Indians Exchange Roles," *New York Times*, August 30, 1964; Jack Hunt, "Land Tenure and Economic Development on the Warm Springs Reservation," *Journal of the West* 9 (1970): 93–109. On relations with the white community and recent efforts at adjustment, see Michael Baughman and Charlotte Hadella, *Warm Springs Millennium: Voices from the Reservation* (Austin: University of Texas Press, 2000).

52 Metzler, "Restless Indian," 12.

53 For explication of the Indian position, see Lawrence Winishut to the editor, Portland *Oregonian*, March 5, 1956. Winishut was a member of the tribal council.

54 A photo published in the Portland *Oregon Journal* on May 2, 1956, showed only Wasco Chief Joe McCorkle turning a spadeful of earth, but all three chiefs participated.

55 Wollner, *Electrifying Eden*, 240.

56 On the McQuinn Strip, see Gordon Macnab, *A History of the McQuinn Strip* (Warm Springs, OR: Tribal Council, 1972). The settlement brought an additional 61,360 acres, much of it timbered, into the reservation.

57 In 1991, the tribal government closed unprofitable Jefferson Plywood, thus eliminating 110 jobs; it was the first closure in the twenty-one-year history of Warm Springs Forest Products. In April 2016, after fifty years of operation, the sawmill also closed, citing an outdated plant and shortage of sawlogs. *Bend Bulletin*, October 4, 1991; and March 9, 2016; Idaho Falls *Post-Register*, April 14, 2016.

58 Ruby, Brown, and Collins, *Guide to the Indian Tribes*, 89–90. For a partial list of tribal enterprises and services, see, www.warmsprings.com/Warmsprings/ Tribal_Community/History_Culture/Chronology.

CHAPTER 14

1 Cox, *Park Builders*, 78–82 (Boardman quotes, p. 80); Samuel H. Boardman, "Oregon State Parks System: A Brief History," *OHQ* 55 (1954): 227–229. See also, Chester H. Armstrong, *History of Oregon State Parks, 1917–1963* (Salem: Oregon Highway Dept., 1965), 6–20. Some years ago I found Boardman's manuscript account of his journey to Bend, but took no detailed notes and have been unable to relocate it.

2   Cox, *Park Builders*, 54–56. See also, Thomas R. Cox, "Conservation by Subterfuge: Robert W. Sawyer and the Birth of the Oregon State Parks," *PNQ* 64 (1973): 21–29.

3   Cox, *Park Builders*, 95–97. See also, Lawrence C. Merriam and David G. Talbot, *Oregon's Highway Park System, 1921–1989* (Salem: Oregon Parks and Recreation Department, 1992), 23–34. Lawrence Merriam was John C. Merriam's grandson.

4   John C. Merriam, "A Contribution to the Geology of the John Bay Basin," University of California, *Bulletin of the Department of Geology* 2 (1901): 269–314; Arnold Shotwell, ed., "Journal of First Trip of University of California to John Day Beds of Eastern Oregon," University of Oregon, *Bulletin of the Museum of Natural History* 19 (1972); Barbara R. Stein, *On Her Own Terms: Annie Montagu Alexander and the Rise of Science in the American West* (Berkeley: University of California Press, 2001), 107–108, 112–113, 308. Merriam became head of the Carnegie Institution in Washington, DC, in 1920, but most of his fieldwork was done while resident in the West.

5   John C. Merriam, *Published Papers and Addresses of John Campbell Merriam* (4 vols.; Washington, DC: Carnegie Institution, 1938), vol. 4: 2165–2264 (quote, p. 2179); Cressman, *Golden Journey*, 409–410. See also, Stephen R. Mark, *Preserving the Living Past: John C. Merriam's Legacy in State and National Parks* (Berkeley: University of California Press, 2005).

6   Cox, *Park Builders*, 84–85 (Boardman quote, p. 93).

7   Cox, *Park Builders*, 96–97; Armstrong, *History of Oregon State Parks*, 205–207; Merriam and Talbot, *Oregon's Highway Park System*, 27; Beckham and Lentz, *Rocks and Hard Places*, 177–181.

8   Cox, *Park Builders*, 96–98 (quote, p. 97), 142–143; Armstrong, *History of Oregon State Parks*, 88–89, 170–172, 217–218; Merriam and Talbot, *Oregon's Highway Park System*, 25, 215, 235.

9   Joseph Wood Krutch, *The Desert Year* (New York: William Sloane, 1952); Joseph Wood Krutch, *The Voice of the Desert* (New York: William Sloane, 1955); Peter Wild, *Pioneer Conservationists of Western America* (Missoula, MT: Mountain Press, 1979), 131–139. Disney's film won the Academy Award for Best Documentary Feature in 1953 and was subsequently selected by the Library of Congress for inclusion in the National Film Registry.

10 Earl Pomeroy, "Toward a Reorientation of Western History: Continuity and Environment," *MVHR* 41 (1955): 579–600.

11 Shaver, *History of Central Oregon*, 648–649; Fussner, *Glimpses of Wheeler County's Past*, 29–30; Stinchfield and Stinchfield, *History of Wheeler County*, 6, 7.

12 Cressman, *Golden Journey*, 401.

13 Carrol B. Howe, oral history interview by Stephen R. Mark, January 23, 1992 (Crater Lake National Park Oral History Series), pp. 2–3, 5, 12–13, www.craterlakeinstitute.com/online-library/oral-history. Anthropologist Theodore Stern published *The Klamath Tribe: A People and Their Reservation* (Seattle: University of Washington Press, 1965) as Howe was completing work on his

own initial study of the Klamaths. Much later Howe produced *Unconquered, Uncontrolled*, which drew on fresh findings and took the tribal story further.

14   Brogan was not the first to appreciate lava country—in 1909 a group traveled from Klamath Falls to the Modoc Lava Flow—Captain Jack's Stronghold— and claimed its grandeur equal to that of Crater Lake. But such reactions were exceptional. Klamath Falls *Evening Herald*, June 28 and 29, 1909; and January 18, 1918.

15   Cressman, *Golden Journey*, 284–285, 287–288, 291, 293–296, 306, 308, 310, 313–314, 316, 333, 340–342, 345–346 (quote, pp. 353–354); Howe, interview, 2, 5, 12–13 (quotes, pp. 12, 13).

16   Howe, interview, 13.

17   Hands, *Jefferson County Reminiscences* (quote, p. 295).

18   *Bend Bulletin*, February 1 and May 28, 2013; Historic Preservation League of Oregon, "Petersen Rock Garden," www.historicpreservationleasgue.org/mep_ PetersenRock.php.

19   Portland *Oregonian*, August 3, 2012; Waterston, *Where the Crooked River Rises*, 21–28.

20   Rockhounding continues, and in 2016 a new group, the Dayville Rock and Gem Club, was added to the groups of enthusiasts. John Day *Blue Mountain Eagle*, December 14, 2016.

21   Tom Bohmker and Eddie Humbird, *Gold Panner's Guide to Eastern Oregon* . . . (n.p.: Cascade Mountains Gold, 2011); Garret Romaine, *Gem Trails of Oregon* (3rd ed.; Upland, CA: Gem Guides, 2009); Armstrong, *History of Oregon State Parks*, 195–196; Alan Watts, *Climber's Guide to Smith Rock* (Helena, MT: Falcon, 1992).

22   Rhoda M. Love, *Louis F. Henderson (1853–1942): The Grand Old Man of Northwest Botany*, Occasional paper no. 2 (Eugene: Native Plant Society of Oregon, 2001); Love, "Pioneer Botanist William Cusick."

23   Sawyer shared an interest in such things; rather than the sweeping lawns usually found in such places, he filled the large front yard of his home on Bend's Drake Road with a jumble of junipers, rabbitbrush, bitterbrush, sagebrush, orange globe mallow, and other native vegetation.

24   Cox, *Park Builders*, 96–97; Merriam and Talbot, *Oregon's Highway Park System*, 215; Armstrong, *History of Oregon State Parks*, 177; Susan R. Kephart, "Morton Eaton Peck: Field Botanist, Poet, and Author of *Manual of the Higher Plants of Oregon*," *Kalmiopsis* 7 (2001): 1–7; James M. Trappe, "Helen Margaret Gilkey 1886–1972," *Mycologia* 67 (March/April 1975): 207– 213; Rhoda M. Love, "Georgia Mason: Eleven Summers Alone in the Wallowas," *Kalmiopsis* 17 (2010): 9–16; Donald H. Mansfield, *Flora of Steens Mountain* (Corvallis: Oregon State University Press, 2000), 19; Jackman and Scharff, *Steens Mountain*, 122–135; Native Plant Society of Oregon: High Desert Chapter website, www.highdesertnpsoregon.org. See also, Georgia Mason, *Guide to the Plants of the Wallowa Mountains of Northeastern Oregon* (Eugene: University of Oregon Press, 1975).

25 *Burns Times-Herald*, May 10, 1946. Sodium fluoroacetate, developed in the 1940s and marketed as 1080, quickly became the poison of choice, especially in coyote and rodent control; a cruel and indiscriminant killer, its use was banned by the EPA in 1972.

26 Gaston, *Centennial History of Oregon*, vol. 1: 478; Klamath Falls *Evening Herald*, March 16, 1929; Oregon Fish and Wildlife, DFW.state.or.us/agency/history.asp. It would be a long time before a new view of the coyote and wolves—and a more holistic view of the natural world in which predators were seen as valuable—would take hold. Works such as Dayton O. Hyde's *Don Coyote: The Good Times and Bad of a Much Maligned American Original* (Westminster, MD: Arbor House, 1986), set in Klamath County, would eventually appear, but public attitudes were slow to change. See also, Jackman and Long, *Oregon Desert*, 176–191.

27 On rabbit drives, see *Madras Pioneer*, December 28, 1911; *Fort Rock Times*, November 11, 1915; Klamath Falls *Evening Herald*, April 21, 1916; March 20 and June 21, 1919; January 12, 1920; February 26 and March 7, 1921; Dorothy Lawson McCall, *Ranch under the Rimrock* (Portland: Binford and Mort, 1968), 39–42; Pratt, *Homesteader's Portfolio*, 146–147; Wilson and Scott, *That Was Yesterday*, 80–81; Parks, *Portraits*, 71, 190.

28 Gaston, *Centennial History of Oregon*, vol. 1: 478.

29 On deer hunting and management in the area, see Edwards, oral history interview; Georgia Gallagher, oral history interview by Maret Pajutee, May 22, 1998, www.sisterscountryhistoricalsociety.org; Cox, interviews with John Shaw, Sam Hewitt, and Doug Hockett, Sisters, Oregon, September 16, 2017.

30 For an analysis of Disney's intentions and the impact of the movie, see Ralph H. Lutts, "The Trouble with Bambi: Disney's Bambi and the American Vision of Nature," *Forest and Conservation History* 36 (1992): 160–171.

31 *Time Magazine* 64 (August 23, 1954): 13–14. See also, Richardson, *Dams, Parks, and Politics*, 83–87.

32 Hansen, "Ecological Survey," 90 (Jewett quote); Paul A. Johnsgard, *Grouse and Quails of North America* (Lincoln: University of Nebraska Press, 1973), 157–160; Jackman and Long, *Oregon Desert*, 195–199; McVicker, *Child of Steens Mountain*, 21; *Burns Times-Herald*, June 28, 1913. For recent environmentalist explanations, see George Wuerthner, "What's Driving the Decline of Sage Grouse?" *Counterpunch*, December 3, 2011; Mac Lacey, "Sage-Grouse Stronghold Threatened by BLM Plan," *Desert Ramblings: Newsletter of the Oregon Natural Desert Association* 23 (Winter 2010): 1–6.

33 Virginia Holmgren, *Chinese Pheasants, Oregon Pioneers* (Portland: Oregon Historical Society, 1964); C. Hart Merriam, "Introduced Pheasants," *Report of the Commissioner of Agriculture, 1908* (Washington, DC: GPO, 1909), 484–488; Frank B. Wise, "A Brief History of the Oregon State Game Commission" (typescript, 1938), dfw.state.or.us/agency/docs, 10; *Burns Times-Herald*, September 13, 1913; and March 12, 1914; Klamath Falls *Evening Herald*, August 24, 1914; and July 23, 1919.

34 Johnsgard, *Grouse and Quails*, 477–478, 492–496.

35 Michno, *Deadliest War*, 240, 314.

36 W. L. Minckley and James R. Deacon, eds., *Battle against Extinction: Native Fish Management in the American West* (Tucson: University of Arizona Press, 1991), 7–21; Bishop, *In Search of Ancient Oregon*, 220–222.

37 Today the trout of these interior waters are generally referred to as redband trout and the coastal form of the same species as rainbow trout. The usage grates on the ear of many old-timers east of the Cascades, who always called their more colorful form rainbow trout and labeled the coastal form speckled trout, which they (myself included) considered not only less colorful but a less challenging game fish.

38 Kittredge, *Who Owns the West*, 30; Minckley and Deacon, *Battle against Extinction*, 43–54. However, Lost River suckers, locally known as mullet, *were* a sportfish in the Klamath Basin in the early twentieth century, as well as a continuing source of native sustenance. *Klamath Republican*, March 25, 1909; Klamath Falls *Evening Herald*, March 4 and 16, 1918; April 7, 1919; and March 16, 1921; Carrol B. Howe, *Unconquered, Unconquerable: The Klamath Indian Reservation* (Bend, OR: Maverick, 1992), 77.

39 Barklow, *Gateway to the Wallowas*, 145–149; Sharp, *Where Rolls the Oregon*, 48, 57, 61–65; Ben Schley, "A Century of Fish Conservation (1871–1971)," www.nctc.fws.gov/history/articles/fisherieshistory; *Burns Times-Herald*, July 29, 1912 (1st quote); Klamath Falls *Klamath Republican*, May 27, 1909; Klamath Falls *Evening Herald*, June 1, September 14, and December 28, 1909; April 21, 1913; May 9, 1918; Kittredge, *Who Owns the West*, 24 (2nd quote); William Kittredge, *Owning It All* (St. Paul, MN: Graywolf Press, 1987), 59–60. Stocking trout in the high Cascades, packed in by horse, also began in 1913. Most of these lakes were previously devoid of fish.

40 Klamath Falls *Evening Herald*, February 16, March 7, and April 15, 1918; January 3, 1919; February 16 and August 6, 1921; March 27 and 28, and December 27, 1929; Wise, "A Brief History," 1, 5–6, 10; Oregon Department of Fish and Wildlife, "Hatcheries," www.state.or.us/fish/hatcheries. A hatchery on Fall River, south of Bend, was also built in 1929.

41 Minckley and Deacon, *Battle against Extinction*, 148–153; Langston, *Where Land and Water Meet*, 136–142; William E. Hosford and Steven P. Pribyl, *Silvies River Fisheries Evaluation*, Information Report 91-2 (Salem: Oregon Department of Fish and Wildlife, 1991), 5; Oregon Department of Fish and Wildlife, *Status and Conservation of Oregon's Interior Redband Trout* (Salem, OR: Dept. of Fish and Wildlife, 2005), 1–34; Kevin Goodson et al., *Oregon Native Fish Status Report* (Salem: Dept. of Fish and Wildlife, 2005), vol. 1: 83–97, 109–115; vol. 2: 368–412, 440–457; Patrick de Haan and Jennifer Von Bargen, *Great Basin Trout Genetic Status Assessment: Final Report* (Longview, WA: USFW Abernethy Fish Technology Center, 2015), 21–31, 34–39, 61. In the ongoing battle of lumpers vs. splitters, taxonomists are divided on whether redband trout are one or more subspecies of *Oncorhynchus mykiss* or separate species.

42 Hugh R. MacCrimmon and T. L. Marshall, "World Distribution of Brown Trout," *Journal of the Fisheries Research Board of Canada* 25 (2011): 2527–

2548; W. M. Chapman, "Alien Fishes in the Waters of the Pacific Northwest," *California Fish and Game* 28 (1942): 9–15.

43   Wallowa County and Nez Perce Tribe, *Salmon Habitat Recovery Plan with Multi-Species Habitat Strategy* (Enterprise, OR: Wallowa County Planning Dept., August 1993, revised September 1999); 1–10; Wallowa County, NRCA, co.wallowa.or.us/community_development_natural_resource_advisory_committee). See also, Sissel Waage, "(Re)Claiming the Watershed: Property Lines, Treaty Rights, and Collaborative Resource Management Planning in Rural Oregon" (PhD diss., University of California, Davis, 2000).

44   On bull trout in Central Oregon during the 1940s and 1950s, see Edwards, Anderson, and Edgington, oral history interviews, www.sisterscountryhistoricalsociety.org.

45   *Seattle Times*, July 9, 2001. For further discussion, see Holly Doremus and A. Dan Tarlock, *Water War in the Klamath Basin: Macho Law, Combat Biology, and Dirty Politics* (Washington, DC: Ocean Press, 2008); Richard A. Slaughter and John D. Weiner, "Water, Adaptation, and Property Rights on the Snake and Klamath Rivers," *Journal of the American Water Resources Association* 43 (2007): 308–321; Doug Foster, "Refuges and Reclamation: Conflicts in the Klamath Basin, 1904–1965," *OHQ* 103 (2002): 150–187; Reid D. Brown, "Giving Suckers (and Salmon) an Even Break: Klamath Basin Water and the Endangered Species Act," *Tulane Environmental Law Journal* 15 (2002): 197–223.

CHAPTER 15

1   Basques, Irish, and Indians received attention, but blacks went largely unnoticed—except in 1911, when bronc rider George Fletcher became a crowd favorite at the Pendleton Round-Up. More typically, Amos Marsh was a member of a body of black loggers in Wallowa County, but Barklow's otherwise thorough *Gateway to the Wallowas* gives no hint of his or other blacks' presence. Bales and Hill, *Pendleton Round-Up*, 73–78; Marsh, "Black Logger's Journey," 500–521.

2   McCall, *Ranch under the Rimrock*, 1–3, 21, 45–50; Walth, *Fire at Eden's Gate*, 29–46. See also, Portland *Oregonian*, March 22, 2013.

3   For context, see Bailey, *Main Street*, 92–100, 129–136.

4   Good, *History of Klamath County*, 74–75; Klamath Falls *Evening Herald*, October 19, 1908; and May 18 and 28, 1909.

5   *Bend Bulletin*, November 13, 2005; and June 20, 2014; Judy Osgood, ed., *Desert Sage Memories* (Bend, OR: RSVP, 2002), 78; Joseph *Wallowa Chieftain*, April 14 and June 7, 2016; St. John, *Oregon's Dry Side*, 131–132, 272; Stephen Dow Beckham, ed., *Statewide Inventory of Historic Sites and Buildings: Wallowa County* (Salem: Oregon State Historic Preservation Office, 1976), n.p.

6   Earl Pomeroy, *In Search of the Golden West: The Tourist in Western America* (New York: Alfred A. Knopf, 1957), 112–131, 146–147, 149; Travel Information Division, "Budget Survey," *Oregon Blue Book, 1947–48* (Salem, OR: State Printing Dept., 1947), 203–204; Beckham and Lentz, *Rocks and*

Hard Places, 193–196; John Day *Blue Mountain Eagle*, December 15, 1966 (quote); March 1, 2017; and May 30, 2018; Kittredge, *Who Owns the West*, 26–27; Klamath County Historical Society, *Klamath Country History*, 35.

7   "Bend Skyliners Lodge," Living New Deal, https:livingnewdeal.org; *Bend Bulletin*, May 25, 2012; and April 12, 2018; Beaverton (Oregon) *Beaverton Valley Times*, September 23, 2017; Jon Rombach, ed., "Gardner Locke Reminiscences, 1993," www.skifergi.com/pb/wp_2b18d . . .; Ian McCluskey, "Step Back in Time at This Small Town Ski Hill," Oregon Public Broadcasting, October 26, 2017; www.spoutspringsskiareea.com/about-2; Emilio Trampuz, "Dixie Summit, The Smallest Ski Area in Oregon," www.youtube.com/ watch?v=11nxSs1X1Y; John Lund, "History of the Crater Lake Wilderness Ski Race," *Nature Notes from Crater Lake* 28 (1997), www.craterlakeinstitute/ nature-notes/vol28.

8   Portland *Oregonian*, September 28, 1997; and May 19 and 31, 2007; *Bend Bulletin*, May 19, 2007; Edwin Battistella, "Les Schwab," *Oregon Encyclopedia*; Les Schwab, *Les Schwab: Pride in Performance, Keep It Going* (Prineville, OR: Les Schwab, 1986). See also, Jean Pierre Bardou, *The Automobile Revolution: The Impact of an Industry* (Chapel Hill: University of North Carolina Press, 1982).

9   Fred Kampo and Carolyn McCreesh, *The History of Retriever Field Trials in America: The Early Years* (Oshkosh, WI: Self-published, 2006), 3–38; Salem *Oregon Statesman*, June 28, 1959; www.city-data.com/city/Fossil-Oregon; www.theRetrieverNews.com/library/HistoricalAchievements. *The Retriever News* incorrectly calls the owner of Bracken's High Flyer George Dudek.

10 Klamath Falls *Herald and News*, November 7, 1958.

11 Bales and Hill, *Pendleton Round-Up*, 14–17, 211, 219–223, 225–230; Pendleton *East Oregonian*, May 16, 19, and 24, 1909; Joseph K. Dixon, *The Vanishing Race: The Last Great Indian Council . . .* (New York: Doubleday, 1913); Zane Grey, *The Vanishing American* (New York: Grosset and Dunlap, 1925); Hanley, *Owyhee Trails*, 149–150. Dixon's work included Umapine's account of his killing of Chief Egan during the Bannock-Paiute War (pp. 51–59).

12 Macnab, *News and People*, 317; www.tamastlikt.org/press-releases/archive; www.nixyaawii.k12.or.us.

13 Ruby, Brown, and Collins, *Guide to the Indian Tribes*, 11–12, 228; *Burns Times-Herald*, August 26, 1904; and March 24, 1906.

14 William Stone, "Fiery Priest Fought for Rights of Paiutes," Portland *Catholic Sentinel*, February 24, 2015; Stowell, "Wada-Tika," 5 (1st quote), 270–271, 274 (3rd quote), 279, 288–305, 308–309, 324–337, 367–369; William Stone, *The Cross in the Middle of Nowhere: The Catholic Church in Eastern Oregon* (Bend, OR: Maverick, 1993), 71 (2nd quote), 88–89, 116, and passim. Reportedly Hines received cutting rights to ten acres of federal timber in exchange for his "gift."

15 Stowell, "Wada-Tika," 285 (Capp quote), 292, 296–299.

16 Stowell, "Wada-Tika, 288–289, 296, 302–306 (quote, p. 305), 308, 334; *Burns Times-Herald*, April 15, 1926; June 9 and May 26, 1933.

17 Stowell, "Wada Tika," 288, 299–303; Stone, *Cross in the Middle of Nowhere*, 88–89 (quote). The bishop arranged for private mass for Father Heuel after his suspension.

18 Stone, *Cross in the Middle of Nowhere*, 114–117; *Burns Times-Herald*, June 5, 1953; and August 22, 1963; 77th Cong., 1st sess., HR 622, July 18, 1941.

19 Stowell, "Wada-Tika," 271, 369–376, 386–387; Stone, "Fiery Priest"; *Burns Times-Herald*, April 28 and May 5, 1999; and June 22 and October 5, 2016; Portland *Oregonian*, December 17, 2000; John Day *Blue Mountain Eagle*, June 22, 2016. Tribal membership fluctuated, but in 2015 stood at 346, with 151 living on the reservation. On the often-overlooked Fort McDermitt Reservation, located on the Nevada-Oregon border (with its headquarters in Nevada, but over half its land in Malheur County), the school remained segregated until 1951.

20 Chris Clements, "Federal Termination and Its Effects on the Land, Culture, and Identity of the Klamath Indian Tribe" (Honors thesis, Rutgers University, New Brunswick, NJ, 2009), 30; Allen Foreman et al., "Termination: A Brief Review of the History of the Dispossession of the Klamath, Modoc, and Yahouskin Band of Paiute Indians through the Termination," www.klamathtribes.org/background/termination, 2–9; Susan Hood, "Termination of the Klamath Indian Tribe of Oregon," *Ethnohistory* 19 (1972): 379–392; Howe, *Unconquered, Unconquerable*, 93–138. There had been earlier efforts at termination. See Otis H. Johnson, "The History of the Klamath Indian Reservation, 1864–1900" (MS thesis, University of Oregon, 1947), 139–140.

21 In accordance with common practice, the term Klamaths is used here to include members of all three constituent tribes/bands on the reservation.

22 Ulrich, *American Indian Nations*, xiv (Skelton quote), 193–202. In the tribal newsletter, Ulrich explained the purpose behind her study: "I wanted to show the effects of policy on people." Chiloquin *Klamath News*, November/December 2010, p. 10.

23 Clements, "Federal Termination and Its Effects," 41–44, 47–55 (Schonchin quote, p. 53); Foreman et al., "Termination: A Brief Review," 3, 6, 10, 12–13, 21–22 (1st quote), 23, 26, 28; Ruby, Brown, and Collins, *Guide to the Indian Tribes*, 145–147; Donald Fixico, "Termination and Restoration," *Oregon Encyclopedia*; Klamath Falls *Herald and News*, July 30, 1979. See also, Charles Crane Brown, "Identification of Selected Problems of Indians Residing in Klamath County, Oregon—An Analysis of Data Generated since Termination of the Klamath Reservation" (PhD diss., University of Oregon, 1973).

24 www.kcsd.k12.or.us; www.oregoncities.us/by. . . . For further analysis, see Patrick Mann Haynal, "From Termination through Restoration and Beyond: Modern Klamath Cultural Identity" (PhD diss., University of Oregon, 1994).

25 Barklow, *Gateway to the Wallowas*, 4, 18–19; Enterprise *Record-Chieftain*, September 30, 1926; *Seattle Times*, November 6, 1996; and June 1, 1997.

26 Ruby, Brown, and Collins, *Guide to the Indian Tribes*, 90; Thomson, *Klamath Tribes Fishery*, 6–12; www.wsfish.org; www.critfc.org; www.fws.gov/warmspringshatchery; John Day *Blue Mountain Eagle*, July 23, 2014; June 22 and October 5, 2016; and May 23, 2018. Although the lower Walla Walla runs through Washington, the stream heads up in Oregon's Blue Mountains, where the main spawning beds occur.

27 Lakeview *Lake County Examiner*, January 8, 1920; Klamath Falls *Evening Herald*, March 3, 1920; Shaver, *History of Central Oregon*, 901; Parks, *Portraits*, 170; Forrest E. Cooper, *Introducing Dr. Bernard Daly* (Lakeview, OR: Lake County Historical Society, 1986), 133–146, and passim.

28 Cooper, *Introducing Dr. Bernard Daly*, 146 (1st quote); Ken Metzler, "Can Education Save Lakeview?" *Old Oregon* 43 (August/September 1963): 8–13 (Conn quote, p. 11); Austin, "Desert, Sagebrush, and the Pacific Northwest," 140–142; Kittredge, *Owning It All*, 41. On Paul Dull, see *Oregon Quarterly* 97 (Winter 2018): 66.

29 www.eou.edu; Portland *Oregonian*, May 20, 2010; La Grande *Observer*, March 2–4, 2018; John Day *Blue Mountain Eagle*, March 14, 2018; Cox, interviews with Ronald Fahl and Archie Dunsmoor, September 30, 1974; and August 3, 1991; William G. Robbins, *The People's School: A History of Oregon State University* (Corvallis: Oregon State University Press, 2017). In time Oregon State University would establish a Cascade Campus in Bend, but it has not assumed the regional role of Eastern Oregon, nor has Oregon Technical Institute in Klamath Falls.

30 *Bend Bulletin*, March 4, 1954; Edwards, oral history interview, op cit.; Jean Nave, "Bill Edwards, A Brief Biography," *Sisters Country Personalities*, www.sisterscountryhistoricalsociety.org; Cox, interviews with Sam Hewitt, Doug Hockett, John Shaw, Kris Kristovitch, and Denny Reese, Sisters, Oregon, September 16, 2017. When Edwards left to teach in Germany in 1956, I took over the school's conservation program.

31 McVicker, *Child of Steens Mountain*, 76–77 (1st quote, p. 77), 83–85; Smyth, *Footloose and Ahorseback*, 63, 142–146; www.greatschools.org/crane/crane; www.opb/programs/oregonstory/ruralvoices/crane (2nd quote); *Burns Times-Herald*, April 29, 1963; and January 20, 1999; John Day *Blue Mountain Eagle*, September 14, 2016.

32 For discussions, see John Day *Blue Mountain Eagle*, January 28, 2015; and April 5, 2017; Martin and Weber, "A Tale of Two Oregons," 37–39.

33 John Day *Blue Mountain Eagle*, September 14 and 28, 2016; www.usnews.com/education/best-high-schools/national-rankings; Klamath County Historical Society, *Klamath Country History*, 90; www.kcsd.k12.or.us; www.oregoncities.us/bly. . . .

34 Letter to the editor, *Old Oregon* 43 (October/November 1963): 30–31.

35 John Day *Blue Mountain Eagle*, August 10, 2016. See also John Day *Blue Mountain Eagle*, March 7 and 14, 2018.

CHAPTER 16

1 Tom McCall with Steve Neal, *Tom McCall, Maverick: An Autobiography* (Portland: Binford and Mort, 1977), 1–5, 64; Walth, *Fire at Eden's Gate*, 41–46, 155–156, 338–340, 469.

2 For a useful summary, see Marsh, *To the Promised Land*, 278–283.

3 Winch, "Tumalo Irrigation District," *Oregon Encyclopedia*; John Hodecker to the author, July 15, 1991; Crowell to author, July 12, 2013 (Cox, personal corres.); Cox, interview with Hodecker, Redmond, Oregon, September 16, 2017 (quote); Martin and Weber, "Tale of Two Oregons," 26; Waterston, *Where the Crooked River Rises*, 73.

4 On Sawyer, see Cox, *Park Builders*, 47–56; William L. Lang, "Robert W. Sawyer (1880–1959)," *Oregon Encyclopedia*. The Sawyer papers are in the University of Oregon's Knight Library.

5 Walth, *Fire at Eden's Gate*, 2–9, 440–441, 446–447, 450–451.

6 Hal K. Rothman, *Devil's Bargains: Tourism in the Twentieth-Century American West* (Lawrence: University Press of Kansas, 1998), 10–28 (1st and 2nd quotes, p. 11), 369–370 (3rd quote). See also Kittredge, *Who Owns the West*, 133–141.

7 Ramsey, *New Era*, 2–3.

8 Kittredge, *Who Owns the West* (quote, p. 159).

9 Kittredge, *Hole in the Sky*, 228 (quote, p. 230); Carl Abbott, "From Urban Frontier to Metropolitan Region: Oregon's Cities from 1870 to 2009," in Hibbard et al., *Toward One Oregon*, 56. See also, Beverly A. Brown, *In Timber Country: Working People's Stories of Environmental Conflict and Urban Flight* (Philadelphia, PA: Temple University Press, 1995).

10 Rothman, *Devil's Bargains*, 26–27, 369–370; Waterston, *Where the Crooked River Rises*, 72–80; Robbins, "Town and Country in Oregon," 74, 75–76 (quotes); Cox, interview with Sam Hewitt, Sisters, Oregon, September 15, 2017. Waterson's "What One Thing?" was originally published in *Oregon Quarterly* 86 (2006).

11 Melanie Tupper, "One Man's Dream for Christmas Valley," www. ChristmasValley.net; Parks, *Portraits*, 199–200; Portland *Oregon Journal*, July 11, 1967; Portland *Willamette Week*, September 19, 1979; Walth, *Fire at Eden's Gate* (quote, p. 244).

12 Brown, *In Timber Country*, 45–46, 51–52, 55–56, 86 (1st quote), 101, 109 (2nd quote), and passim; Walth, *Fire at Eden's Gate*, 366–367 (3rd quote); Cox, discussions with David Welch, Margaret Sommers, and Anne Welch, Redmond, Oregon, August 4 and 5, 2001.

13 Langston, *Where Land and Water Meet*, 148–150, 164–165; Abbott, "From Urban Frontier," 55–56.

14 Their experiences are traced in Kirkpatrick, *Homestead*, and other works.

15 McCarthy, *History of Oregon Sheriffs*, 225–227; Carl Abbott, "Utopia and Bureaucracy: The Fall of Rajneeshpuram, Oregon," *PHR* 59 (1990): 77–103; Hugh B. Urban, "Zorba the Buddha: Capitalism, Charisma and the Cult of Bhagwan Shree Rajneesh," *Religion* 26 (1996): 161–182. See also, accounts by

Les Zaitz in the Portland *Oregonian*, the first starting in July 1985; a second on April 14, 2001; and a third on April 15, 2011.

16 As a leading chainsaw manufacturer, Omark had long been tied to the lumber industry; through it and family fishing and camping trips, Gray had come to know Central Oregon intimately.

17 Architectural Foundation of Oregon, 2008 Honored Citizen, af_oregon.org/pd2008_Sponsor_AFO_HC.pdf (quote); www.oregonproducts.com/pro/company/history; *Bend Bulletin*, March 16, 1966; August 2, 1968; and March 12, 1969; Eugene *Register-Guard*, July 7, 1985; Portland *Daily Journal of Commerce*, October 17, 2008; James W. Quinn and Paul Redding, *Sunriver: The First Twenty Years* (Medford, OR: Commercial Printing, 1990); Osgood, *Desert Sage Memories*, 76–77, 123–125. To keep the development from growing overly large, Sunriver was eventually reduced from 5,500 to 3,300 acres through sale of land to the Forest Service.

18 "Mike Hollern" (quote); "Carole Campbell Crail," *Sisters Country Personalities*, Sisters Country Historical Society, www.sisterscountryhistoricalsociety.org.

19 Black Butte Ranch, www.blackbutteranch.com/about-us/history; "Ed Denniston," *Sisters Country Personalities*, www.sisterscountryhistoricalsociety.org; Sisters *Nugget*, April 28 and May 3, 2015.

20 *Bend Bulletin*, May 15, 2012; Andy Kiersz, "The Middle Class Is Vanishing in America's Cities," *Business Insider*, May 14, 2016.

21 Publications of the Eastern Oregon Visitors Association, especially its annual visitors' guides, are good indicators of the scope of developments.

22 Mead, *History of Union County*, 24–26.

23 On the barn, see, Kittredge, *Owning It All*, 43–45; Oregon State Parks, *Southeastern Oregon Historical Sites* (Salem: State Parks Department, 2004), 4.

24 Beckham and Lentz, *Rocks and Hard Places*, 200–201.

25 Fussner, *Glimpses of Wheeler County's Past*; Kenny Moore, *Bill Bowerman and the Men of Oregon* (Emmaus, PA: Rodale, 2006), 17–25, 415; Portland *Willamette Week*, September 7, 2016; Jim McGraw, "Remembering Larry McGraw," *Pomona* 38 (Summer 2005): 22–28.

26 Kitzhaber's environmental record has been less noted than those of McCall and Straub, but one authority considers him "Oregon's foremost environmentalist" between 1987 and 2002. Marsh, *To the Promised Land* (quote, p. 465), 475.

27 Kittredge, *Who Owns the West*, 34. Lake Abert dried up to the point that its salinity was so high it could no longer support even brine shrimp and talk of making it a bird refuge ceased. By 2019, the lake had refilled; it is still classified by the BLM as an Area of Critical Environmental Concern.

28 Langston, *Where Land and Water Meet*, 143–146, 149 (Marlett quote); William G. Robbins, conversation with the author, Tulsa, Oklahoma, October 15, 1993.

29 Oregon Natural Desert Association, *2011 Annual Report* (Bend, OR: ONDA, 2011): vol. 2; Waterston, *Where the Crooked River Rises*, 98. No data on the

membership of the ONDA is available, but the board was made up of urbanites from Bend, Portland, and out of state. It seems likely those from Bend were, like Marlett, recent transplants.

30   Becky Hatfield-Hyde, "Roaring Springs," *Range Magazine* 7 (Summer 1999): 42–43, 45 (Marlett quote, p. 43).

31   Kittredge, *Who Owns the West,* 17–19 (1st and 2nd quotes); Smyth, *Sunshine, Shadows and Sagebrush,* 78; Gerald (Skip) A. Miller, "45 Years of the Wild Horse and Burro Act of 1971," 4–6 (3rd quote, p. 5), 8–9, www.hors-sens. com/mustang/45_years_of_whb_act_of_1971.html.

32   J. Edward de Steiguer, *Wild Horses of the West: History and Politics of America's Mustangs* (Tucson: University of Arizona Press, 2011), 151–207.

33   Dan Flores, review of de Steiguer's *Wild Horses of the West,* in *Southwestern Historical Quarterly* 115 (2012): 418 (quote).

34   Altogether eighteen herd management areas would be established in Oregon, all of them east of the Cascades. See PBS, *Oregon Field Guide* Episode #2508: "Mustangs of Oregon," February 6, 2014.

35   Bureau of Land Management, press release, June 30, 2017, blm.gov/press-release/blm-introduces-new-partnership-approach.

36   Laura Leigh, statement, August 1, 2017, *Wild Horse Education* (1st quote); Portland *Oregonian,* November 2, 2015; *Bend Bulletin,* November 3, 2015 (2nd quote).

37   Todd Forbes, telephone interview, August 4, 2017 (notes in Cox personal files).

38   Forbes, interview; Bureau of Land Management, "Beatys Butte Wild Horse Gather, Fertility Control, and Training Facility," blm.gov/programs/ wildhorse-and burros/partnerships/beatys butte-wild-horse-partnership.

39   Randy Parks to the author, August 1, 2017; Jimmy Hall to the author, August 2, 2017 (Cox, personal corres.); Forbes, interview. Former mustanger Skip Miller, one of the observers, was impressed with how the gather was handled. Miller, "45 Years," 11–12.

40   The term "shill" is Jack Shepherd's. See Jack Shepherd, *The Forest Killers: The Destruction of the American Wilderness* (New York: Weybright and Talley, 1975), 31–110. See also Hirt, *Conspiracy of Optimism.*

41   Harold K. Steen, *Jack Ward Thomas: The Journals of a Forest Service Chief* (Seattle: University of Washington Press, 2004); Thomas, *Wildlife Habitats,* 10–21, and passim; Arran Robertson, "The Instability of Stability: Remembering Jack Ward Thomas," *Oregon Wild,* June 2, 2016 (quote).

42   John Day *Blue Mountain Eagle,* March 30, 1995; and June 26 (quotes), September 11, and October 23, 2002; Grant County General Election Ballot, November 5, 2002; Kathy McKinnon, Grant County Clerk, "Measure Detail Report," November 8, 2002 (copy in Cox, personal corres.). For the larger context, see Samuel P. Hays, *Wars in the Woods: The Rise of Ecological Forestry in America* (Pittsburgh, PA: University of Pittsburgh Press, 2006).

43   Tony Davis, "Cows, Ballot Measure Gunned Down in Oregon," *High Country News,* November 25, 1996; Tony Gheno, "Cattle Grazing," *High Country*

News, November 10, 2008; Jeff Barnard, "Oregon Man Takes Aim at Cattle Along with Open-Range Law," *Los Angeles Times*, October 26, 1997.

44 *State v. Hinton*, Court of Appeals, 209OrApp 210, 147 p3d 345 (2006); ONDA, "South Fork of the Crooked River," www.onda.org/where-we-work/central-oregon/whychus-deschutes-wilderness; *Burns Times-Herald*, April 9, 2014; Ron Aeschbacher, conversation with the author, Medford, Oregon, March 15, 1998.

45 John Day *Blue Mountain Eagle*, June 26, 2002; Walth, *Fire at Eden's Gate*, 450; Kittredge, *Who Owns the West*, 159–162. See also, Kittredge, *Owning It All*, 15–18, 68–70.

CHAPTER 17

1 Zalunardo, conversation with the author (first quote); Paula Elmes, conversation with the author, Salt Lake City, Utah, May 13, 2016; www.ktvz.com/news/crooked-river-roundup, May 19, 2016 (2nd quote); Waterston, *Where the Crooked River Rises*, 29–30, 34–35, 127–128 (3rd quote, p. 128).

2 www.fs.fed.us//HiRes/Ch3/Case_Studies/Grande_Ronde_River.

3 Nils D. Christoffersen, *Wallowa River McDaniel Habitat Restoration Project* (Enterprise, OR: Wallowa Resources, 2006); Enterprise *Wallowa County Chieftain*, June 30, 2015; La Grande *Observer*, April 17, 2015; www.wallowaresources.org/index.php/what-we-do/stewardship-work/who-we-are/our-story.

4 On Jackson Hole, Wyoming, see Rothman, *Devil's Bargains*, 279–286, and passim.

5 John Springer, letter to the editor, Portland *Oregonian*, March 18, 2011.

6 www.bluemountainconservancy.org/index; www.wallowalandtrust.org/index.php/about-us/mission-and-programs; La Grande *Observer*, February 28, 2001; Portland *Oregonian*, March 17 and 21, 2011. A second easement later expanded the Wolfe Ranch project to five hundred acres. On the LCDC, see Walth, *Fire at Eden's Gate*, 242–249, 355–361, 414–416, 451–463; Marsh, *To the Promised Land*, 296, 313–314, 329.

7 John Day *Blue Mountain Eagle*, August 24 and September 14, 2016; Enterprise *Wallowa County Chieftain*, August 25, 2016. The National Conservation Easement Database reports annual acreage.

8 Cox, *Park Builders*, 92.

9 The Metolian, Facebook page (quote); Portland *Oregonian*, April 7, 2009; Salem *Statesman-Journal*, June 18, 2009; www.friends.org/trail/metolius; "Metolius Preserve," deschuteslandtrust.org.

10 *Bend Bulletin* May 27, 2008; and February 25, March 16 and 28, and April 2 and 3, 2009; Portland *Oregonian*, June 20, 2008; and March 16 and 25, April 2, 3 and 7, and December 1, 2009; Sisters *Nugget*, February 25, March 10, and April 3, 2009; Portland *Oregon Business Journal*, July 24, 2010 (quote). 1000 Friends of Oregon (www.friends.org/news) covered developments. This was a new issue in the region. When I served on the Sisters City Council in the 1950s, such things never intruded into discussions.

11   Portland *Oregon Business Journal*, July 24, 2010; and November 2, 2012; *Bend Bulletin*, January 26, 2014; John Day *Blue Mountain Eagle*, December 6, 2017. Of the state's eighteen destination resorts in 2010, eight were in Deschutes County and four in neighboring Crook. Jefferson County, which encompassed the Metolius Basin, had none.

12   For descriptions of Colorado's problems, see Bill Obermann et al., *Tracking Agricultural Land Conversion in Colorado* (Denver: Colorado Department of Agriculture, 2000); Chris Frasier, "Too Many Homes on the Range," *Alternet*, December 16, 2005; Hal Walter, "Too Many Homes on the Range," *High Country News*, March 9, 2010.

13   Carrie MacLaren et al., *Too Many Homes on the Range: The Impact of Rural Sprawl on Ranching and Habitat* (Portland: 1000 Friends of Oregon, 2004 [?]), 1–2 (1st quotes), 11–13, 15 (2nd quote).

14   Ben Gordon et al., *The New Face of Farming: Shaping Policies That Support Today's Agricultural Practices* (Portland: 1000 Friends of Oregon, 2012), 3 (quote). See also, Beverly Wolverton, *A Hundred and Sixty Acres in the Sage: Homestead History of the Immediate Post Area* (Post, OR: Self-published, 1984).

15   Gary J. Lettman et al., *Forests, Farms and People: Land Use Change on Non-Federal Land in Oregon, 1974–2009* (Salem: Oregon Department of Forestry, 2011); Lettman et al., *Land Use Change on Non-Federal Land in Oregon and Washington* (Salem: Oregon Department of Forestry, 2013). See also, Portland *Daily Journal of Commerce*, October 7, 2008.

16   MacLaren et al., *Too Many Homes on the Range*, 8–9.

17   Becky Hatfield-Hyde, "Welcome to the New Millennium in the Klamath Basin: Water, Whiskey, Murder, and Hope," *Terrain.org: A Journal of the Built and Natural Environments* 10 (2001), www.terrain.org; Portland *Oregonian*, April 5, 2005; *New York Times*, July 30, 2011; Eugene *Register-Guard*, December 31, 2012; Klamath Falls *Herald and News*, June 26 and July 12, 2013; *Los Angeles Times*, December 11, 2015; *High Country News*, February 8, 2016; Thadeus Greenson, "Uncharted Waters," *North Coast Journal* 27, no. 2 (January 14, 2016): 12–17; Yreka (California) *Siskiyou Daily News*, December 29, 2016. More modest efforts at dam removal occurred on Whychus Creek (formerly Squaw Creek) near Sisters and the Umatilla River. As on the Klamath, these aimed to restore fish runs and healthy ecosystems. With less at stake, they met limited opposition and, when implemented, soon showed positive results.

18   *Burns Times-Herald*, April 1 (4th quote), 15, 22 (1st quote), and May 6 (2nd quote), 1992; *High Country News*, November 22, 1999 (3rd quote).

19   Langston, *Where Land and Water Meet*, 144–146.

20   Doc Hatfield and Connie Hatfield, "The Trout Creek Mountain Project, Oregon," *Natural Resources and Environmental Issues* 5 (1995): 53–58; Tom Knudson, "The Ranch Restored: An Overworked Land Comes Back to Life," *High Country News*, March 1, 1999; "About the Trout Creek Mountain Working Group," *The Aurora Project* (Prineville, OR: Bureau of Land

Management, 2000); Dan Wheat, "Healing Rangeland Leaves Grazing Scars," Salem *Capital Press*, June 28, 2012.

21   Steven Steubner, "'Multiple Use Is Still the Best Concept,'" *High Country News*, November 22, 1999 (Davies quote); Hatfield-Hyde, "Roaring Springs" (Marlett quote).

22   Langston, *Where Land and Water Meet*, 146–148 (quote, p. 148), 164–165; Alice Elshoff, "Bringing Back Our Native Desert Fish," *Desert Ramblings*, newsletter of ONDA 11 (Summer 1998); *Seattle Times*, December 14, 1997. On Davies, see Peter Walker, *Sagebrush Collaboration: How Harney County Defeated the Takeover of the Malheur Wildlife Refuge* (Corvallis: Oregon State University Press, 2018), 105–107.

23   *Seattle Times*, December 14, 1997; Portland *Oregonian*, July 27, 2008 (quotes); US Fish and Wildlife Service, "Candidate Conservation around the Nation," 5–6, www.nctcfws.gov/Pubs9/esa_candconserve.pdf; Environmental Stewardship, "2007 Environmental Stewardship Award Winner, Region V: Roaring Springs Ranch, Frenchglen, Oregon," www.environmentalstwardship. org/regionv-roaring springsranch.aspx.

24   *High Country News*, May 12 and November 22, 1999.

25   Steubner, "Multiple Use"; Marlett, "Clinton Signs Steens Protection Act!" *Desert Ramblings* 13 (Fall 2000), 1, 4–5 (quote, p. 5); Langston, *Where Land and Water Meet*, 148–150, 164–165. For his part, Marlett was thrilled with the idea of national monument status for the Steens—so long as ranchers were bought out to end grazing thereon.

26   Public Law 106-399-Oct. 30, 2000 (114 Stat. 1655). For ONDA's claims, see http://onda.org/where-we-work/steens#sthash.com.; Walker, *Sagebrush Collaboration*, 114–116.

27   ONDA, *2011 Annual Report*, 3, 6; Brent Fenty to Jerry Perez and Robyn Thorson, November 8, 2013, attachment in onda.org/where-we-work/ oregon-desert-trail; *Burns Times-Herald*, April 9, 2014 (quotes); and December 30, 2015.

28   John Day *Blue Mountain Eagle*, February 24, 2016 (Walden quotes); Enterprise *Wallowa County Chieftain*, October 25, 2016; Greg Walden, speech in US House of Representatives, January 5, 2016, opb.org/news/ series/burns-oregon-standoff-bundy-militia-news-updates. . . . For a reaction to Walden's speech, see La Grande *Observer*, January 20, 2016.

29   Portland *Oregonian*, July 27, 2008; John Day *Blue Mountain Eagle*, June 28, 2017; Waterston, *Where the Crooked River Rises*, 99, 101–103; Langston, *Where Land and Water Meet*, 154–160.

30   Driscoll, *Gilchrist*, 158–161; *Bend Bulletin*, December 27, 2015; Crowell to Cox, December 12, 2013 (Cox personal corres.). The company town and sawmill were not included in the sale.

31   www.conservationfund.org/projects/gilchrist-state-forest.

32   www.conservationfund.org/projects/gilchrist-state-forest (quote); *Bend Bulletin*, October 12 and December 10, 2009; March 6 and June 3, 2014; and November 21, 2015.

33 For discussions, see Robbins, *Landscapes of Conflict*, 178–212; Cox, *Lumberman's Frontier*, 363–375.

34 Klamath Falls *Herald and News*, January 3, 2005; *Bend Bulletin*, November 21 (quote) and December 27 and 30, 2015; and March 9, 2016; Idaho Falls *Post-Register*, April 14, 2016. Perhaps overoptimistically, Gilchrist Forest was projected to generate a $14 million annual increase in tourism and recreation dollars.

35 Oregon Board of Forestry, *Achieving Oregon's Vision for Federal Forests* (Salem, OR: Dept. of Forestry, 2009), 5, 51; *Scientific American*, June 9, 2013; Oregon Forest Resources Institute, *Federal Forestlands in Oregon*, 10; Northwest Interagency Coordination Center, *Northwest Annual Fire Report, 2012* (www.nwccweb.us), 5, 9, 12; National Drought Mitigation Center, *Oregon, 2012*, www.droughtmonitor.unl.edu; Oregon, Fire Protection Division, *Fire Season Report for 2015* (Salem: Oregon Department of Forestry, 2016); Skovlin, *Fifty Years of Research*, 38–39; Portland *Oregonian*, October 12, 2012; and August 19, 2015; *USA Today*, July 17, 2014; John Day *Blue Mountain Eagle*, August 17, 2016. In Grant County, the Waterman fire complex burned 12,250 acres in 2014, and the Canyon Creek complex the following year burned 110,442 acres and destroyed forty-three homes.

36 Portland *Oregonian*, September 14, 2012; and November 12, 2016; John Day *Blue Mountain Eagle*, January 28, 2015; March 2, 2016; and December 6, 2017; *Baker City Herald*, December 18, 2009; Oregon Forest Resources Institute, *Federal Forestland in Oregon* (Portland: OFRI, 2010), 4, 11; Oregon Board of Forestry, *Oregon's Vision for Federal Forestlands*, 21, 50.

37 John Day *Blue Mountain Eagle*, March 30, 1995; and March 2, 2016 (2nd quote); Jack Ward Thomas, "Thoughts on Ownership of America's Public Land," speech to Outdoor Writers Association of America, Chattanooga, Tennessee, June 26, 1995 (1st quote); Harold K. Steen, "An Interview with Jack Ward Thomas," Forest History Society, Durham, NC, 2002; Arran Robertson, "The Instability of Stability: Remembering Jack Ward Thomas," *Oregon Wild*, June 2, 2016.

38 John Day *Blue Mountain Eagle*, March 2, 2016 (1st quote); *Baker City Herald*, November 23 (3rd quote) and December 18, 2009 (2nd quote).

39 Oregon Solutions, "Solving Community Problems in a New Way," www.orsolutions.org; La Grande *Observer*, June 6 and 8, 2012. For another view, see Michael Hibbard, "Issues and Options for the Other Oregon," *Community Development Journal* 24 (1989): 145–153.

40 Oregon Board of Forestry, *Oregon's Vision for Federal Forestlands*, ii–iii (1st quote), 3 (2nd quote), 14, 17. See also, *Baker City Herald*, November 23, 2009.

41 *Baker City Herald*, December 21, 2009 (quote).

42 Blue Mountain Forest Partners website, www.bluemountainforestpartners.org/about, 2015; "Malheur National Forest: Blue Mountain Forest Partners (OR)," www.westernlaw.org/our-work/wildlands/forests; "Blue Mountain Forest Partners," www.sustainablenorthwest.org/what-we-do/success-stories/blue-mountain-forest-partners; Susan Jane Brown and Mark Webb,

"Restoring Forest Health: Collaboration as Responsibility," *Oregon State Bar Newsletter* (Winter 2012); John Day *Blue Mountain Eagle*, September 5, 2012; June 19, 2013; March 26, 2014; April 13 and December 27, 2016; Portland *Oregonian*, September 14, 2012.

43 John Day *Blue Mountain Eagle*, August 22, 2012 (quote).

44 Portland *Oregonian*, June 15, 2009; August 29 and September 14, 2012; John Day *Blue Mountain Eagle*, August 22 (quote), September 5, and December 5, 2012.

45 Press release, Senator Jeff Merkley, September 11, 2012, www.merkley.senate. gov/news/press-releases/wyden-merkley-announce; John Day *Blue Mountain Eagle*, September 12, 2012 (1st quote); January 6 and 25, September 9, and November 20, 2013 (2nd quote); May 4, 2016.

46 John Day *Blue Mountain Eagle*, September 12 and December 5, 2012 (1st quotes); March 26, 2014 (2nd quote); February 18 and March 4, 2015 (3rd quote); May 25, 2016; June 6, 2018; Portland *Oregonian*, September 14, 2012.

47 Blue Mountain Forest Partners website; "Blue Mountain Forest Partners," Sustainable Northwest website; Brown and Webb, "Restoring Forest Health," *Oregon State Bar Newsletter* (Winter 2012).

48 These included the Harney County Restoration Collaborative, Lakeview Stewardship Group, Umatilla Forest Collaborative Group, and Wallowa County Resources. Oregon Forest Resources Institute, *Federal Forest Lands in Oregon*, 19. See also, Walker, *Sagebrush Collaboration*, 111–121.

49 In addition to Hatfield's operation, members of the co-op were from Prineville, Fossil, The Dalles, Crane, Plush, Drewsey, Vale, Antelope, Baker, Unity, and Seneca. In time they added a feedlot—Beef Northwest Feeders—in Boardman. It was thus very much a child of Eastern Oregon even though it eventually spread beyond the state and became Country Natural Beef.

50 Joe Roybal, "The Naturals," *Beef Magazine*, November 1, 2009 (quote), www. beefmagazine.com/beef-quality/1101-hatfield-beef-trailblazers.

51 Roybal, "The Naturals" (quotes); *Capital Press*, March 22, 2012; Doc Hatfield and Connie Hatfield, "Country Natural Beef . . . 'an Idea to Be Constantly Examined,'" Range Beef Cow Symposium, Fort Collins, Colorado, December 11, 2007 (University of Nebraska, Lincoln, digital commons).

52 Ed Marston, "A Final Hats Off to Rancher Doc Hatfield," *High Country News*, April 27, 2012 (quote). For an illustration of Hatfield's concern for the land, see Patton, "Cutting Down Junipers to Save Desert Water," Oregon Public Broadcasting, October 27, 2010. Hatfield was a founding member of the Oregon Watershed Improvement Coalition and later a member of Oregon's Watershed Enhancement Board.

53 Oregon Public Broadcasting, Hatfield obituary, March 21, 2012 (1st quote); Marston, "Hats Off to Doc Hatfield," *High Country News*, April 27, 2012 (2nd quote).

54 Rik Dalvit, "Doc Hatfield: A Man of Passion, Vision," Salem *Capital Press*, March 28, 2012 (quotes); *Bend Bulletin*, March 22, 2012; *High Country News*, April 27, 2012. His health failing, in 2009 Hatfield passed leadership of the co-op to Roaring Springs Ranch's Stacy Davies, who had ideas similar to the

Hatfields—indeed, he had worked for Hatfield before being hired to manage Roaring Springs—but he had not been an original member of ONB.

55 John Day *Blue Mountain Eagle*, September 28, 2016 (quote); Peter Donovan, "A Conversation with Jack Southworth, 1995," www.managingwholes.com/ Southworth.html.

CHAPTER 18

1 *Burns Times-Herald*, November 2, 1988. Cubic feet per second, cfs, is the standard measure of water rights.

2 *Burns Times-Herald*, August 10 and 17, 1994 (1st quote); Portland *Oregonian*, January 5, 1996; *San Francisco Chronicle*, January 9, 2016; Zoe Carpenter, "Inside the Bundy Brothers' Armed Occupation," *The Nation*, January 5, 2016 (2nd quote); Jerry Miller, "Looking Back: The Hammonds and Bundys," *Range Magazine* 24 (Spring 2017): 20; Paul Larmer, "Modern Sagebrush Rebels Recycle Old Western Fantasies," *High Country News*, January 25, 2016; Walker, *Sagebrush Collaboration*, 18–25. The Harney County Library in Burns maintains a sizeable folder of materials on Hammond in its Claire McGill Western History Room.

3 *Burns Times-Herald*, August 10 and 17 (1st quote), 1994; March 24 and June 7, 1995; Kathie Durban, "Ranchers Arrested at Wildlife Refuge," *High Country News*, October 3, 1994 (2nd quote).

4 US Dept. of Justice, US Attorney's Office, District of Oregon, news release, October 7, 2015; *Burns Times-Herald*, June 27 and November 7, 2012; October 14 and December 30, 2015; Portland *Oregonian*, January 5 and 7, 2015; Salem *Capital Press*, June 26, 2010; and October 22, 2015; *Bend Bulletin*, January 6, 2016; Joseph Ditzler, "Harney County Ranchers Stand Trial in Pendleton Federal Court," Oregon Public Broadcasting, June 13, 2012; Hank Vogler, "Enemies of the State: A Good Family Burned by the Feds," *Range Magazine* 20 (Spring 2013): 36–38. For a timeline of events, see Portland *Oregonian*, February 5, 2016.

5 *Burns Times-Herald*, November 2, 1988; and August 9 and 19, 1994; Salem *Capital Press*, August 11, 1994 (quote); *High Country News*, October 3, 1994.

6 *High Country News*, October 3, 1994; *Burns Times-Herald*, June 27, 2008; Nampa *Idaho Press-Tribune*, January 1, 2016; Klamath Falls *Klamath Voice*, January 4, 2016; Portland *Oregonian*, January 5, 2016; Associated Press, January 7, 2016 (Oregon Farm Bureau quote); Vale *Malheur Enterprise*, July 26, 2016 (Walden quote).

7 Portland *Oregonian*, January 2 (quote) and 5, March 8, and December 30, 2016. See also Sarah Childress, "The Battle over Bunkerville: The Bundys, the Federal Government, and the New Militia Movement," *Frontline*, May 16, 2017; Stephanie L. Witt and Brian Laurent, "Go Away Closer: A Collision of Culture and Governance," in Judd and Witt, *Cities, Sagebrush, and Solitude*, 69.

8 Portland *Oregonian*, February 5, 2016 (quote). The adjacent Malheur Field Station, owned by the Great Basin Society, closed in the face of approaching militiamen, but since the field station failed to fit the view of a federal versus private confrontation, it failed to gain a place in news coverage; it was

abandoned, but never occupied by the militia (although there are reports it was used for target practice). It did, however, eventually serve as a base for federal investigation teams. Portland *Oregonian*, January 22, 2016; interview, Karen Nitz, Burns, Oregon, April 25, 2017.

9   Carpenter, "Inside the Bundy Brothers' Armed Occupation." Of those in Bundy's group, apparently only one was from Oregon, and he from Irrigon, miles to the north near the Columbia River. However, see Christopher A. Simon, "The Oregon County Supremacy Movement and Public Lands in Oregon," in Brent S. Steel, ed., *Public Lands Management in the West: Citizens, Interest Groups, and Values* (Westport, CT: Praeger, 1997), 111–128; Keith Nantz, "I'm an Oregon Rancher: Here's What You Don't Understand about the Bundy Standoff," *Washington Post*, January 10, 2016; and Portland *Oregonian*, February 17, 2016.

10 James Pogue, *Chosen Country: A Rebellion in the West* (New York: Holt, 2018), 129 (1st quote); La Grande *Observer*, January 20, 2016 (2nd quote).

11 Salt Lake City *Deseret News*, January 4, 2016 (2nd quote); *Religion News Service*, January 7, 2016; *World Religion News*, January 8, 2016; Pocatello *Idaho State Journal*, January 26, 2016 (1st quote); July 22, 2018; *Salt Lake City Tribune*, January 31, 2016; Portland *Oregonian*, January 6 (4th and 5th quotes), January 20, 2016 (3rd quote). James Pogue and Peter Walker saw the connection, but their analyses appeared only later: Pogue, *Chosen Country*, 60–66, 168–175; Walker, *Sagebrush Collaboration*, 50–52. See also, James Aho, *Far Right Fantasy: A Sociology of American Religion and Politics* (New York: Routledge, 2016).

12 *Burns Times-Herald*, January 13, 2016; *USA Today*, January 29, 2016.

13 Portland *Oregonian*, January 11 and 20, 2016; *Burns Times-Herald*, February 3 and 10, 2016.

14 *Christian Science Monitor*, January 6, 2016; *Washington Post*, January 7, 2016 (quotes); Pendleton *East Oregonian*, May 27, 2016; Walker, *Sagebrush Collaboration*, 35–36.

15 Carpenter, "Inside the Bundy Brothers' Armed Occupation," *The Nation*, January 5, 2016 (quote); *Burns Times-Herald*, February 10 and 17, and May 18, 2016; Portland *Oregonian*, June 28, 2016.

16 Samantha Swindler, "A Rural Paper's Decision on the Voice of Harney County," www.oregonlive.com/oregon-standoff/2016/04 (quote); Walker, *Sagebrush Collaboration*, 33–35.

17 Portland *Oregonian*, January 20, 2016; *Los Angeles Times*, February 12, 2016 (1st quote); John Day *Blue Mountain Eagle*, January 28 and February 16, 2016 (2nd quote).

18 *Burns Times-Herald*, January 28 and February 17, 2016; Portland *Oregonian*, January 21 and March 8 and 23, 2016; Pocatello *Idaho State Journal*, January 26 and 29, 2016; John Day *Blue Mountain Eagle*, January 28 and February 16, 2016; *Salt Lake Tribune*, March 11 and July 4, 2016.

19 *Burns Times-Herald*, May 18, 2016; Pendleton *East Oregonian*, May 27, 2016 (1st quote); Portland *Oregonian*, January 6 and June 28, 2016; Spokane

Spokesman-Review, July 5, 2016; *Guardian*, January 9, 2016 (2nd quote); *High Country News*, February 6, 2017. After several terms, Grasty had already announced he would not run for reelection. The recall effort was thus largely symbolic.

20   *Burns Times-Herald*, May 25, 2016; Portland *Oregonian*, June 28, 2016 (quote); *Bend Bulletin*, July 7, 2016; Spokane *Spokesman-Review*, July 7, 2016.

21   Bill Morlin, "'Constitutional Sheriff' Richard Mark Hoping to Capitalize on Oregon Standoff," Southern Poverty Law Center website, February 16, 2016 (quote); Portland *Oregonian*, June 28, 2016; *Burns Times-Herald*, April 6, 2016; William G. Robbins, "The Malheur Occupation and the Problem with History," *OHQ*, 117 (2016): 596–597; Walker, *Sagebrush Collaboration*, 50–52, 55–56, 153, 156. The Hammonds received a sort of vindication too. On July 10, 2018, President Donald Trump issued them a pardon, and they were freed from prison. *New York Times*, July 10, 2018; *Burns Times-Herald*, July 11, 2018.

22   John Day *Blue Mountain Eagle*, March 30, 1995.

23   John Day *Blue Mountain Eagle*, June 26, September 11, and October 23, 2002; Grant County, General Election Ballot, November 5, 2002; Kathy McKinnon, Grant County Clerk, "Measure Detail Report," November 8, 2002 (copies in Cox, personal correspondence).

24   John Day *Blue Mountain Eagle*, March 26, April 16, July 29, August 1 (2nd quote), and September 3, 2014; January 16, 2015; April 13, 2016 (1st quote); Pendleton *East Oregonian*, March 25, 2014; Enterprise *Wallowa County Chieftain*, June 18, 2014; and January 19, April 5, and October 25, 2016. The plan encompassed the Malheur, Wallowa-Whitman, and Umatilla national forests and part of the Ochoco, in all some 4.9 million acres.

25   John Day *Blue Mountain Eagle*, August 1, 2014; January 28, February 18, and March 4, 2015 (3rd quote); April 6 (2nd quote) and 13, 2016 (1st quote); May 3, 2017.

26   John Day *Blue Mountain Eagle*, July 14, 2015; April 13 and 27, 2016; February 22 and May 24, 2017; August 15 and 22, 2018.

27   Portland *Oregonian*, February 9, 2016 (1st quote); Pendleton *East Oregonian*, October 9 (2nd quote) and 14, 2015. The Constitutional Sheriffs organization insisted county sheriffs were the highest law enforcement authorities, superseding federal authorities on public lands. The argument required considerable twisting of Article IV, sec. 3 of the US Constitution, a document they professed to be defending, and ignored a host of legal precedents. See Constitutional Sheriffs and Peace Officers Association, CSPOA.org.; Christopher A. Simon, "A Crucible or Populist Resistance: Tracing the Roots of the Sagebrush Rebellion," in Judd and Witt, *Cities, Sagebrush, and Solitude*, 98–102.

28   John Day *Blue Mountain Eagle*, May 29, 2013; January 23, 2015; January 26, April 27, and August 31, 2016. For this and other purposes, including a "public land patrol," Palmer deputized a total of sixty-nine people, a huge number for such a lightly populated county. In an odd move, Palmer did not place his management proposal on the county commission's agenda as an

action item, but presented it during the public comment portion of a meeting. His motives for so doing are unclear. John Day *Blue Mountain Eagle*, October 14, 2015; and February 3, 2016.

29 Portland *Oregonian*, December 22, 2016.

30 Grant County Ordinance 2013-01; John Day *Blue Mountain Eagle*, July 14, 2014; March 18, 2015; February 8, 2017 (quote).

31 John Day *Blue Mountain Eagle*, January 26, June 28, July 6, and August 3, 10, and 17, 2016; Rylan Boggs to author, August 31, 2016 (Cox, personal corresp.).

32 John Day *Blue Mountain Eagle*, October 24, 2014; March 23 and May 25, 2016.

33 John Day *Blue Mountain Eagle*, September 21, October 26, and November 8 and 16, 2016; February 1, 2017. A road-closure ordinance of 2013 was open to the same charge, eventually leading former commissioner Mark Webb to push the county court to rescind it. John Day *Blue Mountain Eagle*, February 8, 2017.

34 John Day *Blue Mountain Eagle*, February 26, March 5, June 2 and 9, and December 29, 2010; January 26 (2nd quote), March 23, April 27 (1st quote), May 4, June 8, July 6, and August 20, 2016; January 25 and August 2, 2017; Spokane *Spokesman-Review*, February 25, 2010; Portland *Oregonian*, February 26 and March 3, 2010; May 6, 2016. Gold rush lawlessness, the strength of pro-Confederate sympathies during the Civil War, a history of vigilantism, and the activities of the sheepkillers early in the twentieth century could have reinforced the image, but were probably not widely enough known to have been factors in drawing the alienated and marginalized.

35 John Day *Blue Mountain Eagle*, May 4, 2016.

36 John Day *Blue Mountain Eagle*, January 12, 19 (Palmer quote), and 26, and April 13, 2016; July 12, 2017; Portland *Oregonian*, January 26 and February 9, 2016; *Washington Post*, April 4, 2016.

37 John Day *Blue Mountain Eagle*, April 6 and October 19, 2016 (quotes).

38 John Day *Blue Mountain Eagle*, August 17, 2016 (1st quote); January 25 (2nd quote) and February 15 2017.

39 John Day *Blue Mountain Eagle*, May 4, 2016 (1st quotes); January 25 (3rd quote), February 1, 8 (2nd quote), and 15, 2017. The meeting of January 28 was organized by Jim Sproul, who proclaimed "federal and state agencies have become outlaws." It was advertised on social media, but not in the press; attendance was estimated at 500–650 with only 250–300 locals. Kay Steele raised the basic question about the purpose of the meeting: Was it for education, as Sproul claimed, or indoctrination? Clearly, she thought it the latter. John Day *Blue Mountain Eagle*, January 25, 2017.

40 John Day *Blue Mountain Eagle* July 14, 2015; June 14 and August 30, 2017.

EPILOGUE

1 Even the authors included in *Toward One Oregon* have difficulty finding evidence that Oregon is a single entity other than in a legal sense, or that the state is moving toward the unity implied in the volume's title.

2   Results are from www.uselectionsatlas.org/Results/state.

3   www.ballotpedia.org/Oregon_State_Senate_elections; www.
    oregonlegislature.gov/ferrioli/Pages/biography. John Day *Blue Mountain
    Eagle*, November 22 and December 20, 2017; January 10 and 31, 2018. Also in
    2008 and 2012, no Democrats ran for the state senate in Districts 27, 28, and
    29.

4   John Day *Blue Mountain Eagle*, October 19, 2016; Portland *Oregon Business
    Journal*, March 25, 2016.

5   John Day *Blue Mountain Eagle*, May 31, 2017 (quote); Salem *Capital Press*,
    July 8, 2017; Salem *Statesman-Journal*, July 7, 2017; www.olis.leg.state.or.
    us/ . . . /SB432; 1000 Friends of Oregon, "Action Alert! Stop Legislative
    Assault on our Rural Lands," www.friends.org/NoSB432; League of Woman
    Voters, "Action Needed! Stop SB 432," www.lwvor.org/ 2017/06/18/action-
    needed-stop-sb432.

6   Ontario *Argus Observer*, May 19 (1st quote) and June 23, 2015; John Day *Blue
    Mountain Eagle*, June 24, 2015; and October 12, 2016 (2nd quote); Pendleton
    East Oregonian, September 27, 2015; Pocatello *Idaho State Journal*,
    September 26, 2015.

7   The Oregon Department of Employment found similar problems in three
    southwestern and three north coast counties. See Oregon Department of
    Employment, *The Unemployment Landscape of Rural Oregon, May 2017*
    (Salem, OR: Department of Employment, 2017).

8   John Day *Blue Mountain Eagle*, February 8 and 22, 2017; Portland *Oregonian*,
    August 19, 2013; January 22 and April 24, 2015; March 1, 2016; Vale *Malheur
    Enterprise*, November 30, 2016, 7; Department of Employment,
    Unemployment Landscape of Rural Oregon, 7, 19, 20–23, 31, 38; www.kcsd.
    k12.or.us./bly; www.oregoncities.us/bly/images/2003 Community Plan.

9   Portland *Oregonian*, August 19, 2013; January 22 and April 24, 2015; March
    1, 2016; *Bend Bulletin*, March 16, 2017. Grant County's figures were nearly as
    daunting: in 2012 unemployment was 13.4 percent and the county had lost
    6.2 percent of its population; in 2016 unemployment was still 7.6 percent.
    Portland *Oregonian*, September 14, 2012; John Day *Blue Mountain Eagle*,
    June 29, 2016.

10 Waterston, *Where the Crooked River Rises*, 72–85 (quote, pp. 84–85);
    Department of Employment, *Unemployment Landscape of Rural Oregon*, 3,
    4. Changes in Deschutes County showed up in another way; according to the
    Pew Research Center, from 2000 to 2014 its middle class declined by over 8
    percent. It and Umatilla County had the highest rates of inequality in Eastern
    Oregon.

11 TownCharts, *Oregon Education Data: Education Data for All Counties in
    Oregon*, www.towncharts.com/Oregon/Oregon-state-Education-data.html;
    USDA, Economic Research Service, *County-Level Data Sets: Education*,
    www/.ers.usda.gov/data/county-level-data-sets.

12 Kittredge, *Owning It All* (1st quote), 41; Kittredge, *Who Owns the West*, 32;
    McVicker, *Child of Steens Mountain*, 30 (2nd quote), 129 (3rd quote);

Metzler, "Can Education Save Lakeview?," 8; John Day *Blue Mountain Eagle*, December 6, 2017.

13 Mark McMullen and Josh Lehner, *Analyzing Demographic and Economic Trends across Rural Oregon* (Salem: Oregon Office of Economic Analysis, 2015), 4–5; John Day *Blue Mountain Eagle*, December 6, 2017; Walker, *Sagebrush Collaboration*, 162–166.

14 John Day *Blue Mountain Eagle*, November 11, 2015; and July 20, 2016; ONDA, "Oregon's Owyhee Canyonlands," www.onda.org/publications/brochures/owyheecanyonlands-brochure; ONDA, "Owyhee Canyonlands," www.onda.org/where-we/work/owyhee; Pew Charitable Trusts, "Your Public Lands: Oregon's Owyhee Canyonlands" (quote); Mike Matz, "5 Reasons to Protect Oregon's Owyhee Canyonlands," Pew Charitable Trusts, www.pewtrusts.org/research-and-analysis/research/2015/10/22/ your-public-lands-oregon-owyhee-canyonlands, October 22, 2015; and September 6, 2016; Wild Owyhee, "Owyhee Canyonlands Conservation Proposal," www.wildowyhee.org/why-protect-it/ConservationProposal.

15 Ontario *Argus Observer*, October 4 and 11, November 3 and 26, and December 8, 13 (quote), and 30, 2015; February 25, April 5, and May 3, 9, and 10, 2016; Salem *Capital Press*, January 27, 2016.

16 Ontario *Argus Observer*, November 6 and 26, and December 10, 2015; February 16 and 21, and March 6 and 9, 2016; Vale *Malheur Enterprise*, July 26, 2016; Salem *Statesman-Journal*, March 10, 2016; January 22, 2017; John Day *Blue Mountain Eagle*, July 27, 2016; and April 18, 2017; Salt Lake City *Tribune*, June 3, 2013; *Christian Science Monitor*, June 13, 2017.

17 *Wildlife News*, April 16, 2012 (quote); and June 7 and 16, 2017; Spokane *Spokesman-Review*, August 28, 2016; Pocatello *Idaho State Journal*, July 30, 2017; George Wuerthner and Mollie Matteson, *Welfare Ranching: The Subsidized Destruction of the American West* (San Francisco: Foundation for Deep Ecology, 2002); George Wuerthner, "Is Ranching Sustainable?" *Western Watersheds Messenger* 15 (Fall 2008): 4–5; Tim Lengerich, "Dispelling the Cowboy Myth: An Interview with George Wuerthner," *Earth First! Journal* 21 (June/July 2001): 19, 56–57; Douglas Bevington, "George Wuerthner: A Bold Voice for Wild Nature," *CounterPunch*, posted April 3, 2017.

18 Cox, conversation with Barbara Vatter, Pullman, Washington, July 31, 1996; Portland *Oregonian*, March 22, 2013; *Los Angeles Times*, April 17, 2013 (quote); Hudson, New York, *Modern Farmer*, January 27, 2017; Irving, Texas, *Western Farmer-Stockman*, June 5, 2017. Boardman Grassland Preserve is also larger than Zumwalt Prairie, but it is a case unto itself, being owned by the US Navy and public access denied.

19 RCPP_Grande_Ronde_Watershed_Conservation_Partnership_Project.pdf.

20 *Oregon Conservation Strategy, 2016* (Salem: Oregon Department of Fish and Wildlife, 2016); nrcs.usda.gov/wps/nrcs/main/national/programs/easements/grassland; growingsolutions.org/eastern-oregon-grassland-restoration.

21 Osgood, *Desert Sage Memories*, 10–12 (quote, p. 12).

Bibliographical Note

This book rests on a foundation of specialized material—local newspaper accounts, technical works, interviews, correspondence, and reminiscences—too numerous to list here, but a variety of more extensive works, named below, address its major concerns.

Although no general studies take the same broad view as this study, Earl Pomeroy, *The American Far West in the Twentieth Century* (2008), and Dennis R. Judd and Stephanie L. Witt, *Cities, Sagebrush, and Solitude* (2015) provide a good foundation. There are also valuable geographically limited works, especially Phil Brogan, *East of the Cascades* (1964); Thomas Vaughan (ed.) *High and Mighty: Select Sketches about the Deschutes Country* (1981); and Gale Ontko, *Thunder over the Ochoco* (5 vols.; 1993–1999).

On Eastern Oregon's geologic past, see Ellen Morris Bishop, *In Search of Ancient Oregon: A Geological and Natural History* (2003), and Thomas Condon, *The Two Islands and What Came of Them* (1902). For efforts to reconstruct its human prehistory, see Luther S. Cressman, *The Sandal and the Cave* (2nd ed., 2005) and his autobiography *Golden Journey: Memoirs of an Archeologist* (1988).

Early Native-white relations are covered in A. B. Meacham, *Wigwams and War-Path* (1875); Sarah Winnemucca Hopkins, *Life among the Piutes: Their Wrongs and Claims* (1883); Gregory Michno, *The Deadliest Indian War in the West* (2007); and Robert H. Ruby and John A. Brown, *The Cayuse Indians: Imperial Tribesmen of Old Oregon* (1972). The introduction to Wilson Wewa's *Legends of the Northern Paiute* (2017) is a treasure trove of information from the Native point of view. Susan Jane Stowell, "The Wada-Tika of the Former Malheur Indian Reservation" (PhD diss., 2008) draws on both Native and white sources.

The period of exploration has been well covered, and the journals of nearly every important explorer have been published. Among the more valuable studies are Gloria Griffen Cline, *Peter Skene Ogden and the Hudson's Bay Company* (1974); John W. Evans, *Powerful Rockey: The Blue Mountains and the Oregon Trail* (1991); Allen Nevins, *John C. Frémont, Pathmarker of the West* (1992); and Keith Clark and Lowell Tiller, *Terrible Trail: The Meek Cutoff, 1845* (1993).

The cattle country is chronicled in George Francis Brimlow, *Harney County, Oregon, and Its Rangeland* (1951); J. Orin Oliphant, *On the Cattle Ranges of the Oregon Country* (1968); and Peter K. Simpson, *The Community of Cattlemen* (1987). More personal, but still highly valuable, are Anne Shannon Monroe, *Feelin' Fine! Bill Hanley's Book* (1931); William Kittredge, *Hole in the Sky: A Memoir* (1992); and Johnie ("Cactus") Smyth, *Footloose and Ahorseback* (1981). Sheep are less well covered, but see Alexander Campbell McGregor, *Counting Sheep: From Open Range to Agri-Business on the Columbia Plateau* (1982).

Gold mining is touched on in numerous works, but few provide a solid overview. A good popular account is Miles F. Potter, *Oregon's Golden Years: Bonanza of the West* (1991). More narrowly focused is R. Gregory Nokes, *Massacred for Gold: The Chinese in Hells Canyon* (2009).

The wheat belt (including its extensive acreage in Washington) is magnificently chronicled in Donald Meinig, *The Great Columbia Plain: A Historical Geography, 1805–1910* (1968). Nard Jones's novel, *Oregon Detour* (reprint, 1990) reflects the insights of a native son. Equally valuable is Arthur H. Bone (ed.), *Oregon Cattleman/Governor, Congressman: Memoirs and Times of Walter M. Pierce* (1981). Also useful is John F. Due and Giles French, *Rails to the Mid-Columbia Wheatlands* (1979).

Homesteading the High Desert has generated a number of reminiscences and other works. Among the best are Barbara Allen, *Homesteading the High Desert* (1987); Eileen O'Keefe McVicker, *Child of Steens Mountain* (2008); and Alice Day Pratt, *A Homesteader's Portfolio* (1922). H. L. Davis's Pulitzer Prize–winning novel, *Honey in the Horn* (1935) captures the pathos magnificently.

Basic to the study of Eastern Oregon's forests is Nancy Langston, *Forest Dreams, Forest Nightmares: The Paradox of Old Growth in the Inland Northwest* (1995). Also useful are Lawrence Rakestraw, "A History of Forest Conservation in the Pacific Northwest, 1891–1913" (PhD diss., 1955); Harold K. Steen, *Jack Ward Thomas* (2004); and John C. Driscoll, *Gilchrist, Oregon, The Model Company Town* (2012).

Tourism and its attendant problems are covered in Hal K. Rothman, *Devil's Bargains: Tourism in the Twentieth Century American West* (1998); Earl Pomeroy, *In Search of the Golden West: The Tourist in Western America* (1990); and my own *The Park Builders: A History of State Parks in the Pacific Northwest* (1989). Hugh Myron Hoyt, "The Good Roads Movement in Oregon, 1900–1920" (PhD diss., 1970) provides useful background.

The evolution of education and government have been little studied, but Urling C. Coe, *Frontier Doctor: Observations on Central Oregon and the Changing West* (1940); Forrest E. Cooper, *Introducing Dr. Bernard Daly* (1986); and James L. Crowell, *Frontier Publisher: A Romantic Review of George Palmer Putnam's Career at the* Bend Bulletin, *1910–1914* (2008) cover some aspects.

Irrigation and hydroelectric power have received considerable attention. Key works include Elmo Richardson, *Dams, Parks, and Politics: Resource Development and Preservation in the Truman-Eisenhower Era* (1982); Karl Boyd Brooks, *Public Power, Private Dams* (2009); and Martin T. Winch, *Tumalo, Thirsty Land: History of Tumalo Irrigation District* (1985). Although short on critical analysis, the Bureau of Reclamation's studies of individual projects are quite useful, especially Eric A. Stene, *Klamath Project* (1994), and *Owyhee Project* (1996); and Robert Autobee, *Deschutes Project* (1996). Katrine Barber's *Death of Celilo Falls* (2005) is a poignant chronicle of the problems one project caused. More contemporary is Holly Doremus and A. Dan Turlock, *Water War in the Klamath Basin* (2008).

A wealth of material deals with the rise of conservation and environmental concerns: Dallas Lore Sharp, *Where Rolls the Oregon* (1914); Stephen Dow Beckham, *The Gerber Block: Historical Developments on the Public Rangelands in Klamath County, Oregon* (2000); and Worth Mathewson, *William L. Finley, Pioneer Wildlife Photographer* (1987) treat individual aspects well. More analytical is Nancy Langston, *Where Land and Water Meet: A Western Landscape Transformed* (2003). Also revealing is Brent Walth, *Fire at Eden's Gate: Tom McCall and the Oregon Story* (2000).

The continuing problems of Native Americans and efforts at their correction are chronicled in Donald Lee Fixico, *Termination and Relocation: Federal Indian Policy, 1945–1960* (1986); Patrick Mann Haynal, "From Termination through Restoration and Beyond: Modern Klamath Cultural

Identity" (PhD diss., 1994); and William Stone, *Cross in the Middle of Nowhere: The Catholic Church in Eastern Oregon* (1993).

Finally, numerous studies address current problems. Peter Walker's *Sagebrush Collaboration: How Harney County Defeated the Takeover of the Malheur Wildlife Refuge* (2018) is unusually perceptive. Also insightful are Ellen Waterson, *Where the Crooked River Rises: A High Desert Home* (2010); Carrie McLaren et al., *Too Many Homes on the Range: The Impact of Rural Sprawl on Ranching and Habitat* (2004); and Oregon Forest Resources Institute, *Federal Forestland in Oregon* (2010).

Index